FIRST SON

FIRST SON

The Biography of
Richard M. Daley

KEITH KOENEMAN

THE UNIVERSITY OF CHICAGO PRESS

CHICAGO AND LONDON

Keith Koeneman is a third-generation Chicagoan. He holds advanced degrees from Harvard University, the University of Chicago, and Northwestern University and writes on Chicago politics, history, and culture for the *Huffington Post*.

The University of Chicago Press, Chicago 60637
The University of Chicago Press, Ltd., London
© 2013 by Keith Koeneman
All rights reserved. Published 2013.
Printed in the United States of America

22 21 20 19 18 17 16 15 14 13   1 2 3 4 5

ISBN-13: 978-0-226-44947-0 (cloth)
ISBN-13: 978-0-226-44949-4 (e-book)

Library of Congress Cataloging-in-Publication Data
Koeneman, Keith.
  First son : the biography of Richard M. Daley / Keith Koeneman.
    pages ; cm
  Includes bibliographical references and index.
    ISBN 978-0-226-44947-0 (cloth : alkaline paper)—ISBN 978-0-226-44949-4
  (e-book) 1. Daley, Richard M. (Richard Michael), 1942– 2. Mayors—Illinois—
  Chicago—Biography. 3. Chicago (Ill.)—Politics and government—1951– I. Title.
    F548.54.D35K64 2013
    977.3092—dc23
    [B]

2012037859

♾ This paper meets the requirements of ANSI/NISO Z39.48-1992
(Permanence of Paper).

To Claire,

my love,

you are the sine qua non

of my existence

CONTENTS

CAST OF CHARACTERS   ix

PROLOGUE   xv

PART 1. *A Kid from Bridgeport*

1. DICK DALEY 3
2. EVERY HAPPY FAMILY IS THE SAME 20
3. CHICAGO VISIONS 33

PART 2. *The Second Generation*

4. FROM FATHER TO SON 49
5. DARWINIAN EVOLUTION 62
6. MAYORAL ELECTION OF 1983 87

PART 3. *Political Calculus*

7. ALL HELL BREAKS LOOSE 97
8. RESTORATION 106
9. CHICAGO, 1989 122
10. A NEW ERA 127

PART 4. *Plugger*

11. CRIME AND GRIME 143
12. TAKEOVER OF CHICAGO PUBLIC SCHOOLS 155

PART 5. *Civilizing Richie*

13. HAS CHICAGO HAD A SEX CHANGE? 171
14. HOUSING WITHOUT HOPE 183
15. BILL DALEY 197

PART 6. *Pride Is the First Deadly Sin*

16. CROSSING THE RIVER 209

17. THE TWO FACES OF RICHIE DALEY 210

18. MILLENNIUM PARK 228

19. CORRUPTION TAX 240

PART 7. *Legacy*

20. GLOBAL CITY, PAROCHIAL COUNCIL 255

21. ONE TOO MANY 268

22. SISYPHUS... 282

23. BLOODLINES 293

24. SUNRISE, NOVEMBER 29, 2011 309

APPENDIX A. CHICAGO MAYORS SINCE 1900   311

APPENDIX B. ELECTION RESULTS OF RICH DALEY'S

POLITICAL CAMPAIGNS   313

APPENDIX C. TIMELINE OF EVENTS IN RICH DALEY'S LIFE   315

ACKNOWLEDGMENTS   325

NOTES   327

INDEX   361

A gallery of photographs begins after page 180

CAST OF CHARACTERS

THE MAYORS

RICHARD J. "DICK" DALEY (DECEASED)	Mayor of Chicago from 1955 to 1976.
JANE BYRNE	Mayor of Chicago from 1979 to 1983. First female mayor.
HAROLD WASHINGTON (DECEASED)	Mayor of Chicago from 1983 to 1987. First African-American mayor.
RICHARD M. "RICH" DALEY	Mayor of Chicago from 1989 to 2011. Firstborn son of Dick Daley.

THE RIVALS

EDWARD "ED" BURKE	South-side Irish-Catholic and second-generation machine politician. One of the two white leaders of the divisive Council Wars from 1983 to 1986. Chicago alderman for over forty years.
JANE BYRNE	See "The Mayors" above.

THE INNER CIRCLE

WILLIAM M. "BILL" DALEY	Youngest brother of Rich Daley. Well-known political consigliore.
MARGARET "MAGGIE" DALEY (DECEASED)	Wife of Rich Daley. Founder of Gallery 37 and After School Matters.
TIM DEGNAN	Bridgeport native who some refer to as the fifth Daley brother.
PATRICK HUELS	Eleventh Ward alderman from Bridgeport from 1976 to 1997.

JEREMIAH JOYCE — Former politician from the south side. Controversial businessman.

FRANK KRUESI — University of Chicago policy wonk who liked to be near the political action.

THE ADVISERS

DAVID AXELROD — Media guru and political adviser for Democratic politicians.

RAHM EMANUEL — Fund-raiser for Daley's 1989 mayoral race who would become well-known in Chicago and in national political circles. Tight with the Daley brothers. Current mayor of Chicago.

NED KENNAN — Psychologist and political strategist who advised both Rich Daley and Jane Byrne.

JOHN SCHMIDT — Attorney with progressive political leanings. Expert on privatization.

DAVID WILHELM — Campaign manager for Daley's 1989 mayoral race. Democratic national chairman from 1993 to 1994.

THE ALDERMEN

TIMOTHY "TIM" EVANS — African-American alderman from the south side who served as Harold Washington's floor leader in the city council from 1983 to 1987.

RICHARD "DICK" MELL — Wheeler-dealer alderman. Father-in-law of Rod Blagojevich.

JOE MOORE — North-side alderman. One of the few independents in the city council.

PATRICK O'CONNOR — Longtime leader in the Chicago City Council.

DAVID ORR — Former north-side alderman. Interim mayor for one week after Harold Washington's death. Cook County clerk for more than two decades after 1990.

EUGENE SAWYER (DECEASED) — African-American alderman. Mayor of Chicago from 1987 to 1989.

EDWARD "ED" VRDOLYAK   Former chair of the Cook County Democratic party known as Fast Eddie. Close ally of Ed Burke. Served a ten-month jail sentence in 2011 and 2012.

WELL-KNOWN POLITICIANS

ROD BLAGOJEVICH   Former governor of Illinois who is now in prison. Son-in-law of Dick Mell.

GEORGE W. BUSH   Forty-third president of the United States. Spent his sixtieth birthday with Rich Daley at one of the mayor's favorite Chicago restaurants.

WILLIAM J. "BILL" CLINTON   Forty-second president of the United States.

JESSE JACKSON   Civil rights activist and minister. Unelected player in Chicago politics for over forty years.

MICHAEL "MIKE" MADIGAN   Powerful speaker of the Illinois House of Representatives. Second-generation machine politician.

BARACK OBAMA   Forty-fourth president of the United States. First African-American president. First president from Chicago.

DAN ROSTENKOWSKI   Second-generation machine politician. US congressman from 1959 to 1995. Old-school dealmaker. Close political ally of Dick Daley. Mentor of Bill Daley.

POLITICOS

GERY CHICO   Prominent attorney. Political bloodlines run from Rich Daley, Ed Burke, and Harold Washington.

JOHN DALEY   Eleventh Ward Democratic committeeman and Cook County Board commissioner. Younger brother of Rich Daley. Bridgeport native who never left.

ALLISON DAVIS   Prominent attorney. Former idealist who turned into a clout-heavy real estate developer. Raised $68 million from City

	of Chicago pension funds to do deals with Daley's nephew Robert Vanecko.
DENNIS GANNON	President of the Chicago Federation of Labor.
VALERIE JARRETT	African-American power player from Chicago with deep ties to Barack Obama. Political bloodlines run from Rich Daley and Harold Washington.
EDWARD "ED" KELLY	Machine politician and former superintendent of the Chicago Park District. Friend of Dick Daley.
DAWN CLARK NETSCH	Independent Democratic politician and liberal law professor. First woman nominated for Illinois governor by a major party.
WILLIAM "BILL" SINGER	Attorney and former alderman who ran against Dick Daley for mayor in 1975. Chicago Public Schools board member from 1989 to 1990.
TODD STROGER	Former president of the Cook County board. Son of and heir to the political office of John Stroger, a longtime African-American ally of the Daley family.

THE CREATIVE CLASS

FOREST CLAYPOOL	Political player with management skills: two-time mayoral chief of staff, superintendent of the Chicago Park District, president of the Chicago Transit Authority. Longtime friend of David Axelrod, Rahm Emanuel, and David Wilhelm.
ARNE DUNCAN	CEO of Chicago Public Schools from 2001 until 2008 who then became US secretary of education. A basketball player, like his friends John Rogers Jr. and Barack Obama.
EARNEST GATES	African-American housing advocate.
FRANK GEHRY	World-famous architect.

JULIA STASCH	Mayoral chief of staff and former commissioner of housing.
CHARLIE TROTTER	Gourmet chef and restaurant owner.
ED UHLIR	Park planner and architect.
PAUL VALLAS	CEO of the Chicago Public Schools from 1995 to 2001.
LOIS WEISBERG	Commissioner of cultural affairs from 1989 to 2011. Friend of Maggie Daley. Political bloodlines run from Harold Washington.
OPRAH WINFREY	One-of-a-kind talk show host.

THE BUSINESSPEOPLE

JOHN BRYAN	CEO of Sara Lee Corporation from 1975 to 2000. Major philanthropic fund-raiser.
LESTER CROWN	Civic leader and billionaire businessman.
MIKE KOLDYKE	Well-known venture capitalist. Founder of the Golden Apple Foundation.
CINDY PRITZKER	Civic leader and member of family that owns hotels, real estate, and manufacturing companies.
JERRY REINSDORF	Owner of the Chicago Bulls and the Chicago White Sox.
JOHN ROGERS JR.	Founder and CEO of Ariel Investments. African-American civic leader who is friends with Barack Obama, Arne Duncan, Valerie Jarrett, and the Daley family.
PAT RYAN	Founder of Aon Insurance. Chairman and CEO of Chicago's 2016 Olympic Bid Committee. Longtime Daley supporter.
JOHN WARNER	Senior executive at Boeing Corporation.

LAW ENFORCEMENT AND GOOD GOVERNMENT VIGILANTES

| PATRICK FITZGERALD | Tough federal prosecutor who arrived in Illinois in 2001. |

DAVID HOFFMAN — Inspector general of Chicago from 2005 to 2009.

MICHAEL SHAKMAN — Attorney who in the 1970s sued to prevent the city and county from hiring and firing employees for political reasons, which became known as the Shakman Decrees.

THE CONVICTED

JON BURGE — Former Chicago police officer raised on the far south side of Chicago. Sentenced to four and a half years in prison in 2011 for lying about his role in torturing African-American suspects.

JOHN CANNATELLO — Businessman sentenced in 2006 to twenty-seven months in jail for his role in the Hired Truck Scandal. The Cannatello family had two generations of ties to the Daley family.

JAMES DUFF — Businessman sentenced in 2006 to nearly ten years in jail for a fraud scheme against the City of Chicago. The Duff family had two generations of ties to the Daley family.

AL SANCHEZ — A leader of the Hispanic Democratic Organization (HDO). Streets and Sanitation commissioner from the far south side found guilty of trading city jobs for political favors. Sentenced to two and a half years in prison in 2011 for his role in hiring fraud at city hall.

ROBERT SORICH — Former mayoral patronage chief and a native of Bridgeport. The Sorich family had two generations of ties to the Daley family. Sentenced to nearly four years in prison in 2006 for hiring fraud at city hall.

DONALD TOMCZAK — City of Chicago water department boss and a native of Bridgeport. Sentenced to four years in prison in 2006 for his role in the Hired Truck Scandal.

PROLOGUE

January 6, 2011. Rich Daley, the mayor of Chicago, stood in front of a podium at Saint Mark International Christian Church in the Austin neighborhood on the far west side of Chicago. African-American community leaders and educators surrounded the mayor as he started a news conference. In a few months, Daley would turn sixty-nine years old and time had dusted his once dark hair with a white layer of color. The mayor announced that the city and its partners would expand the Safe Haven activities program so that more than a thousand grade school students could participate during after school hours. "We all want our young people to stay safe from violence, stay away from a life of violence and achieve their full potential in life. And among the most important things we can do to help are to give them the best education possible and give them plenty of positive activities after school," said Daley.

The serious tone of the news conference took a sudden, more lighthearted turn, however, when the mayor fielded a question about his brother Bill Daley. He smiled. His eyes brightened. His body relaxed. The president of the United States had held a press conference and named his brother as White House chief of staff. Rich Daley was clearly proud of his younger brother. The mayor fielded questions from news reporters, one of whom inquired whether his sibling's appointment confirmed that the "Chicago [political] mafia" controlled Washington, DC, and national politics. Daley rejected the suggestion, noting that most presidents had brought advisers to Washington that they trusted and respected. The mayor and the black leaders on the stage laughed lightheartedly as Daley used his familiar style of public speaking—

clumsy but heartfelt—to compare the current president's decision to those of Kennedy, Nixon, Reagan, Bush, and Clinton.

When Daley spoke of US presidents and their exercise of the powers of office, he spoke of a subject that he knew well. The Daley family had exerted political power on the local and national stage for nearly sixty years. His father, Dick Daley, was one of the most dominant American politicians of the twentieth century—a kingmaker, a president picker. A political talent so influential that Rich Daley and his brothers grew up visiting presidents, sleeping at the White House, and having private, intimate conversations with the highest elected officials in the United States of America.

Yet for all his talents, Daley's father had been a flawed leader. Dick Daley started his political career in 1919—the same year as Chicago's infamous race riots—and as he aged and increased in power he grew more reactionary, especially on the issue of race.

Rich Daley also knew how to exercise power. He served as mayor for nearly twenty-two years, and his legacy included transforming Chicago from an ethnic Midwestern urban center to one of the world's truly global cities. As mayor, he also tried to repair the mistakes of his father by improving race relations, fixing the public schools, and resuscitating public housing. Rich Daley plugged away for more than two decades, trying to finish the unfinished business of the Daley family.

There were certain paradoxes, however, in the two winter press conferences that day that discussed the appointment of a Daley to high political office—one in Washington, DC, and one in Chicago. In the nation's capital, President Obama announced the selection of a fellow Chicagoan as his chief of staff and admiringly described Bill Daley's deep knowledge of politics as a "genetic trait." Obama—the nation's first black president—had brought in a pragmatic Daley to try to shape up his administration and win greater approval from the American public. Moreover, four of the other most senior advisers to the liberal black president—Rahm Emanuel, David Axelrod, Valerie Jarrett, and Arne Duncan—had grown up politically in Chicago as advisers to Bill Daley's brother, the no-nonsense mayor. On the west side of Chicago, Rich Daley stood surrounded by black leaders and educators as he once again tried to improve public education and reduce crime. Daley appeared completely at ease in the company of these African-Americans, a group with whom he had spent much of the last two decades.

Three months prior, the mayor had announced that he would not run for reelection and would retire at the end of his sixth term. This decision made Daley the first Chicago mayor in over eighty-five years to voluntarily retire from office. He would not die in office like his father had done.

Yet the Daley clan would continue to exercise political power even as Rich Daley prepared to retire. Bill Daley and the president's other senior advisers from Chicago would continue to perform on the world's stage. In Chicago, Rahm Emanuel—a person who the normally close-mouth mayor had once described as the most focused and effective person he had ever worked with in public life—prepared to replace Daley and ascend to the city's mayoralty. Chicagoans abhorred a political vacuum, and it was likely that the smart and pugnacious Emanuel would govern with a strong hand. A new era called for a new leader. The Daleys and their protégés, however, would continue to exercise power at the highest levels of American government, in ways both visible and unseen by the public. A nearly century-old political dynasty would continue to influence the lives of many.

Rich Daley had grown up as the firstborn son of Dick Daley, the Irish-Catholic political boss who fine-tuned the Chicago political machine and ruled over a city of three million people. Dick Daley was a political genius but was power hungry and a flawed leader. His son Rich inherited his great love of Chicago and a belief in the Democratic machine. But growing up in his father's shadow, the younger Daley seemed insecure and lacking of his father's talent or charisma.

Early in his professional career, the younger Daley was part of the Chicago Democratic machine and completely dependent on his father for his positions and accomplishments. He was also emotionally immature, intellectually unexceptional, and a bit of a bully. After his father's death, however, Rich Daley began a dramatic personal evolution. He matured emotionally and intellectually, becoming more open to new people and new ideas. He also became a public policy aficionado and gradually gave up his belief that the Democratic political machine was essential to advancing his own career goals.

One key event in Rich Daley's life greatly contributed to his disillusionment with the machine: the Cook County state's attorney race of 1980. During this election, Daley fought successfully for his political survival by winning a classic political battle—against a lifelong rival, the machine politician Ed Burke—that essentially became a civil war within Chicago's Democratic Party. After he won, Daley continued to mature in his new office, developing fresh credibility as a public servant and effective executive.

But Rich Daley then made a big mistake: he decided to run for mayor in the Chicago election of 1983. Impatience—a lifelong trait of his—provides a partial explanation for his choice. But the key to Daley's bad decision was something deeper: the hubris of a still emotionally immature man who grew up as the privileged son of Chicago's most powerful politician. Daley lost his campaign for mayor in 1983, and the City of Chicago anointed Harold Washington its first black mayor. Six years in the political wilderness followed for Daley.

Yet a crucial aspect of Rich Daley's personality and long-term success was his ability to persist. Daley had started his early life with people having low expectations for him—he was not a great student, talented athlete, or charismatic leader of his classmates. Because of this, Daley became a "plugger," developing the fortitude to persist even after suffering repeated disappointments. In 1989, Rich Daley took back Chicago's mayoral seat for the Daley family.

As mayor, Daley retained his great political skills but also took big risks and evolved into a highly effective chief executive of the city. His legacy would not only include finishing the unfinished business of the Daley family—improving race relations, public schools, and public housing—but also the aforementioned transformation of Chicago into a global city. During his years in office, Daley physically resurrected the downtown area and Chicago's lakefront. Out went the gritty, worn-down postindustrial Midwestern capital. In came a beautiful, sophisticated city: Millennium Park, refurbished neighborhoods, a lakefront Museum Campus, wrought-iron fences and landscaped gardens, attractive downtown colleges, and a renewed Navy Pier. Daley's revitalized, beautified, high-quality-of-life Chicago became the model for many cities in America and throughout much of the world.

But Daley was not a perfect mayor. Rather, the arc of his career was consistent with what a study of human nature would predict: a steep learning curve; a decade of disciplined work leading to mastery; the accumulation of power; and, finally, hubris and mistakes. Daley's legacy would unfortunately also include a pension crisis, the midnight destruction of Meigs Field, persistent corruption within city government, high levels of crime, and financial mismanagement during his last years in office.

Despite his imperfections, over a thirty-year period Daley evolved tremendously as a person and as a professional. This evolution, however, did not prevent him from governing Chicago as the ultimate pragmatist, a leader who used "brass knuckle" tactics to improve the city he loved or to protect his own power. At times this meant falling back on tried-and-true Chicago politicking: rewarding loyalty with favors, using city government resources to overwhelm opponents, and tolerating political corruption. Sometimes his Machiavellian "the end justifies the means" operating style left hurt feelings, especially among colleagues and friends who had spent years serving him and the people of Chicago. "What's not his nature??? He's just a mean, cold-hearted little prick," said one of Daley's long-time political allies in describing the mayor's modus operandi. Yet Daley's family, his friends, and many, many long-time associates believed that he was a man of humor and perspective, a somewhat sensitive man, a leader who had loved his city in a way that was truly exceptional.

Even though the mature Daley had largely resolved the conflicts between his Bridgeport roots—conservative, parochial, machine-dominated—and his own evolving belief system, the conflicts were never completed resolved. Daley—the man of history—remains a complex man and a man of occasional contradictions. Sensitive and tough, impatient yet persistent, a street-smart, cutthroat policy wonk who completely self-identifies with Chicago, the city by the lake. Despite his imperfections, Rich Daley surpassed his father's accomplishments in office and became one of the most influential mayors in the last hundred years of Chicago, now one of the world's truly international cities.

PART I

A Kid from Bridgeport

CHAPTER I

DICK DALEY

Lillian Dunne Daley gave birth to Dick Daley, an Irish-Catholic kid from Bridgeport, on May 15, 1902, during the third term of Mayor Carter H. Harrison II. During Chicago's "age of Harrison," the Irish quietly ascended to the top of the political ladder. For most of Dick Daley's life, the Irish would rise and rise and rise and then, finally, control Chicago politics. It was as if all of the ethnic groups in the city decided to play a real life, twentieth-century game of king of the hill. Like kids scrambling up a snowy, icy pile on the grade school playground— pushing, kicking, punching, crawling over the backs of each other to make it to the top—the Irish, German, Polish, and Italians, as well as a few tough blacks, struggled and struggled to overtake one another. The game would end with Dick Daley on top of the heap, surrounded by his Irish buddies. He was, at his death in 1976, king of the hill.

But that glory was far off in the future.

Turn-of-the-century Bridgeport was a gloomy, ethnic, working-class neighborhood. Industry had created its most prominent physical features: railroad tracks to the east, the Union Stock Yards to the south, and Bubbly Creek to the west. Each day, the neighborhood inhaled the nasty smell of the stockyards. The tangy odor of blood and manure overpowered newcomers, but many long-time residents ceased to sense it or told their children the smell was healthy. Bubbly Creek, a gaseous, waste-filled section of the south branch of the Chicago River, was equally repellent. In 1906, four years after the birth of Dick Daley, Upton Sinclair's famous expose of the stockyards, called *The Jungle*, described the creek as "a great open sewer."

Despite this tough environment, Dick Daley experienced many positive influences in his childhood, including good parents. His mom,

Lillian Daley, was thirty years old when she gave birth to her first and only child. She always dressed her son in fancy clothes, an unusual luxury in working-class Bridgeport. Like many only children, throughout his life Dick Daley retained an inner sense of his own specialness, an immutable feeling that he probably intuited from his mother's great joy at his very existence. Even as a mature adult, he delighted in celebrating his own birthday, along with family, friends, and his city hall employees. Like many firstborn children, young Dick Daley was a "striver." He showed up on time, worked hard, respected authority. According to his grade school teacher, the nun Sister Gabriel, "[Dick Daley] was a very serious boy. A very studious boy. He played when he played. He worked when he worked. And he prayed when he prayed."

Daley's mom was the dominant personality in their household. She was a high-energy woman, possessed a good sense of humor, and displayed more charisma and aggressiveness than most women in the early twentieth century. On St. Patrick's Day, Daley's mom joked with her young son that she needed to go down to city hall to have her "behind painted green." Lillian Daley also regularly marched in parades for women's right to vote, sometimes bringing her son with her. The Nineteenth Amendment to the US Constitution granted this right to women in 1920, when Dick Daley was eighteen years old. His mom also was tough on him, letting her son know that she had high expectations for his career.

Daley's dad, Mike Daley, was a quiet and reserved man who worked as a business agent for the sheet metal workers union. Though a man of few noteworthy accomplishments, he was even tempered and a good listener. His son, who had fond memories of his father, would later emulate Mike Daley's reserve and ability to listen without voicing his own views. These traits—along with the energy, sense of humor, and charismatic aggressiveness he inherited from his mother—served Dick Daley well when he entered his career in Chicago politics.

The Bridgeport of Dick Daley's youth was an ethnic enclave, an Irish-Catholic village in the midst of a great, unforgiving city. This community had its own churches, schools, stores, and saloons. Like other of the city's south-side neighborhoods, Bridgeport was a miniature world of its own. As Daley aged, he learned that the Irish portion of Bridgeport contained a trustworthy clan: a small group of friends and relatives whom he always depended on for the support he needed. These people—the Irish-Catholics of Bridgeport—became Daley's tribe. He would never leave them.

Daley's family attended mass at Nativity of Our Lord parish, where he was also a student and an altar boy. An early photo showed him in his white vestments, with hands crossed and Bible between his thumbs. Young Daley had a round face, a serious look, and a disciplined stance but did not appear exceptional.

For most ethnic Catholic families of the time, the local parish represented both the religious and cultural center of the neighborhood, and the Daley family was no different in this respect. Between 1900 and 1930, student enrollment at Catholic elementary schools in Chicago tripled, surging from approximately fifty thousand to more than 145,000, as first- and second-generation ethnic Chicagoans registered their children. These parents looked to parishes such as Nativity of Our Lord primarily to train their kids in Catholic morality and proper social conduct. The second major attraction of parish schools for Catholic parents such as the Daleys was the schools' ability to transmit a specific ethnic culture. Nativity of Our Lord, which was founded by the Irish-born Father Michael Lyons, was an Irish-Catholic institution that sought to preserve the cultural heritage brought over from Ireland. The curriculum, which focused on penmanship, memorization, and rote learning, was of tertiary importance for many parents.

After graduating from Nativity of Our Lord, Dick Daley attended De La Salle Institute, a Catholic high school run by the Christian Brothers. De La Salle provided a solid, practical education that emphasized business courses, such as bookkeeping, business law, and typing. De La Salle was an all-boys, all-white, largely Irish school just east of Comiskey Park, home of Dick Daley's beloved Chicago White Sox baseball team. Like most of the other all-boys Catholic high schools at the time, De La Salle emphasized discipline, and the black-robed Christian Brothers who ran the school did not hesitate to punch a teenager who acted up.

Though De La Salle only opened its doors to white Catholics, the school stood in an impoverished neighborhood on the "wrong" side of the street that separated Bridgeport from the black neighborhoods to the east. This quirk of fate—in a city such as Chicago where nearly all the neighborhoods were ethnically and racially divided—unsettled De La Salle's teachers, students, and parents. According to an authorized school history, "The school was surrounded by tenements and by low life. It was a white school as an island surrounded by a black sea." By 1920, the neighborhood encircling De La Salle on the south side of Chicago would contain nearly 85 percent of the city's black population.

This sea of African-Americans in Chicago would grow larger and larger throughout Dick Daley's lifetime. Starting during World War I, blacks living in the Southern United States left their rural homes and headed for big Northern cities such as Chicago to escape Southern hostility and to look for jobs. Due to surging wartime production and a lack of new immigrants from Europe, Chicago factories hired blacks as permanent employees for the first time. This Great Migration of blacks in the United States lasted from 1916 until 1970, with its two strongest phases starting during the two world wars. Partly due to the availability of industrial jobs in areas such as the Union Stock Yards, the African-American population in Chicago surged from 2 percent of Chicagoans in 1915 to 38 percent by 1975.

The historical record indicates that Dick Daley found this demographic change deeply unsettling. Later in life he reportedly tried to use his political power to preserve a city where whites and blacks each stayed in their own neighborhoods. Seven years after his death, blacks interviewed in focus groups during a Chicago mayoral election expressed the view that Dick Daley used his power to create unjust policies because he "hated the goddamn niggers." That type of open racial controversy was far off in the future, however, from his De La Salle days.

In addition to attending school and working at part-time jobs, during his teenage years, young Dick Daley joined the Hamburg Athletic Club, only a short walk from his Bridgeport home. The Hamburg Club, like other such groups throughout the city, organized social activities and sporting events. At the club, Daley developed a reputation as a serious and competent manager of the baseball teams. He set up the matches, determined lineups, and coached the teams during the games. Club members apparently noticed Daley's skill and conscientiousness, electing him president of the organization in 1924, a position he held for the next fifteen years.

In addition to organizing sporting and social events, the Hamburg Athletic Club actively supported local politicians during campaigns, as well as functioning like a tough, turf-protecting local street gang. The club had an illustrious history as a training ground for successful Eleventh Ward Irish politicians such as Tommy Doyle and Joseph Mc-Donough. Young, testosterone-filled club members were often willing to get out the vote during Chicago elections, applying physical force if necessary. Members of the Hamburg Club also used violence to enforce unwritten ethnic and racial boundaries, especially against blacks. This type of extreme parochialism likely contributed to the race riots of 1919, the worst such unrest in Chicago's history.

The race riots that summer started when a black kid in Lake Michigan made the mistake of swimming across an invisible racial barrier at the Twenty-Ninth Street Beach. Whites stoned him and he drowned, setting off intense racial street battles. Beatings, shootings, and arson raged for seven days on the south side, with Irish-American gangs playing a central role. The Eleventh Ward politician Joseph McDonough—patron of the Hamburg Athletic Club and soon to be Dick Daley's political mentor—actively inflamed the fears and angers of his Bridgeport neighborhood during the riots. The Irish-dominated Chicago police force, sympathizing with the whites, held back and let the racial battle rage, leaving thirty-eight dead and more than five hundred injured. For the rest of his life, Dick Daley—disciplined as ever—remained silent on what occurred in summer of 1919 when he was seventeen years old.

Dick Daley started at the bottom when he began in politics in 1919. His first position in Chicago's Democratic Party was as an Eleventh Ward precinct captain in the upcoming mayoral election. Like all precinct captains, the Democratic Party assigned Daley the responsibility of personally getting out the vote for approximately five hundred voters on specific city blocks in his neighborhood.

Though the Democrats lost this race to the Republican candidate Big Bill Thompson, during the 1920s young Dick Daley began his slow, steady rise in politics. When he became an Eleventh Ward precinct captain, he joined the Democratic Party of Cook County, which insiders called "the organization" and everyone else called "the machine." The Chicago machine was a political organization with a shared ethos that focused on winning political elections and maintaining the group's own power. In the machine, precinct captains reported to ward committeemen, who reported to the chairman of the Cook County Democratic Party. Despite this focus on hierarchy, within the machine there were many differences of opinion and personal feuds. These disputes typically were handled behind closed doors by pragmatic, nonideological men who focused overridingly on preserving their own power.

Dick Daley intuitively understood the way the machine functioned, and he quickly aligned himself with big Joe McDonough, the three hundred pound Eleventh Ward political boss from Bridgeport. McDonough, a colorful alderman in the Chicago tradition, was an outgoing man known for his large appetites and authentic concern for his constituents. Though he was an elected official and ran a real estate firm and a saloon, McDonough was not known as detail oriented. Savvy and street smart, the Bridgeport politician therefore made Dick Daley his personal assistant. As boss of the Eleventh Ward, McDonough could have picked nearly any young Irish Democrat he wanted, but big Joe must have seen qualities in Daley that eventually made the younger politician's reputation inside the machine: an ability to master detail, faithfully follow orders, keep his mouth shut, and work, work, work.

McDonough rose through the ranks of the Democratic Party and Daley rose with him. Daley's first job downtown was working in the Chicago City Council where he reviewed proposed bills and budgets for McDonough and other aldermen while also attending night school. In this position, Daley not only learned how the city council worked but also developed his lifelong low opinion of the ethics and talents of most Chicago aldermen. According to one neighborhood friend, "I always went out dancing every night, but Dick went home to study law books. He would never stop in the saloon and have a drink."

Though he avoided paperwork and most managerial decisions, big Joe McDonough made shrewd political alliances. The most important partnership was with Anton Cermak, the clever, deeply ambitious Czechoslovakian politician. Cermak became president of the Cook County Board in 1922, chairman of the Democratic Party in 1928, and mayor of Chicago in 1931. Though mean tempered and a poor public speaker, Cermak had the genius to build a disciplined, multiethnic political party. He started by organizing saloon owners and alcohol drinkers, most of whom were first- or second-generation Catholic immigrants from Europe. After earning the nickname "wettest man in Chicago," Cermak reached out to key Irish, German, Polish, and Jewish politicians to create a multiethnic coalition as his political army. Cermak also wrapped himself in the mantle of blue-ribbon good government reform and gradually instilled a results-oriented discipline in the Chicago machine. His favorite saying was "Only lazy precinct captains steal votes."

In 1930, Cermak's political organization backed McDonough for county-wide office as treasurer. Daley, along with the party's other precinct captains, worked for the team and got out the vote for big Joe McDonough. The potential election of his mentor meant more to Daley than the other political workers and he was known to lead campaigners in song, using his strong Irish voice.

McDonough won and brought Daley along with him as his deputy in the treasurer's office. In his new position, Dick Daley—conscientious and hard-working as ever—began mastering budgeting and municipal finance, as well as learning about the tight relationship between patronage hiring, campaign contributions, and running municipal government. McDonough did not frequent the treasurer's office—preferring the saloon and the racetrack—and Daley inherited significant responsibility.

In 1934, big Joe McDonough developed pneumonia and died. At the age of thirty-two, Daley had lost his key mentor in politics. Many attended McDonough's funeral at Nativity of Our Lord Church in Bridgeport even though his own obituary admitted that McDonough was no angel. McDonough's death, along with the assassination a year earlier of Mayor Anton Cermak, left Dick Daley's career prospects exposed. Apparently, Mayor Cermak was not angelic himself; nearly $1.5 million in cash was found in one of his safe deposit boxes after his death.

Far from failing after the loss of his political patrons, Daley began a twenty-year rise through the ranks of the machine that ended with him on top, like the pope in the Catholic Church or a five-star general in the US Army. Few people outside of local politics realize how dull the field is. Routine—an endless series of small decisions, small acts, bad meals. Repetitious—endless waiting for an important electoral contest or a consequential policy decision. Dick Daley, like most of the survivors of this type of environment, became the complete political bureaucrat: patient, detail oriented, calculating, and cutthroat. He reviewed budgets, marked up legislation, made lists, and filled out paperwork. He waited. He went to the Eleventh Ward office, did favors, and counted votes as a precinct captain. He waited. He attended government sessions, political meetings, funerals, weddings, and wakes. He waited. He kept his thoughts to himself like his father, but always looking for the next opportunity up the ladder.

Daley's first big break happened in 1936 when locals backed him as a write-in candidate for the Illinois House of Representatives. Daley ran a strong campaign and won with the help of his Hamburg Athletic Club buddies. Sitting in Springfield, the Illinois legislature was similar to the Chicago City Council in that many of the elected officials were corrupt or maintained a low level of professional competence. In addition, the state capital had a social culture filled with temptations: cash-carrying lobbyists, easy women, and lots of alcohol. Dick Daley avoided these temptations and mastered the legislative process. Though he focused on supporting the Chicago machine's legislative agenda, Daley also took some progressive positions, such as trying to replace the state sales tax (which was a burden to the poor) with a system of income taxes.

During his years in Springfield, Daley built such a positive reputation that by 1945 a respected newspaper editor described him as "the best exhibit of the hard-working, decent, honest organization politician that the [Chicago] machine can provide." The Democratic Party also recognized Daley's talents, appointing him as deputy Cook County controller in 1936. This office, along with his continuing position as an Eleventh Ward precinct captain, allowed Daley to collect a second salary as well as to keep his active ties within the world of street-level Chicago politics.

By the mid-1930s, the key pattern of Dick Daley's career had emerged: dual existence. Daley would publicly master every office to which he was elected or appointed: city council clerk, Cook County deputy treasurer, Illinois state representative, deputy Cook County controller, Illinois state senator, state revenue director for Governor Adlai Stevenson—and, eventually, mayor of Chicago. In these offices, he worked hard and in good faith, executing his responsibilities and serving the public. But quietly and beyond the public eye, Dick Daley took control of the levers of power, and his ferocious grip never let go: Eleventh Ward precinct captain, Eleventh Ward committeeman, member of the Cook County Democratic Central Committee, chairman of the Cook County Democratic Central Committee, and—ultimately—the Boss. Dick Daley's duality—great skill on the one hand, an unquenchable thirst for power on the other—was the source of both his greatest successes and most tragic failures during his six decades in politics.

In 1938, Daley moved up to the Illinois senate, where he began representing the legislative interests of the Chicago machine—now known as the Kelly-Nash machine—in Springfield. Pat Nash, the leader of the Irish wing of the party and a well-liked elder statesman, had chaired the Cook County Democratic Party since 1931. Nash held a reputation within the local Democratic Party as a fair and skillful leader. On the assassination of Anton Cermak in 1933, Nash picked Edward Kelly, an Irish-Catholic from Bridgeport, to become the new mayor of Chicago. Kelly—tall, handsome, athletic—had worked for decades at the Metropolitan Sanitary District in Chicago, where his control of large sewer and construction contracts enriched both Nash and himself. The Chicago machine knew that Kelly was a man with whom it could do business. Party members also respected his strong leadership skills and his past managerial performance. At the Sanitary District, Kelly transformed and beautified Grant Park, constructed Soldier Field, and refurbished the Museum of Science and Industry. Dick Daley soon emerged as the Kelly-Nash go-to guy in the Illinois senate, becoming minority leader of the senate Democrats in 1941.

The Kelly-Nash machine built on the party apparatus established by Anton Cermak. These leaders of the Chicago Democratic Party held together Cermak's disciplined, multiethnic coalition, while adding three new avenues of expansion: the black community, an alliance with organized crime, and New Deal programs from the federal government. The shrewd Dick Daley observed these Kelly-Nash innovations up close and did not miss their implications for increasing the power of the local Democratic Party. Within two decades, the Kelly-Nash machine would be known as the Daley machine.

By 1943, Ed Kelly had served ten years as a successful and popular mayor, but the Chicago machine began quietly to undermine his leadership. This revolt transpired as a two-step drama. First, Pat Nash, the popular party chairman, died. Kelly took over leadership of the party, but his temper and domineering style alienated many, and the Chicago Democratic Party soon replaced him as party chairman with Jacob Arvey, the Jewish Twenty-Fourth Ward committeeman with mafia connections. The second step in the drama then played out. Though Kelly had allowed taxes to rise, corruption and mafia ties to slip into city government, and Chicago schools to become an ineffective political wasteland, leading Chicago Democrats had a different worry: race. With the Great Black Migration continuing to increase the African-American population of Chicago, Arvey and the rest of the party's leaders were deeply concerned with Mayor Kelly's real and consistent support of "open housing," a policy that allowed Chicago's growing black population to live in any neighborhood of the city. Arvey ordered a telephone poll on the open housing issue to learn how it affected

Mayor Kelly's popularity with voters. The results of the poll indicated that Kelly had lost the support of most white ethnic groups.

In 1947, the Chicago machine dumped Kelly over the open housing issue, as well as repeated political scandals and his administration's poor delivery of city services. The local Democratic Party replaced Kelly with Martin Kennelly, a conservative businessman who actually believed in good government. Depending on one's point of view, backing Kennelly was either a clever or a largely cynical move on the part of the local Democratic Party. Though a civic leader and an Irish-Catholic from Bridgeport, Kennelly was politically naive and without an independent base of supporters. During Kennelly's two terms as mayor, the machine kept him as a figurehead of good government for the party. Due to Kennelly's political ineptitude, this largely succeeded. Corruption blossomed in the city council. The machine reasserted its control of housing and education and effectively eliminated the progressive stance on nondiscrimination against black citizens that the previous mayor had supported. Racial tensions increased dramatically.

For Dick Daley, Martin Kennelly's eight years in office as a weak mayor greatly increased his own political power. In 1947, Daley became the Eleventh Ward committeeman, finally taking his place as the political Boss of Bridgeport. His role as a committeeman meant that Daley also automatically joined the Central Committee of the Cook County Democratic Party, becoming part of the inner circle that ran Chicago politics. His public profile also increased from 1948 to 1950 while serving successfully in the Illinois cabinet of the liberal Governor Adlai Stevenson. In 1953, at the age of fifty-one, Daley was elected by the local Democratic Party to serve as chairman of Cook County Central Committee. The Irish-Catholic kid from Bridgeport had become the most powerful politician in Chicago.

Once Dick Daley held power in his hands, he did not hesitate to use it. For the 1955 mayoral election, Daley's hand-chosen slate-making committee—whose job it was to pick the Democratic candidates for office—refused to support Mayor Kennelly and instead selected Dick

Daley as its candidate. "I guess we wanted him," explained Alderman Tom Keane, who soon became Daley's highly effective floor leader in the city council. "That was part of it. But he wanted it and he went after it. You don't get drafted for an office. Ha! You don't sit around waiting to be anointed. You go after it, and he wanted it more than anybody else did, and he worked at getting it, and that's how he got it. I don't think he had originally set his goal specifically at becoming mayor. He would have gone for governor or anything else. He wanted power and an office."

On the eve of the most important milestone of his life, Dick Daley maintained the appearance of a prosperous, fifty-something Chicago corporate or civic leader. Well-dressed and immaculately groomed, radiating confidence, with wide, stocky shoulders, Daley had a firm handshake and a pleasant, understated smile. An intense but disciplined man, Daley had blue eyes and a direct gaze.

Dick Daley sought the mayor's office by employing the political machine, which he controlled as chairman of the Democratic Party. He truly believed in the Chicago machine, not just as a political organization, but also as a way of improving Chicago, the city that he loved. Daley felt that the secret of politics was to combine good candidates and timely issues, along with a dedicated force of party loyalists who went door-to-door talking to their neighbors and friends.

Daley had two strategies for the 1955 mayoral race: to fire up the local Democratic Party so that it would deliver the citywide vote and to capture the black vote through an alliance with Bill Dawson, the black south-side boss. Daley personally met with many of the party's three thousand precinct captains and made it clear that he was their type of guy. "My opponent says, 'I took politics out of the schools,'" Daley told one group of raucous campaign workers. "[He says] 'I took politics out of this and I took politics out of that.' I say to you: There's nothing wrong with politics. There's nothing wrong with good politics. Good politics is good government."

The machine delivered for Daley, and he beat sitting-mayor Kennelly in the crucial Democratic primary. The key to this victory was the five black south-side wards under the influence of Dawson, which produced enormous vote margins for Daley in both the primary and general elections. Commenting on the election, the *Chicago Daily News* captured a piece of the duality that marked Dick Daley's career: "Some of the finest, high-principled men in the Democratic Party worked for Daley in the election. So did some of the most notorious rascals in politics anywhere. Both kinds helped to deliver the votes to the winner. Daley knows which is which. We pray he has the strength to govern himself and the city accordingly."

From the perspective of history, 1955 marked an important landmark in Chicago politics for two reasons: blacks became a bedrock of the Democratic Party and Dick Daley, one of great political talents of twentieth-century American politics, became the new mayor of Chicago. Like Halley's comet, this second event marked something exceedingly rare in history: when a person of enormous talent has the good fortune to find a career where his talents and passions intersect. The emergence of Dick Daley as mayor of Chicago was one of these exceptional occasions.

Though most contemporary observers in Chicago failed to recognize the importance of this epochal political event, a few shrewd, street-smart politicians did. "Let me tell ya, this Daley—he's going to be one tough sonofabitch," said Charlie Weber, the Forty-Fifth Ward alderman. An even more colorful alderman, the 275-pound, saloon owner named Paddy Bauler, accurately predicted how one man would soon dominate the entire local Democratic political organization.

"Keane and them fellas—Jake Arvey, Joe Gill—they think they are going to run things," said Bauler. "Well, you listen now to what I am sayin': they're not gonna run nothing. They ain't found it out yet, but Daley's the dog with the big nuts, now that we got him elected. You wait and see; that's how it is going to be."

As the new mayor, Richard J. Daley did run things, both the Democratic political party and city government. In fact, the new Mayor Daley quickly used his mastery of politics to tame the machine. Having grown up in Chicago politics during the Kelly-Nash era, Daley fully understood the necessity of harnessing the local party and he was not afraid to function as a political boss. His first decision in office, therefore, was to break one of his campaign promises: he would not give up his position as chairman of the Cook County Democratic Party. He would run the party as well as the city, and for many years, this dual authority made Daley highly effective.

Daley swung into action with great energy and skill. This dynamism was hugely important because Chicago, like other large American cities during the 1950s, had started to suffer a drain of its citizens and its tax base. Poor blacks continued to migrate to Chicago from the South, while wealthy whites bought cars and moved to the suburbs. Business headquarters and factories later followed the whites to the suburbs and, later still, to the sunbelt.

Daley used his contacts in Springfield, Illinois, to obtain an increased sales tax and a new utility tax for the City of Chicago. Many believed that at least a partial explanation for this quick victory was that Daley promised the Republican governor William Stratton that the state Democratic Party would run a weak candidate against him in 1956. If true, Daley's skillful exercise of influence helped Chicago financially and himself politically.

With money for his city secured, Daley promptly de-fanged the Chicago City Council, quickly pushing through reforms that took away the council's authority to prepare the city budget and to approve all city contracts of $2,500 or greater. Daley also removed the authority of ward aldermen to grant driveway permits, which were a great source of under-the-table income for ward politicians. Daley centralized these types of favors, as well as nearly all patronage hiring, at the mayor's office on the fifth floor of city hall. These changes in Chicago's political structure, combined with Daley's power to slate all Democratic candidates for office, took much of the venom out of the city council cohort previously known as the "grey wolves." The mayor soon dominated the legislative body, and most aldermen voted as they were instructed by Daley.

The energetic, action-oriented mayor focused on both small issues and large strategic plans. Having started in politics as a precinct captain in Bridgeport, Daley knew that voters cared about mundane city services, such as garbage collection, snow removal, street lighting, and paving. His party organization helped to take care of these services, following Daley's instructions: "Don't worry if they're Democrats or Republicans. Give them service and they'll become Democrats." Daley also made sure to initiate actions that were visible to the voting public: adding policemen, firemen, and road construction crews.

Daley did not limit himself, however, to the small but important details of running the city. During his first decade in office, he also made big, bold proposals and established himself as Chicago's great builder mayor. During the late 1950s and throughout the 1960s, Daley stimulated the new construction of both public and private modern high-rises in Chicago's downtown Loop district, which reached a total value of $8 billion by the time he died. He also promoted great public investments, such as McCormick Place Convention Center, a system of expressways, the University of Illinois at Chicago campus, and the expansion of O'Hare Airport. These initiatives and Daley's dynamism combined to rejuvenate downtown Chicago. This great growth period also inspired the business community while also increasing Chicago's tax base and laying a long-term foundation for future economic growth.

This success was not preordained. By the 1960s, the city had lacked substantial downtown development for over twenty years, and many areas near the lakefront had deteriorated and suffered from neglect. This discouraged suburbanites and tourists from visiting. Much of the real estate construction that began in Chicago during this time period reflected the business community's confidence in Daley and his mayoral leadership.

Though Daley deserves much of the credit for this vibrant growth period, he also enjoyed some friendly winds at his back. In 1955, the Prudential Building rose in downtown Chicago, making it the first completed high-rise in the city since the depths of the Great Depression. This event excited Chicagoans, and within a year one million guests had visited its observation deck. The same year also marked the completion of the initial section of the Eisenhower Expressway and the first commercial passenger flights at O'Hare Airport, two other projects that started prior to Daley's election.

Soon after entering office, Daley formed the Public Building Commission, a hand-picked group that he stacked with influential businessmen, architects, financiers, and labor officials. Under Daley's leadership, the Public Building Commission initially focused on the development and construction of the Civic Center of Chicago (now called the Daley Center). When completed in 1965, the Civic Center stood across from city hall as a modernist, forward-looking high-rise that not only served the city but also signaled to private developers that downtown Chicago was a smart bet for their own buildings. Moreover, Mayor Daley made sure Chicago's key banks and architecture firms were involved in most of the new development projects planned for the city's downtown area.

This mayoral leadership inspired the necessary confidence for the business community to develop risky commercial high-rise buildings. Over the next decade and a half, the city's businessmen felt confident enough to start creating one of the world's most magnificent skylines: First National Bank Building (now Chase Tower), Standard Oil Building (now the Aon Center), John Hancock Center, and the Sears Tower (now the Willis Tower). "The golden age of building happened under Richard J. Daley," said John Vinci, a Chicago architect. "Some really good buildings came out of it, some of the best buildings in America."

As impressive as was Daley's role in this architectural and building renaissance, his expansion of O'Hare Airport into the busiest airport in the world was even more important to the long-term success of Chicago and its suburbs. Daley had the foresight to see the strategic and economic importance of the airline industry for Chicago. He also personally negotiated with airline executives, financiers, suburban mayors, and state and federal government officials in order to expand O'Hare. Daley won most of the negotiations due to his persistence and financial sophistication, as well as his deep knowledge of human motivations and the workings of federal, state, and local government. By 2010, O'Hare generated 450,000 jobs and $38 billion in annual economic activity for the greater Chicago region. From the perspective of history, Dick Daley's twentieth-century expansion of O'Hare Airport allowed Chicago to continue as one of the world's great cities. It was the most important accomplishment of his long career, and one which equaled Chicago's great railroad expansion in the nineteenth century.

His first decade in office clearly demonstrated that Dick Daley was an immense talent, both as mayor of Chicago and as a once-in-a-generation political phenomenon. If Daley had left public office at the height of his game—like the marvelous pitcher, Sandy Koufax, who retired his unstoppable pitching arm in 1966—then historians may have quickly anointed him one of the most significant mayors in American history. But Daley did not retire after his first two terms in office, or even after his third. He held on to power for more than an additional decade. This extra passage of time would reveal another side of Dick Daley—a man not only of vast abilities but also of Shakespearean flaws.

CHAPTER 2

EVERY HAPPY FAMILY IS THE SAME

For their first real date, Dick Daley took Eleanor "Sis" Guilfoyle to a White Sox baseball game at Comiskey Park. Daley, of course, was a politician—Bridgeport born, but somewhat liberal, a New Deal, FDR-Democrat. In his personal life, Daley could be warm and charismatic, and he probably made a good impression on his date. Bill Marovitz, a young family friend of the Daleys who himself later went into politics, recalled his youthful feelings for Dick Daley: "You know, he had the most wonderful smile, robust laugh. I just loved being around the guy. . . . When he was out at family time or social stuff, he was wonderful to be around. If we were at a White Sox game together, he would be yelling and screaming just like I was. Just like any fan would be. He would be yelling and screaming for the Sox, and at the umpire, but he would have kids on his knee and he was just a warm, affable guy in social situations."

In the summer of 1936, Dick Daley married Sis Guilfoyle at St. Bridget's Church in Chicago's Bridgeport neighborhood. On the next St. Patrick's Day, the couple had their first child, Patricia. Soon, Sis gave birth to a second, and then a third, daughter: Mary Carol and Eleanor. In November 1939, Dick and Sis moved from their Bridgeport apartment to a house they bought at 3536 South Lowe Avenue in Bridgeport, where they lived together for the next thirty-seven years. Part of the attraction of the house for Dick Daley was its close proximity to Nativity of Our Lord, the Catholic school and church where he learned to read, to write, and to follow the Catholic catechism.

On April 24, 1942, Dick and Sis were blessed with their firstborn son, Richard Michael Daley, who they named after his father. Later, the couple added three more boys—Michael, John, and Bill—to complete the family of nine. Sis was a homemaker and the disciplinarian of the children. "I'll take credit for that," she said, "because I was home all the time. I don't think Dick would ever say no to them. If they asked me for something and I said no, they'd try to work on the father. All kids do. But Dick would say: 'Well, what did your mother say?' And then he didn't have to say no. I always said, 'Well, they'll never forget me—for the number of times I've said no.'"

Though Dick Daley truly loved it, Chicago in the early 1950s was a drab, worn-out city. Years of neglect—stretching from the Great Depression through the end of World War II—had led to a lack of investment in both downtown and the neighborhoods. This deterioration combined with the city's heavy industrialization and gave Chicago a dull, gray feeling.

Chicago in the 1950s was also a world of strong communities built on largely unquestioned authority. People tended to stay in the same neighborhoods, same jobs, and same homes for most of their adult life. Parents, priests, bosses, elected officials, and school principals made decisions, the vast majority of which were never challenged. Religion and political party were a constant. Children became whatever their parents were before them. For most, this meant Catholic and Democrat. The permanence of this world was like the two sides of a coin. On one side, simplicity, lasting relationships, and strong communities. On the other side, inflexible hierarchy and a world of limited choices.

The bedrock of 1950s Chicago was Catholicism. The city's archdiocese was the largest in America, containing more than 2 million practicing Catholics. In four hundred Roman Catholic parishes, there were two thousand priests, nine thousand nuns, and nearly 300,000 parochial school students. Religious vocations and enrollment in Catholic schools had surged to near an all-time peak.

For Catholics, local parishes became the center of each community. The Chicago archdiocese targeted a parish for each square mile of the city, and most priests and nuns taught that their parish was a sacred space. This meant that the best way to build a Christian community was to stay local: keep your home within the parish, send your children to the parish school, and patronize neighborhood establishments. Make a life and a community together.

Sunday mass in the 1950s was a passive experience, with ritual as its distinctive feature. The priest stood on the altar with his back to the congregation and celebrated the ceremony in Latin. Catholic worshipers did not sing, perform gospel readings, or respond to the priest. Their one act of participation was to receive the Eucharist. When the communion bell rang, each parishioner filed forward, knelt on a red cushion, and accepted a wafer in the mouth as an altar boy slid a silver platter under the chin to catch any slivers of falling communion. Silent prayer was the norm, and no one expected a change of pace or any expression of individuality.

Parochial schools in Chicago focused on transmitting the Catholic faith and indoctrinating children with the proper values. The core educational idea was that children need discipline in order to be prepared to live a moral and successful life. Independent thought or behavior was frowned on. Children wore uniforms and needed permission to go to the bathroom, answer a question, or move about the school. Nuns drilled the students endlessly in spelling, grammar, penmanship, and the Catholic faith. Rote memorization was encouraged.

Life in Bridgeport in the 1950s was a small-scale version of the city itself: Catholic and Democratic, a tight-knit community where continuity and hierarchy were the norm. By Rich Daley's boyhood, Bridgeport had peaked economically. Most of the meat packers had left the Union Stock Yards, taking with them many jobs. Upwardly mobile whites moved to the suburbs. Despite these challenges, the community maintained its vibrancy and its local pride. Modest Chicago-style two-flats and bungalows filled Daley's boyhood neighborhood, along with many City of Chicago employees, who had spent most of their adulthood working for his father's political organization. Neighborhood locals described Bridgeport as a miniature melting pot where people looked out for each other and moms knew who all the kids were.

After spending decades climbing his way through the local Democratic Party, Rich Daley's father was elected mayor of Chicago in 1955, a few weeks before his eldest son turned thirteen years old. On arriving home at midnight on the day of the election, after defeating the sitting mayor in the crucial Democratic primary, Dick Daley was greeted by Sis shouting, "Here he is, kids!" Daley hugged his children and promised to take them fishing to celebrate.

In his victory statement for the Democratic primary, Daley referenced his Catholic faith, pronouncing to Democrats gathered at the Morrison Hotel, "I shall conduct myself in the spirit of the prayer of St. Francis of Assisi: 'Lord, make me an instrument of thy peace.'" Later, however, he attributed much of his success to the Democratic Party, saying that "without the party, only the rich would be elected to office."

Dick Daley had much success and power in his career, but he also loved his family and was a dedicated father and husband. He made his home in Bridgeport a sanctuary from the outside world. "We never used our home for political meetings or bringing people in," said his eldest son, Rich. "It was strictly my father's friends. And that was very important. My father protected us, in many ways. He knew that the sons and daughters of political figures start being used by people. And that was one area that was sacred. It was very beneficial to us, I think, in our upbringing, that no one could get in there."

Young Rich grew up in this protective nest of the Daley household. For most of his childhood, the family's modest ranch house contained ten people, including his parents, his six siblings, and his paternal grandfather Mike. Like most of their Bridgeport neighbors, the Daley children developed in a home where personal privacy was a rare commodity.

Described as naturally shy by his brother Bill, Rich Daley had a happy childhood, with no record of any special achievements. Sports were the primary focus of his grade school years, including unorganized pick-up baseball games in the park and basketball in the alley behind the house. Daley's boyhood also included neighborhood friendships, chores, and errands, as well as fun family events, such as Lake Michigan fishing trips or professional baseball outings. The Daleys were a close family, and there was love and affection in their home.

Rich Daley—like his father—attended Nativity of Our Lord, a parish founded in 1868, thirty-one years after the City of Chicago incorporated. Standing at the corner of Thirty-Seventh Street and Union Avenue, Nativity was a short walk from his boyhood home: one and a half blocks down Lowe Avenue or through the alley. Like the other Daley children, Rich walked home from school for the lunch his Mom made him each weekday. He was a well-behaved, clean-cut kid who fit in well at his conservative parochial school.

"Nativity was the quintessential Catholic grammar school," said Ted Villinski, a boyhood classmate of Rich Daley. "Everybody walked to school—there was no busing or anything like that. There was no lunch program. The nuns were the authority. The Pastor of the parish was a fella by the name of Murray who was a stern disciplinarian. Our lives just circled around Nativity of Our Lord. Richie Daley and I played on the Nativity of our Lord basketball team at the Valentine's Boys Club, which was at Thirty-Fourth and Emerald Street. Our first loves were basketball."

Just as basketball and Nativity of Our Lord were important facets of Rich Daley's youth, so was the Chicago White Sox baseball team. Comiskey Park, standing at Thirty-Fifth Street and Shields Avenue, loomed over Bridgeport. South-side Chicagoans—mostly white, Catholic, and working class—made pilgrimages to the park built on a former City of Chicago dump site. But for the Daley family, the journey was short: half a block up Lowe Avenue, turn right onto Thirty-Fifth Street, and then five blocks to the "Baseball Palace of the World." Emerging from the railroad underpass just west of Shields Avenue, the Daleys would begin to see the first glimpse of Comiskey under the setting sun. The boys, along with their father, would hear the ballpark rustling with energy and feel the anticipation of the crowds.

The White Sox were an exciting team during Rich Daley's boyhood. Between 1952 and 1965, when he was twenty-three, the team won consistently. It was known for good defense, solid pitching, and aggressive base running. In 1959, the White Sox won the American League championship, and the league awarded second baseman Nellie Fox its Most Valuable Player Award.

Due to his success in politics and his love of the team, Dick Daley possessed a private box along the third base line at Comiskey Park, immediately next to the Sox's on-deck circle. He frequently brought his four boys to that box. "My dad loved to take us to ballgames," said Rich Daley. "We could talk, catch up with each other, and watch the game. It was a real joy. I still enjoy the games."

A photographer captured Rich's joy on film. The 1955 photo, taken shortly after Dick Daley won an election to become Mayor Daley, shows Rich smiling as he stands next to his father, who leans slightly forward over the third-base wall and crosses his arms to simultaneously shake the hands of both the White Sox's and the Cubs' general managers. Mayor Daley is wearing a formal hat and a full suit and tie. His three young boys—Bill, Michael, and John—are slightly to the side, looking somewhat in awe. His firstborn son, Rich, stands at his right shoulder, smiling, leaning in, directly between the mayor and Chicago's south-side and north-side baseball skippers. A great public relations shot for a newly elected politician. A happy memory for a family. The photograph is a two-for-one.

Photographs, of course, are only a glimpse of one fleeting moment in time. They can reveal or obscure the truth. Sometimes—as in the case of a smiling, thirteen-year-old Rich Daley standing next to his dad along the third-base line at Comiskey Park—a photo does both.

Rich Daley did have a largely happy childhood and he loved his father, his family, and sports. David Axelrod, the well-known Democratic political strategist, described this facet of Daley's youth: "To hear [Rich] Daley and his family tell it, his childhood was rather unremarkable—a sort of urban, Irish Catholic version of 'Leave It to Beaver'— marked by a rich family and religious life and the typical innocent pursuits of youth, primarily sports."

However, there were other truths as well, other facets of growing up as Rich Daley. His father was a very powerful man and young Daley grew up not only with a proximity to political power but also with a complete immersion in a world in which one man—through personal savvy, hard-won expertise, and force of will—exerted his dominance over a city of more than three million people. So Rich—first as a boy, then as a teenager, and afterward as a young man—grew up in his father's shadow, like a young sapling at the base of a giant redwood. Alderman Ed Burke, another Irish-Catholic, second-generation Chicago politician—who turned out to be one of Rich Daley's lifetime rivals—captured the weight of this type of paternal shade: "I don't know that the influence of my dad ever wears off."

With time, the elder Daley's shadow grew. Young Rich Daley did not establish himself as a superior student, a great athlete, or a charismatic leader of his classmates. Yet like most adolescents, Rich not only wanted his father's love, he also desired the respect and appreciation of the man he admired most. According to Ned Kennan, a friend of the Daleys and a prominent psychologist who advised government leaders and politicians throughout the world: "The Daleys never saw Rich Daley as being the genius of the family. He was always taken by his father as being a nice guy, but not too smart, not too powerful, and he's never going to go anywhere. And he obviously, little [Rich] Daley, was not happy with such an image. He really wanted to have the respect of his father." This desire for paternal approval would gnaw at Rich throughout his life.

Like his father, Rich attended De La Salle Institute. Given his Bridgeport upbringing, this was a natural choice since at that time there was a strict division between children who attended Catholic schools and those who attended public ones. The nuns at grammar schools such as Nativity of Our Lord insisted that their parish boys went to De La Salle and that their female graduates attended one of the Catholic high schools for girls.

Founded in 1889 by the Christian Brothers, De La Salle was a mission-based, Catholic institution. On a day-to-day basis, the Christian Brothers implemented this moral mission through discipline and a tough-love type of environment. "The Christian Brothers were very stern, strict disciplinarians," explained Ron Gralewski, a De La Salle classmate of Rich Daley. "Having had a Catholic parochial background, most kids understood what they needed to do to survive in that type of environment. Basically, keep your mouth shut and do your work. De La Salle had corporal punishment back then, but if you got it, you deserved it. If you got smacked, it's because you did something that you deserved to get smacked for. We all lived with that and it wasn't a problem."

"Ya' know, Rich and I once both got paddled by a teacher," added Gralewski proudly.

Gralewski and Daley were sitting in bookkeeping class, whispering about the spreadsheets they were supposed to be working on independently.

"Is that an asset?" murmured Gralewski to Daley.

"Mr. Gralewski, Mr. Daley, step up here please!" boomed the voice of the Christian Brother in his black suit and white collar.

"Haw haw haw!" roared the class in anticipation of the smack that was sure to follow.

Rich Daley and Ron Gralewski walked slowly to the front of the room, like prisoners marching to their own execution. Facing outward to the class, each leaned over and placed his hands on his knees, supporting all of the body weight.

"Now, I'm not going to get in trouble with your father, am I?" asked the Christian Brother with a smile as he raised his arm in the air and struck Rich with the paddle.

"Smack!!" it goes on Daley.

"Smack!!!" it goes on Gralewski.

"The paddle was kind of like the arm part of an old-fashioned school desk, and it hurt," recalled Gralewski more than fifty years later. "That was the only time a Christian Brother ever smacked me with a paddle, but I had it coming."

In the 1950s, De La Salle was a blue-collar, all-boys school making a reputation for itself as the training ground for politicians and judges. The culture of De La Salle, however, did not focus on politics or even on academics. Sports dominated the De La Salle environment. According to Gralewski, basketball, football, and baseball were "like the three seasons" and the thing to do on Friday night was to attend a basketball game.

Rich Daley's commute from his parent's house to his high school retraced the path to Comiskey Park—half a block up Lowe Avenue, right onto Thirty-Fifth Street, and then five blocks to the stadium. When he reached the intersection of Shields Avenue and Thirty-Fifth Street, Rich continued heading east a few blocks and then crossed over into Bronzeville, a predominantly black, poor neighborhood. Bronzeville stretched from Thirty-First to Thirty-Eighth Street on the south and past Calumet Avenue on the east. High-rise public housing was going up in Bronzeville, and within a few years of Daley's high school graduation the heavy concentration of public housing would dominate portions of the south side of Chicago. In 1962, Rich's father, as mayor of Chicago, made sure that the newly constructed Dan Ryan Expressway, a fourteen-lane highway, separated Comiskey Park and Bridgeport from Bronzeville and the blacks.

"The neighborhood De La Salle was in was surrounded—it was a black neighborhood," recalled Ron Gralewski. "You could get mugged. I don't think it was high crime. It was just the danger of being in a neighborhood *like that.*"

Ted Villinski provided a more nuanced recollection of race relations in Bridgeport. "In Bridgeport we were sort of isolated from racial tension," said Villinski. "We knew gang activity existed between the whites and blacks, but didn't know anyone who was personally involved. At De La Salle, we had a few blacks but not a lot. We didn't really focus on the question of race very much, other than De La Salle not allowing us to walk through black neighborhoods to and from school. But I think we were naive, which was why the whole issue of race did not resonate very much with us."

But the question of race for teenagers on the south side of Chicago in the late 1950s was actually more complicated than remembered. It was true that the small percentage of black students at De La Salle were treated fairly in the tough love manner of De La Salle. These blacks were classmates, athletes, and Catholic young men just like the rest of the student body. But outside of school, there was a different reality in south-side Chicago. Racial segregation was the norm and working-class, blue-collar adults—including the white, Catholic parents who sent their children to De La Salle—could not conceive of a world in which blacks and whites integrated regularly. One practical implication of this was that racial dividing lines existed, and these boundaries were faithfully enforced. Blacks needed to stay on their side. "Wentworth Avenue was the dividing line," recalled John Monacella, another De La Salle classmate of Rich Daley. "Blacks never crossed Wentworth. Whites could go anywhere they want."

In the late 1950s, the rapidly growing black population in Chicago made these racial borders more difficult to guard, and racial tension increased. In 1957, for example, seventeen-year-old Joseph Schwartz used a hammer to murder seventeen-year-old Alvin Palmer as he waited at a bus stop in the evening. Palmer was black, a good high school student who was actively involved in his school. Schwartz was a white kid who had dropped out of De La Salle and became active in a Back of the Yards street gang. Schwartz and Palmer were both two years older than Rich Daley. The president of the Illinois NAACP Gerald Bullock publicly stated that the murder represented "many Chicago attitudes toward racial minorities," and the *Chicago Daily Defender* newspaper editorialized about "the powder keg of racial tensions."

Despite the uncomfortable racial undercurrent, Daley had positive memories of De La Salle: big, open windows that let in the sounds of the nearby screeching el train tracks, sweaty, lunchtime basketball games, and warm spring afternoons.

Daley also played varsity basketball in high school, where he focused much of his energies and time. In the 1950s, the Chicago Catholic League had two varsity divisions, called the Lights and the Heavies. Any player who stood five feet eight inches or under in height played for the Lights and the rest joined the Heavies team. Daley played for the Lights. Given Daley's modicum of talent, many in the De La Salle community believed that the position of his father as mayor of Chicago had an impact in his making the much-sought-after basketball team. According to a professional sportscaster in Chicago who attended De La Salle at the same time as Rich: "He wasn't exactly blessed with great athletic skills, but he worked and worked on his game. By his senior year, he was a really key part of that team. Rich wasn't brilliant out there. He was just a real plugger."

A plugger has a number of essential characteristics. Strong work ethic. Moderate talent in a specific endeavor. Determination. Toughness. Persistence in the face of challenges. These are resources that a plugger taps into when confronting adversity. Long-distance runners, mountain climbers and a certain type of boxer tend to be pluggers. As he matured and progressed in his life, many contemporaries witnessed these characteristics in Rich Daley.

During his senior year of high school, Daley ran for class president but lost. "He just wasn't a guy who was out there with the boys. He hung with his own group of people," said Ron Gralewski in explaining Daley's lack of popularity with his classmates. "His personality was that he was very reserved. He was a quiet, pretty nonassuming guy. Not at all boisterous."

In his 1960 graduating high school yearbook, Rich said his ambition was to become a great lawyer and politician. His high school classmates bestowed on him the nickname of mayor, but that designation may have had ironic connotations. "From the time that Rich was in high school, he wanted to be a politician because that's what he knew," explained Gralewski. "The only thing that Rich ever knew was that someday he wanted to be mayor of the City of Chicago. His nickname in high school was 'mayor' because his father was mayor. I don't know that any of us ever felt that Rich was going to be mayor someday."

After graduating from De La Salle, Rich enrolled at Providence College, a small, Catholic school in Rhode Island. This decision was the first in his life that did not clearly follow in his father's footsteps. At Providence, during his freshman year Daley met Ray Flynn, an Irish-Catholic sports star at the college who later became mayor of Boston and the US Ambassador to the Vatican. Flynn believes that Daley was greatly influenced by the philosophy of social and economic justice of the Dominican priests who ran Providence. This philosophy emphasized that each person must take personal responsibility for creating a society that recognizes human dignity and distributes economic goods in a way that allows all people to meet their basic needs. Flynn, who maintained his relationship with Daley for the next thirty years, said that Rich Daley took this philosophical and religious guidance seriously because that was the nature of his personality: "Richie was rather shy, rather quiet, and very, very serious about life."

Though Flynn loved Providence College, it did not stick for Daley. After two years, Rich moved back to Chicago and enrolled at DePaul University, the alma mater of his father. According to his brother Bill Daley, "I guess that's when it was pretty clear that Rich was going to follow through and go into politics. That's why he came back." At DePaul, he earned a bachelor's degree and a law degree, graduating in 1968.

During law school, Daley joined a study group that met weekly. Larry Daly, one of DePaul Law School's most popular professors, took an interest in Rich, as he did in many of his students, and he encouraged him to work with a group that included Ron Banks, Howie Carroll, Marty Russo, Fred Levinson, Bob Bernstein, and Joe Bernstein. The group usually met at Ron Banks's house in Oak Park on Thursday nights and studied in the basement. They were serious, hard-working commuter students who wanted to get through law school, pass the bar, and become practicing attorneys. Though it was far off in the future, many of the group would become judges, politicians, and labor union officials.

The Banks study group would always take a break for the home cooked meal that Mrs. Banks prepared for them and her family. Heaping plates of braciole—thin slices of steak stuffed with cheese and breadcrumbs and covered with pasta sauce—homemade pasta dishes, and meatballs made from scratch were typical. Rich Daley had a tremendous love of Italian food, and he would pile his plate high as he talked passionately about his family and changes going on in the city. With the other students, he also discussed law cases, talked about girlfriends, and chitchatted with Mr. and Mrs. Banks. After dinner, Mr. Banks shared Churchill cigars with Daley and the others before the group headed back into the basement for more hours of study.

After graduating law school, Daley sat for the Illinois bar exam, but failed it on his first two attempts. Though painfully embarrassing at the time, thirty years later he directly addressed his lack of academic achievement, demonstrating an astute sense of himself. "I know who I am. I'm comfortable with myself," said Daley. "Yeah, I had to take some reading and math courses on Saturdays. So what? So, I flunked the bar. But I passed the third time. I stayed with it and overcame that. . . . There are smarter people than me. I know that. I've met a lot of 'em. A lot of 'em told me that, too—how smart they are. I don't say too much. I just listen and try to figure out where they're coming from."

CHAPTER 3

CHICAGO VISIONS

The walk from the Daley family home to the Eleventh Ward Democratic headquarters was an old and familiar route: one and a half blocks down Lowe Avenue, turn right onto Thirty-Seventh and walk two blocks past Nativity of Our Lord until you hit Halsted Street. Turn the corner and this plain, brick building proudly announces, "ELEVENTH WARD DEMOCRATIC PARTY." Here, Rich Daley's dad received his political education, grew strong, and then powerful. As a young precinct captain, it was in this building that Dick Daley learned how to understand human motivations, dispense jobs and favors, and count votes. At the Eleventh Ward headquarters in the 1920s, Dick Daley became part of the Chicago machine, which depended on economic transactions for much of its political strength. Basically, the machine secured city jobs for its political workers in exchange for their vote-generating efforts.

By the time Rich Daley was five years old, his dad ran this office as Eleventh Ward committeeman, controlling as many as two thousand of these political patronage jobs. This meant that many, many dads in Bridgeport owed their livelihood to his dad. Growing up as the eldest son of such a powerful man may have contributed to the sense of entitlement that some would later discern in Rich Daley. His father, Dick Daley, expected these patronage workers to support the Eleventh Ward Democratic Party. They voted for the party's candidates and sold fund-raising tickets to dinners, golf outings, and other official events. Every year, for example, more than twelve thousand Eleventh Ward residents attended the annual indoor picnic at the International Amphitheatre in Bridgeport. At this event, children and their parents— just like the Daley family—would be treated to free soda and ice cream, along with rides on the Ferris wheels and merry-go-rounds. In 1952 and 1956, and then again in 1968, the vote-delivering power of Daley's Eleventh Ward Democratic Party would help to bring the Democratic National Convention, along with the attention of the entire country, to the International Amphitheatre in Bridgeport.

As Rich Daley grew older, his father—driven by ambition and increasing responsibilities—attended a constant stream of political outings, including countless weddings, wakes, funerals, and retirement homes. Shortly after becoming mayor, he went to eight weddings in one weekend. One political strategist described the enticing proximity to power that Rich Daley and his brothers glimpsed in their formative teenage years. "While the Daley boys were shielded from the glare of publicity as children, they still were afforded an early and seductive inside look at politics and political power," wrote David Axelrod. "They joined their father at meetings, rallies, and . . . often rode with their father in his limousine as the mayor went to evening meetings or wakes, the traditional rites of urban politics."

In 1960, Mayor Daley brought eighteen-year-old Rich and the rest of the family with him to attend the Democratic National Convention in Los Angeles. From the perspective of history, this convention and the presidential election of 1960 became the highlight of the elder Daley's fifty-year career. Over a decade later, Dick Daley reflected on the 1960 convention and his role in the selection of the first Irish-Catholic president of the United States. "I was thinking of my four sons," said the mayor of Chicago, "and I wanted John Kennedy to be their President."

From Chicago, the Daley family boarded a private car on the Santa Fe Chief train, which took them to Los Angeles. At their hotel, a welcoming party of Chicago politicians greeted the family and a live band played the song "Chicago (That Toddlin' Town)."

Political insiders expected Mayor Daley to be the kingmaker at the convention, and he was courted by the supporters of Senator John F. Kennedy of Massachusetts, Adlai Stevenson of Illinois, and other candidates. Daley greatly admired Kennedy. However, Stevenson—the liberal, Democratic nominee in 1952 and 1956—was a longtime ally, and the convention hall began to be filled with Stevenson banners and with calls of "We want Stevenson, we want Stevenson, we want Stevenson." Eleanor Roosevelt herself asked to meet with Daley to make a personal appeal for Stevenson. Mayor Daley accepted the invitation and traveled to meet her in Pasadena, along with two of his sons, Rich and Mike. Daley listened to her appeal for two hours, but then delivered his disappointing verdict.

"It's too late," Mayor Daley told Roosevelt. "We made our commitments. I asked Adlai over a year ago whether he would run. He told me no. We aren't budging."

Daley would be kingmaker at the 1960 convention, and he supported Kennedy, the handsome Irish prince. "That was a special day, a real honor," recalled Rich Daley. "We were able to have experiences like that because of who my dad was."

The Democratic convention in Los Angeles lacked the acrimony that would soon become commonplace at national political meetings. Mayor Daley used his masterful skills as a backroom politician and coalition builder to form an alliance with other powerful Democrats, including Governor David Lawrence of Pennsylvania, New York machine-boss Carmine DeSapio, and Governor Michael DiSalle of Ohio. Senator Kennedy won the Democratic nomination on the first ballot. He then narrowly defeated Richard Nixon in the general election to win the presidency, helped by a remarkable voter turnout in Chicago. Many observers supposed that Mayor Daley stole the Illinois election for Kennedy.

In Washington, DC, politicians invented jokes to explain Mayor Daley's power and what had occurred in the 1960 presidential race. One popular yarn featured President Kennedy, Secretary of State Dean Rusk, and Mayor Daley on a lifeboat in the middle of the Pacific Ocean with only enough food for one of them. The three men agree that two must go overboard. Kennedy said, "I am the president of the United States of America—I'm too important." The secretary of state echoed the president, saying "It's the Cold War—I am essential to the nation."

With a poker face, Dick Daley suggested a compromise: "Listen, gentlemen, the only democratic thing to do is to vote." The mayor won the vote by a count of eight to two.

Rich Daley may have heard this joke or others like it. His dad was a very powerful man. As a young adult, Rich became more and more exposed to his father's dominance. In the early 1960s, politicians in Chicago repeated a story about how one day Mayor Daley interrupted a meeting at city hall when he turned to his bodyguard and said, "Rich needs a haircut. He looks like a hippie. Make that kid get a haircut today." According to Abner Mikva, an ex-Congressman and federal judge, "When Mayor Daley ordered something in Chicago, it was done. And that is hard on a kid."

Another thing that was hard on Rich Daley as he matured into adulthood was his father's relationship with Jane Byrne. When Dick Daley first met five-foot-three-inch Byrne at Queen of All Saints parish, she was a thirty-one-year-old, Irish-Catholic cutie. Daley—mayor of Chicago, who had the rounded face and sturdy girth of his sixty-two years—immediately liked her and invited Byrne to come see him at city hall. Daley and Byrne—both of whom combined political toughness with warmth and charisma—would quickly develop a lasting emotional bond. Over the next twelve years, Dick Daley would uncharacteristically anoint Byrne his protégée, making her a professional in Chicago's antipoverty department, then commissioner of the Department of Consumer Affairs, and eventually co-chair of the Democratic Party of Chicago. On the surface, it seemed as if Daley had gotten what he had wanted from Byrne: a feisty female mascot for his male-dominated political party. But he had actually miscalculated. Three years after the death of Daley, Byrne—a high-energy campaigner and political free spirit—would become the first female mayor of Chicago, a position for which she was temperamentally ill-suited. According to the mayor's press secretary Frank Sullivan, "Jane Byrne was the supreme misjudgment of Richard J. Daley's life."

Young Rich Daley also misjudged Byrne. He could not recognize the positive qualities that his dad saw in the woman he affectionately called Janie. Resentful of Byrne, Rich was blind to the talents of the woman who competed with him for the favors and affection of his father. This initial feeling became a deep-seated jealousy in the younger Daley and contributed to his later underestimating Byrne.

In order to be a great politician, a person must be savvy about human nature and aware of humanity's frequent self-serving behavior and concealed personal agendas. To survive and thrive, politicians must make accurate judgments about the many, many people they meet. Over their long careers, the Daleys—father and son—became known as particularly skillful practitioners of the art of sizing people up. Except for Jane Byrne.

Despite this rare misjudgment, Dick Daley dominated almost everyone with whom he came into contact, including well-known politicians and famous civil rights leaders. At the height of his powers, Daley possessed a rare, very valuable talent: the ability to give rivals an apparent victory while privately "cutting their balls off." This skill allowed Daley to appear publicly conciliatory on sensitive issues, thereby maintaining the support of most voters, while behind closed doors he weakened an opponent and protected his own power. Of course, race was the single most sensitive issue for a politician during the 1950s and 1960s. It is not surprising, then, that two of the great black political figures of that era—Bill Dawson and Martin Luther King Jr.—received this invisible castration treatment from Daley.

Daley and Dawson started off as political allies. When Dick Daley had first won election as mayor in 1955, the black wards under the influence of south-side political boss Bill Dawson delivered him key vote margins. Daley, however, did not trust a man as ambitious as Dawson. Throughout the 1950s, therefore, Daley curbed Dawson's political power. One way Daley accomplished this was by supporting weaker black aldermen as a counterweight to Dawson. This ineffectual group earned the nickname "the silent six." As a face-saving measure, Daley allowed Dawson to maintain his prestigious positions as a Chicago committeeman and US Congressman.

With compliant black politicians in place, Daley focused on rebuilding the city that he loved during his first eight years in office.

He spent his time and political capital on skyscrapers, expressways, airports, and schools. Of course, most of the building that Daley did benefited downtown or white neighborhoods. Black voters passively accepted this and delivered him large voter margins in the 1955, 1959, and 1963 mayoral elections. These black voters also largely put up with the Daley machine's policy of racial segregation in public housing and schools. This passive behavior by blacks reinforced real estate practices sustaining racial segregation in neighborhoods.

After the mayoral election of 1963, however, Daley switched from treating black Chicagoans with benign neglect to more actively disfavoring them. His reasoning was simple and compelling for a man who cared deeply about his own power: Daley had lost the white vote in 1963 to a Polish-Catholic politician, Benjamin Adamowski, who actively opposed open housing for blacks. From 1963 on, therefore, for the rest of his career, Daley not only shed the New Deal liberalism of his youth but also his midlife political moderation. He became much more of a reactionary, especially on the issue of race. He consistently signaled to white voters that he was tough and that he would use his power to "draw the line" with respect to black civil rights. When black Chicagoans in 1963 began protesting the overcrowded, rundown condition of public schools in their neighborhoods, for example, Daley refused to let black students attend white schools that had plenty of openings. Instead, his handpicked school board put mobile classrooms at the overflowing black schools. Nicknamed "Willis Wagons" after Benjamin Willis, the inflexible white superintendent of schools, these temporary structures inflamed the black community and caused a series of school boycotts. Daley—a product of white, private, Catholic schools—was unmoved personally and politically. Daley's own press secretary used to joke that Mayor Daley believed that equal opportunity meant "nine Irishmen and a Swede."

"The more blacks picked on Willis, the more popular he became among the whites," explained a former aide to Daley. "If Daley gave in, the whites would have been mad. He figured he'd always get the black vote, but the whites had already shown that they'd go for somebody else when they went for Adamowski. Besides, Willis was useful to Daley. If the civil rights people kept after Willis, it kept the heat off of Daley."

And so as America's civil rights revolution kicked off and then accelerated, Dick Daley became more backward looking, a sixty-something-year-old man who used his power to defend his own, deeply engrained vision of Chicago: well-ordered white communities, clustered around their large Catholic churches.

Martin Luther King Jr., however, had a different vision of American society—including large, northern cities like Chicago. After winning a number of important civil rights victories in the south, King contemplated bringing his quest for civil rights and an integrated society north to Chicago. King's famous "Letter from Birmingham Jail," written in 1963, partly explained his thinking. King wrote that white moderates blocked progress on civil rights more than outright racists and that "shallow understanding from people of good will is more frustrating than absolute misunderstanding from people of ill will."

King came to Chicago in the summer of 1965 and made twenty speeches in two days as he pondered whether to take his civil rights organization, the Southern Christian Leadership Conference, to the north. The city may have seemed like an appropriate target of direct political action because it combined some of the worst black slums in the nation with a political situation in which King would only have to negotiate with one, all-powerful ruler.

"King decided to come to Chicago," explained Reverend Arthur Brazier, a black minister from Chicago, "because he thought Chicago was unique in that there was one man, one source of power, who you had to deal with. He knew this wasn't the case in New York or any other city. He thought if Daley could be persuaded of the rightness of open housing and integrated schools that things could be done."

When King announced his group would move to the Midwestern city in early 1966, the clever mayor of Chicago reacted as if he had just heard good news. "I'm always happy to have help and assistance in resolving difficult problems of housing, education and poverty," said Daley. "No one has to march to see the Mayor of Chicago. The door is always open and I'm here 10 to 12 hours a day."

When King moved to Chicago in early 1966, he began calling his group the Chicago Freedom Movement and announced that "our objective will be to bring about the unconditional surrender of forces dedicated to the creation and maintenance of slums." Over the next six months, King and his followers organized downtown rallies, gave speeches, and held high-level meetings with the mayor and his city hall staff. These efforts did not lead to much success, however, as Mayor Daley announced the city's own, highly visible plans to address urban blight and also worked behind the scenes to co-opt many of Chicago's black political leaders.

Two events during the summer of 1966 changed the political equation and put increasing pressure on Daley. First, during a summer heat wave, City of Chicago workers turned off the fire hydrants where black children cooled down in the huge west-side ghetto. Five days of rioting and looting ensued, and Mayor Daley called in the National Guard, which brought more than four thousand armed soldiers to the city. The second event was the Chicago Freedom Movement's decision to launch a series of marches through all-white southwest-side neighborhoods bordering the black ghetto. This decision posed a serious political threat to Daley because many of the white ethnics who lived in these areas felt directly threatened by Chicago's growing black population.

"White power!" "Polish power!" "Burn them like Jews," yelled the white residents during one of King's marches.

"Two, four, six, eight, we don't want to integrate!" "Kill those niggers!" screamed other residents during another march.

After getting hit in the head and knocked down by a rock at one march, King compared Chicago to his experiences in the Southern United States. "I've been in many demonstrations all across the south," said King, "but I can say that I have never seen—even in Mississippi and Alabama—mobs as hostile and hate-filled as I've seen in Chicago. I think the people from Mississippi ought to come to Chicago to learn how to hate."

Though unsympathetic to King's desire for racial integration in Chicago, Mayor Daley worried deeply about the political implications of continued marches by King and the Chicago Freedom Movement. "It seemed to me," said one contemporary observer, "that Daley was not trying to figure out how to deal with the broader race and housing problems in Chicago. It was about stopping the marches which were tearing at the heart of the Democratic party."

Using one of his great talents, Daley decided to negotiate. Rather than directly face King, however, in August 1966 he put together a forum under the auspices of the Chicago Conference on Religion and Race, a group composed of religious, business, labor, and other civic leaders. The negotiations at the Palmer House Hotel pitted the Chicago Freedom Movement against the Chicago Real Estate Board. Daley had shrewdly aligned himself and the business community with King, positioning the real estate industry as the roadblock to open housing for blacks. After a series of negotiations, the two sides agreed on a document that appeared to meet most of the Chicago Freedom Movement's demands for open housing in Chicago.

King, tired and worn down, praised the agreement and soon left Chicago. "Never before have such far-reaching and creative commitments been made and programs adopted and pledged to achieve open housing in a community," said King.

The document was not legally enforceable, however, and Daley did not intend to honor it. "My father came home and said, 'I could just see the mayor decide at that moment how he was going to handle King,'" recalled Anthony Downs, the son of Mayor Daley's key housing adviser. "'That he was going to lie to him. I could just see the moment in which Daley decided the only way he could get rid of the guy was to tell him a whole lot of lies.'"

During these turbulent years of the 1960s, Mayor Daley continued to draw his oldest son into politics. After graduating from law school, twenty-six-year-old Rich Daley was invited by his father to attend the 1968 Democratic National Convention in Chicago. American society was experiencing a tumultuous, unsettling decade, and much had changed since the 1960 Democratic National Convention attended by the younger Daley. A growing anti-authoritarian, youth-oriented counterculture. The civil rights movement. Black power. The assassination of John F. Kennedy. Student protests on college campuses, including Berkeley and Columbia. Lyndon Johnson's war on poverty and the Great Society, which the president introduced in Chicago. Medicare. The Civil Rights Act of 1964. Race riots in the cities. The Voting Act of 1965. More race riots in the cities. The US Supreme Court, in *Griswold* v. *Connecticut*, establishing a right to privacy and ensuring that married couples could not be prevented from using contraceptives. A 1965 protest against the Vietnam War, with twenty-five thousand students converging on Washington, DC.

In Chicago, 1968 seemed to start on a better note. Unemployment was low and Chicago's economy was growing rapidly, due to government defense contracts from the Cold War and the high social welfare expenditures of the Great Society programs. As the second largest city in the country, Chicago provided attractive jobs and a high quality of life to many of its 3.5 million citizens. Its mayor was a powerful national figure, and he had brought a national convention back home where the major political parties had held twenty-three of the prior fifty-six conventions.

The larger societal forces of 1968 soon overwhelmed the upbeat mood. In January, the Tet offensive began in Vietnam as the Vietcong attacked South Vietnamese cities and towns. In February, Eugene McCarthy, the student-backed, antiwar candidate for president, mounted a strong challenge to President Johnson in the New Hampshire primary. In March, Mayor Daley spoke on the phone from his Bridgeport home with the White House and then joined his family in the living room and watched Johnson on television tell the American public that he would not seek another term as president.

On April 4, an assassin shot and killed Martin Luther King Jr. Afterward, black Americans raged, and riots broke out in more than 130 cities. In Chicago, forty-eight hours of burning and looting occurred in the black west-side ghetto, leading to injury, death, and more than two thousand arrests. Mayor Daley issued his infamous "shoot to kill" order, earning his place in American history as a reactionary and possibly racist autocrat. The civil rights activist Jesse Jackson, in a memorial service at Chicago's city hall, publicly chastised the city's political leaders, "The blood is on the chest and hands of those that would not have welcomed King here yesterday." In May, students in Paris rioted violently and soon after American college students followed suit. In 1968, more than two hundred major campus demonstrations occurred throughout the country. In June, an assassin shot and killed Robert Kennedy, as he campaigned as a Democratic candidate for the US presidency.

Despite all of this turmoil, Rich Daley's father looked forward to the 1968 convention, and believed that he could control the students, hippies, and antiwar protestors. "No thousands will come to our city and take over our streets, our city, our convention," the mayor of Chicago said publicly.

The convention, which once more would take place at the International Amphitheatre, was a way to highlight Chicago's achievements under Daley's leadership, as well as to boost his Democratic slate of candidates in the November election. Rich Daley's father believed deeply in the Democratic Party. He also loved the power and pageantry of political conventions and parades. The mayor therefore anticipated the Chicago convention with great personal pride. "I would say that it is an important sign of faith to the American people for this national convention to be held here, not in some resort center, but in the heart of a great city where people live and work and raise their families—and in one of the biggest neighborhoods in Chicago—my neighborhood!"

The more than ten thousand protestors who came to Chicago in late August did not share Daley's enthusiasm. Their leadership was called the National Mobilization Committee to End the War in Vietnam and Students for a Democratic Society, and they believed that the 1968 Democratic National Convention was essentially a pro-war rally. With Lyndon Johnson having announced his retirement, they focused their anger on Mayor Daley. These young people believed that Daley—a sixty-six-year-old, big-city political boss—embodied "the Establishment" views that they had come to confront.

"I was an organizer of a large, antiwar demonstration in the spring of 1968 where the Chicago police attacked the demonstrators in Daley Plaza, which led to four hundred arrests," recalled Marilyn Katz, who later became a public relations adviser to Rich Daley. "It was totally unprovoked—a lot of injuries and some kids were beaten into the subways. It was totally brutal. And Daley—the old man—hated us. He didn't want anyone to challenge his authority. The Democratic National Convention was coming soon and he thought the protests were an embarrassment for Chicago. The student movement was a real thorn in old man Daley's side. This was post the assassination of King and it was a crazy, crazy time."

Unfortunately, Mayor Daley's recent actions did nothing to defuse the younger generation's anti-authoritarian point of view. His "shoot to kill" statement after the death of King had signaled to both protestors and police officers that Daley did not intend to restrain his police. In addition, the mayor's decisions leading up to the convention indicated that he stood prepared to keep blacks from rioting and dissidents in line: nearly twenty-five thousand Chicago police, Illinois National Guardsman, federal antiriot army troops, and private security guards would soon arrive.

For a week in late August 1968, the culture wars of the 1960s were fought on the streets of Chicago. The students and other protestors represented the antiwar, anti-authoritarian segment of society who believed that they fought for social justice and a more participatory democracy. The police and Mayor Daley defended the traditional order against the young radicals who they saw as dirty, lawless troublemakers. This fight in Chicago became one of the fiercest and most public cultural disputes of twentieth-century America. Mayor Daley emerged as a hero to some Americans, but a villain to others.

After the convention ended, the federally appointed Walker Commission described the actions of the Chicago Police as a police riot. However, from the perspective of history, both sides deserve shares of the blame. Gathered in Lincoln Park, the young demonstrators were themselves itching for a fight. They taunted the police with phrases like "pigs eat shit!" and were represented by some leaders who espoused violence.

Despite sharing culpability with Daley and the police, some of the demonstrators remembered the Lincoln Park confrontation as an event that the police force instigated through aggression. "You could see them at the edge of Lincoln Park," recalled Marilyn Katz. "They started to come toward us—police in front, tear gas mounted on fire engines and big, blaring lights—and they just marched from the west of the park, followed by the cops beating the shit out of kids and forcing the kids out of the park. This was right [across from the Children's Zoo] where the Green Market is today in Lincoln Park. When people started to get beaten, some started to fight back and then it spilled over onto LaSalle Street. The advent of a really big street fight with the cops then mobilized every kid in the city by the time the convention got to Wednesday night. It was the place to be. So then that became the Battle of Chicago."

On August 28, 1968, convention delegates would choose a Democratic nominee for president. On the same day, television cameras in the South Loop captured Chicago police violently beating demonstrators in what would be known as the Battle of Michigan Avenue. Television transmitted the fury and the blood into living rooms across America, frequently portraying Mayor Daley and his Chicago police as the aggressors.

Meanwhile, as the Battle of Michigan Avenue raged, Mayor Daley tried to control the politicians inside in the convention hall. These party officials, like many Americans, were divided. War versus peace. Traditional values versus a new social order. One convention delegate referred to the street battle as a "police state terror," inflaming Rich Daley to scream insults at him. At this stage in his life, young Daley remained emotionally and intellectually tied to his father's conservative point of view. Challenging the police in public was wrong.

Another leader at the Democratic convention spoke and denounced "the Gestapo in the streets of Chicago." This incited Mayor Daley's Illinois delegates to leap out of their seats and make sour-faced, thumbs-down motions. The senior Daley also lost his self-control. Rising out of his seat, he addressed the US senator on the podium—Abraham Ribicoff of Connecticut. "Fuck you, you Jew son of a bitch," he shouted. "You lousy motherfucker, go home."

Despite the rancorous atmosphere, the convention picked the Establishment candidate, Vice President Hubert Humphrey, who both Daley and Lyndon Johnson supported. After a two-day debate, the delegates also adopted a pro-war plank. In November, without carrying a single large city, Richard Nixon won the election and become president of the United States. Many Americans would retain bad memories of Mayor Daley and Chicago in 1968. The political fallout from the convention also injured the national Democratic Party until well after the Watergate scandal. But Chicagoans backed their mayor overwhelmingly. Across the city, bumper stickers on cars proclaimed, "We Support Mayor Daley and His Chicago Police."

The divisiveness and bitterness of the 1968 Democratic convention was a scarring emotional experience for Rich Daley, and it may have evoked cognitive dissonance in the still maturing young man. On the one hand, young Daley was pained to see his father—a man whom Rich loved and respected—suffer such intense public criticism. His natural reaction to this sort of familial insult was to fight back against the opposition, unquestioningly rejecting their complaints. Rich's tendency to reject the protestors was reinforced by the fact that their unequivocal denunciation of his father's authority and belief system threatened his own worldview. On the other hand, Rich Daley represented a different generation than his father did. He had matured into adulthood during the 1960s, a decade that tended to focus on self-expression and to reject traditional authority. On some gut level, the complaints of the young protestors and the zeitgeist of the 1968 convention must have resonated with him. It would be many years before Rich Daley worked through these conflicting ideas.

PART 2

The Second Generation

CHAPTER 4

FROM FATHER TO SON

As he matured into adulthood, Rich Daley tended to emulate his father. Not only did he live in Bridgeport and attend his father's schools—Nativity of Our Lord, De La Salle, DePaul—he had also depended on the elder Daley for each professional position he held up until his dad's death. In 1966, US District Judge William Lynch hired Rich Daley, then a law student, as a court crier. Judge Lynch was the son of a Bridgeport precinct captain, an old friend of the mayor, and Dick Daley's first law partner. In 1968, the City of Chicago hired Rich Daley directly out of law school as assistant corporation counsel. In 1969, with one year of experience, he left the city job to found a law firm with Ray Simon, a smart attorney from Bridgeport, who had worked for the City of Chicago as Mayor Daley's primary legal adviser. The mayor's clout helped his eldest son's unproven law firm attract politically connected legal assignments. This continuing pattern of dependence linking Rich to his father raised the question of whether the son could ever succeed on his own, or if he and his brothers would become another example of pampered offspring of the highly successful.

On April 23, 1969, Rich Daley's dad became the longest-serving mayor in the history of Chicago. At a city hall celebration, Rich joined his brothers in the receiving line to accept the many congratulations. His father, with Sis by his side, addressed the gathered group. "I've had the blessing of a fine wife and family, and I've tried to do the best I could while I was mayor. None of us is perfect. But as my good mother and dad would say, do the best you can."

A series of financial crises in the 1960s led voters to call an Illinois constitutional convention in December 1969. Mayor Daley had much at stake in the outcome of this convention. He wanted to ensure that

Chicago gained "home rule," which is the power for a city to determine its own structure of government and city policies without interference from the State of Illinois. Chicagoans had unsuccessfully sought home rule since the creation of the last Illinois constitution in 1870 and had even talked of succession from the state over the issue in the 1930s.

Mayor Daley instructed his twenty-seven-year-old son Rich to run as a constitutional convention delegate as part of his political grooming. With help from his brothers, he ran an all-out campaign, even though his father's political clout ensured his election. "We never had a chance to really get involved in a big way in my dad's campaigns," explained Bill Daley. "So Rich's campaign became our little project. Sure, we knew he was going to win, but we took it seriously anyway. I remember going with him to pick out bumper stickers and debating what colors would be the best. It was fun for us."

On election night, Mayor Daley greeted a collection of friends, neighbors, and political workers in the backroom of the Eleventh Ward Democratic headquarters. His son Rich had won his race, receiving nearly 90 percent of the vote, and the elder Daley was deeply moved by the promising start of his oldest son's political career. "I hope and pray to God," said Dick Daley with emotion in his voice, "[that] when he's on the floor of the convention he'll always remember the people from whence he comes, and that he'll always fight for the people." The mayor's voice broke at the end, and he wiped tears from his eyes.

The Illinois Constitutional Convention of 1970 dealt with many of the same issues that the Founding Fathers of the United States addressed in 1787: the role of government in society, the proper relationship between levels of government, and the appropriate methods of taxation and government financing.

Rich Daley received more votes than any other constitutional delegate in the State of Illinois, but lacked the experience to deal with these weighty constitutional issues. His ineffectiveness generated significant resentment from the other delegates. The younger Daley's professional passivity may partially have been a result of his relationship with his father. "It was almost as if there was a glass shelter around him—or he was in a cocoon or something like that," recalled Dawn Clark Netsch, a convention delegate and law professor, in describing how Rich's relationship with his father constrained his development. "There was da' mayor's kid and nobody could touch him. Everybody treated him with kid gloves."

Mayor Daley also sent Mike Madigan, another of his handpicked constitutional convention delegates, down to Springfield. He expected Madigan to make sure his eldest son did not get into trouble and to protect the mayor's political interests. Though the twenty-seven-year-old Madigan was the same age as Rich Daley, he was more professionally mature. He stood as the youngest ward boss in the city, an Irish-Catholic product of the Thirteenth Ward, where his father had also served the Chicago machine. Madigan, whose professional relationship with the younger Daley would experience ups and downs over the next forty years, was a disciplined, tough politician who soon ruled over the Illinois House of Representatives.

Daley was frank in admitting that he followed his father's lead with respect to the Constitutional Convention. "I would say that he influenced me much more than I influenced him. My father has served in the state house, as Senate minority leader, state revenue director, county clerk, and mayor since 1955. Of course he influenced me. He pointed out the issues and gave me the benefit of his advice. He asked me about many specific points and we would discuss them. He helped me reach my decision."

Other convention delegates echoed Daley's view that the convention participants weighed the substantive constitutional issues carefully and that much compromise was necessary. "Mayor Daley thought long and hard before he threw his troops behind the constitution in the referendum," recalled a downstate delegate. "But he finally decided there was more good than bad in it, and the whole thing was a great accomplishment. When you look at what was happening in other states with failures, conspicuously in New York at that time, Illinois was outstanding in writing a new constitution that then was adopted by the voters."

When the voters of Illinois ratified the new constitution on December 15, 1970, Mayor Daley achieved his home rule and taxation goals. This change not only dramatically altered the relationship between Chicago and the State of Illinois but also directly influenced the more than six thousand cities, counties, townships, and school districts across the state. Home rule governments now had taxing, borrowing, and licensing powers with few restrictions from Springfield.

The 1970 Illinois Constitutional Convention had historic importance for one other reason. Michael Shakman, an attorney and unsuccessful independent candidate for a convention delegate seat, filed a lawsuit against the Democratic machine claiming that Chicago's system of patronage politics put nonmachine candidates at an unconstitutional disadvantage. "It was obvious that there were hundreds and hundreds of patronage workers who were out in the district working against me because they were instructed [by the machine] to do so," recalled Shakman. "I just felt the system was wrong and illegal. I lost by about 600 votes out of about 20,000 cast." As a result of Shakman's lawsuit and subsequent litigation, over the next forty years a series of negotiations, court orders, and settlements—known as the Shakman Decrees—limited Chicago mayors from significant politically motivated hiring and firing.

The Chicago machine was considerably weaker in the post-Shakman world. "None of this has ever been personal though," explained Shakman. "I've never had a grudge against Daley—the father or the son. I just thought then, and I think now, that they were running a system that was grossly unfair to voters and to candidates. It required people to give up their political freedoms in order to get government jobs and to keep government jobs. And it prejudiced the candidates and voters from getting a fair chance at an election."

In 1970, Rich Daley left his law practice and joined his brother Michael as a partner in the law firm Daley and George, which their father founded. At the full-service law firm, both of the Daley boys benefited from their dad's citywide clout, and Michael practiced law there for more than forty years. In the early 1970s, the press criticized Rich and Michael for receiving highly paid court appointments from local judges.

Around the same time, in February 1973, the press reported that Mayor Daley had directed more than $1 million in no-bid City of Chicago insurance business to Heil and Heil Insurance Agency on behalf of his twenty-six-year-old son John Daley. Direct avarice of this type was out of character for the elder Daley. However, the mayor was anxious that his sons get rich in the insurance and law businesses. This politically connected insurance arrangement may have seemed natural to the Daley family for another reason. In Chicago, generations of politicians had used implicit threats to coerce real estate developers, tavern owners, and other businessmen to purchase insurance from the politicians' relatives. In a sense, therefore, Daley and his sons were following in this well-worn tradition. Yet these scandals continued to boil over in a climate of more aggressive, TV-driven media coverage.

Mayor Daley did not back down though. In speaking to his colleagues at a meeting of the Cook County Democratic Committee, he angrily defended the father-son arrangements. "If I can't help my sons, then they can kiss my ass. I make no apologies to anyone. There are many men in this room whose fathers helped them, and they went on to become fine public officials. . . . If a man can't put his arms around his sons, then what kind of world are we living in?" Daley expressed a characteristic machine view: one of the great strengths of the organization was its self-help mechanisms, its ability to take care of its own family and friends without aid or interference from outsiders. Daley exhibited two flaws in his thinking, however. First, the money used to pay the Heil and Heil insurance contract actually belonged to the people of Chicago, not to the local Democratic Party. Second, the awarding of favors to insiders, such as Daley's son, systematically excluded anyone who was not also a politically connected insider. But this type of unbiased thinking was beyond Dick Daley in matters regarding his sons.

In July 1973, the news media reported that two of the mayor's sons, John and Bill Daley, had opened their own insurance brokerage, called Daley and Daley Insurance. They located the office across from Nativity of Our Lord Church in Bridgeport, just down the street from their boyhood home. Bill Daley soon left the insurance business and pursued careers in law, politics, and finance. John Daley, however, continued to live and work in Bridgeport, where he sold insurance and made a minor career in politics.

In the early 1970s, the elder Mayor Daley kept helping his firstborn son in other ways, making sure, for instance, that thirty-year-old Rich Daley was elected to the Illinois senate in 1972. This required the mayor to convince the sitting Illinois state senator to retire and then to motivate his political party to deliver his son a landslide victory. However, the younger Daley received a cold reception from his new colleagues, just like he had at the Illinois Constitutional Convention of 1970. Legislators assumed he spoke for his father. "Rich didn't have the luxury some of us had to cut our teeth down there in semi-obscurity," recalled one Illinois state senator. "Every time Rich twitched, people were wondering whether or not the mayor was sending them a message."

As it turned out, the theory that the mayor of Chicago controlled the voting and behavior of his newly elected son was a sound one. Each Friday, when Rich Daley returned from Springfield to Chicago, he went directly to see his father at city hall. One week—without consulting the mayor—the younger Daley had introduced a bill in the Illinois legislature to allow artists to get a share of the proceeds when their works were subsequently resold. His idea was that the State of Illinois would protect the interests of artists. Rich Daley introduced the artist protection bill and received significant support from legislative cosponsors.

"Interesting week? Did you do anything down in Springfield?" asked the mayor one Friday afternoon as he looked carefully at his son sitting in a chair in front of his mayoral desk.

"No," Rich answered, "Not really."

"Did you introduce any bills?" the mayor persisted.

"Yea, well, I did introduce one bill," said Rich.

His father opened a drawer and removed a stack of messages. "I have calls here from the president of the Art Institute," said the mayor. "I have a message here from someone in Paris who called, who's involved in the art world. I have a call from the CEO of Consolidated

Foods, who's a major art collector. And they're all reacting to a bill that you introduced this week in Springfield."

From Dick Daley's perspective, there were a number of compelling reasons not to like the proposed bill. First, his son had not cleared the idea with him before introducing it. The elder Daley believed in party discipline and hierarchy and could be unsympathetic when legislators wanted to follow their own personal preferences. Second, rich and influential interests did not like the bill. Though he had started out his career with some enthusiasm for FDR, by the seventh decade of his life Dick Daley had become completely focused on maintaining his own power. Offending potent interests did not square with that goal. Finally, helping artists simply did not resonate with Dick Daley on any personal level. He had a tough disposition and an analytical mind, and neither his heart nor his intellect was drawn to the idea of an artist protection bill.

"Well, you know, I think it's a pretty good idea," responded Rich. The younger Daley possessed an emerging aesthetic sensibility that was attracted to the idea of helping artists. His first major legislative proposal suggested that Rich Daley might also have very different policy inclinations than his father.

"You can think that's a good idea. And someday when I'm long gone, you could introduce that bill," said his father with a quiet intensity. "Maybe you'll be able to pass it, but for the moment I think you ought to withdraw the bill."

"Okay," his son nodded. And, like a good Catholic schoolboy, the younger Daley obeyed his father and dropped the subject. Even though he was in his thirties, Rich still needed his father's approval and he was not yet independent enough to chart his own professional course.

Rich left city hall and returned to his Chicago office, immediately phoning down to the clerk's office in Springfield.

"I want to withdraw this artist protection bill," Senator Daley said to the clerk.

"You know, senator, that bill has never been introduced," answered the clerk after checking through his stack of files.

"Well, I introduced it," said Daley testily.

"Yea, but there were no cosponsors," replied the clerk. "You need at least one cosponsor."

"Ok," Daley agreed quickly.

Rich Daley hung up the phone, realizing that his father had gotten all of the cosponsors to drop off. His artist protection bill had already been shot down.

Though one newspaper described the younger Daley as a plugger, Rich quickly became known in Springfield as arrogant and something of a bully. The younger Daley earned this negative reputation largely due to his abrasive personality, but it was also partly a result of some of his legislative positions. According to the *Chicago Tribune*, Daley routinely opposed government ethics bills in Springfield, while consistently supporting legislation "seemingly designed to enhance the opportunity for vote fraud." At this stage of his career, the younger Daley tended to focus on the political implications of legislation, rather than its policy effects or its impact on the lives of individual people. More than ten years later, reflecting on this period, Daley would say, "I would do a lot of things differently. But you don't look back, you look ahead."

During this period in the early 1970s, Rich Daley received the nickname that stuck with him for the rest of his career: Dirty Little Richie. Dawn Clark Netsch, who had also served with him in the Illinois Constitutional Convention of 1970, gave him the nickname after the Chicago machine had once again undermined one of her liberal legislative proposals. "I was furious," Netsch recalled more than thirty-five years later. "Since the [machine Democrats] had just killed another one of my bills. They were consumer bills, the kind of bills that Democrats would normally be for. I was very angry and was talking with the press about the dirty tricks that the machine played. . . . And back then in the 1970s, virtually everybody called him 'little Richie.' That name got morphed together by the press with the 'dirty tricks' description and it became the infamous Dirty Little Richie."

Unfortunately for Daley, the nickname stuck. And there was a reason that it did: the dirty little Richie label captured how Illinois legislators perceived the firstborn son of Dick Daley in the early 1970s. The "Richie" diminutive indicated that they viewed the younger Daley as a boy, instead of a peer or respected legislator. The "little" description showed even less respect and pointed to a person viewed as parochial and perhaps spoiled. Finally, the "dirty" epithet signified that Illinois legislators believed that Rich Daley was a person who focused on hardball politics and winning at any cost. They did not see any higher purpose in his behavior.

On some level, Daley knew how his fellow legislators felt about him. The struggling politician explained his low reputation during this rocky 1970s period as a result of three factors: his innate shyness, his lack of socializing in Springfield, and the belief by many contemporaries that he was a political instrument of his father. "I guess that doesn't make for great popularity," recalled Daley.

In addition to his election as an Illinois senator, the decade of the 1970s was important for Rich Daley in other ways as well. His father gave him day-to-day responsibility for the Eleventh Ward Democratic Party and its Bridgeport headquarters. This meant that Rich now controlled thousands of patronage jobs and could directly influence election outcomes by getting troops to deliver the votes he wanted. He also married Maggie Corbett, a devout Catholic girl from a large family who worked as a sales executive with Xerox Learning Systems. The couple met at a Christmas party in 1970 and would settle in Bridgeport. They would maintain a traditional marriage in which Rich focused on his career and Maggie ran the home. Yet over time Maggie would become a subtle but important influence on Rich's cultural and professional evolution. Their marriage would age like a fine red wine, becoming more complex and full of nuance over the next thirty years. The pair would have four children.

Despite his love of Maggie, in the early 1970s Rich still had a great attachment to his parents and his boyhood home, as one of his favorite stories illustrates. During his newlywed days, Daley caught a severe flu, and he called his wife from his law office to tell her. "Honey, I'm sick," Rich whispered to Maggie over the phone. "I'm going home."

Worried, his wife also rushed home to Bridgeport to care for him. Once in their converted two-flat, she called his name and began looking for him.

"Rich," she said from the living room.

"Rich?" she called as she walked quickly into the bedroom.

"Rich!" she yelled as she raced frantically to check in the bathroom.

Daley was not anywhere in the house, however. Maggie was worried, wondering what might have happened to her husband. After a while, she returned to her car and drove a few blocks to her mother-in-law's house at 3536 South Lowe Avenue. Out front, a police car guarded the mayor's home.

"Where's Rich?" Maggie asked as she came through the front door.

"Downstairs," Sis Daley answered calmly.

When Maggie went downstairs and entered Rich's boyhood bedroom, she could smell chicken soup and Vicks Vapor Rub.

"Hi, honey," murmured Rich feverishly as he closed his eyes.

Maggie stood silently for a while, hands on her hips, her emotions oscillating. She had just learned what "home" meant to a Daley.

Despite the continuity and stability of the Daley family, American society continued to suffer great instability in the early 1970s. The culture war endured, and even accelerated, as long hair, miniskirts, drugs, and loosened sexual mores spread throughout America. In January 1973, the US Supreme Court ruled in *Roe v. Wade* that abortion should be legal in most states. In that same month, Secretary of State Henry Kissinger negotiated a final cease-fire agreement in Vietnam and the United States ended the military draft. In March of that year, the last American troops departed from Vietnam and in June the US Congress and the press exposed the Watergate cover-up. The price of a barrel of oil also rose dramatically, shooting from $1.77 in October 1973 to $10 in early 1974. During the early 1970s, the US economy sickened, combining inflation with high unemployment to create stagflation. Heavy industry suffered sharp declines in production and the Midwest began to be known as the Rust Belt. In August 1974, faced with impeachment, Richard Nixon resigned as president. A month later, President Ford created much controversy by giving Nixon an absolute pardon.

Despite the many changes in American society, in the backwaters of Springfield, Illinois, the Democratic Party—safely insulated from most of the country's turmoil—continued its traditional, machine-style politics. In 1975 the Democrats appointed the relatively inexperienced Rich Daley as chairman of the Senate Judiciary Committee, an influential post. In Chicago, politicians still made decisions based on ethnicity, ties to the Catholic Church, and old-fashioned power politics, while much of the United States wrestled with increasing pluralism and a growing focus on individual rights. When one of the more senior candidates for the judiciary position complained, he was told, "Look, you're name is Nudelman, your name isn't Daley." Rich Daley became much more aggressive in this committee, as well as on the Senate floor, even to the point of offending his father's political allies. During this time period, some legislative colleagues continued to view Daley as arrogant, vindictive, or simply mean. This bullying behavior by Daley may have been a result of the stress and the insecurity he felt in his new position, as well as his great desire to impress his father and his legislative colleagues that he was a substantial person.

In the culture wars of the early 1970s, the younger Daley sided with the traditionalists and had particular disdain for the more liberal legislators in the senate, as he explained to associates in a Springfield restaurant. "That [Illinois senator] Katz is just another phony liberal. We're going to cut him up the next time he shows up in judiciary. We'll take him apart. He'll be defenseless."

"I don't make any bones about the fact that he was pretty awful back then," said Dawn Clark Netsch. "It was hard for someone like me to get anything through his committee or others he was on. It got very petty and very mean."

In December 1975, the president of the Illinois senate stepped down in order to run for attorney general in the state. Political insiders believed that Dick Daley wanted his thirty-three-year-old son to step up to the Illinois senate presidency in order to complete his political grooming before taking over for the senior Daley and running for mayor in the next Chicago election. Instead, legislators in the Illinois Senate refused to support this promotion of the younger Daley. Many in the legislature believed that Rich Daley was too divisive and had not displayed the characteristics of a real leader.

The following December, Mayor Daley died in office, having served the citizens of Chicago for more than twenty years. "We had just bought our house," said Rich Daley, "and my wife and I were home working on it that day. I remember a policeman from my father's detail came knocking on the door and told me something had happened, that my dad was sick. We rushed out of there—I remember I was still wearing blue jeans and work boots—and went to the hospital they were supposed to take him to, but he wasn't there. So we went to his doctor's office on North Michigan where he had collapsed. The whole family was there, my mom and brothers and sisters, and Father [Timothy] Lyne from Holy Name. We said some prayers. Then I rode in the ambulance with my dad's body. It was a shock. It was sad."

The following day, which was bitterly cold, the Daley family held the wake at Nativity of Our Lord Church in Bridgeport. More than twenty-five thousand Chicagoans saw the body of Mayor Daley in his casket, after lining up and waiting outside in the thirteen-degree temperature as the winds drove the cold under their winter coats. Like good and obedient sons, Rich Daley and his brothers stood in the receiving line for seventeen hours and shook each hand.

The next day, political dignitaries, including President-Elect Jimmy Carter, Vice President Nelson Rockefeller, Senator Teddy Kennedy of Massachusetts, and former Democratic Party presidential nominee George McGovern arrived to attend the funeral and to pay their respects. These four national figures knelt together in the first pew on the right-hand side of church, a few feet from the late mayor's casket. Chicago's future mayor Jane Byrne, the elder Daley's political protégée, walked down the center aisle and sat behind them in the second pew, even though an usher had tried to escort Byrne to the middle of the church. The dead mayor's family sat across the aisle on the left.

For many politicians at the funeral, Daley's death felt like the loss of their own father. US Congressman Dan Rostenkowski, a longtime Daley protégé, delivered a personal eulogy to machine insiders over the weekend of the funeral." Mayor Daley was a man who could put you down in a second, and he could also make you soar to heights you never believed you could attain," said Rostenkowski. "Mayor Daley sometimes scolded. But when you were feeling low, he would really come through. You remember, I had an election in the United States Congress with a very disappointing result. [I was not chosen for a House leadership position]. The phone rang. I got on the line, and his voice said, 'Danny, what did they do to you? What can I do for you, Dan?' That was the kind of man he was."

Dick Daley was buried at Holy Sepulcher Cemetery alongside his parents. An eight-foot-high granite tombstone in the shape of a cross dominated his gravesite. It was chiseled with a quote from the prayer of Saint Francis of Assisi, Daley's favorite. *Lord, make me an instrument of your peace . . .*

CHAPTER 5

DARWINIAN EVOLUTION

Historians may be tempted to say that Rich Daley learned politics
at his father's knee, and there is some truth in that view. Yet to
stop there would fail to reveal the whole truth. The complexity of the
man. The differences between the father and the son. Dick Daley had
dominated almost everyone in his life and lived with conviction in his
beliefs. The Democratic Party, the Catholic Church, his south-side
Irish tribe—these were his bedrock foundations and he rarely doubted
their strength or his own rightfulness. But his son was different. Rich
Daley had less confidence in his own talents than his father did, and
he sometimes displayed an emotional insecurity that made him a more
mercurial personality than was his father. At times he also struggled
with key aspects of the Daley worldview that he inherited. These glimmers of doubt in the younger Daley would alternate with fierce familial
pride and a cockiness that occasionally led him to make bad decisions
or to create enemies unnecessarily. But one of Rich Daley's defining
characteristics was persistence, a dogged tenacity even in the face of
long odds.

The years after his father's death saw Daley wandering in the des-
ert, like an Old Testament sufferer exposed to the heat of a biblical sun.
He won one epic battle in 1980. He lost one great campaign in 1983.
And then he wandered again for six years, searching for that place in
the shade that he had always taken for granted.

During the Bridgeport wake, funeral, and memorial service for his father, Rich Daley and other Chicago politicians gathered in little groups
and made phone calls. Deals were cut and votes counted, but without

Dick Daley to anchor these week-long negotiations the old ethnic and racial divisions reemerged.

The description of the leading candidates to replace the mayor sounded like the beginning of a bad joke. Question: What do you get when the mayor of Chicago dies? Answer: An Irishman, two Croatians, a black, and a Pole. Eddie Burke. Michael Bilandic. Ed Vrdolyak. Wilson Frost. Roman "Pooch" Pucinski. None of these contenders was really in the running, though, based on leadership qualities or the policy positions he held. Rather, succession politics in 1976 Chicago was simply a pie-splitting contest based on ethnic and racial coalitions.

Here's how the pie was split. Mayor: a Croatian, Michael Bilandic, from Daley's own Eleventh Ward. Vice mayor: a Pole, Casimir Laskowski. Chairman of the city council finance committee: a black, Alderman Frost. President pro tem of the city council: a Croatian, Alderman Vrdolyak.

In all of the political jockeying and deal making that went on over the week of Christmas holidays, Rich Daley, an Irish-Catholic from Bridgeport, emerged as the official Eleventh Ward committeeman. His appointment to this important party post, along with Daley's seat in the Illinois senate, would help as he tried to build a political base for himself over the next few years. "The committeemen respected Rich and the other Daley boys. Because of the father—what the father did for all of them," remembered Ed Kelly, Dick Daley's close friend and the Forty-Seventh Ward committeeman at the time. "We reciprocated to protect Rich and the Daley family. My intentions were to protect the Daley boys anyway I could."

The good intentions of Chicago politicians toward Rich Daley may have been sincere, but these nostalgic feelings did not last long. Soon, leaders in the local Democratic Party decided it was better to kill him off politically.

In January 1977, just weeks after the death of the late mayor, Rich Daley tried to protect his career prospects as a politician. With the help of his allies, he attempted to elect Thomas Hynes—his Spring-

field roommate—as president of the Illinois senate. Hynes and Daley would be close political allies over the next twenty years and the
senate president race was not the last time that the cautious, lawyerly
Hynes would be accused of serving as a front man for Daley's political
aspirations.

However, members of two legislative groups, the black caucus and
the independent Democrats, resisted Hynes and Daley fiercely, calling for greater "participatory democracy" in the upper chamber of the
Illinois General Assembly. The two leaders of these groups, Harold
Washington and Dawn Clark Netsch, were former classmates from
Northwestern Law School. Washington, who led the black caucus,
was angry that the Chicago City Council had not made Alderman
Frost mayor after the death of the elder Daley. Netsch, who led the
independents, was tired of the Chicago machine's domineering legislative style.

At one point, the legislative fight for a new president of the Illinois
senate appeared to reach a stalemate. The battle lasted five weeks, with
186 ballots cast. Eventually, the Illinois Senate selected Hynes as its
president and brokered a settlement that gave more power to the independents and the black caucus. Hynes's victory strengthened Rich
Daley politically by installing a key ally in a powerful position.

The political settlement failed to satisfy Harold Washington, Chicago's most prominent black politician. The dissatisfied Washington
broke with leaders of the local Democratic Party and filed as a candidate against acting-mayor Michael Bilandic in the upcoming special mayoral election. Washington focused most of his campaign on
African-American neighborhoods on Chicago's south side. "There is
a sleeping giant in Chicago," said Washington, "And if this sleeping
giant, the potential black vote, ever woke up, we'd control the city."
Washington struggled with fund-raising, however, and lost to Bilandic
in the Democratic primary. Afterward, he called Bilandic "a third-rate
boss Daley" and said that the machine appointee lacked "Daley's skill
as a balancer of conflicting needs and interests."

Despite Washington's bitterness, the younger Daley's political victory in Springfield helped him to begin establishing his own political

viability within Chicago's Democratic Party. He also began to realize that he needed to improve his reputation and his relationships with other elected officials. "Back at Con-Con—the Illinois Constitutional Convention of 1970—Rich Daley was a mean little prick. He thought the world revolved around him because of Daddy," recalled Don Rose, the political strategist. "He was a total little bastard and this continued when he got into the Illinois senate."

Soon after the death of his father in 1976, however, Rich Daley's behavior began a dramatic transformation. Rose—a tough but insightful political observer—referred to this period as "civilizing Richie," a process of broadening the horizons of a protected, Irish-Catholic scion of Chicago's most formidable political family. David Axelrod, who would eventually become a key Daley adviser, described the evolution of Rich Daley in the late 1970s in more diplomatic terms. "I think that any human being who doesn't change from their mid-20s to their late 40s is an unusual and troubled person," said Axelrod. "I think there's no question that he matured, and that, starting in 1977, he needed to make his own way in the world. And there were an awful lot of people rooting against him, because they felt that he had undue advantages when his father was so powerful. And when his father died it was sink-or-swim time—and Daley swam. I think that a lot of things—personal adversity, political adversity and the people around him—contributed to his growth. Probably one of the best things that you can say about him is that very few public officials have shown the degree of growth, and the ability to grow, that Daley has, from the time that he got to the legislature until [the late 1980s]. The growth has been unusual and enormous."

Rich Daley sought out new advisers, embraced more progressive policy positions, and started to form different political alliances. One fresh focus was a major rewriting of the Illinois mental health law. Working on this reform legislation, Daley developed relationships with John Schmidt, a respected progressive attorney who served on the Governor's Commission on the Mental Health Code, and Frank Kruesi, a University of Chicago policy wonk. Daley also began repairing his relationship with Dawn Clark Netsch, the independent lawmaker with whom he had previously battled in the Illinois senate. These three—Schmidt, Kruesi, and Netsch—are the individuals who deserve considerable credit for "civilizing Richie" within the political sphere.

When Daley chaired the mental health law committee, Netsch encouraged him to hire Kruesi as the committee's key legislative aide because she knew that Kruesi was a bright man with deep knowledge of mental health policy issues. Daley surprised Kruesi, a PhD candidate in political science from the University of Chicago, when he approached him. "I was amazed, and so were my friends in academe, when he called me," recalled Kruesi. "Here I was, a University of Chicago, Hyde Park type with no political background, and he called me out of the blue. He said he wanted to work on this issue and was looking for help and that my name had been recommended. So I went, somewhat skeptically, and I was pleasantly surprised. Everything we gave to him, he read. When the hearings were held, he knew his stuff. He knew the subject inside out."

Netsch also noticed Daley's enthusiasm and the marked change in his behavior. "What happened was that Rich Daley got very interested in this mental health topic," remembered Netsch. "It was the first time he'd ever been involved in his public career with something that had no political end result and was nonpartisan and was very substantive, involving real people and their families. Rich really did get very, very interested in it and did spend a lot of time on it." This period of Daley's legislative career—when he worked with Netsch, Schmidt, and Kruesi on substantive policy reforms—marked a key milestone in his professional evolution. Freed from his father's domineering influence, Daley began to realize that he actually enjoyed focusing on public policy issues.

Kruesi soon entered Daley's inner circle of advisers and the two men developed a friendship that lasted more than thirty years. "It was very interesting to see Frank, who was much younger at the time, actually mesmerized by being part of this power circle, the Daley circle," observed Netsch. Daley's recruitment of Kruesi into his inner circle—along with his rapprochement with progressives like Netsch and Schmidt—was the first outward sign of his personal evolution. Progressive politicians tend to favor reform of the political system and more liberal policies, attitudes that were new for Daley. Careful observers also began to notice that the Bridgeport-raised politico had loosened up and lost much of the mean edge that had previously soured his reputation in the Illinois senate. Daley's growing amiability may have indicated that he found more fulfillment in concentrating on policy reforms than he had when fixating solely on the game of politics.

In addition to mental health reform, Daley also sponsored progressive legislation on nursing homes and juvenile justice. Legislators and political operatives began to develop a new respect for Daley's judgment and political intuition. "They say Rich isn't bright, and it's true that he isn't what you would call an original or creative thinker," said Kruesi. "But he assimilates information and new ideas from the people around him very well, and he has a knack for setting the best political course to accomplish the things he wants to get done. When we were handling legislation, he could look down the road and tell you just where all the problems would be and how to deal with them. You can't do that and be stupid."

Rich Daley also grew his hair longer and began visibly to support Netsch. One important symbolic act was his surprise visit to her September 1977 fund-raising event, a Forty-Third Ward softball game attended by intensely independent Democrats. "I didn't for one minute think Rich would come to the softball game, but he showed up," Netsch recalled more than thirty years later. "It was so much fun to see these people who had spent half of their lives badmouthing the Daleys standing around with their mouth[s] open when Rich was there. After the softball game, a lot of them came back to my house in Old Town, including Rich. My guests were just sort of awestruck I think. It was just so much fun to watch. The joke was that Daley had never been north of North Avenue before in his life."

In February 1979, Chicago Democrats picked Jane Byrne over Mayor Michael Bilandic as their next nominee to run the city. Byrne was a charismatic, high-energy campaigner. Her victory resulted from both simple and complex political forces. The immediate cause was that Bilandic mishandled the snowstorms of January 1979. A series of winter storms had hit Chicago, including nearly nineteen inches of snow that had fallen over a two-day period. The inclement weather caused CTA elevated trains to freeze in their tracks, buses to become overcrowded, and O'Hare Airport to close. In addition, the Bilandic administration alienated some black citizens during the snowstorms by having CTA trains skip a number of south-side and west-side stops. During this weather crisis, many Chicagoans grew angry with Mayor Bilandic and decided that he lacked the competency necessary to lead their city. But there were also larger political forces that contributed to Byrne's victory over Bilandic. Many blacks, a key voting block for Democrats, felt that Mayor Bilandic was hostile to their race, and so they shifted their votes to Byrne. In addition, the Chicago machine's ability to turn out the vote and win elections—which had already started to decline under the first Mayor Daley—continued to weaken after his death.

The selection of Jane Byrne as mayor greatly worried the male-dominated local Democratic Party, as well as much of the Chicago business community. Byrne thought of herself as an outsider, even though she had risen through the ranks of the Democratic organization. Party leaders and powerful businessmen preferred to deal with insiders, people who knew and respected the unwritten rules of a private club. Rich Daley wanted to position himself as a leader within the party. He therefore attempted to insert himself as the organization's primary representative in negotiating a detente with Byrne. "When Richie and I met in my brother's office later in the week, the purpose of the visit quickly became obvious," remembered Byrne. "Richie was then serving as a state senator, but his head was hardly in Springfield. He had dreams of reorganizing the city council from behind the scenes, of choosing the chairs of the various committees himself. These creatures of the machine . . . all were after the same things: power, money, patronage. I stopped listening to his schemes, but Richie persisted. Soon I gratefully excused myself. I was late for a campaign stop. We agreed to meet again."

After Chicagoans elected her as the city's first female mayor, the fraught relationship between Byrne and Rich Daley did not improve. In fact, it would soon worsen. The political issue that precipitated their growing feud was taxes. Mayor Byrne, along with Governor Jim Thompson, had crafted a plan to gradually eliminate the sales tax on food and drugs over a three-year period. Daley, in his capacity as an Illinois state senator, pushed for the immediate repeal of these taxes. This sales tax fight between Byrne and Daley boiled over in late 1979. "Richie Daley and I didn't speak again during my four-year term," said Byrne. "My sales tax position prevailed in the legislature. Only much later would I realize he had been positioning himself for the opening salvo in his race for mayor."

Seven months after Byrne started her mayoral term, thirty-seven-year-old Rich Daley shocked the political establishment by announcing that he would run as a candidate for Cook County state's attorney. Daley's announcement surprised many because he still had a somewhat underwhelming professional reputation—a parochial south-sider obsessed with the game of politics—while the state's attorney position was considered an important and serious office.

Not only was she surprised, but Mayor Byrne also worried that Daley planned to use the state's attorney office as a stepping stone to run against her for mayor in 1983. Though she was a high-energy campaigner and a successful politician, Byrne seemed to lack the right temperament to govern a city the size of Chicago. Her public style was brusque and mercurial, rather than calm and patient. She suffered through a difficult first year in office, with large budget deficits; high inflation, driven by prices set by the Organization of the Petroleum Exporting Countries; and strikes by the city's teachers' union, transit union, and firefighters. By March of 1980, Byrne's dislike of Rich Daley had grown into feverish paranoia.

Struggling with this anxiety and the challenging economic climate, Mayor Byrne recruited Alderman Ed Burke—a mainstay of the Chicago machine—to challenge Daley. Byrne engineered the party's endorsement of Burke in the Democratic primary for state's attorney. "Byrne could see Rich Daley over her shoulder who she perceived to be a threat to her," confirmed Burke. "She was not exactly secure in her position at that point and so she definitely wanted a viable candidate to run against Daley. I was it."

Some political insiders believed that Daley could have prevented a battle royal within the Democratic Party by securing the endorsement for himself. "Rich was running as an independent," recalled Ed Kelly, slate-making chairman and Dick Daley's old friend. "We had Democratic slate-making and Rich never came before us. Daley never even called me. Never even called me. Neither he nor Billy [Daley]. Never called me—to this day, I have no idea why. I think Rich made a mistake. He would have been endorsed if he came. I would have endorsed him."

Daley did not seek out the Democratic Party's help, however, and 1980 essentially became a civil war within the party. On one side stood those currently in power, including Mayor Byrne, Ed Burke, and forty-five of the fifty city council aldermen. On the other side stood the Daley family, along with Bridgeport's alderman and Michael Sheahan from the Nineteenth Ward. The Daleys started out as underdogs, but they had earned a reputation for having long memories and they let it be known that—if they won—they would remember who had supported them.

Ed Burke and Rich Daley shared similar personal backgrounds. Burke grew up in the Back of the Yards neighborhood on the south side of the city, two miles south and just west of where Rich Daley grew up. His family belonged to Visitation parish, which was located on the prestigious Garfield Boulevard. Visitation maintained a prominent Catholic church and school that had a long history of producing influential Democratic politicians. Like Rich Daley, Ed Burke walked a few blocks to get from his boyhood home to the central institution in his neighborhood, the local Catholic parish.

Visitation parish was so central to the community that since 1933 every Fourteenth Ward alderman had attended religious services at the church. This meant that every political leader from the Fourteenth Ward was not only Catholic but white and Irish as well. Judge John J. Sullivan had organized the Democratic Party in his ward, picking candidates and dispensing city jobs. Judge Sullivan also developed a brilliance for selecting political candidates for citywide office, and he helped to strengthen the Chicago machine during the 1930s and 1940s. Two more Visitation parishioners—Judge James McDermott and Clarence Wagner—followed Sullivan as political bosses of the Fourteenth Ward. McDermott and Wagner worked to position the Fourteenth as a political counterweight to the Bridgeport dominated Eleventh Ward. In 1950, Wagner became chairman of the finance committee in the Chicago City Council and the leader of a group of aldermen, known as the grey wolves, that effectively ruled Chicago during the weak reign of Mayor Kennelly. In 1952, McDermott and Wagner mounted a challenge to Dick Daley for the chairmanship of the Democratic Party, but their campaign collapsed when Wagner died in an automobile accident. Daley took over the Chicago machine and ran it for the rest of his life.

The political tradition that developed in the Fourteenth Ward was based on personal relationships. Men like Sullivan, McDermott, and Wagner would help their constituents obtain jobs or promotions, manage their finances, or get out of jail. "Chicago neighborhood politics was a social safety net in a time when there weren't a lot of other agencies to whom people that were in trouble could go. That's the way it worked," remembered Ed Burke. "That's the way the system worked and it wasn't a bad system. It was helping people and it was giving somebody a chance that might not otherwise get a chance."

Ed Burke's father, Joseph Burke, became alderman of the Fourteenth Ward in 1953, when Ed was ten years old. The elder Burke, a former policeman, continued in the ward's tradition of personal politics, providing favors for his white, Irish-Catholic constituents and attending many weddings, wakes, and other social obligations. His son Ed joined him in many of these activities. "Politics was kind of in my blood from a very early point," remembered the younger Burke.

The maturing Ed Burke soon developed a positive reputation. Proud of his Irish-Catholic heritage, he was well-dressed and polite, a smooth communicator who worked to make a personal connection with people. He was also smart. Burke attended DePaul University for both college and law school while also working as a policeman in the state's attorney office.

At DePaul, Ed Burke became reacquainted with Rich Daley, who attended the university at the same time. The two Irish-Catholic students from political families socialized and carpooled together. Through his acquaintance with Rich, Burke also developed a closer relationship with Daley's father, the most powerful politician in Chicago.

The year 1968 was to be critical in Ed Burke's life. At twenty-four years old, he was nearly finished with law school and engaged to Anne Marie McGlone, a south-side Catholic girl. While Burke studied for the bar exam, his father became sick with lung cancer and died three months later. Burke's future soon diverged from how he had imagined it. "In all likelihood, what would have happened is that when I finished law school I maybe would have been a potential candidate for the House of Representatives or that sort of thing, assuming of course that [my father] would be alive and would be mentoring me," said Burke. "But that process became undone when he died. I was left with the decision to either run to succeed him or forget about politics because in Chicago politics you have to move when you have the opportunity or forget about it."

The young Burke decided to petition the Democratic Party and ask that it appoint him to fill the Fourteenth Ward committeeman position left vacant by his father's death. According to Burke, Dick Daley telegraphed to the committee his opinion that the aspiring politician would be a good successor to his father. Burke won by three votes. "In those days people looked for 'the smoke to come from the Vatican' so to speak—whether it was white or black—and so the signal from Richard J. Daley that I would be acceptable permitted me to be elected committeeman and then to be elected alderman some nine months later," recalled Burke. The second generation politician adhered closely to his father's belief in the Democratic machine and his focus on arranging favors for his white, Irish-Catholic constituents.

In the Chicago City Council, the young alderman soon became known as a high-caliber legislator. During council meetings, Burke frequently spent his time memorizing *Robert's Rules of Order* as his colleagues dozed off or left the chamber. He was also intelligent and hardworking, a strong public debater, and an extrovert who generally got along well with his colleagues. In these respects, Burke may have modeled himself after Dick Daley, a commanding man whom he respected.

But Burke had other qualities as well. He was a dapper dresser who made every effort to look like the movie version of an accomplished legislator. He entertained his colleagues at parties by playing Irish tunes on the piano. He gave long, ceremonial speeches. Ed Burke took himself very seriously. His actions suggested someone with an inflated sense of his own self-importance.

In the early 1970s, Ed Burke aligned himself with Ed Vrdolyak, the young, magnetic alderman of a far south-side ward. "To know him is to have an opportunity to view one of the most charismatic and most persuasive individuals that you could ever run across," said Burke. "I have never seen anybody like him. Never seen anybody that can inspire people the way he did. Never seen anybody that could demand loyalty the way that he did. He was a unique and admittedly colorful part of the political culture of Chicago."

Vrdolyak and Burke led what came to be known as the "coffee rebellion" in the Chicago City Council. This 1972 effort by young aldermen to gain more political power relative to the first Mayor Daley met with mixed results. Vrdolyak gained a seat on the powerful finance committee and Burke was selected to publicly defend the administration's positions on the council floor, but Dick Daley continued to run the city.

In early 1975, a south-side congressman died and a seat in the US Congress opened up. Ed Burke believed that he had a good chance at being selected by the Chicago machine as the Democratic candidate in the upcoming special election. The first Mayor Daley asked Burke to serve as a pallbearer at the congressman's funeral, a public sign that many politicos interpreted to mean that Burke would become the new US representative from Chicago. "As Daley was wont to do, he led me to believe that I was going to be the successor," recalled Burke. Daley changed his mind, however, and selected John Fary, an older Polish politician from Burke's own Back of the Yards neighborhood. "I will go to Washington to help represent Mayor Daley," declared the sixty-four-year-old Fary on the night of his election. "For twenty-one years, I represented the mayor in the legislature, and he was always right."

Burke believed that the seventy-two-year-old Daley made this decision to select Fary in order to protect the seat for Rich Daley or one of his other boys. "There was a sense that he didn't want to commit to making me a congressman and foreclosing the possibility that he could send one of his kids to Congress," said Burke. "It was clear that John Fary was a temporary seat warmer."

The professional interests of Burke and Rich Daley had diverged in the 1975 congressional election, but in the next important election—the 1979 Democratic primary for mayor of Chicago—the two politicians found themselves on the same side. Both supported the low-key Mayor Michael Bilandic over his challenger Jane Byrne. This political bet did not pay off for either when the feisty Byrne won the primary and general elections.

When Jane Byrne became mayor of Chicago, the political interests of Ed Burke and Rich Daley soon took dramatically different paths. After a brief battle in the city council, Burke and Vrdolyak made political peace with Mayor Byrne. Daley's relationship with Byrne never improved and he became livid with her, Burke, and Vrdolyak. Because Byrne believed that Daley represented her greatest political threat and that he would challenge her in the 1983 mayoral election, she started firing city employees from Daley's Eleventh Ward, reducing his clout and weakening his political campaign apparatus. Rich Daley's back was up against the wall. Without a political office independent of Mayor Byrne, he faced the possibility of political extinction. Daley chose to run for Cook County state's attorney.

The 1980 Democratic primary for state's attorney featured two Irish-Catholic heirs to political dynasties: Rich Daley and Ed Burke. Both were public officials who had long been mentored in political families. At this stage in their careers, however, Daley—like a finch adapting to life on the Galapagos Islands—began to evolve faster than Burke, becoming a more disciplined candidate, a tougher politician.

"Burke has got a glorified vision of himself," Forty-Ninth Ward Alderman David Orr observed five years later. "There's a struggle going on within Ed Burke to go beyond his background. Even Rich Daley has managed to move beyond the limiting aspects of his upbringing. Roots are fine and Ed Burke has deep political roots. But roots are supposed to grow into something bigger. . . . He's got the power, but the tragedy of Ed Burke is that he's using it for a day that's passed him by."

Byrne's backing of Burke for state's attorney had two significant implications. First, it allowed Daley to run as an independent Democrat and an anti-machine, anti-Byrne candidate during a period when many voters thought poorly of both Byrne and the local Democratic Party. Second, the break with the party forced Rich Daley to build his own team and political campaign apparatus, which became invaluable to him as his career progressed.

Daley's inner circle of advisers had evolved since his father's death. From the family branch of Rich Daley's holy trinity—family, government, and politics—Bill Daley emerged as his brother's closest adviser. The youngest Daley brother had great judgment, keen political insights, and the courage to speak up and say things that made people uncomfortable from time to time. From the government branch, the brainy Frank Kruesi joined the Daley inner circle as he worked as a staffer in the Illinois senate. From the politics branch, Daley identified two new talents who became integral to his career success: Tim Degnan and Jeremiah Joyce.

Approaching his fortieth birthday, Degnan was a tall, big-shouldered native of Bridgeport. Like his father before him, Degnan had served as Chicago's commissioner of Streets and Sanitation. A chain smoker with a raspy voice and a square jaw like John Wayne, Degnan became known as Daley's political enforcer. He also served Daley as a behind-the-scenes political operative with deep connections—some of them unsavory. Nearly thirty years later, Degnan's relationship with Rich Daley was described as so personal that he was considered the fifth Daley brother.

Jeremiah Joyce was even more colorful than Degnan. He was an Illinois state senator who previously worked as a police detective, a high school history teacher, and alderman from Tom Hynes's southwest-side Nineteenth Ward. Joyce had a creative streak, a genius-level IQ, and a family lineage as the son and grandson of two rugged, well-known labor leaders. Described as having the personality of a Doberman pinscher, Joyce was known as a tough and wily political organizer—so tough and so wily that even some of his closest allies feared him.

Three other new members of Daley's political team were Richard "Dick" Devine, Paul Stepan, and Phil Krone. Devine, a skilled trial attorney, was a star athlete in high school at Loyola Academy. After earning a JD from Northwestern Law School, Devine followed in his father's footsteps and went to work for the City of Chicago, accepting a position as executive assistant to the late Mayor Daley. Over the next thirty years Devine held executive positions in the state's attorney office and Chicago park district. Stepan, a thirty-six-year-old lawyer and real estate developer with ties to Daley's father, specialized in Democratic fund-raising. The thirty-eight-year-old Krone was a shrewd and experienced political strategist.

According to Krone, Daley initially faced long odds in his quest to become the new state's attorney. "I saw everybody who would have kissed Rich Daley's ass at noon on the corner of State and Madison when his father was alive, turn their backs on him and knife him in the back," said Krone. "I figured I would make up for that and work for him. The Democratic Party, the Republican Party, the crime syndicate were all working against him. . . . That was the only major campaign that I put a lot of time in from which I didn't take any compensation. The Daleys had by then become my close friends."

Paul Stepan also had a personal connection to Rich Daley. Stepan had attended Catholic high school at Loyola Academy and played on the Lights five-foot-eight-and-under basketball team, where he became friends with Dick Devine. Devine introduced Stepan to the late Mayor Daley. Though Paul Stepan was a civil rights supporter, the mayor won him over. "I'd stayed in touch with Dick Devine all these years, and he was working for Richard J. Daley and told me he was a great guy," said Stepan. "I trusted Dick, and when I met the mayor, I was converted. He was a really warm man. That's how I got involved."

In January 1980, Rich Daley's campaign ran into financial difficulties. The younger Daley mortgaged his house and loaned $100,000 to his own campaign to keep it viable. During this crisis, Daley and Stepan discussed the financial problems of the campaign.

"Rich, this is a mess," said Stepan.

"Ok, you're in charge [of finances]," replied Daley.

Though Stepan turned out to be a talented fund-raiser who ended up collecting more than $600,000 in political donations during Daley's 1980 campaign for state's attorney, he initially felt a lot of pressure as the campaign's financial point man. "You have to understand, this was really personal. I felt like I had to raise that money to make sure Rich wouldn't lose his house. That's how personal this all was."

Chicago politics during this time period was in a state of transition. The machine's power was ebbing, as signaled by Byrne's upset victory for mayor. Moreover, with the death of Dick Daley, powerful ward committeemen, such as Ed Burke and Ed Vrdolyak, were reasserting their parochial interests over the general needs of the city. In particular, Vrdolyak—rich, aggressive, self-made "Fast Eddie," who would become chairman of the Cook County Democratic Party—would exert tremendous influence in the city council. Furthermore, TV ads and professional fund-raising soon came to dominate political campaigns.

In the great election battle of 1980, however, the Democratic Party engaged in a civil war, an old-fashioned, get-out-the-vote, Chicago-style street fight. "You break it all the way down to the precinct level," recalled one Daley political operative. "Like in Mike Madigan's Thirteenth Ward, there were eighty precincts. When we started out in 1980 we probably had three or four people that went in there—but then on Election Day we probably had three hundred and fifty people who worked the Thirteenth. We really, really did drive them crazy. They hated us. Hated us. They would slash the tires on our cars. They would call up your house in the middle of the night and say, 'We're going to kill you' and all this kind of shit. There were times where it was really, really bad. . . . There was a lot of tough stuff, a lot of fights that went on. . . . We just basically tortured Madigan, day and night."

Even though Chicago politics was in the midst of a political civil war, the 1980 Saint Patrick's Day parade—filled with the rituals and pageantry of old-time electioneering—still attracted the Democratic Party faithful. Mayor Jane Byrne stood on the reviewing stand, watching the floats, the hand-lettered signs, and printed posters. The Irish-Catholic Byrne proudly waved a green-tasseled shillelagh as she watched the teamsters, the pipefitters, and the sanitation workers stream past, followed by a team of bare-legged shivering cheerleaders.

"Where's Daley already?" someone asked.

"He's coming, he's coming," came the hoarse reply.

As the March snow fell, the Daley float soon emerged, an enormous flatbed with matronly ladies waving. On the side of the float, an image hung—like a religious icon—of the late Mayor Daley. Behind walked Rich and Maggie Daley, their hair flaked white with snow.

"Hi, mayor," Rich Daley said to Byrne with a wave of his hand.

"Hi," she answered crisply with a stiff wave.

Soon, a column of Daley supporters marched in front of the mayor, chanting their message at her, like soldiers on review: "Da-ley, Da-ley, Da-ley, Da-ley." But Jane Byrne, a spitfire as always, leaned over the railing and began mimicking them. "Da-ley, Da-ley," she chanted. "Da-ley, Da-ley."

Despite her bravado, Byrne's candidates—Ed Burke and presidential candidate Teddy Kennedy—lost decisively in the Illinois Democratic primary of 1980. Rich Daley not only beat Burke in every geographic area in the City of Chicago but also earned more votes than Burke in suburban Cook County, which had previously held strong anti-Daley feelings when his father was mayor.

After this impressive primary win, Daley expected to receive support from the local Democratic Party in the November general election against the sitting Republican state's attorney, Bernard Carey. However, Mayor Byrne blocked this pro forma endorsement due to her belief that the entire Daley family was challenging her leadership as mayor. Many Democrats believed that Byrne even lent her behind-the-scenes support to Carey, the Republican incumbent. Rich Daley—rejected by the political machine his father had fine-tuned—took fairly conventional election positions in the general election. "Let's get tough-on-crime." "We need to professionalize the office of state's attorney." He also began to very skillfully use Byrne's attacks against him to gain votes and to improve his own reputation.

In October 1980, Rich Daley attended the Democratic Party's pre-election campaign lunch at the Bismarck Hotel. Held the Tuesday before the general election, this longstanding event was designed to energize the local party. Political operatives filled a crowded room, smoked, and talked. Ward committeemen and precinct captains could read the campaign signs hanging overhead: CARTER MONDALE 1980. RE-ELECT OUR METROPOLITAN SANITARY DISTRICT TRUSTEES. All of the faithful Democrats waited for the requisite political sermons. Rich Daley shattered the upbeat mood, however, when he started his campaign speech by accusing Mayor Byrne of "McCarthyism" and a "ruthless desire for power."

"There isn't a precinct captain, a Democratic worker, a business-man or professional," said Daley, "who does business with the city who does not fear Mayor Byrne, and everyone in this room knows it."

Turning the election into a referendum on Byrne, Rich Daley won in November. Ironically, the firstborn son of Dick Daley had defeated the Chicago machine as an independent Democrat. Rich Daley's victory demonstrated his emerging political talents, as well as the growing strength of his own brand.

Yet across the country Republican candidates beat Democrats, riding on the coattails of Ronald Reagan. The former actor and governor of California had focused his political message on tax cuts and the need to roll back the cultural excesses of the 1960s and 1970s. The Democratic Speaker of the US House of Representatives provided a vivid analysis of Reagan's broad political appeal. "A tidal wave hit us from the Pacific, the Atlantic, the Caribbean, and the Great Lakes," said Tip O'Neill.

Despite this nationwide Republican tsunami, Rich Daley won a close race. He beat the Republican incumbent by sixteen thousand votes out of the two million cast. The race was so close that it wasn't clear until the next morning that Daley had officially won.

Don Rose, the campaign manager for the Republican candidate, provided his own postdefeat analysis. "What went wrong was that a mayor intruded herself in this race in a way that she thought, in her own politically ignorant way, would assist in defeating her enemy, Rich Daley," said the frustrated Rose. "Instead, she succeeded in the last ten days in building up a massive block of votes for him. Jane Byrne did more for Richard M. Daley than Richard J. Daley ever did. Richard J. Daley just gave his son a state senate seat and a name. Over the last year or so, Jane Byrne, through her intemperate attacks, has built him into a folk hero."

Daley's state's attorney victory was a key event in his professional life. Not only had he broken politically with the Chicago machine and won, he now had an important office with which he could build his own credibility as a public servant. His great victory did not cause Daley to abandon his wily political instincts, however. He made sure that Tim Degnan—his close ally from Bridgeport—filled his old seat in the Illinois senate for the next nine years.

On his first day in office as state's attorney, Rich Daley drove to the criminal courts building at Twenty-Sixth Street and California Avenue. This court building was located in Little Village, a Hispanic neighborhood that once was filled with Poles and Bohemians. During the 1980s, Little Village quickly became an epicenter of Chicago's Mexican culture, a lively strip of stores, *carnicerias*, *taquerias*, *panaderias*, and Mexican nightclubs. Getting out of his car, Daley walked up to the front of the courts building with energy in his step. Without saying hello, the pot-bellied security guard at the door patted Daley down and searched him. Rich Daley's face turned bright red, a physical sign of the temper that he would later be known for professionally.

"That's Richie Daley, you idiot," a policeman in the lobby bellowed at the guard.

Daley quickly developed a reputation at the state's attorney office for skill as an administrator. On learning that much of the support staff was low quality and unprofessional, the new state's attorney ordered skills assessments. He also changed the culture of the office. Secretaries no longer cooked meals at their desks, walked the office in stocking feet, curled coworkers hair, or played the radio and danced in the hallway.

Daley also started to become known as a leader who was interested in ideas. "Rich has a lot of ideas about things," recalled Dick Devine, who served as Daley's first assistant state's attorney. "He liked to bounce those ideas off people before making a decision. But he was also at that time [in his career] a very good listener. He wanted to hear from the people in the office that had relevant experience and get ideas from them. It was really a very good atmosphere in the sense that there was a lot of discussion about the priorities for the office and what we were going to do."

Daley also showed a certain low-key passion for the work. "I've found that this job is very challenging," said Daley. "Very rewarding, and very depressing. It's rewarding to see dedicated people in this office, the police department, and the communities work together on problems. It's depressing to see so much violence. You can understand why prosecutors sometimes overreact when they look at pictures of a 65-year-old man who was beaten to death. But I like the job."

After his first year in office, Daley had developed a reputation as a professional, competent state's attorney who ran a tightly controlled organization. "Daley's performance has been a pleasant surprise," said one staff lawyer. This characterization of Daley's management style would hold true as he progressed in his political career.

Rich Daley also built an exceptionally good team of professionals at the state's attorney office, combining key members of his inner circle with other talented individuals. In addition to appointing Dick Devine, he also kept on Bill Kunkle, a tough Republican career criminal prosecutor, as his chief deputy. He chose Cathy Ryan, an exceptional person who was both a nun and a lawyer, to become head of the juvenile division. Daley also named Frank Kruesi to a key policy-making position. "I think his political judgment was that his political interests were in showing that he could run a very strong, professional office," explained John Schmidt, Daley's transition chief at the state's attorney office. "But I also think that he wanted to operate that way and so he began to develop a style of getting very strong people, being willing to support them. That style of wanting to get good people and wanting to deal with them at a personal level—that developed at the state's attorney office."

In the early 1980s, Daley's political evolution continued, and at this stage in his career he showed a curious mix of conservative and liberal tendencies in office. As a professional administrator, he showed a liberal bent by making high-quality legal appointments and by signing the Shakman decree, a court-negotiated agreement preventing political hiring and firing of government workers. On other issues, however, Daley still appeared as an old-fashioned Chicago Democrat, failing to prosecute voting fraud and eventually disbanding the state's attorney vote fraud group. Like his father, he also took tough-on-crime policy positions, such as advocating the prosecution of teenagers as adults for serious crimes.

Though Daley had a largely positive start in office as state's attorney, he suffered a personal tragedy during 1981. His son Kevin died before his third birthday. Kevin Daley had a medical condition called spina bifida, a developmental birth defect of the spinal cord. For the rest of his professional career, a memorial card from Kevin's funeral sat prominently on Daley's desk, alongside the memorial card from his dad's funeral.

Kevin's thirty-three months of illness and death were a traumatic experience for Rich Daley and his wife Maggie but they tried to focus on the positive. "I like to think the experience with Kevin affected us in a good way," said Maggie. "We learned to appreciate what's really important and to ignore the superfluous things. Kevin taught us to take each day and enjoy that day and each other."

"I'm forty years old now, not twenty-eight or thirty," explained Rich a year after his son's death. "Sure, you mature. The fact of life is that the loss of my father, the loss of my son, these things affect you. The loss of a son affects you in your relationship with your wife and children. And it changes the way you think about other children who are sick and the parents who don't have insurance to take care of them. I think you become a little more sensitive."

Rich Daley had endured the five most traumatic years of his life: his father had died, his son had died. These events had moved him deeply and he became a more empathetic man. The local Democratic Party had tried to kill him off politically and he felt betrayed by Ed Burke and many other men whom he had known most of his life. In becoming state's attorney, Daley won for himself an important office where he had started to mature as a leader. But Jane Byrne—a woman he disliked intensely—still held the office of mayor of Chicago, a position he had coveted since his teenage years at De La Salle high school. This fact made Daley—a man who had evolved into a tough and persistent politician—livid. He would not wait long to act on his feelings.

Approximately a year after Daley had become the state's attorney, Chicago superintendent of police Richard Brzeczek had forwarded to him a letter from Dr. John Raba, the medical director of Cermak Health Services at Cook County Jail. Police Chief Brzeczek had written that the doctor's letter concerned the physical mistreatment of Andrew Wilson, a black man accused of murdering two Chicago police officers, and noted that he was "seeking direction" from Daley on how to proceed.

Prison Health Services
2800 South California Avenue
Chicago, Illinois 60608
Telephone 633-5782/5783

February 17, 1982

Richard J. Brzeczek
Superintendent of
Chicago Police Department
1121 S. State Street
Chicago, Illinois

Re: Examination of Andrew Wilson

Dear. Mr. Brzeczek:
I examined Mr. Andrew Wilson on February 15 and 16, 1982. He had multiple bruises, swellings, and abrasions on his face and head. His right eye was battered and had a superficial laceration. Andrew Wilson had several linear blisters

on his right thigh, right cheek and anterior chest which were consistent with radiator burns. He stated that he had been cuffed to a radiator and pushed into it.

He also stated that electrical shocks had been administered to his gums, lips, and genitals.

All these injuries occurred prior to his arrival at the Jail. There must [be] a thorough investigation of this alleged brutality.

Sincerely,

John M. Raba, M.D.
Medical Director
Cermak (Prison) Health Services
cc: Mr. William M. Doyle
Mr. Leonard R. Bersky, Director
Sheriff Richard J. Elrod
Mr. Phillip T. Hardiman, Executive Director
Department of Corrections
JMR/fm:

In time, it would become clear that one police officer had been in charge during the February 1982 interrogation of Andrew Wilson: Jon Burge, a Chicago cop and a decorated former military policeman during the Vietnam War. In his free time, Burge navigated his boat, dubbed *The Vigilante*, on Lake Michigan. Slowly, police investigators begin to piece together how Burge treated Wilson on the day of his arrest. The following description came from an official police investigation.

Burge then entered the room and said, "fun time." He was carrying a little bag with him. Burge put an extra set of handcuffs on Wilson's arm that had not been handcuffed; he also placed a set of cuffs on Wilson's ankles. He placed the bag in the garbage can and left. A short time later, Burge returned, this time accompanied by an officer with a scar whom Wilson . . . later identified as Officer Hill. Burge took the bag from the garbage can and pulled out the black box. He clamped the wires to each of Wilson's ears. Then he cranked. Wilson testified that he repeatedly rubbed the wires off and that, at one point, the shocking knocked him off his chair.

After this occurred several times, Burge and Officer Hill un-handcuffed one of his arms, stretched him across the radiator that was adjacent to the ring on the wall and rehandcuffed his freed arm to something on the opposite side of the radiator. . . . They placed the clamps attached to the wires on each of his little fingers, and while Wilson was kneeling against the hot radiator Burge cranked the black box. . . . [Wilson] further stated that at this time, he was hollering and screaming out, saying he hadn't done anything and calling "Somebody help me."

Wilson testified that during this shocking episode, while in the kneeling position, his legs, chest and face made contact with the radiator. Wilson also stated that while he was stretched across the radiator, the big officer with the scar, whom he referred to as "Burge's partner," kicked him in the back. Another officer, whom he described as short and whose identity he did not know, was also kicking him at this time.

The next part of the incident that Wilson recalled was when Burge pulled a second device out of the brown bag. Wilson described this device as black, round, with a wire and an electrical cord sticking out from it. He said it resembled a "curling iron with a wire." In his testimony, Wilson described how Burge plugged the device into the wall, then ran the wire "real gentle" between his legs in the groin area. Wilson stated that he was standing, spread-eagled at this time. Burge then jabbed the wire into Wilson's back, slamming him into the grill over the window, causing Wilson to fall back.

Wilson stated that when he began to spit blood, the torture stopped and the officer put the objects back into the brown bag.

Officer Burge served as a Chicago Police Department commander in a largely black neighborhood on the south side of the city, and his service during the 1980s coincided with persistent rumors—and then later news reports, lawsuits, and criminal trials—about the systematic torture of black suspects in Chicago police stations.

There is no record that State's Attorney Daley or his staff ever responded to the letter from Police Chief Brzeczek. Doctor Raba soon received a phone call from George Dunne, the chairman of the Cook County Board. The board not only controlled the county jails but also Raba's employer, Cermak Health Service. Dunne advised Doctor Raba not to get involved in the Andrew Wilson matter. For the next thirty years, whispered reports of Jon Burge and his south-side activities would haunt the career of Rich Daley.

CHAPTER 6

MAYORAL ELECTION OF 1983

Rich Daley's life experiences—including his personal tragedies and professional successes—were part of his evolving character as he considered whether to run for mayor of Chicago in the upcoming 1983 election. If he did run, Daley would start the campaign with a mixed public reputation and a collection of uneven strengths and weaknesses. On the positive side, the voting public associated the Daley name with growth, jobs, and high-quality infrastructure improvements. The City That Works image inherited from his father was a significant asset for Rich Daley. Unfortunately, some Chicagoans also associated the political heir of Dick Daley with negative images: declining race relations, corruption, and the intolerance of a powerful political boss at the 1968 Democratic National Convention.

Daley's personal traits were also mixed. On the positive side, he had become an experienced public figure and a tough and very instinctual politician who had tutored under one of the great political geniuses of twentieth-century American politics. Daley also had a gift for identifying and nurturing talent and had great discipline with respect to managing human relations. He knew how to compartmentalize and control his life's holy trinity—politics, government, and family—and how to nourish the circle of advisers that fed in from each of these roots. As state's attorney, Daley also had started to develop into a skilled administrator, a trait that the voting public would soon recognize. He also possessed a healthy ego and a deep desire to reclaim the mayor's office for the Daley family.

But Rich Daley was also an awkward public speaker—a significant liability in a society where TV increasingly dominated the political dialogue. He also had a red-faced temper, did not like feedback, and felt a great sense of entitlement to the office of mayor. These signs of possible hubris aggravated another serious personal flaw: his animosity toward Mayor Jane Byrne.

The mayoral race of 1983 actually started with three strategic mistakes made by Mayor Byrne, one each in 1980, 1981, and 1982. Each misstep had racial connotations. First, Byrne supported a district remapping in 1980 that reduced the political power of black and Hispanic voters. Second, in 1981 she replaced two African-American members of the Board of Education with two white women. Third, in 1982 Byrne replaced a number of black Chicago Housing Authority (CHA) Board members with whites, despite the fact that more than 80 percent of CHA tenants were black. Even though Mayor Byrne cynically calculated that these political moves would gain her more white votes than any black votes she lost, she had miscalculated. Each of these decisions by the mayor alienated black voters, one of her key political bases. In July 1982, this led the political activist Jesse Jackson and other prominent black politicians to organize a boycott of the city's Chicago Fest at Navy Pier. "It is better to boycott with dignity," said Jesse Jackson in a radio interview, "than to sing and dance in shame. We are not bound by Chicago plantation politics. We must aggressively and militantly use our dollars and our votes."

The Chicago Fest boycott became a catalyst to energize and mobilize the black community, which soon started its own voter registration drive. By April 1983, Chicago would have nearly 670,000 registered African-American voters, approximately 150,000 more than in 1979.

White politicians, such as Jane Byrne and Rich Daley, had difficulty in seeing this growing black political power, however. In announcing his candidacy, Daley focused on Byrne. "People are worried about the future of Chicago," said Daley, "because they have experienced the results of mismanagement. People are worried about the future of Chicago because they know the city has ineffective leadership."

As a black politician, Harold Washington, in contrast, knew what was occurring in his community. His landslide reelection to the US House of Representatives took him into the churches, homes, and neighborhoods of African-Americans. He felt their rising anger at Mayor Byrne and President Reagan. "Black voters hate Ronald Reagan with a vengeance, and they will turn out," predicted one Democratic pollster in late 1982.

"Chicago is a divided city," said Washington in announcing his candidacy. "Chicago is a city where citizens are treated unequally and unfairly. Chicago is a city in decline. . . . Since 1955, women, Latinos, blacks, youth and progressive whites have been left out of the Chicago government."

"I have compassion for the terrible plight of our people," thundered Washington, "And a vision for its future. I honestly believe that of those candidates mentioned, only I can rebuild Chicago by rallying Chicagoans to create a city in which every individual will receive his or her full measure of dignity."

Though none of the white politicians realized it at the time, black Chicagoans were in a fever, an almost religious thrall. "They saw Harold Washington not as a political person," remembered Ned Kennan, who Jane Byrne had hired to advise her 1983 campaign. "They saw Harold Washington as representing deities, as representing religion. . . . And I began to realize that if Harold was smart enough to augment this image, the spark that had already ignited was going to become a major fire that no one could fight politically because it will be totally out of the political context."

Neither the local Democratic Party nor any of the white candidates recognized the growing fervor of the black community. When the party gave Byrne its tepid endorsement in late November 1982, the field was complete. Byrne, Washington, and Daley would compete in the Democratic primary to become the next mayor of Chicago.

It would be an ugly, mean-spirited campaign.

Daley got off to a good start. In November, he received his first endorsement from the Forty-Fifth Ward Democratic organization, which represented white, Catholic voters in Chicago's northwest-side Bungalow Belt. "I've been a Daley man right along," said the Forty-Fifth Ward committeeman. "I was for his father, and I'm for him." Daley soon received other endorsements from old-school white politicians who had supported his father, such as Dan Rostenkowski, the influential US Congressman.

Rich Daley also had the backing of wealthy, influential members of the Chicago business community, including the Pritzker family; Robert Abboud, former chairman of First Chicago Corporation; and Ben Heineman, president of Northwest Industries. "I'm a very strong supporter of Rich," said J. Ira Harris, general partner at Salomon Brothers. "I think we need strong chief executive leadership, which I believe Rich would provide, and we cannot continue to have a situation of a revolving door in top management. My feeling is that Rich looks at the position [of mayor] as that of a chief executive who must surround himself with very competent, talented people who have the ability to develop a business plan. The crux of the whole campaign is going to come down to management. It's not different from running any other $2 billion business. No one person runs a corporation and no one person runs a city. I have known Rich for many years, and I have watched his career. I am convinced Rich looks at it this way." This emerging consensus that Daley possessed chief executive leadership and a talent for administration would eventually become one of his most enduring political assets.

In 1983, however, the vindictiveness of the campaign would overshadow such thoughtful, substantive pronouncements. Racial, ethnic, religious, and sexist slurs would soon waft through the political battle. "It's a racial thing, don't kid yourself." "Ditch the bitch and vote for Rich." "It's our turn now." "We want it all, we want it now." "Epton! Epton! He's our man; we don't want no Af-ri-can."

To his credit, Daley tried to downplay such sentiments, especially those that touched on race. "The fear, the hysteria he's using. . . . It isn't good for the city," said Daley, after Democratic Party chairman Eddie Vrdolyak made his infamous "it's a racial thing" comments to white precinct workers.

Yet Jane Byrne and Harold Washington refused to turn down the racial animosity heating up in Chicago. Byrne's campaign workers began, as early as January 1983, scaring voters and telling them that she was the "white hope" candidate that could "stop the nigger." Other Byrne leaflets showed photos of Jesse Jackson and claimed he would be the "real mayor" unless the voters kept Byrne in office. "There are some who believe that I should avoid the race issue," said Washington at the final debate between Byrne, Daley, and himself, "But I will not avoid it because it permeates our entire city and has devastating implications. . . . I'm running to end Jane Byrne's four year effort to further institutionalize racial discrimination in this great city."

While Byrne and Washington fought a battle on race and competed for black votes, Rich Daley ran a parallel campaign that targeted white voters. According to political scientist William Grimshaw, the 1983 Democratic primary was not a three-way race. Instead, it was two separate contests, each with two candidates. Byrne versus Daley for the white vote. Washington versus Byrne for the support of African-Americans. Some white voters and politicians would later blame Daley for running against a sitting white mayor and dividing the white electorate.

Washington caught two big breaks that helped drive black voters to come out and support him. First, Mayor Byrne agreed to a series of debates because she was focused on Daley and believed that he would demonstrate his weak public-speaking ability. Byrne was right about Daley. But she failed to anticipate how well Washington would present himself. Polls of white voters after the first debate showed that Byrne had gained six points, Daley had lost nine, and Washington had gained one. But polls of black voters after the same debate indicated that Washington had gained eight points, Byrne had lost six, and Daley lost two. The first debate clearly had helped Washington demonstrate to black voters that he had the capacity to govern. Washington's second big break came near the end of the campaign. His staff gambled and organized a political rally at a large venue, the University of Illinois Pavilion. The event drew more than twelve thousand enthusiastic supporters and helped to transform Washington's candidacy into an almost religious movement for black Chicagoans.

In competing for the support of white voters, Rich Daley decided that one of his most effective tools would be his mom, Sis Daley. White

Chicagoans had a great nostalgia, an unmet yearning for the simplicity of the Daley mayoral era. In a thirty-second television commercial, Sis stood in front of family pictures in the living room of her Bridgeport home. "That's Rich," says Sis. "He's the eldest [son]. I'm very proud of him. I'm sure that if his father was alive, he'd be very proud of him. He'll be a professional mayor of Chicago and a good one."

In the final debate at Roberto Clemente High School, Rich Daley also tried to connect himself to the earlier Daley era. "I make no apology for my name. I am proud of my family name, and I'm proud of my father and my mother. From them I learned a love for this city. I look back to my father's life with pride."

Daley collected prominent endorsements, including those of the *Chicago Tribune*, the *Chicago Sun-Times*, and his one-time nemesis, Dawn Clark Netsch. He also received the endorsement of Walter Mondale, former US vice president, a few days before the Democratic primary voting would occur.

The Mondale endorsement of Daley enraged Jesse Jackson. "Realistically," said Jackson, "we have to recognize that racism reduces our options to the point that we cannot hope to be elected president or senator or governor; therefore, we have to increase black political participation where we can. You would think that a liberal like Mondale would understand and appreciate this."

"I'm an old friend of Rich Daley's," responded the former US vice president, "And I promised him, long before Harold got into it, that I would help him. It's the first time I've been in a race when there's a black candidate on the other side, but I made a commitment and I believe, in politics as in anything else, you keep your word."

About six weeks before the Mondale endorsement of Daley, Jane Byrne sat in a small loveseat at the mayor's office, wearing a beautiful dress. With her legs folded under her derriere, she looked very charming and queen-like as she led a key campaign meeting before the 1983 Democratic primary. The room was filled with high-level advisers and staff of all kinds. Ned Kennan, the psychologist and political adviser, stood at the front of the room making a presentation with an overhead projector.

"Jane, I'm not so happy to say this, but I think you're going to lose the election," Kennan said bluntly with his thick Israeli accent.

"Fucking Daley can never win. He's only, like, 24 percent of the vote," replied Mayor Byrne confidently.

"No, no, Daley's not going to win the election," answered Kennan directly. "Harold is."

"Ned, I know that you're a genius and I always present you as such," said Byrne, looking directly at Kennan. "I always believe what you say, but right now you are full of shit."

"I've been full of shit on many occasions," agreed Kennan, "But trust me, you're going to lose to Harold Washington. He's going to win because he is the voice of the black people. The voice of God, the voice of church, the voice of the righteous thing to do. The voice intermingles with excitement, a voice intermingled with ecstasy. A voice intermingled with being in a trance. And the fact of the matter is, Jane, if the fire of this voice catches on, all they have to do is go to the polls and you lose."

"You're full of shit," said Byrne caustically. "I mean, you're really full of shit. Go learn something new." Kennan left the meeting and went back to his hotel, eating dinner by himself.

On February 22, 1983, Harold Washington beat Byrne and Daley to become the nominee of the Democratic Party for mayor. Washington had decisively won the black wards, while Byrne and Daley had divided up the white neighborhoods. Washington ended up with 36.3 percent of the vote, while Byrne had 33.6 percent and Daley had 29.7 percent.

In retrospect, Daley not only lost the actual 1983 election, he also lost the fund-raising competition. Daley only raised $3 million, while Jane Byrne collected more than $5 million and Harold Washington over $4 million. This mistake would not be lost on Daley or his chief fund-raiser Paul Stepan. "We learned a lot about what not to do in that campaign," said Stepan. "Don't wait until the last minute; don't ignore any community in the city; don't ever take no for an answer. Because we just didn't raise enough money that time. Maybe if we had, we could have made more TV buys and knocked Byrne out of the race.

In a two way contest, people in Chicago vote race, we know that, and I think we probably could have won."

In front of a heavy-hearted room of supporters at the Hyatt Regency, Rich Daley asked "all neighborhoods and all people" to support the next mayor. Daley's speech was heartfelt and authentic, conveying an obvious and genuine love for the City of Chicago. This authenticity and passion for the city would make an impression on the crowd. In later years, many Chicago voters would come to agree that he had the city's best interests at heart.

"By your vote," said Harold Washington in his victory speech later that evening, "The Democratic Party has been returned to the people. We shall have an open and fair government in which people of all colors, races and creeds are treated fairly, equally and equitably."

Despite Washington's rhetoric, the general election was even nastier and race-focused than the primary. Bernard Epton—a wealthy, Jewish Republican—would benefit from voter backlash against Washington, as many whites decided that they needed to "Vote Right, Vote White." On Palm Sunday, shortly before the election, Harold Washington attended mass at Saint Pascal's Roman Catholic Church. While he prayed inside with the congregation, some of Epton's supporters spray-painted the words "NIGGER DIE" on the church doors.

"The big thing is fear," said Saint Pascal's pastor, Father Francis Ciezadlo. "People have either heard of neighborhoods changing or have lived in neighborhoods that changed. . . . It's really a black-white thing. We cannot deny that there is prejudice."

On April 12, 1983, the citizens of Chicago cast their ballots for mayor. The final voting—hugely polarized by race—resulted in Chicago's closest mayoral election since 1919. Harold Washington had won 51.7 percent of the vote, overcoming the prejudice of many and defeating Epton to become the first black mayor of Chicago.

PART 3

Political Calculus

CHAPTER 7

ALL HELL BREAKS LOOSE

Harold Washington was a great campaigner—charismatic, full of life—and a wonderful orator. Washington was also a pathbreaker for black Chicagoans, inspiring a belief that the local Democratic Party could be changed and made more open and diverse. Unfortunately, Washington turned out to be relatively ineffective as mayor of Chicago for two reasons: he was a weak administrator and he did not understand—or, perhaps, did not care—how power worked in white Chicago.

"Well, I loved Harold, but he didn't know power," explained Marilyn Katz, a liberal Democrat who actively advised and supported Washington. "He opened up the city, ushered in a whole era of change, but he was a south-side Congressman with no real relations with the business community. We didn't have any friends in Springfield or in the city council. Washington didn't have any real idea how things worked, so the only way we could ever get anything done was to organize around issues, which was something new in Chicago."

"Prior to Harold, a bunch of white men ran the city—the Civic Committee and the Commercial Club and the mayor and five politicians," added Katz. "So Harold's greatest accomplishment was to break open the political process. We did some incredibly groundbreaking policy innovations during that time."

Washington may have "broken open the political process" and helped to provide more opportunities to blacks, women, and other minorities, but to many longtime white Chicagoans his reign as mayor appeared to be complete chaos. The city council fought bitterly and launched a political civil war known as the Council Wars, while the already fractious City of Chicago started to become known as Beirut on the Lake. From the outside, the Council Wars appeared to be a black-versus-white political civil war. The group of aldermen that held twenty-nine votes was led by Ed Vrdolyak and Ed Burke and included twenty-eight white aldermen. The group of aldermen that had twenty-one votes was led by Mayor Washington and had seventeen black aldermen. For three years, the city council waged an embittered power struggle and achieved very little of substance.

"I would never describe myself as a bitter or hateful person," asserted Alderman Ed Burke twenty-five years later. Since 1983, Burke was known for his city-funded, twenty-four-hour-a-day bodyguards and gangster-looking black sedan. "I think that a lot of the stuff that you read about my political career developed in the conflict with Harold Washington in the '80s, but frankly, that was more of a political struggle than a struggle of black and white. If he would have agreed to compromise with us, it would have been business as usual."

Wednesday, November 25, 1987, approximately 12 Noon. The traffic on Lake Shore Drive was slow as David Orr, Forty-Ninth Ward Alderman, tried to drive south toward downtown Chicago. Off to the left, Lake Michigan looked gray and foggy, with a thin mist of rain blowing across the waves. The chilly forty-five-degree temperature made it seem as if another Chicago winter was starting.

Orr, a progressive politician, was out in his ward when he heard a rumor that Mayor Harold Washington had suffered a heart attack. He returned to his house to change out of his casual clothes and told his wife that he had no idea when he would come home. Orr then started driving toward the mayor's political office in the Loop.

Orr had been one of only four white aldermen to support Mayor Washington during the 1983–86 Chicago City Council Wars. Over this long Thanksgiving weekend and into the next week, as interim mayor he would stand at center stage in what some consider to be one of the most interesting scenes in the annals of US urban politics. As events unfolded, the drama turned into a succession battle, a knockdown, winner-take-all, Chicago-style political fight. Ego and power. Secret meetings and side deals. Broken rules and dashed expectations.

Above all, though, this spectacle turned on the issue of race: black and white.

As Orr drove downtown, however, he did not know how the coming political battle would unfold. Sporting a thick mustache and nicknamed "Mr. Goody Two Shoes," he still looked like the assistant history professor who taught college for ten years before entering politics. His academic training probably gave Orr perspective, though, making him aware of the parallels between the unfolding drama and the day that Richard J. Daley, the famous Boss Mayor of Chicago, died eleven years earlier in 1976. Both had heart attacks at work just before the holidays. Both were rushed to Northwestern Memorial Hospital and were treated by Dr. John Sanders, a cardiac surgeon.

Orr's knowledge of history may also have made him aware, as he drove downtown from his multiethnic Rogers Park ward, of the years of instability that followed Daley's twenty-one-year reign. How Michael Bilandic, the low-key Eleventh Ward machine alderman from Bridgeport who was supposed to keep the mayor's seat warm for Rich Daley, could not handle the great snowstorms of January 1979, paralyzing the basic functioning of the city. How Jane Byrne, the five-foot-three-inch political free spirit who "beat the whole god-damn machine singlehanded" to win the mayoral election, but was unable to hold together the business-banking-labor nexus that Chicagoans preferred. How race became everything in 1983.

"A vote for [Rich] Daley is a vote for Washington," Ed Vrdolyak had said to a group of white precinct workers in 1983. "It's a two-person race. It would be the worst day in the history of Chicago if your candidate . . . was not elected. It's a racial thing. Don't kid yourself. I am calling on you to save your city, to save your precinct. We are fighting to keep the city the way it is."

Orr certainly knew how Harold Washington, a former machine politician, inspired an overwhelming African-American turnout to beat both Byrne and Rich Daley and become Chicago's first black mayor. Chicago's progressives and African-Americans rejoiced, but a group of largely white aldermen fought Washington bitterly for three years.

When Orr reached the mayor's political office, he joined Washington's chief of staff and other political operatives, as well as Eugene Sawyer, the long-serving south-side African-American alderman and president pro tempore of the city council. Sawyer had started his political career as a machine politician, a former precinct captain and water meter reader handpicked for his loyalty by Mayor Daley during the civil rights turmoil of the early 1970s. He maintained strong ties to the Democratic organization but was also politically astute enough to become the first alderman to support Washington's 1983 mayoral bid. Sawyer seemed very well-informed as to Washington's health prognosis.

"The mayor is dead," Sawyer told the group, long before the official phone call.

Sawyer had received his information from Ed Burke, who had learned it from a fireman. At this stage in his political career, Burke was a study in contrasts. Well-dressed and articulate, Burke was a hard-working legislator who had mastered *Robert's Rules of Order*. He was also a former policeman who chaired the city council's police-fire committee and was known to have deep connections with cops and fireman throughout Chicago. But unlike Sawyer, during the Council Wars Burke had used his powerful chairmanship of the finance committee to let him serve as a point man for anti-Washington attacks. By now, a number of his colleagues and members of the press believed that Burke was a living relic of the once dominant Chicago machine: a white Irish-Catholic politician who truly believed that the Democratic Party should be run by white Irish-Catholic politicians.

Later in the afternoon, on the day before Thanksgiving, the fireman-to-Burke-to-Sawyer rumor was confirmed when the mayor's press secretary announced from Northwestern Hospital that Mayor Harold Washington had died. For attentive fans of Chicago politics, the early, intimate conversations between Sawyer and Burke indicated that the succession battle to succeed Washington started before the public knew of his death. Burke and the remnants of the old-line machine— which had gradually loosened its grip on power during the Byrne and Washington administrations—were already working to take back the mayoral throne.

Washington's political advisers, however, insisted on delaying the official press conference until Tim Evans, Fourth Ward alderman, could attend, along with Orr in his capacity of interim mayor. Evans, an African-American from the south side, had served as Washington's floor leader in the city council. A former machine politician during the Daley era, Evans had evolved into a progressive who many blacks considered Washington's rightful heir. Washington's political advisers were true believers in his reform agenda—"you're talking about people for whom this man was like a god," according to Orr—and were willing to play political hardball to give Evans the best chance of becoming acting mayor.

Washington, the charismatic African-American leader who had declared the machine "dead, dead, dead" after his first mayoral victory had now permanently passed beyond Chicago's borders and its political divisions. His aides scheduled the funeral for Monday morning, with Washington's body to lay in state over the weekend. While Chicagoans lined up for blocks and blocks to attend his wake, Sawyer, Burke, Evans, and other big-time Chicago politicians began making phone calls, holding secret meetings, and jockeying to succeed Washington.

Dick Mell, a white alderman from the northwest side, was one of those wheeler-dealer politicians who looked in the mirror and saw the next mayor of Chicago. Though described by some as a charismatic field marshal, Mell was given more of a back-handed compliment by Sawyer: "He's not the kind of guy who would stab you in the back; he'd stab you in the chest." Mell was a former businessman, and now was known as a scheming, clout-heavy ward boss. Within three years of Washington's death he would also become father-in-law to an obscure traffic court prosecutor, Rod Blagojevich, who would later follow him into local politics.

The city council, in the meantime, needed to select one of its own members to serve as acting mayor—just as it did eleven years earlier when Dick Daley suddenly died—until Chicagoans could vote in a special election. Sawyer, Evans, Burke, and Mell had support from various aldermanic colleagues. Sawyer represented the black old-school Chicago politicians. Evans aligned with Washington's progressive coalition and had overwhelming support in the African-American community. Burke inspired strong loyalty among the white politicians but was considered a mayoral long shot due to his divisive, anti-Washington offensives during the Council Wars. Mell got off to a fast start and was pushing and cajoling to get the necessary twenty-six city council votes as quickly as possible.

"Dick Mell called me several times to ask me to support him for mayor," said Orr. "Mell implied that he [already] had twenty-four votes. . . . You read the papers, you saw the stuff Mell was offering everyone. Dick is like that. He asked me straight out what I wanted to be. What it would take to get my vote."

Reverend Jesse Jackson—the influential black Chicagoan who had run for US president in 1984 and would run again in 1988—flew in from the Middle East and begin holding press conferences and meeting with well-known African-American and Hispanic aldermen. On Sunday afternoon, Jackson organized one such meeting at city hall, excluding all white aldermen. Jackson started the meeting by joining hands with the participants and singing "We Shall Overcome" before taking the group into a side room. Though Jackson attempted to represent himself as a neutral kingmaker, his speeches and organizing activities were designed to unite black aldermen behind Evans.

The white aldermen also held secret meetings, including two at the home of a northwest-side alderman. Since none of the white aldermen could secure enough votes to ensure victory at that point, Mell also reached out to Luis Gutierrez and the bloc of four Hispanic aldermen. He supposedly offered important positions, such as vice mayor, Hispanic control of the park district, and a Hispanic chief of staff, but the Gutierrez bloc remained uncommitted.

On Sunday, November 29, as the Chicago Bears defeated the Green Bay Packers, Mell met secretly with Sawyer, who may have already locked up eleven votes from black aldermen unwilling to face certain defeat at the polls by supporting a white candidate. Mell, who controlled sixteen white votes, decided the next day to back Sawyer. "I could support a black man, but Sawyer in his community could not support me," Mell explained.

This calculation by the white leaders within the Democratic Party, which was neither high-minded nor race-blind, reverberated through Chicago politics for years and years. Moreover, the motivation for this political decision was very important: Mell and his white aldermanic colleagues supported Sawyer because they were attracted to his flaws. These politicians realized that, if they chose Sawyer as mayor, his election would drive a deep wedge into the black voting bloc that Washington had constructed because, they calculated, Evans would almost certainly challenge Sawyer in the next mayoral election, thereby dividing black voters.

With a twenty-one gun salute and cries of "Harold! Harold!" Chicago buried Washington at Oak Woods Cemetery on Monday, November 30, 1987. "He loved people—black, white, brown, red, green, whatever color," said Washington's pastor, the Reverend Herbert Martin, who was a keynote speaker. "And for those whose backs were pressed against the wall, Harold always had a word of hope."

Washington's political advisers chose Evans as another keynote speaker, because they believed Evans most closely matched this progressive perspective. A Monday night memorial service for Washington at the pavilion on the University of Illinois at Chicago campus also became a political rally for Evans, with shouts of "We want Evans" and "No deals!"

However, Chicago politicians, both black and white, had already agreed on a deal: Sawyer would be the next mayor. The city council set a special meeting for 5:30 PM on Monday, just hours after the final ceremonies honoring Washington. Washington's supporters got wind of the meeting and began to show up in support of Evans. Crowds started arriving at city hall. Three thousand people packed the city council chambers, with thousands more raucous, emotional supporters out on LaSalle Street. The city council floor itself also became chaotic, with open shouting matches between supporters of Sawyer and Evans. At one point, Dick Mell screamed, "What a sham! What a sham!" and then jumped up on his aldermanic desk in a vain effort to get recognized by Orr, who as interim mayor had the responsibility of presiding over the special city council meeting.

Washington's supporters that day felt betrayed. As they still dealt with the pain of the late mayor's funeral, many black Chicagoans suspected that the city council would jam a new mayor down their throats. African-American aldermen that supported Sawyer started to receive death threats.

As the wild city council session progressed, Sawyer—an African-American who represented many of the upset black Chicagoans in the crowd—began to lose his nerve for taking the mayoral throne. "Dick, I can't do it. I gotta pull out," Sawyer told Mell on the floor of the city council. "Okay," Mell replied with a fake sigh, "But you should tell the people who backed you. That's the least you owe them."

Hours afterward on that same night, Mell and his colleagues elected Sawyer at 4 AM with a roll call vote: twenty-nine in favor of Sawyer, nineteen for Evans. One abstention was also cast—by Pat Huels, the Eleventh Ward Alderman from Bridgeport. Rich Daley, Cook County state's attorney, controlled the abstaining alderman and therefore could later continue to claim to be above political infighting.

"I said to former Mayor Washington that I would not involve my office in the Council Wars," said Daley. "I told him that the people want the state's attorney to run a professional office and not get involved in petty politics."

Political insiders knew, however, that the Eleventh Ward alderman had followed Rich Daley's orders to vote with the block backing Sawyer on all procedural votes and then to walk off the council floor and get recorded as an abstention during the final vote that the news media would report to Chicago's public. In November 1987 Rich Daley already knew that he would run again for mayor in the 1989 mayoral election, but he did not want to leave any fingerprints during the succession battle.

Dick Mell later explained the floor conversation he'd had with Sawyer as a head fake, a calculated political tactic. "It was a ruse to get him in the room with us!" gloated Mell. "Once inside, I slammed the door and locked it. I thought, 'Now we gotcha, you son of a bitch!' Then we climbed all over him. When we walked out, he was so weak he wobbled like this—whoa!—and we had to steady him. But he was ours."

The City of Chicago now had its forty-fourth mayor: Eugene Sawyer. Sawyer had a reputation of being a nice guy, and some even called him "Gentleman Gene." With sixteen years of city council experience, and few enemies, political observers expected the new mayor to have early accomplishments. As legislator-in-chief, Sawyer did have some quick successes: allowing lights in Wrigley Field; passing a 1988 budget; breaking the taxi monopoly; developing land near O'Hare Airport; and shepherding a gay rights ordinance through the city council. However, his effectiveness as a leader of Chicago continued to be hamstrung by the political fallout from the backroom deals and racial divisiveness of that late night, special city council meeting.

Between April and July of 1988, the white Democratic aldermen took active steps to reassert their control of Chicago city government. In April, they increased the financial budgets of allies on key city council committees. In May, they unceremoniously dumped Alderman Orr as vice mayor, replacing him with Terry Gabinski, the protégé of old-time machine politician Dan Rostenkowski. In July, the white party leaders purged Evans and all of his major supporters in the city council of their committee chairmanships, as well as their patronage jobs and discretionary funds. According to Sawyer's press secretary, after the July meeting, Aldermen Burke and Mell washed their hands in the bathroom off of the city council chambers and gloated.

"The niggers will never get together after this," Burke predicted to Mell in the men's bathroom.*

---

*Quoted in *Restoration 1989* (Lyceum Books Inc., 1991) and in *The Mayors: The Chicago Political Tradition* (Southern Illinois University Press, 1987). Though Alderman Burke has claimed that he never used racial epithets, the historical record indicates otherwise. For example, before he died in 2010 the political strategist Phil Krone characterized Alderman Burke as one of his best friends. In the same conversation, Krone said, "Now, Eddie was a racist. There's no 'ifs,' 'ands,' or 'buts' about it." For a similar take on Burke, see *When Corruption Was King* by Robert Cooley (Carroll and Graf Publishers, 2004).

CHAPTER 8

RESTORATION

Allies of Tim Evans filed a lawsuit in April 1988 to force a special mayoral election the following year. With the memory of Harold Washington still fresh in the minds of Chicago voters, Evans's supporters felt the earlier date would aid their candidate and prevent Mayor Sawyer from consolidating his new powers of office. On November 21, 1988—one year after Washington's death—the Illinois Supreme Court ruled the election would be held in 1989. The decision was based on the technicalities of state election law.

"This is a great victory for all the citizens of the city," declared Evans.

"I had a closer relationship with Harold Washington than [Sawyer] did." he added.

In addition to Evans and Sawyer, quite a few other candidates would eventually throw their hats into the electoral ring. Ed Burke. Ed Kelly. Danny Davis. Lawrence Bloom. Juan Soliz. Rich Daley. All of the candidates except for Daley were members of the Chicago City Council. Unimpressed, one Chicago newspaper called the group "the Seven Dwarfs." Later, Ed Vrdolyak, the larger-than-life, divisive former chair of the Democratic Party, joined the race as a Republican. New leadership for Chicago did not seem promising.

Eight months later, Rich Daley summoned his brother, Bill Daley, and his chief fund-raiser, Paul Stepan, to a meeting to discuss whether he should campaign for mayor in the upcoming election. Though the news media did not recognize it yet, Daley had grown tremendously since his failed 1983 bid for mayor. He was more experienced and humbler and had a better team of advisers.

"I'm going [to run again]," Rich told his brother.

Turning to Stepan, the recently reelected state's attorney then asked, "How much can you raise?"

A month earlier, Rich Daley had amassed formidable vote totals in getting reelected—not only sweeping the city's fifty wards but also winning in the Republican suburbs.

"How much do you need?" responded Stepan, as he made eye contact with the younger brother.

"One million by January," responded Bill Daley.

"We'll do it," Stepan promised the Daleys, and he did. The campaign amassed $1.4 million by the time of its first TV ad in January 1989.

The Daley campaign went on to raise more than $7 million, swamping the fund-raising efforts of the other candidates. The Daley brothers—Bill and Rich—subscribed to their father's philosophy for political campaigns: winning big. "It's not just important to win elections, it's important to win them big—by smashing margins so that you have such a huge mandate that nobody will dare challenge you," said the seasoned journalist Bob Crawford in explaining the Daley's electoral philosophy.

Recalling the pivotal meeting years later, Paul Stepan would say, "Billy [Daley] is a political genius." In sophisticated political circles, this had become the consensus view of Bill Daley by 1989. He played a critical role in his older brother's mayoral campaign for two reasons. First, Rich Daley was carefully suspicious of most of his political advisers because he realized that human beings tend to have hidden agendas, even when they appeared helpful. Bill Daley was an exception to this self-serving behavior, and Rich trusted him completely because his brother had proven to be a person who provided advice with love and affection and loyalty. Second, in terms of political acumen and strategic insight, "Billy was the smartest of them all." Over time, he had established himself as a complex thinker who could see more than one side of an issue, trend, or poll.

As he reflected on the Daley brothers and the fund-raising success

of the 1989 campaign, Paul Stepan said, "[We raised] more than anyone had ever raised in that period of time in a local race, ever. We were
just the best. No one had ever done it better than we did."

Large contributors included the progressive lawyer John Schmidt,
who initiated the campaign funding with a $150,000 loan. The reform-
minded Schmidt had established his liberal bona fides at the 1972
Democratic National Convention when he humiliated Rich Daley's
father by designing a credentials challenge that ousted Mayor Daley's
convention delegation and substituted it with delegates led by the Reverend Jesse Jackson and the alderman Bill Singer. Schmidt now made
a bet on the Boss's son, hoping that he could guide Rich Daley to more
progressive policy positions. But why did Daley associate himself with
Schmidt, a man whom his father likely would have despised? Daley
respected Schmidt, and as a pragmatic politician understood that he
gave him credibility with two important constituencies: politically active attorneys and white lakefront liberals.

The business establishment also placed a large wager on the sitting
state's attorney. Two traders in financial markets, Richard Barnes and
Richard Dennis, each gave $100,000. Paul Beitler, a real estate devel-
oper who lived in the northern suburb Winnetka, also gave $100,000.
Pat Ryan, the founder and chief executive officer (CEO) of Aon Insurance, gave $100,000, even though he was also a Republican who lived
in the suburbs. Over the next twenty-plus years Ryan and Rich Daley
would develop a close, mutually beneficial relationship.

There are at least two theories why contributors opened their check-
books for Daley. The first focused on his competence and one-on-one
charisma, as well as their shared political ideology with the candidate.
"It was him, it was Rich," said Stepan. "People used to think he was
this slow, funny-talking south-side guy. But I kept bringing important
people, like Richard Barnes, in to talk with him, and afterward they'd
give us money every time. Rich just has that effect on people."

A second theory of Daley's political fund-raising success rested on
the concept of influence-buying. This view held that political groups,
including business people, donated money to Daley to ensure that he
listened to their views, identifying them with a key center of power in

Chicago. "They want to be on the list," said Forrest Claypool, who would soon become a key Daley aide. The list—Daley's financial disclosure report for the 1989 campaign—included more than ten thousand names of individuals and companies.

Many large donors on the Daley list were real estate developers, lawyers, financiers and other suburban business contributors. This type of contributor was associated with what is known as "pinstripe patronage" in Illinois, a term that had developed during the administration of Big Jim Thompson, the Republican governor of Illinois from 1977 to 1991.

"We're not out to buy a piece of Chicago," said real estate developer Philip Klutznick in explaining why his group gave to Rich Daley. "We already own a substantial piece of Chicago. The property that we own pays more property taxes as a single building than most communities [in Chicago]. The unfortunate thing is since we don't live in the city, we don't have any right to vote and participate in the decision making process. . . . Most of those who gave do not live in the city. The only way we can make our voices heard is to support financially the best candidate who will do the best job for creating a city environment that will be fertile ground for development and business. That's why we're here in the city. . . . But ping-pong legislation from city government has jilted the development community's ability to get international investment. We have to put a halt to that and bring stability. If you call that selfish, damn right, it's selfish."

Miriam Santos, whom Rich Daley later appointed as city treasurer in 1989, agreed with the influence-buying theory and emphasized that large contributors expected favors, including investments from the City of Chicago pension funds. "They thought that they were buying their way in, that they'd be getting things in return," said Santos after serving as city treasurer for three years. "Not just access. They thought they'd be getting preferential treatment from me. It was so blatant. All these financial types seemed to think that, by supporting the mayor in 1989, they deserved special treatment [after the election]. One man screamed at me when I said no and told me I didn't understand how the system works."

There is also a third theory of why Rich Daley broke fund-raising records in his 1989 mayoral campaign: Rahm Emanuel, a passionate, aggressive twenty-nine-year-old force of nature. Like a Category 5 hurricane, Emanuel would blast into the Daley election office, plaster a telephone to his ear and quickly develop powerful wind speed.

"Five thousand dollars!?" stormed Emanuel into the telephone. "You, you, you—I wouldn't embarrass you by having it listed that you only gave $5,000. You're a $25,000 person; better to give nothing and say you were out of town. If you want to give $5,000, fine, but don't call me when people start asking you if you're going bankrupt. People of your stature are giving $50,000."

At this stage of his career, Emanuel, who served as finance director for the Daley operation, was a progressive who brought an intense cause-oriented perspective to the election battle. "It's that sense of aggressiveness," said Hurricane Rahm, in an attempt to explain his gale force intensity. "That's an attribute people say I have—I'm 'too aggressive.' I don't see it. I just keep pushing, that's all."

Forrest Claypool, who had worked with Emanuel on political campaigns for liberal office seekers, described it another way. "He talks tough to people—'Here's what we need, here's why we need it, and we can't take any less from you.' A lot of these people are used to folks dancing around the subject and being overly polite, and no one's ever accused Rahm of that."

After helping the Daley campaign, Emanuel would power on to great career success and a fair amount of controversy. Savvy political operative. Senior adviser in the White House. Investment banker. Member of the US House of Representatives. Architect of the Democratic Party's 2006 takeover of the US Congress. White House chief of staff. One colleague from the White House colorfully captured Emanuel's Chicago-style toughness: "He's got this big old pair of brass balls, and you can just hear 'em clanking when he walks down the halls of Congress."

Over time, Emanuel's collection of friends and allies expanded to include many familiar names, such as Daley, Clinton, and Obama. Emanuel also became well known for his aggressive style and his profanity. "You've got to have a thirst for winning," explained Emanuel. This uncompromising approach would earn Emanuel the nickname of "Rahmbo."

Emanuel and Daley maintained their professional connection over the next twenty years of their careers. The fruition of Daley's relationship with Emanuel was far off in the future, however. The special mayoral election of 1989 was what Emanuel, Daley, and the rest of the campaign team were focused on now.

History will remember three things about the Chicago mayoral election of 1989. First, Rich Daley would clearly spell out his policy preferences in a series of speeches and written press releases named "The Daley Agenda for Chicago's Future." The Daley Agenda closely followed the political blueprint of Harold Washington: progressive, inclusive, and focused on the "spirit of renewal." Remarkably, over the next twenty years Daley consistently—almost relentlessly—attempted to address and solve the policy challenges highlighted in the Daley Agenda. Second, Daley expanded his circle of advisers to include a number of young, gifted liberals. He built a truly exceptional team. The new additions—including Rahm Emanuel, David Axelrod, and David Wilhelm—combined with Bill Daley, Tim Degnan, Frank Kruesi, and Jeremiah Joyce to create a dominant political squad that few could match. Finally, the political demographics in 1989 turned out to be the mirror image of Harold Washington's 1983 victory. In 1989, one battle-tested white candidate faced two African-Americans and the black electorate became seriously divided.

On December 5, 1988, Rich Daley held a press conference at the Hyatt Regency to announce his candidacy for mayor of Chicago. Physically, Daley was unexceptional. No movie star looks, no imposing physique or towering stature. Short and stocky, the former five-foot-eight-and-under basketball player wore conservative suits, nondescript ties, and white shirts. Though known as a stiff, formal speaker by the public, in private Daley had a shake-the-windows laugh. "Rich has a very hearty and wonderful laugh, and you can always find him in a room," said his wife, Maggie. Rich Daley smiled broadly but with a nervous energy. Viewed from the side, he appeared warm and friendly. If viewed straight on, however, his smile appeared slightly crooked and had a certain indefinable cockiness. Twenty years later, some would see the same imperceptible quality in the smile of George W. Bush, another heir to a political dynasty.

On this forty-degree day in December 1988 Daley's short announcement speech acknowledged the need for racial healing but primarily focused on his public policy agenda.

> Today, I proudly announce my candidacy for the Democratic nomination for mayor of Chicago. I do so aware of both the great challenge and the great opportunity the next mayor will find. Let's face it: We have a problem in Chicago. The name-calling and politics at City Hall are keeping us from tackling the real issues. It's time we stop fighting each other, and start working together. I'm not interested in running as "the white candidate," or in serving as mayor of half the people. Fighting crime is not a white issue or a black issue. Good schools are not a white issue or a black issue. Protecting taxpayers against waste is not a white issue or a black issue. Working to build Chicago's economy is not a white issue or a black issue. Competent government is not a white issue or a black issue. It's time to say, "Enough is enough." But let's begin by recognizing how much more we can do by lowering our voices and raising our sights. It's time for a new beginning in Chicago. I may not be the best speaker in town, but I know how to run a government, and how to bring people together. . . . Chicago needs to rise above the politics and the name-calling. And I know we can. To my fellow Chicagoans, I say, "Let's begin today."

The text of the Daley Agenda built on this concise speech and clearly laid out his policy priorities. Three key themes would emerge. First, Daley emphasized quality-of-life issues with, in particular, middle-class voters in mind. Education. Crime. Effective government. Economic development. Neighborhoods and housing. An insightful politician, Daley instinctively knew that the middle class were *his* voters. The rich he could co-opt. The poor did not vote.

Second, Daley followed the progressive Washington blueprint with respect to policy issues, but he stripped these subjects of racial and ethnic connotations. While he focused on quality of life for middle-class Chicagoans, he did so regardless of their group affiliations. "I think I'm very progressive." said Daley. "When I was a state senator [I worked] for nursing home reform, the elimination of the state sales tax on food and medicine, mental health reform and child abuse reform, and [I fought] gangs and drugs as state's attorney. I'm very progressive. That's a new word we're using, and I think that can apply to me. You can be black, white, Hispanic, male or female and be progressive on your record—not on speaking—but on your record. I have a good record as state's attorney. That is not a record that is moving back. That is a record of moving forward. Everybody is trying to run off of somebody else. What I'm asking is for people to judge me on my record and my experience and what I'm talking about for the future of this city."

Third, Daley emphasized accountability and getting things done. "This should be the essence of the campaign for mayor," said Daley, "confronting the important issues facing Chicago, and offering specific proposals to deal with them." This focus on effective government came to differentiate Daley from Harold Washington, who as mayor had been full of good ideas but ineffective as a manager of the city.

Finally, in a way that is unusual for politicians, Rich Daley was very specific about ranking his main policy concerns. "Education is the top priority for Richard M. Daley," he would say over and over again. Speaking directly to the middle class, he would tap into the American Dream of creating a good life for our children. Rich Daley painted an old-fashioned, family-centered, neighborhood-centric vision of living in Chicago.

"I want each school in Chicago to be the heartbeat of its neighborhood and its community," said Daley, "And I want each school in Chicago to stand as a beacon of hope for every child who attends it. They may not live in the best neighborhoods. They may have problems with their families. But when those children are in school, I want it to be a place of pride, hope, and accomplishment. Children don't vote in the election for mayor. But they have more at stake than anyone. They need a mayor who recognizes their potential, and has the experience and commitment to help them reach it. The future of our children is the future of our city. Each of our citizens has a stake in that future, and we all must work together to attain it."

Daley's expanded circle of advisers had helped him to craft and to communicate his vision for Chicago. In addition to the strategic insights of Bill Daley and Rahm Emanuel's intense fund-raising expertise, the Daley campaign also relied on two other major talents: David Wilhelm and David Axelrod.

Wilhelm, Daley's campaign manager, was a liberal, thirty-one-year-old wunderkind. Having grown up in central Appalachia, Wilhelm claimed that he had become COMMITTED to politics at the age of seven when as a supporter of Lyndon Johnson he got into a fist fight with a classmate backing Barry Goldwater. Years later, in a speech to college students Wilhelm succinctly described his campaign philosophy, "If you want to win, always be the aggressor. Always. Get on the offense and stay there."

Wilhelm brought an important set of skills to Rich Daley's 1989 campaign for mayor. Wilhelm was a nuts-and-bolts political operative who brought a calm, upbeat demeanor to the campaign. He also had a close relationship with Forrest Claypool, and the two men would act as the best man at each other's weddings. Wilhelm also brought with him tight relationships with David Axelrod and Rahm Emanuel, both of whom he had worked with in US Senator Paul Simon's successful 1984 campaign. Rich and Bill Daley were not the only up-and-comers who recognized Wilhelm's talents as a political operative. Within a few years, he would become the Democratic National Committee chairman.

David Axelrod was a thirty-four-year-old political media consultant and former news reporter with a bandito mustache and a rumpled, just-rolled-out-of-bed style of dressing. Axelrod, a hard-core liberal Democrat, had a genius for molding language and the media's impressions of key political issues. "My expertise is in the areas of language and how to shape issues," explained Axelrod, "and in the course of a campaign my role is to work through with [Daley] and [his] staff what the fundamental messages of that campaign are going to be, and then come up with ideas and with language and ultimately with media that bring those messages home."

Axelrod, who in the late 1980s and early 1990s was in the process of developing a reputation as a political consultant with the magic touch, further described his approach to advising a candidate such as Daley. "Every campaign begins with essentially the same process," said Axelrod, "and that process is a gathering of as much information as possible about your candidate, about your opponents, and about the political environment in which you're working. What we're about is the business of developing a message for that campaign. And by message I mean an argument, much as a lawyer would develop a case or an argument for a courtroom—except in this case the jury is that electorate that you're trying to influence at the polls. And so you ought to go into a race pretty much understanding what your comparative advantages are, what issues work to your benefit, where your strengths are, [and what are] your opponent's weaknesses on issues that are important to people. And then you try and drive the debate that way, and make the race about the issues that you want the race to be about. You do that through a combination of free media—in other words, press conferences, speeches, debates—and paid media, which are commercials, which tend to come later in the campaign."

In 1989, this process led Axelrod and Rich Daley to focus on the public's then current perceptions of the state's attorney. "We made one adjustment at the beginning of the campaign," said Axelrod. "We made a commercial, and in it Daley addressed the camera and at one point he said, 'I may not be the best speaker in town, but I know how to bring people together and run a government.' And that one line was quite useful for us, because it showed some self-awareness and it was important for us to separate out the fact that Daley is not always the most articulate speaker from the issue of whether he was bright and capable."

According to John Callaway, the host of the political news show *Chicago Tonight* from 1984 to 1999, Rich Daley ended up mastering the television medium in a way that his political competitors failed to do. Apparently, Daley had internalized the media and public relations lessons from Axelrod and his other advisers. "He is the master of the short bite," said Callaway. "He also has the ability to say something with his face. He is coached on what to say, but how he says it is pure Richie. We got him on *Chicago Tonight* and every time we asked a question, he'd throw it back to us. We asked, 'How could a guy who lived in Bridgeport be sensitive to the needs of black people?' and he came back with 'This is misjudging Bridgeport, we're not a wealthy neighborhood,' and so forth without once addressing the question. To put it mildly, Richie just beat the shit out of us."

Besides David Wilhelm, the political prodigy, and David Axelrod, a wordsmith with a genius for media, Daley's exceptional team of advisers included several other key players. Rahm Emanuel was a fundraising force of nature. Bill Daley was a mastermind strategist with excellent people skills. Tim Degnan was a big-shouldered political enforcer with deep, ward-level connections. Jeremiah Joyce was a tough and crafty political organizer. Frank Kruesi was a University of Chicago policy wonk who liked to be near the action. Rich Daley also made one symbolically important appointment: Avis LaVelle as his press spokesperson. The presence of LaVelle, a highly respected black reporter for WGN radio, signaled to key swing voters—including lakefront liberals, gays, and Hispanics—that Daley had changed since 1983. He was now willing to represent all Chicagoans. Like any championship team, Daley's squad also had high-quality role players—such as Paul Stepan, Phil Krone, and Forrest Claypool—who loyally performed their campaign duties. In terms of skills, Daley's campaign team had it all. Media. Fund-raising. Issues-based policy politics. Ward-level, backroom deal making. In terms of ideology, the new advisers were progressives who supported a liberal agenda. The old south-side advisers were nonideological. Pragmatists, they cared only about winning.

"The thing about the Daley operation that is impressive to me," said Axelrod in the early 1990s, "is that he has a lot of good people around him, and there is a lot of collegiality and group decision making. While [Rich Daley] is pretty strong willed, and the final arbiter in all matters, generally a consensus emerges among the people around him and he's presented with a recommendation which he either accepts or rejects. So my role is often to work within that group to forge a consensus if I have a strong feeling about something. But ultimately it's his call."

The 1989 mayoral primary was scheduled for February 28, 1989, and the general election for April 4, the same day as the Chicago Cubs' home opener at Wrigley Field. Most of the early candidates—Ed Burke, Ed Kelly, Danny Davis, Lawrence Bloom, James Taylor, and Juan Soliz—would drop out of the race prior to Democratic primary. They knew that they were no match for Daley, his money, and his team. In private, some of the white politicians—particularly Ed Burke— admitted that they did not want to repeat their mistakes from the 1983 mayoral contest by dividing the white electorate again.

With Burke out of the picture, three candidates would continue to challenge Daley: Mayor Eugene Sawyer, Alderman Tim Evans, and Ed Vrdolyak, who had switched to the Republican Party. However, Vrdolyak was a fringe candidate by this stage of his career, someone only supported by hardcore reactionary whites. In 1989, therefore, Rich Daley—a tough, veteran white candidate—would essentially battle two African-Americans, Sawyer and Evans. The black voting public in Chicago became critically split, and the political demographics in 1989 ended up as the mirror image of Harold Washington's 1983 victory.

Jesse Jackson tried to prevent the black community from splintering because he believed that Rich Daley would capture the office held by his father for two decades unless Sawyer or Evans dropped out of the race. "[Daley] certainly has the money and the name recognition, and most of the traditional party is rallying around him," Jackson said. "He certainly would have an edge." Though Evans aroused more visceral support from many of Harold Washington's African-American backers, Sawyer had used the clout of the mayor's office—jobs and contracts—to gain backing from the black business community and had amassed a $3 million campaign fund by the beginning of 1989.

Buckling to pressure, Evans dropped out of the Democratic primary on December 29, 1988. He refused to endorse Sawyer, however, and announced that he would run in the general election for mayor as the standard-bearer of the Harold Washington Party.

It appeared that Gentleman Gene Sawyer would be no match for Rich Daley. Either Sawyer did not understand the political math it took to win or he was too nice to make it happen. In December, Daley took the leashes off of his fund-raisers, Emanuel and Stepan, and the campaign money began to flow in. He also set loose his team of political advisers. Daley, a south-sider who grew up in the culturally conservative Bridgeport, then encouraged his allies on the Chicago City Council to support a gay rights bill, known as the human rights ordinance. In January, Daley's TV ads—written and choreographed by David Axelrod—aired across Chicago. In that same month, Daley received the political endorsement of Alderman Luis Gutierrez the well-known Puerto Rican American politician whose election had firmed up Harold Washington's progressive coalition. The Gutierrez endorsement, combined with Hispanic nostalgia for the first Mayor Daley and a desire to back a winner, would start to pull Hispanic voters into Rich Daley's camp.

Sophisticated TV ads. Lots of political cash from the pinstripe patronage crowd. Growing support from Hispanics, gays, and lakefront liberals. White politicians who did not want to repeat the mistakes of the 1983 mayoral election. Apparently, Sawyer would be no competition for Rich Daley.

It seemed that Daley was unstoppable. In spite of this, the worst fears of the Daley campaign appeared to come true shortly before the Democratic primary. "You want a *white* mayor to sit down with everybody," Rich Daley had said at a southwest-side campaign rally. A campaign watchdog group quickly censured Daley. Eugene Sawyer and other black politicians almost immediately claimed that Daley's campaign rhetoric of racial reconciliation was merely an act, a way for the Bridgeport prince to hide his true feelings on race. The Daley campaign issued denials and claimed that the candidate had misspoken. Luckily for Daley, many Chicagoans believed him and the incident eventually blew over.

While the Daley camp continued to worry about the campaign incident, a few days before the primary Eugene Sawyer sat and ate his usual breakfast at his favorite breakfast joint, Ms. Biscuits, a seven-table south-side restaurant. Biscuits. Ham sausage. Grits. Scrambled eggs. Menthol cigarettes.

"Campaigning citywide is brutal," said Sawyer. "I enjoy campaigning, but it is different from running for alderman. We had it down to a science. You've got to remember, I ran five times; I've never lost an election."

"I think people want some peace and tranquility," continued Sawyer. "People want somebody who'll run a good government, but with a gentler demeanor. They want someone who'll get everybody to lower their voices. . . . I never thought I'd run for mayor—I thought Harold would be mayor for twenty years and then I'd be too old. I had some thoughts about running for Congress. . . . I could have walked away from all this. You wouldn't believe the things that went through my mind. I talked with my family, my minister. The thing for me was keeping what Harold had accomplished. That was the only thing that mattered. That was it. The night I got elected [mayor by the city council], I was watching TV and I just couldn't understand who they were talking about. Then I realized it was me, and I couldn't believe it. I've never done anything to hurt anybody in my life. Those speeches on the floor were horrible. They really hurt. It hurt me, it hurt me real bad. I cried actually. There were lots of times afterward, I just laid in my bed, going through all sorts of frustration."

A few days later, Sawyer badly lost the Democratic primary to Daley. Fifty-six percent of voters went with the Democratic prince from Bridgeport. As expected, Rich Daley won the traditional white vote, while Eugene Sawyer received the black ballots. In a dramatic shift from the 1983 election, Daley also swept the lakefront and Hispanic wards. North-side, gay-identified precincts voted for the south-side-born supporter of the White Sox by overwhelming margins.

In Chicago, as everyone knows, winning the Democratic primary is the whole ballgame. The city had not elected a Republican as mayor since Big Bill Thompson lost in his 1931 attempt to secure a fourth term in office.

In the general election, Daley faced Tim Evans and Fast Eddie Vrdolyak. The result was essentially the same as the Democratic primary. Daley by a landslide. Again, he won the votes of Hispanics, liberals, and gays. Again, working-class whites voted for Daley. Again, many blacks stayed home. Rich Daley had become the first white politician ever to defeat an incumbent, big-city black mayor. Seventeen months had passed since the death of Harold Washington, and his coalition was now dead. More than twelve years had tolled since the death of Rich Daley's father. A new era had started.

Wednesday, April 5, 1989, approximately 10:15 PM. In the grand ballroom of the Hyatt Regency Chicago, it seemed like Oscar night in Hollywood. Six thousand Daley supporters, glittering and upbeat. A live band. Wine and beer flowing. A laser light show as the Daley family entered the sparkling ballroom. The mayor-elect of Chicago had arrived to celebrate.

An hour before, Rich Daley had watched the election returns in another room in the hotel with three hundred big-money campaign donors. A *très chic*, exclusive event. VIP only.

Daley then returned to the twenty-eight floor of the Hyatt Regency, where his wife Maggie, his mother Sis, his three children, and a few of his closest advisers also monitored the day's voting on TV. At around 10 PM, Daley received a phone call from his competitor, Tim Evans, who conceded that Daley had won. Daley hung up the phone, smiled, and waved his arms wildly to signal to his family in the other room. We've won! We've won! We've won! Everyone hugged.

After the celebrating subsided, one of Daley's advisers, the psychologist Ned Kennan, walked up to him and put his hand on his shoulder.

"Come with me," said Kennan.

Daley and Kennan walked together to the twenty-eighth-floor window. They could see Lake Michigan, the Chicago River, and the city's skyline stretching before them. The night sky was clear and blue, and the April temperature was a crisp forty-four degrees.

"Look at this beautiful city. Richard, this city is yours right now," said Kennan.

"Yeah," Daley agreed.

"Please don't fuck it up."

"I promise you. I promise," whispered Daley, as if to himself.

Kennan knew that it was true. Knew that Rich Daley would persist. Knew that Daley would love and care for Chicago because Kennan believed that Daley had "this enormous desire to do something good for the city. Because for him, doing something good for the City of Chicago meant doing something to justify him as an accomplished person in the eyes of his father."

CHAPTER 9

CHICAGO, 1989

It was April 24, 1989, and Rich Daley—Richard M. Daley, the new
mayor of Chicago—just completed his first inauguration address at
Orchestra Hall. A who's who of Chicago stood and clapped and smiled
when he spoke. Excitement, expectation, and human intensity filled
the hall.

What was Chicago like when Rich Daley took office in 1989? If the
new mayor could have seen the entire city—every person, street, and
neighborhood—here's what he would have witnessed on his first day:

Chicago stretches north and south and west, covering more than
two hundred square miles.

To the east is Lake Michigan with Gary, Indiana, dirty and neglected, off in the distance.

The expressways his father built—the Kennedy, Dan Ryan, Stevenson, and Eisenhower—extend north and south and west into the
white, white suburbs.

To the southwest is McCormick Place North, the convention hall's
new annex. It is the first day of the National Design Engineering
Show, and the halls bustle with out-of-towners looking for the latest
technology. Later the men will head up north to Rush Street, eat steaks
at Gibson's, and seek extracurricular entertainment.

Bridgeport, his own neighborhood, is to the south and west of the
convention hall. Comiskey Park—with its monster scoreboard—sits
proudly in Bridgeport at Thirty-Fifth Street and Shields Avenue. In
two weeks the construction crews will break ground across the street
and start building the new Comiskey stadium.

The heart of Robert Taylor homes sits dilapidated just east of
Bridgeport and a mile or so south. In the twenty-eight high-rise build-

ings along a two-mile stretch of State Street little black kids play in unlit stairwells. Their teenaged brothers, who have joined the Black Kings gang, roam the public-housing development. They harass young women and sell crack cocaine to out-of-work black men.

To the southeast, the gothic University of Chicago campus is busy with students scurrying to class. In the nearby Kenwood and Oakland neighborhoods, professional, middle-class blacks are rehabbing old homes in the rundown area. One of the African-American fixer-uppers is excited about the changes, "I've not had any problems with people [already living] in the community. . . . Even though they realized that the gentrification was taking place, they were happy and pleased that it was someone black."

In South Chicago, on the far southeast side of the city, sits South Works, home of the dying, once-gigantic US Steel plant. The derelict facility stretches over more than six hundred acres, from Seventy-Ninth Street to Ninety-Second Street, along the lakefront. Back in the day, twenty thousand men and women sweated and labored here, producing steel beams at the mouth of the Calumet River. As a teenager, one Polish man took a high-paying job here and became a steelworker like his father. "My old man—I remember around the table—he didn't want me to go into the mill. 'Don't go in that goddammed place. Get an education. Stay out of it,' he'd say." The new Mayor Daley doesn't know this yet, but in a few years, the building's doors will permanently close.

Just south, in the Lake Calumet area, sits a gross, polluted industrial wasteland. It was once home to the Wisconsin Steel plant, the Torrence Avenue Ford plant, and a mountain range of salt, scrap iron, and coal. Today it is a graveyard of railroad cars and empty factories ruled over by Fast Eddie Vrdolyak. Daley will soon propose building a third airport there.

To the north and west, Midway airport rests in this once white and ethnic, but now changing, neighborhood. The airport itself—the belle of the ball from the 1930s until the 1960s—now weakly brags about Midway Airlines, an outfit that will go bankrupt in two years.

On Twenty-Sixth Street, in the Mexican neighborhood known as

Little Village, a street food vendor hawks her carne asada tacos. "Tener un hambre canina," her customer says quietly. She nods silently, scoops steaming grilled beef and cilantro onto a corn tortilla and then tightly wraps it in tin foil.

To the east sits Pilsen, another Mexican neighborhood, bumping up against Bridgeport. The hallways and cafeteria of Komensky Elementary School, which soon will be renamed Manuel Perez Jr. Elementary, are overcrowded with Mexican kids. Third graders there are nearly an entire year behind on reading abilities. Danny Solis, a community organizer who Rich Daley will appoint alderman in 1996, is pushing for ten new schools in overcrowded Hispanic neighborhoods. According to Solis, "The money can come from desegregation funds. The Chicago School Board spends about $70 million a year busing kids from one neighborhood to another. That's a failed program from the '60s. I think that money should be used to build good schools in the neighborhoods where people live. Then they should fire the bureaucrats and use the money saved in salaries to build new schools."

Further to the east is Dearborn Park, an integrated, middle-class residential community of houses, townhomes, parks, and condominiums. This "suburb in a city" in the South Loop has started to replace grimy, long-abandoned rail yards. The new middle-class parents of Dearborn Park are fighting bitterly with nearby public-housing residents and the Board of Education over whose kids will be served by the local school. Within a year many of the new neighbors will be left with sour feelings. "What the Board of Education got with all of its bungling and indecisiveness was just another ghetto school," says one white mom.

The West Loop has problems of its own, never having really recovered from the massive street rioting and property destruction after Martin Luther King Jr. died during the reign of the first Mayor Daley. The impoverished neighborhood also contains the Henry Horner projects, a collection of seven CHA high-rises near Chicago Stadium. Two boys, aged fourteen and eleven, are hunting for snakes along the el tracks near the projects. The boys, brothers, are African-American and their older brother is already in jail for armed robbery. When a train passes, its suburban commuters see the boys outside and discreetly slide away from the window, fearing sniper shots.

On the far west side are the Austin, Lawndale, and Garfield Park neighborhoods, depressing slums filled with crime, violence, and drugs.

To the north is Bucktown, a gentrifying community. On Damen, just off of the Milwaukee and North Avenue intersection, sits Sophie's Busy Bee Cafe under the el tracks. Old Polish families are sharing the counter space with hipster artists and young professionals. All are eating pierogi, potato pancakes, blood sausage, and sauerkraut.

O'Hare Airport stands fourteen miles to the northwest. Part of Roman "Pooch" Pucinski's domain, this is the whitest ward in the city. The airport is massive and noisy, with planes on runways and cars circling to drop off passengers. O'Hare's suburban neighbors will soon become a thorn in Daley's side—always willing to fight airport expansion.

To the north and east sits Rogers Park. A diverse, multiethnic neighborhood filled with South Asians, Koreans, Haitians, and Jamaicans, as well as blacks and whites. Loyola University anchors the lakefront, but crime is a problem elsewhere. Teenaged drug dealers fire gunshots outside Rogers Park Grade School. For ten months parents have tried in vain to get the City of Chicago to put up antidrug warning signs near the school. "We know the signs won't stop all the drug activity, but they would make a statement," says one Latina mom. "It would only cost about $35,000 for all the signs. The city wastes more than that on council committees."

To the south is Wrigley Field, home of the Cubs and an iconic spot for fans to attend day games and drink beer in the sun. Unlike Comiskey Park, the new mayor had not spent a lot of time at the north-side baseball venue.

In nearby Lakeview, known to its residents as Boys Town, adult entertainments abound. The Pleasure Chest, an adult novelties shop. Victor/Victoria, a female impersonator bar. The Second Story All Male Emporium.

In neighboring Lincoln Park, the yuppies long ago replaced the hippies. Quality of life is arriving as well. Beautiful brownstones. The park, Lake Michigan, and the beach. The zoo. Charlie Trotter's restaurant. Children's Memorial Hospital. In this living-the-good-life neighborhood, the public school is good, as is the Catholic school, Saint Clement. Even Daley's alma mater, DePaul, is on the rise.

To the south lies Cabrini-Green, a nightmare CHA housing project. Bumping up against the Gold Coast and gentrifying Old Town, Cabrini-Green is a lost civilization, a no-man's-land of gangs and gunshots.

Back in the Loop, the John Hancock Building, the Sears Tower, and the rest of the skyline stand tall. The sun shines bright. The sky is blue. Lake Michigan glimmers off to the left.

In the Tribune Tower near the river, Al Voney is shining the shoes of reporters. A fifty-seven-year-old from the south side, Voney longs for the old days, "In the last ten years, since [Dick] Daley died, Chicago has become like Detroit—a dead man's town. The bars are closing too early. The city is dilapidated. There's nothing to do."

Just to the south sits the stately Prudential Building, overlooking the lake and a twenty-four-acre site wasted on the gray, abandoned Illinois Central Railroad tracks. A tremendous eyesore in the middle of the Loop.

A few blocks to the west lies the infamous, cursed Block 37, a square block of precious land in the Loop's epicenter. Within a year, fifteen of its buildings will be demolished for redevelopment and Daley will tell Chicagoans, "We take a giant step forward today to rebuild our central business district." More than twenty years later, Block 37—like an incurable patient—will still not be restored to health.

City hall is just down the street from Block 37. Rich Daley—the new mayor of Chicago—will soon sit in his father's building. He is home.

CHAPTER 10

A NEW ERA

During his third week in office, Mayor Daley declared that city hall "should not be a pigpen. Let's get some pride back into city buildings." The new mayor then ordered a complete housecleaning of all city offices. "The first thing I found when I opened my drapes was that the blinds were dirty and, secondly, that the windows were dirty," said Daley. "They should be keeping the Hall clean from the washrooms to the hallways. Unfortunately, when they sandblasted the building, someone forgot to tell them to clean the windows." High standards and an obsessive focus on details would mark Daley's first term in office.

The new mayor first needed to overcome many challenges. The city had suffered through nearly thirteen years of political instability. This period of weak leadership had drained confidence from businesses and families. Crime had risen and prisons were nearly full. The City of Chicago suffered a $120 million budget deficit in 1989. City departments were union heavy, bloated, and weakly run. The city also did a poor job of revenue collection. Basic services such as snow removal, garbage collection, and street repair had significantly deteriorated. Chicago was littered with abandoned automobiles and vacant buildings. Jobs and families continued to move to the suburbs, as they had for forty years. Public schools and public housing offered little hope to children—mostly blacks and other minorities—who had no other options.

But Rich Daley was developing a knack for governing and got off to a fast start. On his first day in office the new mayor signed thirteen executive orders, signaling to voters that he would continue many of the progressive political reforms initiated by the late Harold Washington. Four of these executive orders were of particular note: a commitment to AIDS education, establishment of a school reform commission, reaffirmation of the existing affirmative action plan for hiring minorities, and a continuation of the city's minority contracting program. Alderman Danny Davis, who was African-American and who would run against Daley as a candidate for mayor in less than two years, expressed initial support for the mayor's actions. "One day does not an administration make," said Davis. "But as of right now, I would give him very good grades. . . . If it is an indication of things to come, then we could look forward to Mayor Daley fulfilling his campaign promises. I for one hope that he does."

The first campaign promise that Daley focused on realizing was his vow to appoint a diverse mayoral cabinet. Thirteen of his initial twenty-five appointments were minorities, including an African-American police superintendent and a Latino fire commissioner. The cabinet also included four holdovers from the preceding black mayoral administrations and one from his father's reign. Within six months the mayor would push out one of the holdovers—Joan Harris, the wealthy and independent commissioner of cultural affairs—and replace her with an appointee who would later become one of the most influential people in Rich Daley's professional life.

The new commissioner of cultural affairs was Lois Weisberg, a dynamic woman who also had served in the administration of Harold Washington. Two other members of Washington's team, David Mosena and Valerie Jarrett, also stayed on and worked for Daley. These three—Weisberg, Mosena, and Jarrett—introduced the political equivalent of genetic variation into the Daley administration, helping it to evolve beyond the Bridgeport roots of the second generation mayor.

Watching Daley make public appointments was a bit like having the opportunity to see Harry Houdini perform magic. The key to a successful magic act is, of course, illusion and misdirection of the audience's attention. While the spectators get caught up in the showmanship and hoopla of the act, the magician performs his trick or discreetly makes his seemingly impossible escape. And so it was in 1989 in Chicago. The Daley cabinet was diverse and competent, but the real power rested in two other places: outside the administration and in the mayor's office.

The outsiders included Bill Daley, David Axelrod, Rahm Emanuel, David Wilhelm, and Jeremiah Joyce. The first four of these—the fearsome foursome from the 1989 campaign battle—had moved on to other challenges. Each, however, maintained close ties to Rich Daley, providing political services and private advice, but they were political operators at this stage of their careers, not government servants. Jeremiah Joyce had also moved on. His goal now was to use his political connections and ties to Daley to make as much money as possible. Joyce—like a hungry Doberman pinscher let off his leash—functioned outside the constraints of government. His business deals brought Daley controversy. But he also served as the mayor's conduit for untraceable decisions, off-the-record discussions, and innovative ideas.

The insiders were political appointees in the mayor's office. John Schmidt was blue ribbon material—smart, capable, and ethical—but he served as Daley's interim chief of staff for only three months before returning to the practice of law. The real power rested with three Daley confidantes, all of whom had a long history with the Daley family and Bridgeport-centric politics: Tim Degnan, Ed Bedore, and Frank Kruesi. The big-shouldered and square-jawed Degnan came out of the old school of Chicago politics. He had deep insights into human nature and people's strengths and weaknesses. Degnan also had a long, close connection to the Daleys. He provided absolutely unadulterated advice to the new mayor because "he was the one person who had no other agenda other than Rich Daley's interest." Daley therefore gave the most sensitive responsibilities to Degnan. As head of intergovernmental affairs, Degnan took care of all relationships with politicians and political operatives, including the city council and the Illinois state legislature. Ed Bedore also had close ties to the new mayor. During the 1960s and 1970s, he served as budget director under the first Mayor Daley. Bedore, like Degnan, possessed traits highly prized by the Daley family: he was both closed mouth and dependable. Frank Kruesi was a policy expert—deep thinking and Machiavellian—who spent more than a decade advising Daley in the Illinois senate and state's attorney office.

Talented advisers were important because the job Rich Daley had won was extremely difficult. Many issues crossed the mayor's desk: financial problems, neighborhood problems, social issues, economic challenges, difficulties with city services. In a city of nearly 2.8 million people, everyone wanted a piece of the mayor. In order to succeed, Daley needed to combine many traits: persistence, wisdom, toughness, shrewdness. He needed to be both methodical and opportunistic, like an Olympic athlete who had trained for many years and now was competing in the championship decathlon match.

The first major challenge for Daley and his team was to focus on the last two months of the Illinois legislative session in Springfield. This was essential because the City of Chicago had a large operating deficit that would require severe budget cuts and a property tax hike if further funding was not forthcoming from the state.

Success for Daley in Springfield depended on two other potent politicians: Governor Jim Thompson and Mike Madigan, the Illinois House Speaker. Though Thompson was a Republican, he was also a committed Chicagoan. He and Daley had good personal chemistry. Madigan and Daley, in contrast, had a much more rocky relationship. They were close friends early in their political careers, but for the last decade had become uneasy rivals. The original source of the tension was Madigan's backing of Jane Byrne in 1979 during her feud with Rich Daley. The Daley-Madigan rivalry deepened over the years as Daley built up his own political organization and Madigan had aligned himself with Eugene Sawyer during his two years as mayor of Chicago.

Daley and Thompson quickly agreed to work together on a state income tax increase that would aid Chicago. Tim Degnan then received his marching orders from Daley: get Madigan, the powerful Speaker of the House, to agree to the Daley-Thompson deal. Degnan had a series of private meetings with Madigan who soon saw the tax increase measure as an occasion to go out of his way to do something for Rich Daley and get back on his good side. Madigan was a politician without any guiding principles or higher calling—other than maintaining his own power and his lucrative, politically connected law practice—and he worried about losing a legislative fight to Daley and Thompson. Soon a bill passed in the Illinois legislature that brought $188 million to Chicago. These new revenues allowed Daley to proceed with his infrastructure initiatives without raising property taxes or dramatically cutting the city budget. It was the political equivalent of winning the lottery.

The Daley-Thompson alliance also generated an unplanned legislative victory for Chicago. Though it was not public knowledge at the time, Governor Thompson anticipated retiring from office in two years, and he had a personal list of objectives that he wanted to accomplish before he retired. One of his goals was to save Navy Pier, the badly deteriorated 3,300-foot long block of concrete and timber extending out into Lake Michigan. In the 1950s, a University of Illinois campus was located at the Pier, and Thompson had studied there before the structure fell into twenty-five years of disrepair. During the end of the 1989 Illinois legislative session, Thompson suggested to Daley that they should join together to save Navy Pier. Daley agreed and the two politicians put together an innovative deal. The City of Chicago would contribute its ownership of Navy Pier to a new entity, called the Pier and Exposition Authority, which would own both Navy Pier and the McCormick Place Convention Center. As part of the agreement, the State of Illinois would grant $150 million to rehabilitate the pier and would share control of the new entity with the city. Though the mayor did not know it at the time, this fortuitous political deal would become the first step in the long-term beautification of Chicago's lakefront that would transform the city during his tenure in office.

The Springfield legislative session was an unequivocal success for Daley and his team, but the City of Chicago still had deteriorated city services that the new administration needed to address. Mayor Daley quickly let city workers know that they needed to perform a full day's work and that basic city services, such as garbage collection and snow removal, needed to be significantly improved. According to Daley's chief of staff Forrest Claypool, the message to Chicagoans was that "the City's back in business folks. We're going to improve services and give you a bang for your buck." Mayor Daley also began to focus intently on the problem of abandoned automobiles. This issue was the number one complaint on the city's phone hotline. These discarded cars were havens for rats, prostitutes, and crime, and the city lost millions of dollars a year trying to tow them off of the streets. The mayor—who had zero tolerance for any symbols of decay in the city—focused intently on the issue.

Rich Daley—with the help of his south-side buddy Jeremiah Joyce—came up with an innovative and effective solution to the abandoned vehicle problem. He would privatize the towing of deserted automobiles. A motivated, for-profit company could pay the City of Chicago a fee and tow more than 150,000 vehicles per year. The neighborhoods could be cleared of abandoned cars, and the city could convert an ineffective, money-losing endeavor into a profitable service that improved communities. A win-win.

The plan was innovative and effective, but unfortunately Rich Daley complicated the situation by giving Jeremiah Joyce and some of his other supporters an inside deal on the towing contract with the City of Chicago. In July 1989, Edward Corcoran and Martin McNally formed Environmental Auto Removal, Inc. Nine days later the company known as EAR received the lucrative towing contract with the city. Corcoran was a Daley supporter and campaign donor. McNally was a lawyer with business ties to Jeremiah Joyce. Another Bridgeport friend of Daley owned one of the auto pound lots used by EAR. A City of Chicago employee with political ties to Joyce was put in charge of the towing program and named deputy commissioner in the streets and sanitation department. A few years later Daley would appoint Eileen Carey, Joyce's sister-in-law, as the city's commissioner of streets and sanitation.

A win-win program for improving the neighborhoods and reducing the budget deficit was transformed into a politically questionable deal for Daley administration insiders. As cars got towed off of the streets, reporters wrote negative stories on Daley's connections to EAR. Good government supporters fumed.

Though the EAR towing scandal was short lived and did not hurt Daley during his first term in office, it had two long-term negative consequences for his reputation. First, Joyce and his cronies would continue to generate political scandals for Daley, both through EAR and other questionable, politically connected business deals at O'Hare Airport. More important, over the ensuing years these types of deals left a portion of the voting public with the impression that Daley favored his buddies and allowed corruption in Chicago. This perception conflicted with the image that Daley had started to build as the "CEO of the city" who always had its best interests at heart.

Despite periodic scandals, Daley worked hard in 1989 to build coalitions and win the support of a wide range of voters. One group Daley targeted was Chicago's gay and lesbian community. Chicago's Lakeview neighborhood hosted nearly a hundred thousand people for the twentieth annual Gay and Lesbian Pride Parade that summer, and Daley had quietly agreed to serve as the parade's grand marshal. Not only was Daley the first sitting mayor to lead the Pride Parade, but he was also the first major politician of any party to participate. The mayor rode in a bold Thunderbird convertible wearing a conservative wool jacket. Masses of men lining the parade route on Broadway Street—shirtless, leather-wearing, or dressed in drag—blew kisses to the mayor, waved and shouted, "Happy Gay Day." The mayor waved back and smiled. "I think it is important for me to take part in this parade to show my support of the gay community, which I believe has contributed to a better quality of life in this city," said Daley after the parade. "I represent all the people and that even means the gays."

Now largely forgotten, this was an epic event—the firstborn son of Dick Daley serving as the grand marshal in the Gay Pride Parade. Old man Daley probably rolled over in his grave. But why did his son Rich do it? Late in her life, Dawn Clark Netsch recalled how Rich Daley's support of the gay community was emblematic of his personal evolution. "Of course, the most dramatic transformation was with the gay-lesbian issue," said Netsch. "The change on that issue has been unbelievably dramatic! What I did see happening with Daley was that the world around him was opening up and he was exposed to more people and more things and he began to absorb it. That, obviously, evolved over time and what's marvelous now is that he's an absolute hero in the gay community. That could have never have happened if his father was alive." So riding in the parade became the right thing for Daley to do—after his father had died and his son had died—to show his support for the gay community as human beings. It was also a calculated move right out of his father's political playbook: whenever a voting group gets strong enough to carry a ward, then a smart politician needs to find a way to support them. Good policy, smart politics—a straightforward decision for a man who had become adept at political calculus.

Daley also showed political skill in dealing with the Chicago City Council. The new mayor—with Tim Degnan as his primary liaison—reorganized the city council and put allies in charge of key committees. Daley also named his own Bridgeport alderman as his whip, or political floor leader in the council. He also temporarily defanged Ed Burke, his slippery political rival.

After the 1989 election, Burke regained his seat as chairman of the finance committee of the Chicago City Council and remained there for over twenty years. Many political insiders believe that Burke cut a deal with the Daley brothers to get back his powerful finance chair. If true, the arrangement with Burke proved to be a smart move for Daley, but a bad result for the people of Chicago. For Daley, the agreement put his rival in a position where he could help Daley's agenda without threatening his power. But for Chicago citizens the outcome came out differently. As finance committee chair, Burke used his political influence to help his clients reduce their real estate taxes, sue the City of Chicago, or negotiate questionable business deals. He also used the resources and power of the finance committee to protect city council aldermen under criminal investigation. Under Burke, the finance committee spent millions of dollars of taxpayers' money defending politicians accused of corruption, as well as bureaucrats charged with malfeasance.

With the city council compliant at the end of 1989, the new mayor pushed through his first budget. The $3 billion budget focused heavily on improving basic city services, as evidenced by its "garbage is votes" theme for the 1990 budget. Daley's budget also increased tree trimming and planting, funded a new 911 emergency system, and formalized the privatized system for towing abandoned cars. Daley also kept taxes low, instituted a hiring freeze in all city departments, and cut departmental spending by seven percent. The Civic Federation—a respected watchdog group—gave Daley's first budget a glowing endorsement.

In early 1990 Daley also began publicly discussing the possibility of building a third major airport in Lake Calumet, a polluted, deindustrialized area on the southeast side of Chicago. Other politicians quickly denigrated the proposal, however, because Republicans in the suburbs and in downstate Illinois did not support giving Chicago another coveted airport. But Daley persisted, repeatedly focusing on the economic benefits a third airport would bring to the area. "Are steel mills coming back?" asked Daley. "I don't see anybody building steel mills. Are factories coming back? You see no one building factories. So we're talking about economic opportunities and jobs." With Daley's backing, a feasibility study was completed on the third airport idea and political negotiations began to take place between the mayor, the governor of Illinois, and other politicians in Springfield.

During his first year in office, Rich Daley showed Chicago voters that he was developing a knack for governing and persistence in pursuing policies that he believed in. "I don't get so disappointed in not accomplishing something that I give up," Daley explained to reporters at the end of 1990. "I stay on it. And I knew that [persistence was important] when I flunked the bar twice. I never gave up on anything in my life. And one person who showed me never to give up on life was my son, Kevin, who fought for his life the entire time he was on this earth. You never give up. . . . My philosophy is [to always] move ahead."

But Rich Daley was more complicated than he appeared to the public. Voters saw a hardworking, sincere man who loved Chicago. He had appointed a diverse and able cabinet. He had repaired the budget and began improving city services. He had reached out to form political alliances with many segments of Chicago society, including gays, Hispanics, lakefront liberals, and blacks. But Rich Daley had also begun to master political calculus and was putting together a personal political army to maintain his own power. This private army of political operatives soon provided Daley a measure of independence from both the Democratic Party and mainstream voters.

Unlike his father, Rich Daley never became chairman of the Cook County Democratic Party. It was somewhat surprising that Daley did not simply take over the local party and its political apparatus. As the firstborn son of Chicago's most famous political Boss, Daley had both the hereditary claim and the personal knowledge to accomplish such a party takeover.

But Rich Daley had three issues with the remnants of the Chicago machine that existed in 1989: a lack of trust, a lack of respect, and a public relations problem. Daley did not trust the party because it abandoned him when he needed it most: during his 1980 campaign for state's attorney. According to longtime Chicago alderman Bernie Hansen, Daley also believed that many of the organization's white ethnic aldermen were still furious with him for paving the way to the election of a black mayor in 1983 who took away much of their power. Furthermore, Daley did not respect the party. He believed that most of the ward bosses were "soft" and had lost the strength to win elections and to rule their wards effectively. After he became mayor, he did not meet with groups of aldermen because, according to Hansen, he considered them "an unnecessary evil created by the state legislature to be a pain in the ass to the mayor." Finally, Daley believed that modern media had created a serious image problem for the machine. Voters no longer tolerated a system of overt political bosses. "[Voters] have their own opinions about candidates," Daley explained in 1990. "I think they want the mayor to be a good mayor. We got too many problems . . . problems with education, problems with housing, problems with healthcare. They want [elected officials] to focus on these problems and not to get involved in the political sector." Daley did get involved in politics, of course, but he did so covertly, away from the public eye.

Daley had actually fathered his own parallel political organization—his election campaign militia—during the 1989 mayoral campaign. Some of these troops were veterans of Daley's many previous campaigns for state's attorney during the 1980s. But Daley's closest confidantes—Tim Degnan, Bill Daley, and Jeremiah Joyce—had also reached out to political mercenaries in Chicago and developed alliances that evolved into potent political patronage armies loyal to Mayor Daley. The Hispanic Democratic Organization. The Coalition for Better Government. Don Tomczak and his roughneck boys from the water department. These embryonic groups had germinated during the 1989 campaign.

The exact birth of the Hispanic Democratic Organization remains shrouded in mystery, but it is safe to say that HDO began life on the south side of Chicago. During Daley's campaign for mayor, a political operative named Al Sanchez met with Tim Degnan at the headquarters of the Democratic Party in the Daley family's native Eleventh Ward. Degnan told Sanchez, "Richard Daley is looking for support in the Hispanic community. He understands they are an important part of the city's fabric." Apparently this message resonated with Sanchez because he and Degnan agreed to meet again with a larger group of Hispanics a week later.

The second meeting took place at a bar called G's, which sat at the corner of Ewing and Ninety-Fifth Street, a short drive from where the mayor later proposed building a third airport in Lake Calumet. G's Bar was a blue-collar, bump-and-a-beer type of place. Jim Beam. Old Style. Chicago White Sox banter during the summer. Chicago Bears exchanges in the winter. Sanchez and his crew arranged the back room of G's Bar with sixty chairs on the dance floor. The room filled up with more than a hundred Hispanic volunteers from the southeast side of the city. Degnan gave a short but effective talk. "We're going to build a Hispanic organization like you have never seen," he said in his deep voice. Sanchez suggested calling the group the Hispanic Democratic Organization (HDO). "That's beautiful," agreed Degnan. Many of the attendees left the meeting believing that they would get city jobs if they helped Daley win the mayoral election.

A couple of years later in the early 1990s, some of Daley's closest confidantes, including his brother Bill and Tim Degnan, began strategizing about how to expand and formalize the Hispanic political organization that had started on Chicago's south side. These strategy sessions included politicians and political operatives who would later hold influential positions in the Daley administration: Victor Reyes, Al Sanchez, Danny Solis, Ben Reyes, Ariel Reboyras, and Luis Gutierrez. By 1993, Victor Reyes—the up-and-coming political protégé of Tim Degnan—had filed papers to officially establish HDO as a political action committee.

Over time, however, HDO assumed a much more active, muscular role in Chicago elections and it developed a formidable reputation— both for winning campaigns and for securing clout-heavy city jobs for its members. Nearly two decades later, during the federal corruption trial of Al Sanchez, Bill Daley distanced himself from HDO and its questionable activities. "You're talking about 20 years ago," he said. "Even if it happened—and I'm not saying it did—things were different. There was nothing illegal about that stuff [back then]." In 1989 scandals involving HDO were still far off in the future. At that time in Chicago the growing Hispanic organization seemed like an effective political vehicle for the Daleys and their allies.

Another political group that supported Daley during this time period was the Coalition for Better Government. Despite its innocuous sounding name, the coalition was run by a controversial figure, Dominic Longo, who made a long career in Chicago as a political operative. The government had already convicted Longo of vote fraud by the mid-1980s. Despite this setback, Longo continued working in local government jobs and using the Coalition for Better Government to produce campaign donations and workers for Chicago politicians. He became a committed Daley loyalist in the 1990s, even as he maintained his close ties to Alderman Dick Mell—the scheming, influence-peddling ward boss—and Rod Blagojevich, his slick, up-and-coming son-in-law.

Donald Tomczak was another seasoned political operative who became a staunch Daley loyalist during the new mayor's first term in office. The political conversion of Tomczak was a huge surprise to hardened politicos in Chicago because Tomczak had betrayed Daley earlier in their careers.

Tomczak had roots similar to those of Rich Daley. He grew up on the south side, attended high school at De La Salle Institute, and received his first machine-backed job in the early 1950s as an asphalt worker in Dick Daley's Eleventh Ward organization. Despite his Bridgeport roots, in the Democratic civil war of 1980 the rough-edged, cigar-chomping Tomczak sided with Jane Bryne.

Rich Daley vowed never to forgive Tomczak, but after he became mayor in 1989 one of his closest advisers helped Daley change his mind. Dan Rostenkowski—the powerful chairman of the House Ways and Means Committee in Congress—convinced Daley that Tomczak's ability to organize city workers for political campaigns was indispensable. Tomczak became deputy commissioner in the water department and used overtime pay and promotions to build a political patronage army of hundreds of men.

Tomczak and his militia of water department workers, along with the Hispanic Democratic Organization and the Coalition for Better Government, became key factors in Daley's political organization during his first term in office. Later, new groups broadened the mix, including black workers in the Streets and Sanitation Department, white workers in the Streets and Sanitation Department, and a political army disingenuously called the Lakefront Independent Democratic Organization. For more than a decade, all of these groups performed well, producing campaign workers and donations for Daley and his political allies. They also largely stayed out of the public eye, though a few pesky reporters and watchdog organizations periodically raised questions about their activities. In the future, tougher foes would challenge these political armies, including Federal Bureau of Investigation (FBI) operatives. Tomczak—as well as HDO leaders, Coalition for Better Government organizers, Streets and Sanitation Department bosses, Chicago City Council members, and high-ranking Bridgeport-born appointees in the Mayor's Office of Intergovernmental Affairs—eventually received federal criminal indictments. But in 1991 at the end of Daley's first term in office, none of this was knowable. The mayor was an effective public leader, popular with voters and politically strong. He was ready to run for reelection.

Daley's campaign for reelection began on December 10, 1990, with his claim that during his first twenty months as mayor "Chicagoans had lowered their voices and moved beyond the destructive policies of [racial] division and name-calling." This claim rang true to most voters, and Daley soon built on the political coalition that he had established in 1989: blue-collar ethnic whites; Hispanics; gays; wealthy, somewhat liberal, lakefront dwellers; and a small group of black voters.

Daley also worked behind the scenes to buy off political opposition in the Chicago City Council and to grease the palms of high-level union officials. He accomplished this in January 1991—in the middle of his reelection campaign—by quietly lobbying Springfield legislators to change the state's pension laws so that Chicago aldermen and union officials would become eligible for large pensions. It did not become public at the time, but this backroom maneuver by Daley would eventually put nearly $58 million into the pockets of aldermen. Even worse, the sweetheart deal would set a pattern for Daley's tenure as mayor: financially irresponsible, politically expedient pension deals that were quietly slipped by the public.

In the 1991 campaign, Daley competed against an over-the-hill Jane Byrne and two black politicians, Danny Davis and Eugene Pincham. His share of the African-American vote rose from single digits to around 15 percent. The incumbent mayor won the election handily, capturing more than two-thirds of the votes. During the campaign, Daley also earned endorsements from prominent African-American preachers and businessmen, as well as the *Chicago Defender* newspaper. The era of competitive politics in Chicago—which had run from 1979 to 1991—came to end. A political master had taken over, and he would run Chicago for many years to come.

PART 4

Plugger

CHAPTER 11

CRIME AND GRIME

During Rich Daley's second term as mayor, the demands were constant. The pressure was intense. Daley loved the job—he had apprenticed his entire adult life to become mayor of Chicago—but the stresses and anxieties of the office sometimes overwhelmed him. At those times, his face would turn a deep red, his voice would rise to a screaming pitch, and he would yell, "You gotta do this! You need to get this done!" Because of these volcanic reactions, he became known at city hall for his merciless temper. High-ranking staff members in the mayor's office referred to meetings with the mayor as "getting a beating." As in, "I'm going to see the mayor and I'm going to get a beating." One city official described the experience this way: "What was it like working for Daley? It's kinda similar to playing basketball for Bobby Knight. You know, you win 100 to 33, and you walk into the locker room afterwards and you get yelled at." By 2008, Hall of Fame basketball coach Bobby Knight had broken more chairs and won more victories than any coach in the history of college basketball. But in 1991 it was not clear that Daley could lead Chicago to victories the way Bobby Knight did with his Indiana Hoosiers.

One of Daley's first challenges after his successful reelection was dealing with the economic recession that started in 1990 shortly after Iraq's invasion of Kuwait. As the first Persian Gulf War accelerated, the price of a barrel of oil spiked from $21 to more than $45. The US economy slipped into an economic malaise that lasted several years. Chicago's economy was hit even harder. The economic downturn lowered sales tax and real estate revenues for the city. The city faced budget shortfalls, at the same time as financial support from the State of Illinois decreased. Chicago also continued to suffer from the ongoing deindustrialization of the Midwest. Corporate headquarters and jobs continued to move to the suburbs and to warm-weather states. Locally based Midway Airlines shut down in late 1991 and four thousand people lost their jobs. Sears, Roebuck and Co., a retailer with thousands of employees in Chicago, chose to move its corporate headquarters to the suburbs. By 1993, thousands of Sears employees would travel northwest of Chicago to Hoffman Estates rather than downtown to the Sears Tower.

In this environment of economic and budgetary stress, Daley frequently met on the fifth floor of city hall with his top staff and pressured them to cut costs and improve city services. One day in 1993, the mayor convened a meeting to discuss the Chicago Air and Water Show, a popular event started by Daley's father in 1958. The Air and Water Show drew two million people to the lakefront to watch the US Navy's Blue Angels and other military crafts perform incredible aerobatic maneuvers. The problem was that the summer event was expensive and a money loser for the city. Several attendees walked into the mayor's private conference room and sat down at the table. Forrest Claypool was the superintendent of the Chicago Park District and had previously served as Daley's chief of staff at city hall. Skinny Sheahan headed up the mayor's Department of Cultural Affairs and Special Events. Lower-ranking officials stood at the margins of the room, but all of the participants could immediately tell that they were about to get a beating.

"Skinny, we're getting rid of the Air and Water Show," said the mayor grimly.

"Oh, that's too bad."

"What do you mean it's too bad?' demanded the mayor. "What do you know about it?"

'I don't know anything about it," answered Sheahan. "I'm just saying I think the show is good. I like the show."

"Oh, you like it. You like it," mocked Daley. "Do you like the fact—Forrest tell him! Tell him how much money you lose! How much money do you lose, Forrest?" screamed the mayor.

"We lose about $750,000 a year," answered Claypool calmly.

"$750,000! $750,000—taxpayers' dollars, so some planes can fly around up in the air," taunted the mayor. "Skinny, they don't know what they're doing. They don't know what they're doing!"

"I don't know about the budget issues mayor, but I tell you the people that go to that show like it," answered Skinny.

"Oh, they do? Why don't we just do whatever everybody likes," sneered Daley. "What about your office—can you do it? Can you do the Air and Water Show?"

"I don't know anything about it, but I'm sure we can do it," agreed Sheahan.

"Forrest, Skinny's doing the Air and Water Show," decreed the mayor. "You are no longer doing the Air and Water Show."

Turning toward Sheahan, Daley discharged another verbal fusillade, "Are you going to lose $750,000?"

"I don't know mayor," answered Sheahan. "I'm going to have to look at the budget."

The meeting soon adjourned, and Daley moved on to his next appointment. Sheahan went back to his office at Special Events and put together a group of analysts to restructure the Air and Water Show as if it were a small, stand-alone business. Out went consultants and extensive perks for the pilots. In came a $150,000 corporate sponsorship from Shell Oil Products. The event broke even the next year while maintaining the same high-quality show.

Even as the mayor dealt with challenges at work, he was also forced to address problems that arose in his personal life. In Grand Beach, Michigan, the police received a phone call at 12:46 AM on March 1, 1992, reporting a fight outside of the Daley summer home.

The Village of Grand Beach was a quiet resort community on Lake Michigan with a population of less than 150 year-round residents. During the summer months, Chicagoans transformed the village into their own neighborhood—a place where fathers golfed, unsupervised children ran around with their friends, and neighbors cocktailed and barbecued together. Families drove golf carts instead of cars in what real estate boosters have dubbed Harbor Country. Two generations of Daleys, as well as many other Irish-Catholics from Chicago, escaped there each summer.

A middle-of-the-night fight was unusual for Grand Beach.

The mayor's sixteen-year-old son Patrick Daley had apparently hosted an unauthorized party while his parents were out of town in New York. Some of his guests had bought beer at a Chicago liquor store, and the group of high schoolers had made the ninety-minute road trip to the Daley summer home for the secret bash. The problems started when some local kids crashed the party and were asked to leave. They left, but then returned to the event with around fifteen friends. A brawl broke out in front of the Daley home: Chicago boys versus local boys. One of the big-city teenagers held a bat in his hand and another may have wielded a shotgun. The Chicago kid with the baseball bat struck a local kid named Andrew Buckman in the head, putting him in the intensive care unit at Saint Anthony's Hospital in Michigan City, Indiana. During the fight, someone also broke the windshield of Mayor Daley's car.

Daley held a Monday morning press conference at city hall to discuss the Grand Beach brawl. The mayor was so shaken by the incident that he could barely read the one-page statement prepared for him. Daley choked back tears and then cried openly in front of a room full of reporters. "I'm very disappointed as a parent would be if their son held a party in their home while his parents were away," said Daley with a breaking voice and a pale face. "I'm more deeply distressed for the welfare of the young man who was injured in the fight." This surge of genuine emotion in the mayor revealed him to be like many of his supporters: regular Chicago guys—firefighters, teachers, cops—who seemed tough to outsiders, but who had tender sides for their family and friends.

At his court hearing, Patrick Daley pleaded guilty to two misdemeanor charges: furnishing intoxicants to minors and creating a public disturbance. The judge sentenced Patrick to six months' probation and fifty hours of community service in Grand Beach.

Shortly after going through this incident with his family, Daley experienced another patch of bad luck. Early in the morning on April 13, 1992, city officials discovered that millions of gallons of water from the

Chicago River had flooded freight tunnels running beneath many commercial structures in the downtown Loop. Electricity was knocked out in much of the city's most important business area. The Chicago Board of Trade—the world's oldest and largest trading exchange of financial futures—shut down. More than $130 billion in daily financial trading was halted and billions of dollars of financial hedges moved to London, New York, Singapore, and Tokyo. Large retailers, such as Marshall Field's and Carson, Pirie, Scott, lost business during the important pre-Easter shopping week. The Chicago Transit Authority closed down the subways serving downtown. Companies sent thousands of workers home early. The Army Corps of Engineers worked around the clock for a week pumping out more than 250 million gallons of water from miles of flooded underground tunnels. Estimates of the final damage ranged as high as $1 billion, and many reporters described it as one of its worst civic disasters since the Great Chicago Fire of 1871.

When all of the facts were uncovered, it turned out that city employees knew about a leak in the Chicago River's retaining wall. The Chicago Flood of 1992 should have been prevented. Mayor Daley was embarrassed and angry. "These people are going to be held accountable," he said at a late night press conference. "Each and every one of those persons who had information will be accountable to me and to the people of the City of Chicago." The mayor and his chief of staff David Mosena took disciplinary actions against eight employees, including firing John LaPlante, an experienced engineer and the first deputy commissioner in the Department of Transportation. "He was really pissed off at me," recalled LaPlante when explaining that he had previously received an inspector's report and photographs that showed damage to the underground tunnels. Years later LaPlante was actually sympathetic to Daley's point of view, even though the mayor failed to discipline politically connected city commissioner Ben Reyes, who boasted strong ties to the emerging Hispanic political organizations in Chicago and could have possibly prevented the civic disaster.

Two months after the great flood, Mayor Daley suffered another disappointment. His two-and-a-half-year effort to bring a third airport to Chicago had failed. At a press conference, a visibly upset Daley called the Lake Calumet airport proposal "flat out" dead. "Sometimes you have to face reality," declared Daley. "We're facing reality. We're going to request another vote, but all the [legislative] leaders said no. The bill is dead."

The mayor and his team had worked diligently to bring a new airport to Chicago, negotiating with airlines, regulators, the governor of Illinois, the governor of Indiana, and countless state legislators and local politicians. In the end, however, the project died for two primary reasons. First, there were more politically active groups against the airport than there were those for it. Environmentalists were against the airport because of nearby wetlands and the fear that construction would stir up hazardous and toxic materials from a hundred years of industrial dumping. Nearby residents were against the airport because it would disrupt their homes and businesses. "For politicians to come in and dictate to people where they are going to live, that's wrong," said one local truck driver. "If Daley wants an airport so bad, why doesn't he put it in his backyard?" Suburban and downstate Republicans were against the Lake Calumet airport because they saw it as an expensive project that would only help Chicago. Mike Madigan, the Speaker of the House, worried that a new airport would hurt his constituents who lived and worked near Midway Airport.

The second factor that contributed to the failure of the new airport bill was that Mayor Daley did not get along with Jim Edgar, whom voters had elected governor of Illinois in 1990. Edgar was a cautious, fiscally conservative Republican from downstate Illinois. Unlike the former governor of Illinois Jim Thompson, Edgar did not have an emotional attachment to Chicago or a personal rapport with Daley. If the mayor had forgotten, Edgar was reminding him that relationships matter in politics. When Daley needed help from Edgar, little assistance was extended, and the Lake Calumet airport bill failed to pass.

Daley did salvage one important victory, however, during his attempt to bring a third airport to Chicago. During the long process, the US Congress had passed a $3-per-flight passenger head tax that was intended to help fund the new airport. This tax ended up generating $100 million a year for Chicago. Two powerful politicians from

Illinois had assisted Daley in its passage: Dan Rostenkowski, chair of the House Ways and Means Committee, and Sam Skinner, US transportation secretary. When the deal to add a third airport fell through, Daley inherited a tax windfall that he could use to improve O'Hare and Midway Airports. With the Lake Calumet airport proposal dead, he asked his chief of staff David Mosena to become the city's new aviation commissioner and to focus on overseeing $1.4 billion in improvements at O'Hare and Midway Airports.

With his consolation prize, the mayor of Chicago focused on another serious problem: the city's recent increase in violent crime. The most serious crimes in Chicago—including murder, rape, assault, robbery, burglary, and theft—had increased significantly in the late 1980s and early 1990s. Arrests had risen as well, and the jails were overcrowded. Despite these enforcement efforts, the public had grown increasingly fearful of crime, and civic trust had fallen. Police morale had also dipped as officers felt a lack of support from the community.

Before Mayor Daley could develop a plan that would address Chicago's crime problem, however, an old controversy arose that would complicate his efforts to make the city safer. The Jon Burge police torture scandal resurfaced. This scandal had significant racial implications because all of Burge's alleged torture victims were black men. In late 1991 one of these men filed a $16 million lawsuit accusing Burge and other police officers of torturing him until he confessed to a murder that occurred during a robbery attempt. Members of the Coalition to End Police Brutality protested at city hall and demanded swift action against Burge. One month later the Chicago police department suspended Burge and recommended that the Police Board fire him. Mayor Daley publicly stated that the police department had taken appropriate action.

The Burge situation created a serious political problem for Daley, one which gave him two unattractive choices. If Daley took no action against Burge, then black voters might be upset with the mayor. Inaction could also hurt Daley politically with various human rights groups. At the same time, taking a stand against Burge could hurt Daley with the politically active, largely white force of more than twelve thousand police officers. For some portion of the force, any action against Burge would be a betrayal of the men and women who risked their lives protecting the neighborhoods of Chicago. During his own Police Board brutality hearing, Burge referred to one criminal suspect as "a piece of human garbage" and his lawyer lectured the Police Board that "you're not allowed to take a man's job away . . . ruin his reputation, take his family's livelihood." This way of looking at things may well have been consistent with the majority view within the police force. Basically, Chicago cops thought Daley should just let the whole thing quietly blow over so that they could get back to "catching bad guys."

The Burge controversy also created a policy problem for the mayor. As he quietly but increasingly took a stand against Burge, many Chicago cops came to feel that Daley did not "have their backs." This sentiment would make the mayor's efforts to decrease crime and to reform the police department more difficult, adding a layer of complexity to Daley's already daunting problem of how to make Chicago safer.

The extent of Chicago's crime problem could be seen at the Cook County Criminal Courts building, just east of the bustling Twenty-Sixth Street commercial strip, the heart of Mexican-American Chicago. This government structure housed the most active felony court in the country, and it was here that Rich Daley served as state's attorney for nine years. During Daley's early years as mayor, the courthouse was almost always teeming with defendants, witnesses, lawyers, judges, and clerks. On a typical day, the courts dealt with fourteen hundred cases and bond hearings. Half of these cases involved drugs. "[They] come in all the time high as a kite," said one deputy at the courthouse. "Don't know where they are. Don't know what [crime] they did." The other cases at court involved violent crime, weapon violations, theft, fraud, and murder.

The scene in a preliminary hearing courtroom one day in early 1993 was typical. A judge, prosecutor, public defender, and clerk occupied a courtroom that focused exclusively on drug offenses. The robed judge sat up on his high perch. The courtroom was large, open, and trimmed in oak. A deputy led twenty-four prisoners into the courtroom and herded them onto the wooden benches in the jury box. The detainees included eighteen black men, five black women, and one white woman. All looked disheveled and exhausted, worn out from a sleepless night in a lockup cell.

A preliminary hearing courtroom revealed the pulse of Chicago's criminal courts process. The tempo was fast and repetitive. The movements were those of a synchronized quintet—clerk, judge, prosecutor, public defender, and deputy—that processed twenty-four prisoners in less than fifty minutes. The clerk called the name of the defendant. The judge reviewed the arrest report and almost instantly announced a finding of probable cause to detain. The prosecutor mumbled the prisoner's criminal background. "Possession of controlled substance with intent to deliver, your honor," he said. "Eleven priors. Delivery of controlled substance, warrant, July of '92. That's the extent of the information, Judge." The public defender requested a reasonable bond for the prisoner and attempted to humanize the detainee for the court. "The defendant is 21 years of age," said the public defender. "He works at Continental White Cap Company. Makes bottles and jars. He's been working there for half a year. He lives with his mother where he's lived all of his life." The judge ruled: "Thirty-five thousand dollar bond, motion, state, August the 11th at 9:30." The deputy placed his hand on the back of the suspect and hurried him out of the courtroom. The clerk called out the next defendant's name.

Fourteen hundred cases and hearings a day, five days a week. The criminal courthouse in Chicago was like a huge, bureaucratic factory that constantly manufactured prisoners. This rising tide of criminals in Chicago contributed to public fear and an increasing sentiment to get tough on crime. This attitude was consistent with national trends. Many states during the 1990s passed "three strikes" laws that required judges to impose tough sentences on criminals who were convicted of three or more serious crimes. In 1993, the US Congress considered the Clinton Crime Bill, a law that would ban the manufacture of assault weapons, fund a hundred thousand additional police officers, and increase the use of the death penalty. Rahm Emanuel—one of Daley's protégés with a high-level position in the Clinton White House—pushed for an anticrime initiative and shepherded the bill through Congress.

In Chicago, Mayor Daley knew that the crime problem needed to be addressed. In October 1992, Dantrell Davis, a seven-year-old living in Cabrini-Green public housing, was shot to death as he walked to school with his mom. The murder was a big story in the news, and black politicians began suggesting that Daley needed to do more to address the city's soaring homicide rate. But Daley struggled to find the right solutions. He had already appointed a new police superintendent in 1992 and proposed restructuring the police department to make it more effective. Neither decision had much of an impact on lowering crime, however.

In 1993, therefore, the mayor and his team tried a new approach to reducing crime. Chicago began experimenting with "community policing," a strategy that encouraged police officers to engage with a neighborhood and solve problems, rather than merely reacting to 911 emergency calls. Community policing assumed that social issues—such as teenage loitering, public drinking, dilapidated buildings, garbage-strewn lots, abandoned cars, and graffiti—contributed to crime. Police officers, therefore, would hold monthly community "beat" meetings and work with residents to eliminate the social problems that contributed to crime. They would also be trained to ride bikes, walk the neighborhood, and actively engage with local people. When the full community policing program was officially rolled out in April 1993, the city gave it the name Chicago Alternative Policing Strategy or CAPS.

During the same month as the launch of the community policing program, Rich and Maggie Daley decided to move from their home in Bridgeport to a new row house in the South Loop's trendy Central Station development. Central Station sat at the southern end of Grant Park, just west of Soldier Field stadium, Meigs Field Airport, and Lake Michigan. There were two reactions to the news. Many politicians and reporters focused on the political implications of the decision, speculating that it might hurt the Daleys' image as a blue-collar family that never lost touch with its roots. The flip side to this point of view was that three out of the other four mayors from Bridgeport—Ed Kelly, Martin Kennelly, and Michael Bilandic—had moved on to other neighborhoods. Only the first Mayor Daley never left his beloved Bridgeport.

The second reaction focused on Maggie Daley and her influence on the mayor. "She wants to be uppity, so let her be up there," said an elderly woman in a babushka picking up leaves in front of her home on South Emerald Street in Bridgeport. "She wouldn't even say hello to anyone. . . . Richie was all right. He'd wave. Not her." Many others felt differently. They saw Maggie as a sophisticated woman and believed that it was natural that she would cultivate finer interests in her husband.

Daley himself downplayed any political significance to the move, emphasizing that it was the right personal decision with his kids off at college. "If I have to worry about my relationship with my wife and my children because of politics, that's the day I'm not a father or a husband," explained the mayor. "I'm a husband and a father first. And that's the value that my father gave to me in my life."

Of all the Daley brothers, only John Daley remained in Bridgeport. He was as a minor politician, homeowner, an active parishioner at Nativity of our Lord Church, and the Eleventh Ward Democratic committeeman. The odds were strong that he would never leave.

Despite resistance from more traditional police officers, the CAPS program met with initial success. "I think it's empowered people," said one police officer. "It's put them in touch with city services. They used to depend on the alderman, which was good if your alderman was strong, but otherwise things didn't get done. That's not true any longer. People can control the policing that occurs in their neighborhoods." During the first several years of community policing, robberies, assaults, and other violent crimes dropped, especially in African-American areas of the city. Mayor Daley could claim some success in reducing crime, even though Chicago continued to have a high murder rate and drug- and gang-related violence would resurge in the early 2000s.

As he worked on Chicago's crime problem, Daley also continued to struggle with economic and budgetary pressures in the first half of the 1990s. Daley administration budgets regularly featured new fees and taxes, employee layoffs, and the privatization of city services. The mayor also tried to address his budgetary problems by pushing legalized gambling as a potential source of new tax revenues. Daley favored the idea of a gambling megacomplex that combined traditional wagering with sports betting, but he also explored the concept of riverboat gambling. The mayor's plan to bring legalized betting to Chicago, though, ended up suffering the same fate as his dream of building a third airport in Lake Calumet. When he needed political support from Governor Edgar and other influential Republican politicians in Illinois, all of his proposals failed to pass.

During Daley's second term in office, he began to experience the rigors of leading Chicago. Many of the most problematic issues that crossed his desk—such as crime and economic development—were intractable. He could only address them through great, great persistence. The sad state of Chicago Public Schools soon rose to the top of his daunting to-do list. Only time would tell if Rich Daley had the stamina to endure such a marathon of stress.

CHAPTER 12

TAKEOVER OF CHICAGO PUBLIC SCHOOLS

Mike Koldyke picked up his phone at Frontenac Company and called down to city hall. It was April 1992 and Koldyke, a well-known venture capitalist, had just been appointed chairman of the Chicago School Finance Authority by Mayor Daley and Governor Edgar.

"Hello," said Tim Degnan in his gravelly voice.

"Tim, this is Mike Koldyke," he replied in his warm, upbeat manner. "I'm the new chair of the school finance authority. Will you see me? I'll come down to city hall."

"Sure," said Degnan. "Eleven o'clock would work."

Koldyke rode the elevator down from his office, exited onto LaSalle Street and briskly took off on the three-block walk to city hall. Koldyke was a liberal Republican from the suburbs, but he was brimming with ideas for improving the Chicago Public Schools (CPS): work-rule changes for the unions, privatization of nonacademic services, school vouchers to encourage competition. Koldyke was a prototypical Chicago businessman—full of energy and ideas—a man who not only founded many companies but had also created the Golden Apple Foundation to honor and fund Chicago's most outstanding teachers. Entering city hall, he rode the elevator up to the sixth floor. Degnan received him in his office.

"Hey Mike, I'm glad you're in that job," welcomed the deep-toned Degnan as he pulled out a chair for Koldyke. "I know you're going to do a good job and I know you have some really good ideas to help the mayor in what he's trying to do."

"Well, there are a couple of things I would like to talk to you about," agreed Koldyke, smiling.

Degnan raised his arm out toward the businessman, like a traffic cop stopping cars so that kids could cross a busy street. "Let me tell you something, Mike," instructed Daley's right-hand man. "I'm sure you have some good ideas, but the first thing you have to realize about the Chicago Public Schools is what you gotta do is blow the fucking place up."

Degnan, of course, meant this figuratively. The deep-seated ineffectiveness of the city's schools, which stretched back to at least the Great Depression, had worsened in the 1960s, 1970s, and 1980s, even as a global, postindustrial economy demanded a more skilled and white-collar workforce. The school system in twentieth-century Chicago had become a bloated bureaucracy focused on protecting the pay and benefits of administrators and teachers. Educating kids was an afterthought. Degnan's warlike metaphor for dealing with the school crisis—what you gotta do is blow the fucking place up—reflected his boss's deep frustration with a dilemma that tore at the very social fabric of Chicago.

But Degnan and Daley both knew that there were no simple solutions to the sad state of the Chicago Public Schools. The fundamental causes of the city's educational failure were too complicated and long standing: racial inequality, broken homes, depressed neighborhoods, entrenched unions. A socioeconomic mess with no clear solution.

A number of these deep-seated problems had significantly worsened during the mayoralty of Daley's father, the first Mayor Daley. After Dick Daley lost the white vote in the 1963 election for mayor, he had become a reactionary leader, especially on racial issues. Furthermore, the aging first Mayor Daley had focused on protecting his own power at all costs.

Dick Daley damaged the Chicago school system in two ways during the 1960s and 1970s. First, he unilaterally granted collective bargaining rights to the teachers' union in 1964. This was a blatantly political decision with serious racial undertones. He did it because he was worried about political demonstrations, race riots, white flight to the suburbs, and the dramatic growth of Chicago's black population. Dick Daley believed that giving bargaining rights to the predominantly Caucasian teachers' union would create a voting bloc that could help him maintain his own power. The consequences of this decision—long term and negative—hurt children and schools for generations. Second, the first Mayor Daley made bad contractual deals with the teachers' union, even though he was financially sophisticated. He repeatedly engineered increases in pay, health care, and retirement benefits when the school system did not have the money to pay for these financial promises.

"What Daley senior was doing—in Enron-style fashion—was hiding and concealing and papering over structural deficits that the school district was experiencing," said Paul Vallas, an expert on municipal budgeting and school finance who the second Mayor Daley would soon name as CEO of the Chicago Public Schools. "And the rating agencies knew about it. And the banks knew about it. And [the accounting firm] Arthur Andersen, obviously, knew about it. But because Richard J. Daley was such a powerhouse, the audits papered over the structural deficits."

In 1979—less than three years after the death of Dick Daley—the Chicago school system became financially insolvent. The State of Illinois gave control of CPS finances to a new entity, called the Chicago School Finance Authority, which soon eliminated many educational programs as part of a cost-saving strategy. A decade of chaos ensued. Five different school superintendents. Five mayors of Chicago. Dramatic turnover of principals and school board members. Teachers strikes in 1980, 1983, 1984, and 1987. In the late 1980s, US Secretary of Education William Bennett labeled Chicago's educational system as one of "the worst schools in the nation."

Bennett's harsh assessment of CPS was justified. Academic performance was disastrous. The standardized test scores of Chicago high schools were in the lowest 5 percent of the country. Violence and gangs were recurring problems. The 400,000-student school system had a drop-out rate of more than one-third, which was partially a function of teen pregnancy. Eight-five percent of the student body was black or Latino, and most were also poor. The essence of Chicago's educational challenge at public schools was socioeconomic.

By the time Rich Daley took office as the new mayor in 1989, he knew that he would need to stabilize the Chicago Public School system in order to begin mending the social fabric of the city. Daley named the city's first-ever deputy mayor for education. He also appointed Bill Singer as a member of the interim board that would run the school system for a short period. Singer had started his political career as a liberal reformer but over time had become one of Chicago's elite Democratic power brokers. The Daley brothers had forgiven Singer for embarrassing their father at the 1972 Democratic National Convention and challenging him in Chicago's 1975 mayoral contest. Singer was a savvy individual, a smart lawyer, and a skillful politician. Rich Daley wanted his assistance in fixing Chicago's shoddy school system.

"Rich was very much interested in reaching out beyond the confines of an old Democratic machine-type cloistered environment," said Singer in explaining why he accepted Daley's offer to join the interim school board. "He wasn't interested in the politics of that [old system]. He was much more interested in those people and community organizations who wanted to make a change in the city."

Daley's desire for educational reform was, in important ways, a rejection of his father's political legacy. The son was choosing to back change rather than defend the political status quo. Rich Daley was aligning himself with children—most of whom were nonvoting minorities—rather than white ethnics or the powerful teacher union.

Singer used his talents to help Daley stabilize the school system. He quickly negotiated a three-year contract with the unions, ensuring that the schools would not suffer another strike in the near term. He also worked to systematically cut unnecessary costs and to complete an inventory of all of the school buildings in the public system. This thorough analysis would convince the mayor that there was a dramatic need to refurbish existing facilities and build new schools.

But it was not just the school buildings that needed a massive overhaul. Administration of the school system was dysfunctional. At the beginning of the 1990 school year, for example, thousands of workbooks, computers, and other educational tools sat in warehouses because the CPS administration failed to complete the authorizing paperwork on time.

Unfortunately, a quirk in Illinois law meant that Singer and the rest of the interim school board would be replaced in 1990 and that Mayor Daley would lose direct control of the Chicago Public Schools. After attending a ceremony to open a new grade school near the end of Singer's term, he and Daley rode together as they headed back to the Loop. They discussed the expiration of the interim school board and all of the challenges facing the schools, agreeing that the Achilles heel of the school reform movement was accountability.

Indeed, for the next five years the Chicago Public School system was like a patient in a coma lingering in a hospital ward for whom no doctor took direct responsibility for his care. While the patient was technically alive, he lacked a productive existence and stood little chance of recovery.

The one vital statistic for the school system during this period was the appointment of Mike Koldyke as chairman of the Chicago School Finance Authority in 1992. Koldyke was smart, full of energy, and willing to stir the pot with new ideas. In 1993, he proposed that the Chicago Teachers Union agree to radical work-rule changes and that the State of Illinois issue bonds to alleviate a financial crisis at the schools. The teachers' union and Republican lawmakers attacked his proposal, and it failed to pass. Koldyke also put forth ideas for making the school system rely heavily on market incentives, such as outsourcing business, engineering, and maintenance functions to private companies while cutting administrative jobs at CPS headquarters. Unions also fiercely resisted these suggestions.

Despite the opposition to Koldyke's ideas by some factions, by 1995 it seemed as if the overall Chicago community was ready for change. Mayor Daley was deeply frustrated with the status quo, as were families with school-age children and the Chicago business community. Daley and his allies began lobbying Republican leaders in Springfield to change state laws in ways that would enable school reform in Chicago.

Unfortunately, the president of the Illinois senate was Pate Phillips, a small-minded ex-marine who had a reputation for intemperate and even racist views. The suburban Phillips did not want to do anything to help Daley, once commenting that giving more money to CPS would "be like pouring money down a rat hole." During one meeting between Koldyke and the white-haired Phillips, Koldyke began to soften Phillips's resistance to Chicago school reform by appealing to Phillips's mean streak. "Listen, Pate," said the energetic and gregarious Koldyke, "you gotta back this [school reform plan] because this is the best way to stick it to the unions." Phillips loved this way of thinking and began to seriously consider supporting school reform.

Around the same time, Koldyke sent a written reform proposal to Dan Cronin, head of the Illinois senate education committee. Koldyke suggested radical reform, including giving the mayor of Chicago control of the school board, eliminating teacher job guarantees, and empowering school principals to hire and fire all teachers and support staff in their schools. A teachers' union representative called Koldyke's plan "ludicrous," while principals praised it as full of "fantastic ideas."

Reform was in the air. With the help of Senator Cronin and other supportive legislators, within weeks Mayor Daley convinced the Illinois legislature to pass a groundbreaking reform bill giving Chicago's mayor the power to name the school board, appoint the CEO of the school system, use state funds more flexibly, and take control of nonperforming schools.

Daley had pushed for these reforms even though he worried about the political backlash from the city's well-organized unions. According to Koldyke, Daley tried to thread a perilous political needle. "He never wanted anybody to say that he was trying to screw the union," recalled Koldyke. "But he did want control of the schools."

Arne Duncan—who later would serve under Daley as CEO of the Chicago Public Schools and under President Obama as US secretary of education—was amazed by the political courage reflected in Daley's final decision. "I think his greatest accomplishment as mayor is that he had the courage to take on school reform in Chicago," said Duncan. "Politically, it was not a smart thing to do. All of his experts were telling Daley that it was going to end his career. But Daley intuitively believed that he had to do this if he wanted to help Chicago to grow and prosper and be successful, whether or not it was the politically astute thing to do. Daley's initial courage has now basically changed the landscape of urban education in the United States. Now, mayors all around the country are also fighting for the opportunity to reform their schools."

Taking a big risk to try to reform the Chicago Public Schools would become one of Daley's most enduring political legacies.

After passage of the educational reform bill, Daley quickly took control of the schools. He appointed Paul Vallas, his top financial executive at city hall, as CEO of Chicago Public Schools and Gery Chico, his mayoral chief of staff, as president of the school board. Both men were ambitious, talented, and loyal to Daley. Vallas—tall, slim, pale, and balding—had the charismatic intensity and charm of an evangelical preacher. A workaholic who was a devout Christian, Vallas believed that reforming education was "the greatest chapter in the civil rights movement." Like a force of nature, he arrived at the Chicago Public Schools in 1995 and changed everything in his path. Chico had other strengths and a different personality. Cool under pressure, he brought great attention to detail and a focus on performance. Self-made, Chico had a track record of not only performing at a high level but also maintaining professional friendships along the way. He was the ultimate insider whose political bloodlines were mixed. On the one hand, Chico had risen through the old-style Democratic machine and become close to Alderman Ed Burke. On the other hand, he had been brought into the Daley administration by David Mosena, a skilled manager who got his start under Harold Washington.

Despite the school reform legislation passed by the Illinois legislature, Vallas and Chico inherited a gigantic mess. Atrocious academics. Run-down school buildings. A structural budget deficit of more than $1.3 billion. Inept management at CPS headquarters. Risk of another strike by the teachers' union.

Vallas started knocking down the challenges like a professional bowler knocking over pins. Within a month, he had delivered a new contract with the teachers, cut more than $150 million in expenses, and designed a five-year balanced budget that eliminated CPS's structural deficit.

Unfortunately, the restructuring of CPS would have a long-term financial cost that would not become apparent for more than a decade. As part of its takeover of the Chicago Public Schools, the Daley administration convinced the Illinois legislature to rewrite the pension code so that CPS would have access to funds that previously were contributed to the Chicago Teachers' Pension Fund. This budgetary freedom helped CPS to balance the near-term budget but created a lasting structural flaw in the funding of teacher pensions. Between 1995 and 2009, this "pension holiday" would cost the teachers fund more than $1.5 billion. Most teachers and taxpayers were unaware of this growing multibillion unfunded liability. Daley's pattern of slyly endorsing financially irresponsible, politically expedient pension deals had continued.

With the mayor's approval and political support, Vallas and Chico then began to use the new financial resources of CPS to fund a huge school-construction program. By the end of their tenure, they had built more than seventy-five new school buildings and renovated 350 more. They did this by creating an independent and competitive bidding process that sidestepped Chicago's Building Commission and eliminated the cronyism and contractual patronage that Chicago politics was known for.

"Daley always flew 'air cover' and protected me," remembered Vallas. "Daley always backed us up, encouraged us to be aggressive and gave us the political cover to really start instituting radical school reform."

Improving academics became a much greater challenge for Vallas than balancing the budget and building schools. Unlike most career bureaucrats, however, Vallas was biased toward action. He closed bad schools, fired bad teachers, instituted mandatory summer school for low performers, and launched the largest early childhood education program in the country.

Approximately one year after taking over the schools, Vallas scheduled a meeting at city hall between the principals' association and Mayor Daley. Knowing that Daley was under a lot of pressure and that he had a very short fuse, Vallas met with the principals beforehand and coached them on the best way to interact with the mayor. "Just go in there and stick to our three key points," advised Vallas. "Don't go off on any tangents. It's also a good idea to thank the Mayor because the schools right now are about 50% better than they were a year ago." The principals listened to Vallas and agreed to follow his advice.

Daley's office on the fifth floor of city hall was divided into two parts. His official space had a formal desk and chairs. Off to the side was a conference room filled with a long table and a big aquarium. Daley did most of his work in this side area, where he sat at the end of the long conference table with no telephone and his stacks of paper in front of him.

Daley held his meeting with the principals in his official office, however, signifying that it was intended to be more of a ceremonial visit than an actual working session. Vallas and the principals entered and sat down in the formal chairs.

The woman who headed the principals' association started by saying, "Before we begin, mayor . . ."

"Great, she's going to thank the mayor," thought Vallas.

"I just want to let you know that there're still some schools that have graffiti on them," said the leader of the principals' association. "And, you know what, I think that it's really important that the city does some more about getting rid of the graffiti on the schools. I have a few principals that still have graffiti on their schools."

Vallas watched as Daley's face immediately changed from smiling and attentive to bright red. Three years earlier, the mayor had started a program called "graffiti blasters" to eliminate all visual vandalism in Chicago. Daley was absolutely obsessed with eradicating graffiti and the program had already had great success. For years, Daley had instructed principals that if a school had a problem with graffiti that they should "just pick up the phone, call 311 and a truck will be there to remove it the next day."

"Oh, you want me to do more about graffiti?" asked the red-faced mayor. "Well, here this is what I'm going to do."

"Oh, no, he wants to choke her," thought Vallas.

Daley turned toward Vallas. "What day is it today, Paul?" asked the mayor.

"It's Thursday, Mr. Mayor," solemnly answered the superintendent of Chicago Public Schools.

"Ok, Paul," Daley said. "Since I don't think they listened to what I've said about the schools and graffiti, I want you to tell *this lady here* to tell her principals that on Monday morning, if a school has any graffiti on it the principal will be fired immediately."

The mayor then turned his head back toward the leader of the principals' association. "Get your stuff and get out of my office!" he yelled. The meeting ended with Vallas and the principals shuffling out of the mayor's office suite in silence.

Just as the Chicago schools started to show signs of improvement, a series of political scandals surfaced in city government. Initially, these ethical lapses seemed to center around Ed Burke. In January 1998, former alderman Joseph Martinez pleaded guilty to collecting $90,000 in salary and benefits from city hall without performing any work. Martinez, an attorney at Burke's law firm at the time, alleged that Burke had masterminded the ghost payrolling scheme in order to avoid paying Martinez's medical benefits. Though Burke denied the allegation, he was soon involved in other controversies. In May, a newspaper investigation revealed that Burke had serious conflicts of interest between his private law practice and his leadership role in the city council. As the chairman of the finance committee, he had used his political clout to help his clients cut their real estate taxes, litigate with the City of Chicago, and broker fishy business deals. Mayor Daley publicly criticized Burke, but stopped short of calling for his resignation. In October, Pat Huels—Daley's floor leader in the Chicago City Council—sponsored a strict ethics code to deal with conflicts of interests in the city council.

A few weeks later, new political scandals popped up, and both Burke and Huels were implicated. The *Chicago Sun-Times* ran articles revealing conflicts of interest between the legislators and SDI Security

Inc., a private security company owned by Huels and members of his family. Burke served as the company's secretary for five years and had used funds from the City Council Finance Committee to pay $476,000 in consulting fees to Michael Pedicone, the man who became president of SDI Security. Burke denied breaking any laws and stated that he had no intention of resigning from the city council.

The conflict-of-interest allegations against Huels were even more serious. The press revealed that Huels had skirted the city's ethics regulations by taking a $1.25 million loan from a large city contractor. In addition, the federal government had put a tax lien on Huels's SDI Security after it failed to pay millions of dollars in federal and local taxes on time. The newspapers were outraged. "Chicago cannot afford to be the City of Sleaze," declared one editorial in the *Chicago Sun-Times*. "There is more than pride at stake. Chicago cannot carry a venal reputation into the new century without losing national and world esteem, meaning fewer visitors, fewer conventions, lost contracts and lost jobs."

A major reason for the press's anger was that Huels was not just another professional associate of Daley's. He and the mayor—both born and raised in Bridgeport—were friends and longtime political allies. Moreover, the city contractor who made the loan to Huels, trucking magnate Michael Tadin, was also a boyhood friend of Daley's. The entire situation smelled wrong to the public.

Huels had attended De La Salle Institute—the same Catholic high school as Rich Daley—and started out his career as a City of Chicago tree trimmer. His loyalty to the Daley family had allowed the go-along, get-along Huels to rise through the ranks of the Democratic Party and become the Eleventh Ward alderman from Bridgeport. Along the way he became part of Daley's inner circle, forging relationships with the Daley brothers, Tim Degnan, Ed Burke, and a wide swath of Chicago politicos. When Daley was elected mayor in 1989, he made Huels his city council floor leader. The nondescript Huels soon began wearing expensive suits, Italian ties, and, by some accounts, silk boxer shorts.

As the ethics lapses by Huels and Burke became public, Daley tried to distance himself from the controversy—saying that Michael Tadin, his boyhood buddy from Bridgeport, was "not my friend"—and pressuring Huels to resign from the city council. Daley took a much lighter touch in criticizing Burke, however. Political insiders speculated either that Burke was too valuable to the mayor in the city council or that Daley feared revenge from Burke, who could possibly use his vast city hall surveillance network to find embarrassing information on the mayor.

In the midst of these scandals, Daley received a small respite from the controversy when President Clinton came to Chicago to visit a school and to praise the education reform efforts that Daley and his team had enacted over the past two years. "I want what is happening in Chicago to happen all over America," said the president of the United States. "What is working in Chicago must blow like a wind of change into every city in every school in America."

"Because of what you are doing, the city that works now has a school system on the move," continued President Clinton as he stood next to a smiling Mayor Daley. "I can remember a few years ago when the only news that those of us who didn't live in Illinois got about the Chicago school system was the annual strike. And now I see [all the positive changes that] have happened."

The presidential visit burnished the mayor's reform credentials, but the public never completely believed Daley's explanation that Huels's lapses in judgment were the alderman's private affair and had nothing to do with the mayor. Over the next ten years, the public perception steadily grew that the mayor was too tolerant of political corruption. And perhaps the public was right. The facts would not come out for another eight years, but in 2006 the names of Huels and Tadin surfaced again as another large political scandal arose in the Daley administration. As for Ed Burke, he continued to hold on tightly to his finance committee position, using his power base to help his old school buddies.

In the meantime, this early flurry of scandals eventually blew over, allowing Daley, Vallas, and Chico to focus their time and efforts on reforming the schools. The trio soon opened two magnet high schools, which became among the very best in the country: Northside College Prep in 1999 and Walter Payton College Prep in 2000. It was very hard work, but reported student test scores also rose every year between 1995 and 2001. Equally important, the adept triumvirate brought hope to thousands of Chicago children, parents, and teachers.

Unfortunately, most good things cannot last forever. Over time, the egos of Chicago's educational troika got in the way. Vallas and Chico increasingly jousted over who should get credit for successful initiatives, while Daley grew jealous of Vallas's extraordinary popularity with the voting public. In 2001, city hall confidantes of the mayor began suggesting to Vallas that he resign and run for governor of Illinois. Also, Daley publicly complained about the number of students reading below grade level, lecturing reporters, "Don't ever believe that one person is the key to everything and is irreplaceable."

Chico resigned, and then Vallas did as well. "I like to think that we have started an education revolution that spread across the country," proclaimed the proud Vallas during his public farewell. But two large questions remained. Could the Chicago schools keep improving without Vallas and Chico? Had Daley made a mistake and turned Vallas into a serious political rival?

PART 5

Civilizing Richie

CHAPTER 13

HAS CHICAGO HAD A SEX CHANGE?

The Amoco Building, an eighty-three-floor skyscraper, overlooked the northern edge of Grant Park, just a bit north and west of Meigs Field Airport. Lake Michigan unwrapped itself to the east, a great inland ocean stretching out into the middle of America. Just to the west sat the Chicago Cultural Center. Further west was LaSalle Street, the financial district, and looming above all the other structures, the Sears Tower. Even farther in that direction, the impoverished West Loop—where Mayor Daley was hosting the 1996 Democratic National Convention—faded into the distance. To the north, Michigan Avenue and the Magnificent Mile shopping district lured tourists and luxury consumers. Eighty-three floors below and just to the south of the Amoco Building lay the naked remains of the Illinois Central Railroad yard, a 150-year-old corpse from Chicago's industrial past.

In planning for the 1996 Democratic National Convention, Mayor Daley had begun two years earlier enlisting the support of Chicago's business community. This group had ended up contributing millions of dollars in private-sector funds to help finance the event, and the mayor and some of Chicago's business leaders had gathered during the political convention for a breakfast meeting at the Amoco Building. It was very important to Daley that the convention function smoothly, lessening America's bitter memories of his father and the Chicago police clashing with protestors during the 1968 Democratic National Convention.

In a few years, the Amoco Building's owners would rename the tower the Aon Center, after the large insurance brokerage founded by Pat Ryan, one of Daley's most generous supporters. In the meantime, Daley and a select group of Chicago business executives met in the building's private conference room, far above the bustling streets. As the participants filled their coffee cups and settled into their seats, the mayor of Chicago walked to the window and motioned for John Bryan, the CEO of Sara Lee, a global consumer products company, to come over. Daley and Bryan looked down and saw the dead rail yard.

"We should build a park there," Daley suggested to Bryan.

Bryan silently nodded his head in agreement, and the two men turned back toward the conference table and the business at hand. Nothing would happen with Daley's suggestion for two years, but the Fates of history had matched Daley and Bryan together. These two men—very different in background and personality, in strengths and weaknesses—would either succeed or fail together.

While Daley mulled over the possibility of a new downtown park and worked feverishly to fix Chicago's public schools, he also had begun physically transforming the downtown area and reshaping the very identity of the city. Chicago—the rough-and-tumble, male-identified city of big shoulders—had started to transform into an attractive, feminine beauty.

This transformation reflected two things. First, there was something inherent in Rich Daley's make-up—a humanistic impulse, an indefinable emotional desire—that drew him toward more creative projects, projects that would improve the quality of life of average Chicagoans. Over his years in power, Daley's instinctual perceptiveness altered the very character of the city he loved. Second, as mayor, Daley sometimes appointed senior aides of great creativity, integrity, and effectiveness. These men and women enabled Daley to fashion a new, more attractive version of the city he had inherited.

The most important of these Daley appointees was Lois Weisberg. Six months after becoming mayor in 1989, Daley drove his first commissioner of cultural affairs out of the administration after a somewhat public dispute over budgeting. He replaced her with Weisberg, a sixty-four-year-old self-starter who had served in the mayoral administration of Harold Washington and who had created the Taste of Chicago festival, the Chicago Blues Festival, and the Friends of the Parks advocacy organization.

Weisberg tended to dress vividly—rhinestone-studded glasses, white leather boots with fuzzy fur around the ankles—and spoke with a warm, throaty voice. She liked cigarettes, coffee, and vodka. More important, Weisberg was a super creative, idea-driven connector of people and events. She developed into one of the most influential people in Daley's professional life.

Though he was seventeen years her junior, Daley enjoyed talking with the unconventional Weisberg. The mayor was full of ideas—ranging from practical to shrewd to downright wacky—and Weisberg seemed exceptional in her ability to understand and embrace his many notions on how to improve the city. "Lois Weisberg is one of those unique people who can think very creatively and very practically at the same time," Daley would say years later in explaining her rare talents. "I can call Lois with an idea and know without a doubt that she will find a way to make it happen."

Weisberg's first major initiative under Daley was to figure out what to do with a nearly century-old building for which she had inherited the task of repurposing. The classically styled edifice stood at the intersection of Randolph and Michigan Avenue, just across the street from the dead Illinois Central rail yard in the corner of Grant Park. For nearly a hundred years, this grand civic building had housed the city's central library until 1991 when the new Harold Washington Library Center was completed in the South Loop. After the library moved, the majestic building was nearly empty, causing Mayor Daley to consider selling it during a period of economic and budgetary stresses. Instead, he had kept it and put it under Weisberg's department of cultural affairs.

The Daley family had a long history with the former Chicago Public Library building. In the mid-1970s, real estate developers had planned to tear down this architectural gem and replace it with a skyscraper overlooking the park. Rich Daley's father—Dick Daley, one of Chicago's great builder mayors—would have normally supported development proposals of this type. Instead, his wife Sis Daley intervened, publicly telling a reporter that "I don't think that would be nice" if the building was torn down. "That's a beautiful site where it is. I'm for restoring and keeping all these beautiful buildings in Chicago," she explained. The skyscraper development was subsequently rejected by the city. One month before the first Mayor Daley died in November 1976, he and the Chicago City Council designated the building a landmark.

In 1991, the second Mayor Daley and Lois Weisberg rechristened the site the Chicago Cultural Center. On entering the building, Chicagoans experienced a trip back to nineteenth-century grandeur: vaulted ceilings, white marble Venetian staircases, and the world's largest Tiffany glass dome. But the physical beauty of the building was not enough to make it the warm and special place that it would become. Under Weisberg's leadership, the Chicago Cultural Center transformed into a haven for artists, culture seekers, and tourists. A retreat and a harbor from the accelerating pace of late twentieth-century living. The center became a free place to experience art, photography, music, dance, theater, film, and lectures. "It's important to the quality of life in the city that people know [that] there is a place that belongs to them where they can experience culture," explained Weisberg on the tenth anniversary of the Chicago Cultural Center. That year, more than 700,000 people agreed.

In 1992, the mayor's wife Maggie Daley joined the cultural center's advisory board, opened her office in the building, and launched a $3 million fund-raising campaign to support cultural programming in the center. Maggie had become close friends with Lois Weisberg during the preceding years. The two women also founded Gallery 37, a unique art-education and job-training program for high school students.

Gallery 37 was created in response to a problem that Mayor Daley had struggled with: what to do with Block 37, a large parcel of vacant land in the heart of the downtown Loop area. A series of real estate developers had failed in trying to get multiuse developments built on the site. Daley worried that the empty expanse of land reduced the vibrancy and attractiveness of his city's central business area. The mayor therefore asked his most senior staff, the city commissioners who ran major departments, to submit ideas for using Block 37 constructively.

Around the same time, Maggie Daley and Lois Weisberg were brainstorming on ways to help Chicago teenagers to find meaningful artistic and cultural experiences. One idea the two women came up with was to use the Block 37 site and create a summer jobs program where teenagers would be taught by professional artists and paid to create art. Weisberg and Daley believed that getting teenagers connected with the arts would improve their confidence and school performance.

A few weeks after the 1991 inauguration for Mayor Daley's second term, the mayor asked his chief of staff David Mosena to update him on the ideas for using Block 37.

"Well, one is to employ high school kids to create art under circus-like tents," explained Mosena.

"What are you talking about?" Daley asked. "That's one of the worst ideas I've ever heard. Whose idea is that?"

"Well, actually, it's Maggie's idea," Mosena answered.

The mayor paused before responding again. "Oh, well, that's a wonderful idea," he then replied. Daley not only loved his wife Maggie, but he also had great respect for her judgment in cultural matters.

And so Gallery 37 was born in the summer of 1991. Block 37 was physically transformed by large, pitched tents and a 488-foot mural created with the help of students. Two hundred and sixty students participated the first year, coming to the Loop and being paid to create murals, sculpture, and music. "This was one of the most boring city blocks, and it's been brought to life by Gallery 37," said Michelle Ivy, a seventeen-year-old high school student who had participated in the program. "It was just an empty block, and [now] everybody's here to see what 260 high school students are doing."

By the fifth year of the Gallery 37 summer program, more than six hundred students participated, and Weisberg had also recruited international artists to come to Chicago and teach the teenagers. "The [International Artists Program] has turned out to be one of the most exciting parts of Gallery 37," explained Weisberg. "The artists bring their culture with them to Chicago. They have many different approaches to art that they share with the students and other teachers as well."

It was not a coincidence that Weisberg had connected international artists with the Gallery 37 high school summer job program. Earlier in the decade, Mayor Daley gave Weisberg the additional responsibility of running the Chicago Sister Cities International Program, whose mission was to serve as a bridge between Chicago and sister cities, businesses, and individuals throughout the world.

Like many of the professional responsibilities that Daley inherited on his election to mayor in 1989, Chicago Sister Cities was a tired and largely ceremonial venture. Though his father had signed the first agreement with Warsaw, Poland, in 1960, over the intervening three decades the program languished without leadership or strategic focus. The second Mayor Daley changed that state of affairs in 1990 when he implemented an executive order establishing a board of directors for the global outreach program. Over the next five years, cities in Germany, England, Mexico, Israel, the Czech Republic, Ukraine, Lithuania, and Canada became associated with Chicago, joining a revitalized program that already included urban centers such as Shanghai, Osaka, Milan, and Casablanca. Mayor Daley and his team built relationships with each of these sister cities, as well as holding twenty parades and receptions a year for Chicago's various ethnic groups. During the 1990s, it also became more common for Chicagoans to hear foreign languages spoken in the city or to meet an artist or businessperson who had moved to Chicago from another country. In 1995, for example, parents from Chicago and France together founded a French international school, the Lycée Français de Chicago, where children began receiving a dual language, bicultural education. The city's steady internationalization was also beginning to be reflected in Chicago's growing global reputation as a place to visit, live, or do business.

At the same time as Weisberg worked to help Daley to make Chicago an artier and more international place, the mayor started dealing with other problems on his desk. Among these was the dysfunctional and rundown Chicago Park District. The mess at the park district stretched back to at least the 1940s when the Democratic political machine turned it into a job patronage agency that served employees and politicians but not the community. The nearly five thousand employees of the Chicago Park District were required to get out the Democratic vote during city elections. During the rest of the year, however, patronage hires at the parks department sat around and collected paychecks without bothering to make the parks safe, fun, or convenient. During most of the 1970s and 1980s, the park district was run by the Forty-Seventh Ward boss Ed Kelly, one of the first Mayor Daley's closest buddies.

By 1993, the old and inefficient patronage system at the parks had become a political liability to the second Mayor Daley. There were two problems, though only one of them was visible to voters. The public problem was that two credible organizations—the Civic Federation and Friends of the Parks—had issued reports that were sharply critical of the Chicago Park District. The Civic Federation was the oldest and most prestigious independent research organization in the city. Friends of the Park was a volunteer watchdog group founded in 1975 by Lois Weisberg that had built significant credibility over the years. Both reports described the park district as a failed organization. This type of characterization drove the middle class away from the city and toward the suburbs. It also hurt Daley's growing reputation as an effective "CEO of the city."

The second problem was out of sight to the voting public, but a serious political concern for Daley. The superintendent of parks who the mayor had recruited from out of town three years earlier had opened up many of the park district's patronage jobs to people loyal to Daley's political rivals, including Illinois Speaker of the House Mike Madigan. These park employees worked against Daley's interests during important elections. This political threat to the mayor, combined with the park system's lack of credibility with the voting public, made fixing the Chicago Park District one of Daley's most pressing challenges.

The problems at the parks were severe. The enormous park district organization included thousands of playgrounds and athletic fields, 550 parks, 250 field houses, nearly two hundred gyms, ninety swimming pools, thirty-one miles of lakefront harbors and facilities, six golf courses, two conservatories, the Lincoln Park Zoo, and Soldier Field sports stadium. Even though it commanded a $400 million budget, the Chicago Park District suffered from gangs, crime, broken equipment, closed or rundown facilities, and unresponsive or absent union employees.

In July of 1993, Daley cleaned house at the park district by naming Forest Claypool as the agency's new superintendent and, as president, businessman John Rogers Jr. Claypool, who previously served as Daley's chief of staff, called for radical changes at the parks. Rogers, a successful African-American money manager agreed, emphasizing that Mayor Daley "told us there are no sacred cows. Anybody can be removed." Daley himself publicly backed the reform sentiments of his new team, saying, "We want to eliminate the bureaucracy and the red tape . . . and end interference, whether from politics or unions."

Claypool was a smart and seasoned political operative but also a man of integrity who had a talent for managing organizations. In less than three years at the park district, he recruited a new leadership team, stabilized finances, improved operations, and began to create a consumer-focused service organization. He also privatized many of the park district's noncore functions, including computer systems, trash disposal, maintenance, engineering services, and concession operations. Claypool's decentralized approach was consistent with Daley's overall philosophy, even though it deeply offended many politicians and labor union leaders. By allowing Claypool to proceed, the second Mayor Daley began to reveal what would become one of his executive hallmarks: he would not tightly align himself with unions like his father had. Rich Daley did not have the same personal bonds to union leaders and was too focused on improving the city to become an old-fashioned union-loving Democrat.

"In moments of crisis, normal politics cannot be allowed to intrude into what's necessary for the city," explained Claypool. "So, to Daley's credit, he gave me carte blanche to go over to the parks and do whatever was necessary. I cut the work force by 25%, cutting 1,000 patronage jobs out of a work force of 4,000. The ward bosses screamed bloody murder. They usually called Tim Degnan or the mayor and screamed at them. To the mayor's credit, he did not buckle, and I never once was told to stop. Of course, I held up my end of the bargain, too—created new programs, brought people back to the parks, put 100 cops on the beat to drive the gangbangers out and rebuilt the parks. So that helped Daley, too, because his vision was finally brought to life. He got a lot of political credit for that, and so it was a partnership [between us]."

By the late 1990s, former critics of the Chicago parks began describing them as "emeralds of the city" and "jewels full of greenery." The Daley administration had planted 200,000 trees during his first decade in office, and Daley began to be known as one of the country's first "green" mayors. "Talk about a tree person! Right here! I'm a tree hugger!" the mayor had proudly yelled at reporters. "Visitors to Chicago often express amazement at the beauty of this city and one reason—though they may not be totally aware of it—is the abundance of trees [here]."

More than five years earlier, a political protégé of the tree-loving Daley had formally announced in 1994 that Chicago would host its first national political convention since the infamous 1968 event held by the mayor's father. Standing on the newly renovated Navy Pier with Lake Michigan and the city's skyline gleaming behind him, David Wilhelm—who now held the title of Democratic National Committee chairman—revealed that his adopted city would soon welcome the Democratic Party's national convention. "I love this city and, so, as a Chicagoan, as a Democrat and as a former precinct worker in the 44th Ward, I am proud to announce that the 1996 Democratic National Convention will be held in the City of Chicago," Wilhelm told the reporters and dignitaries assembled at Navy Pier. "Chicago is in the heart of the nation, in its location and in its values. It is the capital of the Midwest and at the center of the heartland states, states that we must win again in 1996," added Wilhelm in explaining why Chicago was chosen.

Daley followed Wilhelm to the speaker's podium. "It's important for us to recognize what this means for Chicago. During this convention, the whole world will be watching our city again," said Daley, casting a positive new spin on the belligerent mantra of the 1968 convention protesters. After more than twenty-five years, a big political convention had once again chosen the city by the lake. Additionally, the completion of the pier's $150 million redevelopment soon turned it into a great success, drawing millions of visitors each year and becoming the top tourist destination in the city. Daley's Chicago was on quite a roll during the 1990s.

In preparing for the convention, the mayor and his team did not rest on their laurels. All of the departments at city hall received word that the 1996 convention was "really important" to Daley and began meeting twice a week for two years in order to prepare for the convention. The mayor himself—an astute judge of his own father's political mistakes—also focused on making the political get-together a successful event. He wanted to showcase Chicago as not only a well-run city but also as an attractive city for tourists. "It was very important for Rich Daley to redo the 1968 convention," explained a senior member of the mayor's cabinet.

One focus of convention preparations was urban beautification. City of Chicago planners added flower boxes, planters, trees, and wrought iron fences along many streets that convention attendees might see as taxicabs drove them to the Democratic confab. Throughout the 1990s, Daley had focused on beautification of the city, but his urge to transform Chicago kicked into overdrive as the big event neared. No detail was too small for the hands-on mayor. Daley, for example, asked real estate owners to light their buildings as brightly as possible because the convention was "about economic development, tourism, and civic pride."

Six months before the Democratic national conference, Chicago achieved another milestone in its efforts to become recognized as an attractive global city. Mayor Daley—with the help of John Bryan, the CEO of Sara Lee—brought Jacques Chirac, the president of France to Chicago for an official visit. Chirac had spurned invitations from New York, Atlanta, and Houston in favor of calling on Daley's hometown. The former mayor of Paris gave Chicago his highest praise by comparing it to his beloved France. "There are some cities that are resolutely turned toward the future," said Chirac. "Chicago is one of them. Its very size, the beauty of its bold, modern architecture, these are the signs of a powerful, dynamic metropolis full of life and activity."

1. Boyhood home of Rich Daley in the Bridgeport neighborhood of Chicago (photo by Joan A. Radtke).

2. 1965 photo of the block where Rich Daley grew up in Bridgeport; the arrow points to the Daley home (courtesy of the Chicago History Museum/Edmund Jarecki).

3. Rich Daley jeering at Senator Abe Ribicoff at the 1968 Democratic National Convention. The culture wars of the 1960s came to a head on the streets of Chicago during four days in August 1968 (Warren K. Leffler, U.S. News & World Report Magazine Collection, LC-U9–19756, frame 31A, Prints & Photographs Division, Library of Congress).

4. The Daleys, father and son, attending a rally in October 1974. Both have their arms folded and looked unusually relaxed (AP Photo/File).

5. Alderman "Fast Eddie" Vrdolyak pointing his finger at Mayor Harold Washington during the "Council Wars." Directly behind him is Alderman Ed Burke, who was known as the "Other Eddie" during the black-versus-white political civil war (Lee Balgemann, U.S. News & World Report Magazine Collection, LC-U9–41471, frame 30, Prints & Photographs Division, Library of Congress).

6. Photo of Rich and Maggie Daley during the 1983 Democratic primary for mayor. The Irish-Catholic political heir from Bridgeport lost badly, finishing third after Harold Washington and Jane Byrne (Chicago Public Library, Special Collections and Preservation Division, Photograph © Richard Gordon 1983, All Rights Reserved).

7. April 1983 "unity luncheon" photo of Harold Washington after he had defeated Jane Byrne and Rich Daley in the Democratic mayoral primary. Washington would go on to become the first black mayor of a major American city (AP Photo/Charlie Knoblock).

8. Mayor Harold Washington presiding over a 1986 event marking the tenth anniversary of the death of Dick Daley. To the right of Washington sits State's Attorney Rich Daley (Chicago Public Library, Special Collections and Preservation Division, HWAC 1986–12–18).

9. In 1989, Rich Daley became the first sitting mayor of Chicago to participate in the Gay and Lesbian Pride Parade. Here, he is pictured sitting in a light blue 1956 Thunderbird convertible. In 2006, he was inducted in the Chicago Gay and Lesbian Hall of Fame as a "Friend of the Community" (photo by Rex Wockner, *Outlines/ Windy City Times*).

10. Mayor Rich Daley sits with his mom "Sis" Daley and his brother Bill during the October 1999 dedication ceremonies for the Richard J. Daley Library at the University of Illinois at Chicago (AP Photo/Matt Ferguson).

11. Aerial photo of the runway of Meigs Field after Mayor Daley ordered its midnight destruction (AP Photo/Brian Kersey).

12. Rich Daley and Barack Obama eating lunch at Manny's Coffee Shop shortly before the ambitious Obama became only the third African American US senator in more than a hundred years (AP Photo /M. Spencer Green).

13. President George Bush celebrating his sixtieth birthday in July 2006 in Chicago with Rich Daley at Chicago Firehouse, one of the mayor's favorite restaurants (AP Photo/Pablo Martinez Monsivais).

14. These two photos show Chicago's evolution into a global city. The first (*A*) captures the intersection of Michigan Avenue and Monroe Street five years before the birth of Rich Daley and sixty-seven years prior to the opening of Millennium Park across the street from the intersection (IDOT_0_0_61, Illinois Department of Transportation

Chicago Traffic photographs, University of Illinois at Chicago Library, Special Collections). The second (B) is a 2006 aerial view of Millennium Park that shows why the park has become known as the physical manifestation of Chicago's transformation (photo by Hedrich Blessing).

15. This 1964 photo of Our Lady of Guadalupe Church on the south side of Chicago also gives a sense of how the city looked before its physical transformation. Next to the church is a wall painted, "Cleanliness Is Next to Godliness." The first mayor Daley actively supported the city's campaign for a cleaner Chicago. (JPCC_01_0060_0590_0021, James S. Parker Collection, University of Illinois at Chicago Library, Special Collections).

16. Obama White House Senior advisers David Axelrod and Valerie Jarrett spent formative portions of their careers in Chicago as advisers to Rich Daley, the long-term mayor of Chicago (AP Photo/Gerald Herbert).

17. Mayor Daley promoting the city's One Book, One Chicago program, which was launched in 2001. To his right is author Stuart Dybek whose collection *The Coast of Chicago* was a One Book, One Chicago selection (Chicago Public Library, Phil Miloitis, photographer).

18. In Copenhagen, Denmark, Mayor Daley pitches Chicago's bid for the 2016 Olympics in front of a backdrop of the Chicago skyline (AP Photo/Charles Dharapak, Pool).

19. Mayor Daley, his wife Maggie, and Patricia Maza-Pittsford, dean of the Consular Corps of Chicago, in 2010 (Chicago Sister Cities International).

20. Mayor Daley with Mayor-Elect Rahm Emanuel at an April 2011 White Sox game. The two men have known each other since the 1980s (AP Photo/Charles Rex Arbogast).

21. Alderman Ed Burke—Rich Daley's most important lifetime rival—during the mayor's last city council meeting (AP Photo/M. Spencer Green).

22. Mayor Rahm Emanuel in 2011 with US secretary of education, Arne Duncan, and Chicago Public Schools CEO, Jean-Claude Brizard. Emanuel appeared to be following Daley's political playbook in trying continually to improve the city's schools (AP Photo/Paul Beaty).

23. President Obama arriving at O'Hare International Airport, along with his chief of staff, Bill Daley, and his senior adviser, Valerie Jarrett. All three had grown up politically in Chicago during the more than two-decade reign of Mayor Rich Daley (AP Photo/Paul Beaty).

24. Mayor Daley as the grand marshal of the 2011 St. Patrick's Day Parade, along with his wife Maggie (Old St. Patrick's Church/Dean Battaglia).

25. Rich Daley and his family escorting the casket of Maggie Daley into Old St. Patrick's Church for a November 28, 2011, funeral ceremony (AP Photo/M. Spencer Green).

Daley said he felt a special kinship with Chirac because the leader had served as a mayor for eighteen years. "He is one who cares deeply about the issues that confront the world's urban centers. He understands that great nations are defined by great cities," explained Daley. Two weeks after the end of the 1996 Democratic National Convention, Chicago and Paris would become sister cities, and a French spokesperson would explain how the City of Light chose Chicago as its first American sister city: "President Chirac discovered Chicago and [became] convinced that Chicago is a very important city—a city with which Paris can share a number of experiences and develop business, government and cultural ties."

The day before the convention started at the end of August, Mayor Daley attended a "healing" ceremony with two thousand other people, including former protestors and radicals who had lived through the tumultuous 1968 convention in Chicago. Jesse Jackson, Tom Hayden, and Black Panther founder Bobby Seale also attended. "The challenges of today are just too great to spend time refighting the battles of the past," Daley said during his formal remarks. "I wanted to be here because I wanted you to know—however, unwelcome you were 28 years ago during a very troubling time in this country—you are welcome here today." Daley's words and presence at the ceremony were illustrative of the political approach that he had matured into in his fifties. He preferred to co-opt rivals and meet them half way rather than to prolong political fights. He did not want to repeat the mistakes of his father.

The 1996 Democratic National Convention in Chicago featured President Bill Clinton at the top of the ticket. Clinton was a natural, the greatest Democratic political talent of his generation. He was also a deeply flawed man who tended to overreach before correcting his mistakes. As the sitting president of the United States, Clinton held the powerful advantage of incumbency, but he and his party were still recovering from the tremendous political losses suffered during 1994. In those elections, Newt Gingrich had put together a conservative "Contract with America" platform that had helped the Republican Party capture the House of Representatives for the first time in forty years.

Between 1994 and 1996, the gifted Clinton had then helped his party to recover by supporting more moderate policies than other Democratic leaders, such as welfare reform and the North American Free Trade Agreement (NAFTA).

The political convention itself was largely uneventful. Unlike conventions of the past, no real decisions or substantive policy making occurred during late twentieth-century presidential nominating gatherings. The four-day event in Chicago was simply a good excuse for putting the faces of politicians on TV.

But the many social gatherings around town were popular events, attended by politicians, businesspeople, lobbyists, and reporters. These affairs included a Blue Jeans Bash, music concerts, VIP tours of the Chicago Bulls locker room, private parties hosted by Daley for big donors, and an extravaganza at Navy Pier for twenty-five thousand convention delegates and members of the press. The mayor's old friend Jack Sandner, now CEO of the Chicago Mercantile Exchange, let the California delegation use the Merc's trading floor for one political shindig. "If you embrace the idea of Chicago playing host to the convention, you have to embrace the responsibility. It's about showcasing the city," Sandner explained. Bill Daley, cochairman of Chicago's host committee, echoed the sentiment. "This convention is not about politics," the mayor's brother said. "It's about civic pride."

And so it was. As the 1996 Democratic convention faded into history, the Daley family had much to be proud of. Quality of life had improved for many Chicagoans, and the local economy was strong. Their city, Chicago, had shown well on the national stage. Young observers at the convention found Chicago an attractive and fun place to visit. But older, more seasoned political veterans left town with deeper insights into a place that they had known in their youth. The character of Daley's Chicago had changed. It was hard to put a finger on it, to explain it, but the city was somehow different and the change was fundamental. Chicago had become more beautiful than they remembered.

CHAPTER 14

HOUSING WITHOUT HOPE

Rich Daley's Chicago was more complicated than the picture presented to visitors and casual observers. A fifth of its citizens—more than 500,000 people—lived below the poverty line. Most of these were black Chicagoans living in south-side and west-side ghettos. Many of them lived in rundown apartments or homes, and more than seventy-five thousand survived in public housing high-rises that were broken down, filthy, and violent. "It's like the boys they run everything," said a female resident of Henry Horner Homes, in explaining how gangs controlled her west-side project near the Chicago Stadium. "You know, pulling guns out, putting them to people's heads, and all that type of stuff. . . . The kids can't come outside and play because everybody [is] fighting and shooting and selling drugs everywhere."

On May 30, 1995, the US Department of Housing and Urban Development (HUD) announced that it was taking over control and management of the Chicago Housing Authority (CHA). Over the years, public housing in Chicago had become dilapidated and dangerous and had helped to create some of the worst neighborhoods in the United States. Henry Cisneros, secretary of Housing and Urban Development, had briefed Mayor Daley on the impending takeover of the CHA. Daley was supportive of the plan for a number of reasons. First, Daley was an action-oriented leader. He preferred to plow ahead with plans to fix problems, rather than focusing on niceties that prevented some people from taking action. Second, Daley wanted Chicago to get the federal dollars that would come with a HUD takeover of the CHA. Third, the mayor of Chicago was in the process of taking over the public school system himself and he worried that this challenge would consume him and his team for the next few years. Finally, the HUD plan would solve a rather tricky political problem for Daley: getting rid of Vince Lane, the African-American who at the time ran the CHA. Lane was a former real estate developer who had brought innovative ideas to the dialogue on public housing. Despite Lane's management missteps, Daley worried that the charismatic black leader could become a political threat if he ever succeeded in turning around the CHA. So the planned HUD takeover of Chicago's housing projects satisfied Daley on a number of levels, and he gave it his support despite the political risks: his loss of control of the CHA and a possibility of rebellion by dissatisfied residents.

Daley had struggled with housing challenges and Chicago's poor neighborhoods since at least 1991. In that year, the mayor completed a sweeping reorganization of his administration, naming David Mosena his chief of staff and Valerie Jarrett as deputy chief of staff. The next year Jarrett became Daley's planning and development commissioner, a position that Mosena himself had held under Daley. Jarrett was a thirty-five-year-old African-American woman who had trained as a lawyer before working her way up the ladder in Harold Washington's and Rich Daley's mayoral administrations. She was a strong thinker who could be both direct and diplomatic at the same time.

Jarrett came from a notable legacy. She was the granddaughter of Robert R. Taylor, the former chairman of the CHA (1943–51) and the namesake of the Robert Taylor Homes on the south side of Chicago. Her father was the first African-American to receive tenure at the University of Chicago Medical School. Her mother, Barbara Bowman, was a national leader in early childhood education. Despite her feminine demeanor, Jarrett was in the process of becoming a sophisticated and tough player within Chicago's inner circles of political and business leadership.

One of Jarrett's early decisions during her Daley administration tenure seemed, at the time, inconsequential, but it would become historic in retrospect. Not just for Jarrett, but also for Daley and for the Democratic political establishment in Chicago and in Washington, DC. Jarrett interviewed a young black lawyer by the name of Michelle

Robinson who wanted to leave the prestigious law firm Sidley and Austin and pursue a career in public service. Jarrett liked Robinson and offered her a job as an attorney working for the City of Chicago. Robinson responded by making a very unusual request of Jarrett. She asked Jarrett to have dinner with her and her fiancé, Barack Obama, who had recently graduated Harvard as the first black president of the *Harvard Law Review*. Obama had reservations about his wife-to-be joining the Daley administration, and Robinson wanted Jarrett to talk through the issues with her and her fiancé. The three of them met at a restaurant called Café Le Loup and had a long conversation. Jarrett and Obama held similar worldviews, and "Barack felt extraordinarily familiar" to Daley's senior aide. Michelle Robinson accepted the job working for Jarrett, and the three soon became very close friends.

As Jarrett developed into an influential player in Chicago over the next ten years, she became the link between Chicago's white north-side elites and the city's black south-side leaders. Jarrett's bridge building and rising influence benefited Daley politically. But it would also become tremendously important to the personal and political rise of Barack and Michelle Obama.

"Valerie is the one," recalled Mike Strautmanis, a former colleague of Michelle Obama's at Sidley and Austin. "She was the one who led [Obama] to the black aristocracy. The lawyers. The business people. The politicians, even. And not only the black aristocracy but all the movers and shakers in Chicago. She invited them to Martha's Vineyard for vacation. She had dinner parties where she had all kinds of important people for Barack and Michelle to meet. She invited them to charity events, to sit on the boards of foundations."

But before Jarrett could help the Obamas begin their rise into influential Chicago circles, she first needed to handle the challenges that Daley set before her as his new commissioner of planning and development. One of the first arose because of a situation that had developed on the west side of Chicago shortly after Daley was elected mayor in 1989. Jerry Reinsdorf and Bill Wirtz—two very rich and powerful Chicago businessmen—had struck a deal to tear down the Chicago Stadium and replace it with a new sports arena. Reinsdorf was a likable real estate entrepreneur who owned the Chicago Bulls and Chicago White Sox. Wirtz was a stubborn liquor distributor who owned the Chicago Blackhawks hockey team. The political issue that developed from this deal was that the proposed sports arena would displace sixty black families whose homes would be demolished for the new United Center stadium. Local residents who organized to protest were led by Earnest Gates, a savvy, large-shouldered African-American business-man who had lived in the west-side neighborhood his entire life. Gates had already earned a reputation as a proven fighter for his community, having defeated a plan by the Chicago Bears to build a west-side sta-dium two years earlier.

Daley publicly took the side of the black residents and the west-side neighborhood. "The priority will be dealing with the people living there," the mayor said. "There has to be a strong commitment that there will be housing immediately for them." Daley's support of the minority residents differentiated him from his father and other previous Chicago mayors, who had tended to support white developers over black com-munities. Even Harold Washington had failed to provide much sup-port for Gates's west-side community when the Chicago Bears sought to build a stadium there in 1987.

Daley then put his political skills to work. First, he refused to meet with Reinsdorf and Wirtz, effectively forcing them to begin bargaining with Gates and his black community. Second, the mayor designated Tom Rosenberg, a close personal friend, as his representative in the negotiations. Rosenberg—who did not work for the City of Chicago in any official capacity—was a real estate developer who later had a highly successful career as a Hollywood movie producer.

Gates worried that the new United Center would push his neigh-bors out of the community, and he therefore insisted that the business-men build replacement housing before the new United Center stadium was constructed. The negotiations got off to a rough start and at one point the businessmen stopped talking to Gates for a year. Eventually, however, Reinsdorf realized that Gates was a man of integrity, and the parties agreed on a fourteen-point plan that included new housing, a youth center, and a computer lab. After Mayor Daley had a private conversation with Gates, the City of Chicago also agreed to build a park and a library and to make other infrastructure improvements on the west side.

Once Daley signed off on the deal between Gates and the business moguls, he instructed city officials to avoid the predictable bureaucratic slowdown and to facilitate the agreed on infrastructure work as quickly as possible. As head of the department of planning and development, most of the city's responsibilities on the west side fell to Valerie Jarrett. She soon put together a program called the Strategic Action Neighborhood Pilot Program (SNAPP) designed to focus various city departments on blighted neighborhoods. The west-side area near the proposed United Center stadium was the first area selected for funding by the program. As the program facilitated improvements in infrastructure, housing, and business, the hope was that private development would follow. "The idea of SNAPP is to make sure it creates a ripple effect for the broader community," explained Jarrett.

As Daley's commissioner of planning and development, Jarrett also worked to improve some of the south-side neighborhoods that were close to where she grew up. "I was just walking through the North Kenwood neighborhood last weekend, and the community looks totally different now than it did when I took over the position with the department," Jarrett recalled proudly. "We were able to entice some developers to go into depressed neighborhoods, to seeing how targeting and focusing city dollars early on leads to enormous private sector investing down the line is very satisfying."

In May of 1993, President Clinton proposed a federal program called empowerment zones that mirrored the Strategic Action Neighborhood Pilot Program's holistic approach to community development in inner city neighborhoods. The difference was that each empowerment zone would be in line for $100 million of federal funding. Mayor Daley wanted neighborhoods in Chicago designated an empowerment zone and he put Jarrett in charge of working with community groups and completing the federal application. Jarrett worked a grueling schedule, calmly dealing with the strong and divergent views on how Chicago should prioritize its development efforts. Two years after the start of the empowerment zone process—and even after President Clinton named Chicago one of the $100 million recipient cities—Jarrett struggled to keep the neighborhood groups, community activists, and local politicians in line for Daley. "We've had some rocky days. We've had some rocky meetings. People scream and yell," Jarrett said. "But I find solace in the fact that so far no one has walked away from the table."

By the time HUD took over the desperate CHA in May of 1995, Daley and his team had had some success in community development and affordable housing, but their cumulative track record was mixed. The west side of the city had received its new housing, library, park, and youth center, and there were promising signs of community revival in the depressed black neighborhood near the new United Center stadium. The City of Chicago was also in the process of largely following through on its 1993 commitment to spend $750 million over a five-year period to create and preserve forty thousand affordable housing units for low-income Chicagoans. But the city's public high-rises remained hopeless. Chicago still held some of the worst public housing in the nation.

Housing and Urban Development took over control of the CHA and installed Joseph Shuldiner, one of its own lieutenants, as the new CHA chairman. In announcing the takeover, Secretary of Housing Cisneros said, "The national system of public housing is on trial in Chicago." Shuldiner was a career professional in public housing and had previously run both the New York Housing Authority and the Los Angeles Housing Authority. His new position at the CHA would give him a unique place in history: he would become the only person ever to work with Mayor Daley in Chicago, Mayor Koch in New York and Mayor Bradley in Los Angeles. As he prepared to move to Chicago, Shuldiner quickly developed a friendship with Valerie Jarrett, who helped him find a home in Hyde Park and get his kids into the University of Chicago Laboratory School, one of the best private schools in the city.

But before Shuldiner could have much of a positive impact on the CHA, a new housing tragedy hit Chicago. In July of 1995, a heat wave struck the city and lasted five days. Temperatures rose into the hundreds, and at one point the heat index exceeded 120 degrees near Midway Airport. Over seven hundred Chicagoans died from the heat. Most of the victims were old and lived alone in black, low-income, high-crime neighborhoods. Dead bodies began to stack up at the morgue, a concrete building just south and west of the new United Center. The response by the City of Chicago was slow, primarily because it took Daley and his team a while to realize that the heat wave was more than just an unusual weather event. The excessively hot temperatures had triggered a rapid, but intense social crisis in Chicago, highlighting the need for more proactive city services and additional affordable housing. But the demands of running a city the size of Chicago were incessant, and when the heat wave ended the Daley administration largely moved on to other issues.

A few months later, Valerie Jarrett announced that she was leaving her city position and going to the Habitat Company as an executive vice president. The relationship between Daley and Jarrett had become frayed. As commissioner of planning and development, Jarrett's work schedule was relentless—nearly out of control—and she faced tremendous pressure from competing groups with access to the mayor. Tensions arose between Jarrett and Daley in part because they had different worldviews. Daley's perspective was anchored by his love of the city and his deeply ingrained sense that Chicago needed to be the best place on earth. He cared about the vitality and quality of life of Chicago, but he tended to focus on the city itself rather than individual people. Jarrett's worldview started from a different place. She saw Chicago and the United States as places within a vast world. Jarrett also had a greater appreciation for diversity of thought than Daley and she tended to focus more than the mayor did on helping specific people and communities. Despite these tensions, the mayor had deep respect for her ability to get things done. "She has been great in a tough job," Daley said. "You often have competing interests, developers, community groups and preservationists. It is not easy finding a balance that's good for the whole city, but Valerie has done it."

Within days of her resignation, Daley appointed Jarrett chairman of the board of the Chicago Transit Authority (CTA), an organization with more than ten thousand employees and a budget greater than $800 million. This high-profile, high-clout appointment—in addition to her executive position at the Habitat Company—signaled to Chicago's movers and shakers that Jarrett had become influential in her own right. The next year, her longtime colleague David Mosena would join her at the CTA as its president. Within five years of becoming chairman of the CTA, Jarrett would sit on more than ten corporate and philanthropic boards, entering the most elite echelon of Chicago's power circles.

In her new position at Habitat Company, Jarrett continued to play a leading role in Chicago's community development efforts. In 1987 a federal judge had appointed Habitat as the receiver for the development of scattered-site public housing in Chicago. This was an outgrowth of the famous *Gautreaux v. CHA* public-housing case. The original landmark decision had occurred in 1969, but the CHA had spent nearly two decades dragging its feet in order to avoid building new public housing in white neighborhoods. The essence of the legal ruling was that the CHA had engaged in decades of racial discrimination by only building public housing in black neighborhoods. Habitat's court-mandated job was to ensure that all new public-housing developments in Chicago were built to a smaller scale and in more diverse neighborhoods. In her new role, Jarrett continued to interact frequently with Mayor Daley and Joseph Shuldiner, the CHA chairman.

Shuldiner had a serious challenge on his hands. He not only was responsible for managing thirty thousand units of decrepit public housing, he also needed to stabilize the CHA's organization and to begin improving the deplorable living conditions of its residents. The CHA had not had a clean financial audit in three years, and the organization was in complete disarray. Shuldiner initially focused on correcting the audit problems and getting the agency's finances in order. He then began to work on reducing the size of the CHA bureaucracy and improving rent collection, security, maintenance and the CHA's Section 8 voucher program. Each of these represented a large—perhaps insurmountable—challenge, especially the voucher program for fourteen thousand families. The voucher plan was the federal government's major program for subsidizing the housing needs of low-income families. "The whole program was a joke," recalled Shuldiner. He privatized the Section 8 program of Chicago. An outside company computerized the program and managed it more efficiently. Over his four years as chairman, Shuldiner also reduced the CHA bureaucracy from forty-five hundred to twenty-seven hundred employees. This last accomplishment saved Mayor Daley from having to spend political capital to reform a dysfunctional organization.

Shuldiner worked to patch up the CHA, just as significant changes with respect to public housing were starting to take place at both the federal and local levels. Importantly, these transformations in policy and prejudice were the mirror image of what had occurred three decades earlier in Chicago. Back in the 1960s, flawed federal housing policy had encouraged cities such as Chicago to build large-scale public high-rises with fatal design defects and fill them up with extremely poor people. During the same era, the racist views of many white voters and politicians in Chicago contributed to the concentration of these huge public-housing projects in black neighborhoods. Flawed federal policy and local racism had become a fatal one-two combination for Chicago public housing in the 1960s. But in the mid-1990s, the trends were reversed. Federal housing policy began to discourage high-rises, preferring low-rise mixed-income housing that was more evenly distributed throughout neighborhoods. And the 1990s generation of Chicagoans did not have the same type of racial prejudices of their forefathers. According to Shuldiner, Rich Daley's leadership with regard to supporting black communities and improving race relations was "remarkable compared to mayors in other cities."

Visible changes in public housing started to occur in Chicago. In September of 1995, the CHA began demolishing high-rises at Cabrini-Green, the infamous north-side project where seven-year-old Dantrell Davis had been shot to death as he walked to school with his mom a few years earlier. On December 12, 1998, four dilapidated public high-rises at Thirty-Fifth Street on the south-side lakefront were imploded rather than repaired. In each of these cases, Shuldiner and Jarrett worked behind the scenes to support the removal of the high-rises. Each believed that Chicago needed to construct a more humane and sustainable public-housing model, and they knew that Daley felt the same way.

Out of the public eye, the new US Secretary of Housing Andrew Cuomo began pushing to return the CHA to local control. Cuomo was a second-generation politician with aspirations for higher public office and he worried about the political fallout—and injury to his own career—that might occur if HUD continued running the CHA. Mayor Daley was not quite ready to take it back, however. "Daley and I said that we willing to entertain the return of the housing authority to local control, but not without concessions," recalled Daley's commissioner of housing Julia Stasch. There were two primary issues: increased funding from the federal government and relaxation of some of Washington, DC's antiquated housing regulations. The negotiations proceeded slowly. Meanwhile, on February 23, 1999, Daley won his fourth term as mayor of Chicago, after securing nearly 72 percent of the vote and defeating Congressman Bobby Rush.

In the interim, Stasch and her team, which included the housing expert Andrew Mooney, spent nine months analyzing the state of the CHA and the living conditions of its residents. The verdict: an F. "The conclusion was that incremental improvement was not possible," said Stasch. "There was no amount of money that could keep these properties ahead of their deterioration. And the living experiences for people in those buildings were intolerable, and so that fed into our conclusion that the only thing possible was to reimagine or reinvent public housing in Chicago." Daley agreed with Stasch's conclusions. "If I don't take this on, then what am I mayor for?" he said to her.

But Daley was not eager to take back control of the CHA until HUD agreed to accept more flexible regulations and to commit more federal money. Even as negotiations with HUD continued, in April 1999 Daley made two big announcements. First, he named Stasch as his new chief of staff. Two days later he announced that the planned takeover of the CHA would be placed on hold until HUD agreed to give the CHA more autonomy and funding. Basically, he wanted to replicate the type of authority he received when he took over the Chicago Public Schools in 1995.

"It's not just money, it's a variety of issues," Daley explained when he put the CHA takeover on hold. "The way I took over education, if I took it over the old way [with a quasi-independent school board selected by outsiders], it'd be a disaster. You know that, everyone knows that. If you took over education with the old system, the old ways, we'd be still in the old ways in the old system. . . . You need latitude. If you don't have latitude and flexibility, it's very difficult [to succeed in transforming a large public agency such as the CHA]."

In naming Stasch to replace Forrest Claypool as chief of staff, Daley made her the first women to hold that position at city hall. Stasch was known as a smart, battle-tested administrator with a track record of success in both the public and private sectors. Her prior experience included senior executive positions at a real estate development firm, at a bank, and in the Clinton administration. Unlike many other of Daley's chiefs of staff, Stasch had career success outside of the world of government and politics and she did not need to rely on Daley for establishing her professional reputation.

"She's definitely no-nonsense," said Andrew Mooney. "One of her favorite expressions is, 'Cut to the chase.' And meetings don't go on forever. She'll start looking at her watch after 10 minutes. Her leg will start bouncing up and down. Then, she'll start wiggling in the chair and fooling around with the ring on her finger. You've got two minutes of pleasantries and five minutes to make your case. Then you'll hear what she thinks and you're out the door."

In June of 1999, the City of Chicago took back control of the CHA, and Daley appointed ten new board members, including Mooney, the community activist Earnest Gates, and Rahm Emanuel. Emanuel had returned to Chicago to work as an investment banker after serving as a senior adviser in the Clinton White House, and Daley welcomed him back by appointing him to the CHA board.

Just as Daley and Stasch started to work on fixing the CHA, the

Daley administration got hit with another potentially big political scandal. In July, a newspaper investigation revealed that a company called Windy City Maintenance had won nearly $100 million of city contracts and may have exploited a program designed to help women and minorities. The political issue was that the company was owned by the Duff family, a clan with longtime ties to organized labor, the mafia, and the Daley family. Federal investigators soon began to look into the allegations, while Daley's chief of staff Stasch later started a thorough review of the city's minority- and women-owned contracting program. Stasch believed in good government and she was willing to ruffle feathers to get to the bottom of the situation.

Despite the scandal, in September Daley's CHA announced a new initiative called the Plan for Transformation. Under this dramatic proposal, the CHA would completely remake public housing in Chicago. More than 60 percent of the housing authority's existing 29,300 family apartments would be demolished, and current residents would receive a housing voucher. All new public housing would be low-rise mixed-income communities. Residents would receive job training, counseling, and other assistance. The CHA would privatize the management of all of its housing developments, further reducing the CHA bureaucracy. Daley's Plan for Transformation, which relied on flexible federal housing rules and innovative financing strategies, was arguably the most aggressive public-housing plan in the country. "The mayor's commitment to actually do something radical was really pretty strong," recalled Stasch.

Daley's plan was not only radical, it was also risky. His bold vision included completely transforming communities, knocking down fifty high-rises, moving tens of thousands of low-income families around the city, and building fifteen thousand new family apartments. A big plan. But the Plan for Transformation was also politically dangerous. Many big-city mayors played it safe by throwing bones to the poor in the form of more social services. Daley was actually trying to improve their lives. But there were two big risks to this approach: the poor might revolt or the middle class might mutiny. A revolt of the poor would take shape if public-housing residents simply refused to move. A middle-class rebellion would entail higher income professionals criticizing the plan as offensive to their sensibilities and demanding that it stop.

But before the CHA and HUD finalized the legal agreements for the Plan for Transformation, the relationship between them began to sour. First, a CHA executive embarrassed the federal housing authority by revealing to reporters stocks of air conditioners that HUD had not used to help tenants. An angry HUD official fired off a fax to the CHA: "What kind of bullshit is this?" A second fax said, "Consider your deal canceled." There were other issues as well. Some at HUD felt that Daley wanted too much independent authority and that he was not giving tenants the opportunity to influence the reform plans.

Negotiations between HUD and the CHA failed to move forward until Daley and Rahm Emanuel began lobbying the White House. Emanuel had a tight relationship with President Clinton and, like Daley, was known for his bulldog persistence. Daley also personally lobbied Clinton in Chicago and at the World Economic Forum in Davos, Switzerland, where he was attending an economic forum. He told the president that he was tired of HUD's recalcitrance with respect to the regulatory and financing reforms sought by Chicago. "There was some pressure coming from the White House for HUD to figure out a way for Chicago to move forward and really attack its public-housing problems," recalled Stasch. By February of 2000, HUD had agreed to support Daley's plan, including helping to finance the necessary $1.5 billion cost. Rich Daley—just like his father—knew how to bring home the bacon from Washington, DC.

Two months later, the mayor was hospitalized at Northwestern Memorial with chest pains caused by fluctuating blood pressure, a condition that increases the risk of stroke or heart attack. Though the press speculated that stress caused the condition in the fifty-eight-year-old mayor, within days Daley was back to working his grueling schedule.

The rest of the year was marked by infighting between Stasch and other senior members of the Daley administration. Within six months, Stasch resigned. "I'm a demanding person. I am. I demand a lot. I work them hard. There's no doubt about that," said the mayor in explaining why he experienced so much turnover in his chiefs of staff.

Daley replaced Stasch with Sheila O'Grady, a protégée of Victor Reyes who had once run Daley's politics-focused intergovernmental affairs department. Reyes was himself a protégé of Tim Degnan, the mayor's original political fixer.

So perhaps Daley's explanation did not tell the whole story. With age and power, the mayor of Chicago had become so confident in his own ideas that he sometimes failed to listen and instead dismissed his subordinates' points of view. But Stasch was too talented and too independent to put up with behaviors that some people who grew up in Daley's shadow were willing to suffer.

And so the socially committed Stasch was no longer part of the Daley administration. Her departure left two Achilles's heels in city government: weakened management and lower integrity. Without her as chief of staff, the administration lacked a strong counterweight to the political operatives at the intergovernmental affairs department or well-connected lobbyists. A political culture soon threatened to take over Daley's city government.

As the mayor looked toward the future, the success or failure of his bold Plan for Transformation remained uncertain.

CHAPTER 15

BILL DALEY

While Rich Daley struggled to make Chicago a better city—in his mind, the best place on earth—his youngest brother Bill became a national political figure in his own right. After serving as the US Secretary of Commerce from 1997 to 2000, Bill Daley became chairman of Al Gore's campaign for the US Presidency.

On election night—November 7, 2000, at 4 o'clock in the morning—Chairman Daley walked out on stage at Gore's Nashville, Tennessee, campaign headquarters. The rowdy crowd of campaign workers cheered loudly at his appearance. Despite the late, late hour, Daley looked professional, like a corporate leader standing to address his annual shareholder meeting. Tailored grey suit. Conservative tie. Hair cut short, discretely deemphasizing his bare forehead and crown.

"I have some news to share with all of you tonight," said Daley as he raised his left hand to quiet the crowd. "And let me say that I have been in politics a very long time, but I don't think that there's *ever* been a night like this one. Just an hour or so ago, the TV networks called this race for Governor Bush. It now appears that their call was premature. . . . With 99 percent of the votes counted, it now appears that there is a margin of only about 1,200 votes out of millions cast, with over 5,000 votes left to be counted. . . . Under Florida state law, this triggers an automatic recount, and as everyone knows in America this race has come down to the State of Florida. Without being certain of the results in Florida, we simply cannot be certain of the results of this national election. Let me add that Vice President Gore and Senator Lieberman are fully prepared to concede and support Governor Bush if and when he is officially elected president. But this race is simply too close to call and until the recount is concluded and the results of Florida become official, our campaign continues."

The speech revealed to a national audience what many political insiders already knew about Bill Daley. He was calm. His perspective tended to be balanced. His projection of professionalism usually mirrored how he actually conducted himself in private.

Over the next five weeks, the Bush versus Gore postelection battle became one of the most extended periods of uncertainty in the history of American presidential contests. In the end, the US Supreme Court stopped the ballot recounting in Florida. Al Gore conceded the election for president of the United States to George Bush, a third-generation political heir. Though his candidate lost in 2000, Bill Daley maintained his reputation as one of the country's savviest political consiglieres.

But why talk about Bill Daley at all? The answer lies in the fact that he plays a critical, offstage-onstage role in his brother's story. Rich Daley's life is like an award-winning movie: filled with subtleties, subplots, and actions that are easy to misinterpret on the first viewing. Sometimes—as in the role of his brother Bill—the film needs to be rewound and watched again from a different perspective.

Bill Daley was born in 1948 and was the seventh child of Dick Daley, the last of America's big-city Bosses. He became a political junkie at an early age and was always more interested in the mechanics of elections—voter polls, demographic studies, get-out-the-vote operations—than was his older brother Rich. He also had a more gregarious, upbeat personality. His recollection about helping his brother run for the Illinois Constitutional Convention of 1970 was that the experience was "fun for us."

After this little victory, Daley stayed active in Chicago politics. In 1980, he and Jeremiah Joyce masterminded his brother's state's attorney election even though Mayor Jane Byrne and the entire local party supported Ed Burke in the Democratic primary. "Bill Daley is really, really smart," remembered one political operative from the 1980 election. "You've got to understand something—these guys, the Daleys—this is in their blood." This was true for Bill Daley. Elections—planning them, fighting them, winning them—was in his blood.

In 1983, Daley managed his brother's campaign for mayor of Chicago. It was like putting together a reunion: Let's get the gang back together and do what we used to do. Except that this time the Irish-Catholic boys from Bridgeport and the rest of the south side got booed off the stage. Their candidate placed third, a crushing defeat. The demographics and politics of the city had changed. Harold Washington became Chicago's first black mayor. Many people felt that maybe the Daleys were done, that maybe old dogs can't learn new tricks.

But Bill Daley did learn how the new game was played. "He was savvy about watching how things got done because he bothered to study it," remembered the longtime political journalist Bob Crawford. "And so he got very savvy in his own right. . . . [His] smarts really come from being politically street smart. And, of course, he and his brothers learned from the best one there was—their father. So they always had that savvy going for them. It wasn't an intellectual kind of skill. It was a political skill. And that's what helps them to survive." In 1984, Bill Daley joined the law firm Mayer Brown as a partner and agreed to help build the firm's government-relations practice. In his new role, he used his gregarious personality and political connections to build bridges to all of Chicago's power players: Ed Vrdolyak, Harold Washington, John Stroger, Ed Burke, and many, many others.

"When I became finance chairman [in the city council], Billy was by that time a lawyer over at Mayer Brown and I was helpful in getting Mayer Brown assignments for bond deals and that sort of stuff," remembered Ed Burke. "I am sure that Billy will tell you if you asked him that there wasn't anything that he needed—that I could help him with—from 1983 on, that I didn't step up and do it. My relationship with Billy Daley is probably a good deal closer than it is with Rich."

Like many other powerful Chicago politicians, Ed Burke felt the younger Daley was someone he could do business with. Billy was candid and would answer difficult questions directly. Billy was also a dealmaker—extroverted, pragmatic—a man with whom you could trade favors or find win-win situations.

Dan Rostenkowski also took a deep liking to Billy Daley. Though Daley was twenty years younger than Rostenkowski, the two men became close friends. Perhaps, it was their common history that originally brought them together.

Rostenkowski had grown up in Chicago's Thirty-Second Ward as a member of Saint Stanislaus Kostka Parish, the city's oldest Polish-Catholic church. His grandfather, Peter Rostenkowski, was a politically active businessman who made home loans and sold real estate insurance. His father Joseph Rostenkowski was a local politician who had served as alderman in the Democratic machine for twenty-four years. "Joe Rusty," as the latter was known, also took over his father's businesses and ran a popular tavern in the front part of his home. He was a well-liked local figure, known for providing jobs, helping his constituents, and supporting basketball and baseball teams in the neighborhood. Though he had a gruff demeanor, Rusty had a reputation for honesty, loyalty to his friends, and dedication to the Democratic Party.

In 1955, Joe Rusty's loyalty was tested. The Democratic machine supported Dick Daley in the mayoral primary. This put Rusty in a difficult position in his heavily Polish neighborhood, since one of the two other candidates was Benjamin Adamowski, a well-known Polish politician. But Rusty remained constant to the Democratic machine and supported Daley. His decision alienated many of the alderman's Polish supporters, and they voted him out of office after two decades of service.

Three years later, Rusty's son Dan ran for an open seat in the US Congress. Though he was only thirty years old, the younger Rostenkowski won. A major factor in his victory was the support of the elder Mayor Daley. "Loyalty was the heart of my Dad's support for Danny," recalled Bill Daley. "This was a nice guy and he was Joe's kid . . . and there was a big chit [that my Dad felt he needed to repay]."

Rostenkowski quickly became known as Mayor Daley's man in

Congress. Most weeks he spent three days in Washington—Tuesday, Wednesday, and Thursday—and then drove back to Chicago through the night so that he could meet with Mayor Daley in his office, give him an update, and receive his new marching orders. After just five years in Congress, in 1964 the thirty-six-year-old Rostenkowski received a seat on the powerful House Ways and Means Committee.

Rostenkowski soon became known as a political powerhouse—an arm-twister, a deal maker, and a vote counter—who could be relied on to deliver results. He preferred compromise and trading favors behind closed doors to delivering speeches in public. "As much as people criticize the back room, the dark room or the cigar or smoke-filled room," said Rostenkowski, "you get things done when you're not acting." No one ever accused Dan Rostenkowski of failing to be sincere or of not keeping his word.

Rostenkowski also became known for his sociability and his appreciation of food and drink. He spent decades cultivating relationships with Washington insiders at fancy restaurants such as Morton's in Georgetown, where his reserved table was known as "Rosty's Rotunda." The big-bodied, six-foot-two legislator would hold court over martinis and thick steaks, talking for hours into the night. Rostenkowski's gregariousness and ability to horse trade helped him to secure billions of federal dollars for his hometown Chicago, including $450 million for the John F. Kennedy Expressway and $4 billion for the Deep Tunnel project to keep sewage out of Lake Michigan. In 1981, he became chairman of the House Ways and Means Committee, the chief tax-writing and revenue-raising unit of the US Congress.

Three years later, Bill Daley had joined Mayer Brown. Daley represented corporate clients before his friend Chairman Rostenkowski and other members of Congress, and he spent a lot of time in Washington, DC. "When Bill was in Washington and you wanted to reach him, you didn't call Mayer Brown's Washington office, you called the chairman's office," remembered a Chicago political reporter.

"Bill is obviously not a lawyer whose strength is in drafting complex documents and arguing nuanced cases in appellate courts," said his law partner John Schmidt. "But the kind of work he was doing in representing companies that dealt with Rostenkowski requires a level of precision and intelligence. It's rare—the ability to know the difference between a conference committee amendment that was going to sail through and one that was going to trigger a reaction from some representative."

Even as he worked as a high-powered attorney, Daley also built up his standing within national Democratic circles. He accomplished this by getting in the game. In 1976 he had served as his father's liaison to the presidential campaign of Jimmy Carter. In 1980, Daley was again a key Midwestern strategist for the Democratic president. In 1984, Daley served as presidential candidate Walter Mondale's close adviser and national liaison with Democratic elected officials. In 1988, Daley held a similar position in the short-lived presidential bid of Delaware senator Joe Biden. In the same election, he advised Al Gore on his presidential bid and traveled as an adviser with Texas senator Lloyd Bentsen, the Democratic vice-presidential nominee. In 1992, he was chairman of Bill Clinton's presidential campaign in Illinois and helped to shape Clinton's strategy for recapturing the Catholic vote that Democrats had lost during the 1980s.

Through his efforts, Bill Daley had established a wide network of national contacts in the Democratic Party. In addition to Rostenkowski, Clinton, and Gore, Daley had political ties to former Democratic National Chairman Bob Strauss; US Senators Joe Biden, Lloyd Bentsen, Bill Bradley, Ted Kennedy, and Chuck Robb; and New York governor Mario Cuomo. Daley had also known the Reverend Jesse Jackson for decades.

When the Illinois Supreme Court ruled that the City of Chicago must hold a special election in 1989 to complete the term of the late Mayor Harold Washington, Bill Daley seriously considered running for mayor. He hired a political consultant to advise him and the *Chicago Sun-Times* reported that he was ready to run. However, the youngest Daley brother changed his mind when his older brother Rich told him that he planned to run again for mayor. Bill deferred to Rich, telling his brother that he would help him to regain their father's office.

According to Ned Kennan, Bill Daley "is a smart person who's able to see more than one side of a phenomenon. A person who is loyal to his brother while at the same time very much aware of his brother's deficiencies."

In his brother's 1989 campaign for mayor, Bill Daley presided over hiring and strategy. On the hiring front, he pushed much of the Bridgeport crowd into the background and brought in younger, smarter, more liberal advisers. David Wilhelm, whom he had met in Iowa during Joe Biden's presidential run, was named campaign manager. His young, liberal buddies—Rahm Emanuel and David Axelrod—were put in charge of fund-raising and media. Bill Daley also brought in Kennan—the brilliant psychologist who advised Jane Byrne of the rising tide of black voters in the 1983 election—to conduct focus groups. John Schmidt, his gifted law partner, was given a prominent role. On the strategic side, Daley established one absolute rule for the campaign: there would be no racial element whatsoever. His brother won. In 1991, Bill Daley directed his brother's mayoral reelection campaign, and Rich won again.

In 1991, Governor Bill Clinton of Arkansas would recruit two of Bill Daley's protégé's in his run for president of the United States: David Wilhelm as national campaign manager and Rahm Emanuel as campaign finance director. The then little-known Clinton would raise $71 million and win. In 1992, Wilhelm became the youngest ever chairman of the Democratic National Committee, and Bill Daley's name was floated as a possible Secretary of Transportation in Clinton's cabinet. Daley was passed over, but he remained on good terms with the Democratic president.

In 1993, Bill Daley received a phone call from President Clinton. He asked Daley to become special counselor to the president for the North American Free Trade Agreement, an accord with Mexico and Canada that the Bush administration had negotiated. Supporters of NAFTA, such as Clinton and Bush, believed that open economic borders between the countries would increase long-term economic prosperity in North America. Detractors, including labor unions and many Democratic legislators, thought that the treaty would cause job losses in the United States. This agreement needed ratification by the US House and Senate, and Clinton worried that he did not have enough votes to win its approval.

Daley accepted the president's offer and moved to Washington, DC, for three months. His friend Rahm Emanuel—now serving in Clinton's White House—helped Daley to set up a "war room" where the two politicos and their staff could manage the campaign for NAFTA approval. Daley was Mr. Outside. Emanuel was Mr. Inside. Very few members of the Clinton administration believed that NAFTA could pass, but Daley and Emanuel attacked the challenge relentlessly.

Bill Daley's friend Danny Rostenkowski became the key to success. The legislation ratifying NAFTA needed to come out of Danny's committee before the full Congress could vote on it. The Ways and Means chairman spent weeks cutting side deals with his fellow Representatives in order to get their vote on NAFTA. Billy and Danny worked closely together. Congressman David Bonior, a Democrat from Michigan who led the Congressional opposition to NAFTA, claimed that the pro-NAFTA team passed out $20 billion in special deals—such as local construction projects and contracts for military airplanes—in order to line up votes. The political strategist Don Rose believed that NAFTA passed because Daley had an "ability to find everybody's price." Many corporations also lobbied for the free trade agreement, which created a political counterweight to union opposition.

The trade agreement made it out of Rostenkowski's committee and passed in the House 234 to 200. Most Republicans were in favor and most Democrats opposed. But a win was a win. Bill Daley gave most of the credit for its passage to Rostenkowski and his ability to get the bill out of committee. But Vice President Gore gave Daley virtually 100 percent of the credit: "Nobody thought that we could get [NAFTA passed], but he was able to pull it out of the bag." The passage of NAFTA would go down in history as one of President Clinton's signature accomplishments.

Daley returned to Chicago and to practicing law at Mayer Brown. In 1994, he was named a cochair of the 1996 Democratic National Convention, which his protégé David Wilhelm had brought home to Chicago. Daley—a natural schmoozer and an experienced fund-raiser—helped the convention to raise $10 million in private-sector funds from the business community. "Rich has always been a loner. I'm not. I'm very different than that," said Daley. The 1996 convention was successful in showcasing Chicago. More important for Bill Daley and his brothers, the 1996 convention helped to diminish the memory of their father's disastrous 1968 Democratic convention.

In late 1996, Bill Daley received another phone call from President Clinton. This time the president asked him to serve as his Commerce Secretary, and Daley accepted. At the press conference announcing his appointment, Daley fainted and tumbled headfirst off of the stage. Deeply embarrassed, but without any serious injuries, he returned to the platform. "Public service often is demeaned and denigrated in these days, but I have a very different view," said the incoming Secretary of Commerce. "I come from a family in which we were taught by word and example there is no higher calling or greater trust."

By most accounts, Daley's three years in the cabinet were success-ful. He had a tight relationship with President Clinton, accompanying him on international trips, state dinners, and golf outings. As the US economy boomed, the Chicago native became known not only as a skilled politician but also as a talented manager and an effective envoy to the global business community.

When Bill Daley ended his term at the US Commerce Department, he was still in his early fifties and many believed that the youngest Da-ley brother would continue with his track record of accomplishments. Perhaps he would become White House chief of staff or a US senator. Or maybe even governor of Illinois.

PART 6

Pride Is the First Deadly Sin

CHAPTER 16

CROSSING THE RIVER

One day, a scorpion needed to cross a river, but he could not think of any way to make it. When he saw a frog sitting by the river's edge, he asked the green amphibian to help get him to the other side.

"Hellooo, Mr. Frog! Would you please give me a ride on your back across the river?"

"Mr. Scorpion, how do I know that if I help you, you won't kill me?"

"Because," the scorpion replied, "If I kill you, then I would die, too, since I cannot swim."

The frog was doubtful and wanted confirmation. "How do I know you will not just wait until we get to the other side and then kill me?" asked the frog.

"Once we are on the other side of the river, I will be so grateful for your help," answered the scorpion. This made sense to the frog, and he agreed to take the scorpion across the river.

The eight-legged, thin-tailed arachnid crawled onto the frog's back, and the frog slipped into the river. The cloudy, rushing water churned around them, but the frog paddled near the surface so that the scorpion would not drown. Near the opposite side of the river, the frog suddenly felt a sharp sting in his back. Out of the corner of his eye, he saw the scorpion remove the lethal stinger. Numbness quickly spread through his webbed feet.

"Why in heaven's name did you do that?" croaked the frog.

The scorpion shrugged. "I could not help myself. It is my nature."

CHAPTER 17

THE TWO FACES OF RICHIE DALEY

The new millennium appeared to reveal Rich Daley's vision of Chicago as a global city. But the mayor of Chicago had a dual nature and his own actions sometimes undercut or complicated his loftier goals. Daley could mingle farsighted, strategic leadership with raw political calculation and the cold-blooded exercise of power. During the first few years of the twenty-first century, his contradictory impulses led to mixed historical consequences for the city he loved.

The turn of the millennium started with a party in Chicago. Lois Weisberg and her department of cultural affairs put together a celebration for guests from 220 nations throughout the world. The festivities included a hundred official parties throughout the city, fireworks along Lake Michigan, and an international dinner. "The idea of the dinner is to promote people reaching out to one another globally and to demonstrate that Chicago is so diverse we really think we can match up every country in the world with someone here from that country," cultural commissioner Weisberg explained.

Three months later, Mayor Daley ordered the City of Chicago to begin construction of thirty-eight-thousand-square-foot rooftop garden on top of city hall. This decision was consistent with his personal preferences and his political instincts. There was something inherent in Daley's makeup that attracted him to nature—the more trees and plants, the better—and following a visit to Europe in 1998 the mayor had promised to make Chicago the greenest city in America. The idea was that the green roof would improve air quality and reduce the heat island effect that occurred in large cities. Daley also believed that city hall should become an example of green practices for private industry and that voters would approve of his environmental initiatives.

The following year, Daley scored another success for his vision of Chicago. In March of 2001, Midway Airport opened a new 678,000-square-foot terminal building that brought state-of-the-art amenities to the south-side facility. "It's going to be a radical change both in terms of the look and feel of the facility," said Thomas Walker, the city's commissioner of aviation. "We're more than tripling in size and adding a lot of new services and amenities that will have a significant effect on the surrounding community." After failing to win support for a third airport in Lake Calumet in the 1990s, Daley had supported the renovation and expansion of Midway. The mayor believed that the $761 million facelift of the airport, scheduled for completion in 2004, would serve as an economic catalyst for nearby neighborhoods. His department of aviation predicted that the annual economic impact of the facility would grow from $2.5 billion to $3.4 billion, bringing more jobs and vitality to the south side.

Even as the Midway expansion was christened, the world's largest aerospace firm Boeing Company initiated a search for a new corporate headquarters. The company had three finalists on its list by spring of 2001: Dallas, Denver, and Chicago. During the 1990s, Boeing had evolved from a Seattle-based maker of commercial airplanes to a global aerospace and defense company. With nearly two hundred thousand employees and $51 billion in revenue, the company did business with 145 countries and had operations in twenty-six US states. With its new global scope and character, the CEO of Boeing, Phil Condit, wanted its world headquarters to sit in a central location where its most senior executives could focus globally and strategically without being distracted by sharing a site with any one of its operating divisions.

Boeing had three primary criteria for selecting a new city: vibrancy of the business climate, air travel capabilities to both US and international cities, and quality of living for its executives. As a global company, Boeing knew that it would need to locate in a place where it could attract high-level talent to live and work.

The City of Chicago made a good first impression on John Warner, the senior executive who led the site evaluation process for Boeing. After e-mailing the mayors of Dallas, Denver, and Chicago to describe his company's relocation process, Warner received only one phone call the next day: Mayor Daley was on the line, along with the governor of Illinois. He told Warner that he would form a blue ribbon committee—chaired by John Madigan, the CEO of the Tribune Company—to convince him that Chicago was the right place for Boeing's world headquarters. "That was stunning to me that Daley did that," recalled Warner a decade later.

The Boeing team visited Chicago the next month. Warner, who had never been to the Midwestern city, brought along his wife, six senior executives and their spouses, and various advisers. The group used helicopters to visit potential corporate sites, in addition to schools and neighborhoods throughout the city and the surrounding suburbs.

On the second evening of the trip, Mayor Daley and John Madigan hosted a reception for Boeing at the Art Institute of Chicago. Sitting on the edge of Grant Park and housed in a Beaux-Arts building constructed for the World's Columbian Exposition of 1893, the Art Institute had become known for its striking collection of impressionist and postimpressionist art. Attendees at the event included the Boeing delegation, governor of Illinois George Ryan, and more than seventy business executives from Daley's blue-ribbon committee. Most of these business leaders were members of the Civic Committee of the Commercial Club of Chicago, a century-old organization composed of senior business leaders.

The reception at the Art Institute impressed Warner on two different levels. First, Mayor Daley and his team had done their homework on Boeing more thoroughly than the other finalist cities. Seated at the head table—in addition to Daley, Warner, Governor Ryan, and various business leaders—were the president of Northwestern University and the executive director of the Steppenwolf Theater. "We were big philanthropic supporters of education, arts and culture," remembered Warner. "They decided to put a variety of people at the head table. I was impressed with the research Daley's team had done." The second thing that left a deep imprint on Warner was the vibrancy of the business community in Chicago and the group's close connection to Mayor Daley. "The people who came to talk to the mayor knew him well," said

Warner. "They were friends—there were jokes, slapping each other on the back. And the interactions the business people had among themselves were similar. They really knew each other. The business culture in Chicago was very, very impressive to me." Warner also believed that Chicago had a high quality of life and excellent cultural attractions, such as the Lyric Opera and first-rate restaurants. "We fell absolutely in love with Chicago," said Warner in recalling how he and his wife grew to feel about the city.

Three weeks later, the CEO of Boeing chose Chicago over Dallas and Denver. The decision was kept secret until May 10 when Warner boarded a Boeing jet headed for Chicago. Mayor Daley agreed to meet Warner at Midway Airport with a large delegation and the Boeing plane circled the airport until the entire audience from Chicago had arrived. Warner kept his remarks brief. "I am glad to be back in Chicago," he said with a smile. The thrilled Mayor Daley gave longer remarks.

"Today's decision confirms to the world that Chicago is a great place to live, work, and do business," he said. "It tells the international business community that Chicago's economy is strong, that our leaders can work together to get things done, and that Chicago can meet the needs of any business in the world—from the largest to the smallest. . . . Boeing's decision reinforces what most of us already know: Chicago has a quality of life that is unmatched by any major city in the country."

Warner and his Boeing delegation toured their new world headquarters at 100 North Riverside Plaza and were thrilled to see the marquee of the Chicago Theatre roaring: "Chicago Wins! Welcome Boeing." Mayor Daley's office also called Charlie Trotter's restaurant and set up a dinner for the Boeing executives and part of the mayor's delegation.

Charlie Trotter's gourmet restaurant had opened in 1987—two years before Chicagoans had elected Rich Daley to his first term as mayor—in an inconspicuous two-story brick townhouse situated in the beautiful Lincoln Park neighborhood on the north side of the city. The world-famous, four-star restaurant was a short walk from DePaul University and upscale shopping boutiques. A self-taught chef, Trotter soon became Chicago's standard bearer for culinary excellence and a flawless dining experience. Trotter was known for cooking with light, creative sauces and fresh, organic ingredients, including a wide variety of exotic game. He was also known for his drive and relentless perfectionism.

The dinner at Trotter's started out front on Armitage Avenue with Mayor Daley, along with the chef's wife and mother, greeting the guests as they arrived at the restaurant. The party of forty were seated on the second floor, where they enjoyed an outstanding meal and Trotter's excellent wines. "We had one of the most wonderful meals I ever had," remembered Warner. "It was fantastic and the signed cookbook from Charlie Trotter's became the keepsake."

Over the next four months, Boeing and its contractors worked feverishly to ready its new headquarters for a September move. The top twelve floors of 100 Riverside Plaza needed to be gutted and rebuilt with new wiring and air conditioning. Chicago's business-friendly mayor assisted this construction process by ordering his permitting department to open an office inside the building. Warner also received frequent calls from Daley asking what else he could do to help the aerospace and defense company in its transition.

Following his success in bringing Boeing to Chicago, Daley soon began aggressively pushing for a modernization program at O'Hare Airport, one of the country's busiest and most congested transportation facilities. Despite serving more than 72 million passengers in 2000, O'Hare had not added a new runway since 1971. Daley's June 2001 proposal for O'Hare included adding one new runway and reconfiguring seven roads to improve airport efficiency.

The mayor's plan received immediate and enthusiastic support from the Civic Committee of the Commercial Club of Chicago. "We have been working for expansion of runway capacity at O'Hare for well over a decade," said Lester Crown, a billionaire executive and chair of the Civic Committee's aviation task force. "O'Hare is the economic engine of the region. The mayor's plan will position Chicago as the national and international aviation center of North America. It will add enormous value to the region, as well as hundreds of thousands of jobs. And it will reduce the delays that are so costly to our businesses and frustrating to air travelers."

"Chicago is known for making big plans—not little ones," added Eden Martin, president of the Civic Committee. "The Burnham Plan at the beginning of the last century was the great American urban plan, and it resulted in a physical transformation of Chicago. Mayor Daley's bold plan for O'Hare—if it is implemented—will occupy a similar place in the history of Chicago and Illinois."

Despite the strong support of the business community, the Republican governor of Illinois, George Ryan, objected to Daley's plan. Many Ryan supporters lived in the suburbs near O'Hare and did not want the additional flight traffic that would accompany a modernization of the airport. But after six months of negotiations, Daley and Ryan agreed to a compromise. The mayor's plan for O'Hare would proceed, but Ryan would get two things he wanted as well. First, the mayor agreed to leave open Meigs Field—a favorite private airport for prominent businessmen and Republican legislators—despite his well-known desire to turn it into a public park. Second, Daley also agreed to support a new airport in downstate Peotone, Illinois, fulfilling a longtime wish of many Illinois Republicans. A win-win deal between two savvy political veterans.

The month before the O'Hare modernization plan was finalized, Mayor Daley helped to bring a glass exhibit of the Seattle artist Dale Chihuly to the Garfield Park Conservatory on the west side of the city. Chihuly's colorful and creative glass installations were in the process of making him an international art celebrity. Daley reached out to John Warner at Boeing, who used the company's deep Seattle connections to convince Chihuly to exhibit in Chicago at the 4.5-acre glass-domed conservatory.

But Rich Daley's Chicago was not just about talented artists, economic development, sophisticated cuisine, and world-class corporations. Instead, both Daley and his city had twofold natures—like the two-faced Roman god Janus—that were capable of maintaining seeming contradictions simultaneously: culture and power; lofty aspiration and ruthlessness; the public good and unrestrained Machiavellian decision making. Daley's willingness to exercise raw political calculation was represented by, for example, his role in the rise of the politician Rod Blagojevich—a role that ultimately had negative historical consequences for his city and his state.

Five months after the start of the Chihuly exhibit, Mayor Daley agreed to serve as general chairman of Rod Blagojevich's campaign to become governor of Illinois. "I'll do anything Rod wants me to do. . . . I am lending my name and my support to him because I believe in what he stands for," Daley said at a crowded news conference at a downtown hotel. The mayor was breaking with his long-standing policy of not meddling in statewide political races. Though it was easy to see what attracted voters to Blagojevich—he combined a sunny disposition with the raw charisma that voters found irresistible—the motives of an experienced public official such as Daley seemed less defensible. The up-and-coming US Congressman was a natural politician who spent his free time relentlessly pursuing campaign donations. According to US Congresswoman Jan Schakowsky, when Blagojevich entered a room "there was this crackle of electricity. Everyone wanted to touch him."

Blagojevich was the son of an immigrant father from Serbia and a mother whose parents had emigrated from Bosnia. He grew up in Chicago in a five-bedroom apartment near Fullerton and Ashland Avenues in a gritty neighborhood. His father worked in various manual labor jobs and had a perpetually rosy, first-generation American outlook on life. When he worked at the steelmaker A. Finkl and Sons, Rade Blagojevich took his sons one August night to feel the heat of the furnaces. "This is how hard I work," he shouted in Serbian. "This is how hot it is here. You guys can choose to work like this. It's honorable work. You can make a good living. Or you can choose to be good in school and be a gentleman." Blagojevich's mother, Millie Govedarica Blagojevich, worked for twenty years as a CTA ticket taker. She was funny, practical, and in love with America. She introduced her sons to Elvis Presley, Clark Cable, John Wayne, Humphrey Bogart, and Jimmy Stewart.

Rod Blagojevich was a mediocre student. Like Rich Daley, his favorite activity in his childhood and adolescent years was playing basketball. But Blagojevich was also personable and ambitious. Despite his lack of intellectual firepower, he graduated from Northwestern University and Pepperdine Law School. He failed his first attempt at the Illinois bar exam, but passed it on the second try after studying seven days a week.

Blagojevich quickly entered the world of old-style Chicago Democratic politics. His first job after law school was as a clerk working in the law practice of Fast Eddie Vrdolyak. Within a couple of years, Blagojevich had used a neighborhood connection to secure a job in Rich Daley's Cook County state's attorney office prosecuting traffic cases. Blagojevich's trial partner, the attorney Curt James, recalled the impression that the young prosecutor made on him. "[He had] an ease with talking to everyone—judges, public defenders, victims, and defendants." Another traffic court prosecutor was similarly impressed. "You knew he was going places," said John Lagattuta. "He was a mover and shaker. He never stood still."

In 1988, Blagojevich was a thirty-one-year-old bachelor with his own small time law practice when he decided to attend a political fund-raiser for Alderman Dick Mell. The Thirty-Third Ward committeeman had held the office of alderman since 1975. Mell saw politics as a game of winners and losers, where the best strategy for winning usually involved cutting a deal. "Mell is interested in the game and winning the game, but he doesn't care for or against any particular policy," said Mike Ascaridis, a ward precinct captain.

The fund-raiser was held at Zum Deutschen Eck, a German restaurant on Southport Avenue in the Lakeview neighborhood. It contained a handcrafted bar made of solid oak, matching wooden doorway arches, and faded paintings of the German countryside. Waitresses wore Bayern dirndl skirts, and on weekends Zum Deutschen Eck was known for its festive sing-a-longs. The restaurant served Bavarian style food: Rahmschnitzel, sauerbraten, spaetzle, beef tenderloin à la Deutsch, roast duckling with red cabbage, wiener schnitzel, Bavarian apple strudel, and steins of beer.

Blagojevich slid easily into the fund-raiser, shaking hands and chatting with many of the attendees. One person to whom Blagojevich introduced himself was Bruce DuMont, a radio and TV personality with a political beat. After chit chatting for a while, Blagojevich asked, "Mr. DuMont, which one is Patti Mell?" DuMont pointed to the alderman's twenty-three-year-old daughter who had recently graduated from the University of Illinois. Blagojevich went over and introduced himself. Something about her attracted him. "If you go out with me, I'm going to show you the time of your life," he promised her during their conversation. Two years later, she married him.

Shortly after their wedding, Patti Blagojevich approached her father and asked: "You know, Rod has always wanted to run for some office—do you think it'll ever come up?" His daughter must have planted a seed with Mell because one Sunday evening in 1992 he called Blagojevich at home and asked him if he would be willing to run for the thirty-third district seat in the Illinois House of Representatives. Mell warned Blagojevich that he was unlikely to win. His opponent in the Democratic primary Myron Kulas had already served in the Illinois legislature for more than a decade. Kulas also had the backing of Mayor Daley, Congressman Dan Rostenkowski, and Ed Kelly, the Forty-Seventh Ward committeeman and a longtime machine politician. Blagojevich asked Mell if he could take his own positions on issues if he won the election. "I don't give a fuck about that," Mell replied. Blagojevich accepted.

During this first political campaign together, it quickly became clear that the team of Mell and Blagojevich was a potent combination. Mell provided campaign workers, fund-raising help, tactical advice, political introductions, and a personal driver to chauffer the candidate around the thirty-third district. Blagojevich turned out to be a master at retail campaigning. Full of energy and a natural gregariousness, he never tired of smiling, shaking hands, and connecting with new voters. Blagojevich rolled over Kulas in the 1992 Democratic primary, taking nearly two-thirds of the vote. Mell took to Blagojevich's boyish charm and began calling his son-in-law "the kid."

In the Illinois House of Representatives Blagojevich accomplished little but became known as an exceptionally personable representative. He attempted to position himself publicly as progressive by supporting gay rights and a woman's right to choose. He also advocated "good government" policies, even as he maintained his close political ties to Mell, a classic old-school Chicago politician.

In 1996, Blagojevich ran for the US Congress in the fifth district, a seat that Dan Rostenkowski vacated two years previously after having held it for thirty-six years. By this time, Mell and Blagojevich had had four years to improve their campaign recipe, but they knew that they needed to take their preparation up to the next level. Mell still brought political muscle—including Dominic Longo and his controversial Coalition for Better Government—as well as his own ceaseless wheeling and dealing. Blagojevich still possessed the physical energy and easy verbal fluidity of a political natural.

But two more ingredients were needed to win a Democratic race for US Congress in Illinois: the support of the mayor of Chicago and the guiding hand of an experienced media guru. In February of 1996, Daley broke his policy of neutrality in Democratic primaries and backed Blagojevich. Why did he do it? His press secretary Jim Williams tried to explain this rare public endorsement by the mayor: "Dick Mell is a longtime ally." But this weak answer fell short, since over the years Daley had regularly declined to endorse other longtime allies. The most powerful politician in Chicago was using his power and professional reputation to support the rise of the up-and-coming politician Blagojevich. Maybe Daley thought it was a two-for-one deal: if he helped Blagojevich, both Mell and his son-in-law would owe him. Or perhaps he had some other motive. One thing is clear, however: Daley did it to help himself.

The second ingredient also came together for Blagojevich. Daley's close adviser David Axelrod signed on as the media adviser to the congressional campaign. Axelrod liked the immigrant blue-collar roots of Blagojevich's family, as well as the candidate's American Dream political rise. He would air absorbing TV ads on Blagojevich that were seen throughout the congressional district.

Tensions soon arose among Mell, Blagojevich, and Axelrod. Mell and Axelrod fought about campaign tactics and strategy. Mell preferred an old-fashioned retail ground campaign, while Axelrod believed that

TV ads and media won congressional elections. Blagojevich and Mell fought about nearly everything and would alternate between screaming at each other and refusing to speak. Axelrod gradually began to worry that working with Blagojevich and Mell might start to hurt his good reputation. He even considered quitting the Blagojevich campaign.

But the team stayed together and Rod Blagojevich was elected to the US Congress. He had few accomplishments in his new office, just like his time in the Illinois legislature. One exception to this mediocrity was a trip he made to Yugoslavia in 1999 with Jesse Jackson where he used his Serbian language skills to help convince the Yugoslav president Slobodan Milosevic to free three American prisoners. Other than this one-off adventure and his efforts spent fund-raising, Blagojevich was bored most of his time in Washington. By 2001, he started conferring with Mell about running for governor of Illinois the next year.

One summer day in 2001, Blagojevich went jogging in his Ravenswood Manor neighborhood. Sitting two miles west of the lake on the north side of the city, Ravenswood Manor contains beautiful single-family homes, including many Victorian and Prairie School residences on extra-wide lots. As he jogged through the neighborhood, Blagojevich saw Rahm Emanuel playing on his front lawn with his kids. Blagojevich stopped to talk with Emanuel, and the two politicos soon turned to discussing their shared calling. Blagojevich told Emanuel that he planned on running for the office of governor.

"Who's going to run for Congress?" asked Emanuel.

"Rahm, you should run for my seat," came the reply.

After Blagojevich smiled and jogged away, Emanuel considered the idea. Smart and aggressive, he was working as an investment banker and serving as a CHA board member, but he had always wanted to win elected office for himself. This seemed like a ripe opportunity, and he knew that he needed to meet with Mayor Daley and seek his support.

Emanuel met with Daley and received his private blessing. The mayor later gave Emanuel a public endorsement and also cut a commercial for the first-time candidate. According to Chicago politicians, Emanuel's race for Congress would become the one time in his long career that Rich Daley went all out to help another politician. Unlike his calculated backing of Rod Blagojevich, Daley's support of Emanuel was based on genuine affinity and respect. "Rich was a big supporter of Rahm's, and he is very popular in that district," said Bill Daley. "The mayor was a strong, strong ally of Rahm's."

Word got around town in the right political circles, and Emanuel had no trouble raising money, securing endorsements, or recruiting campaign volunteers. His old friend David Axelrod advised him on political media and advertising, and a seasoned political operative managed Emanuel's campaign. The same operative would also manage Mayor Daley's next reelection campaign. Though neither Emanuel nor Daley ever admitted a connection, both politicians benefited from a militia of political mercenaries, including those controlled by the City of Chicago water department boss Don Tomczak.

As Emanuel geared up his campaign effort for Congress, so did the Democratic candidates for governor of Illinois. In August of 2001, much of the Chicago media speculation focused on whether Bill Daley would run for governor. Private polling conducted on behalf of the youngest Daley brother suggested that he had a good chance of winning the statewide political contest. The same polling also indicated that Bill Daley and his older brother Rich had distinct identities with voters and that the mayor of Chicago possessed some of the highest voter approval ratings of his career.

"Rich Daley is a very strong and established figure in Chicago and Illinois politics," said David Axelrod, a close confidant of both Daley brothers, "and I don't think that transient political events [such as his brother running for governor], even of this magnitude, are going to change that. It's based on people's long-standing observations of him as mayor."

Rich Daley then surprised some political observers by privately giving his younger brother the green light to run for governor. He also publicly rejected suggestions that another Daley in high political office would place too much power into the hands of one family. "He was secretary of commerce, and I didn't take over the United States," said the mayor dryly.

Important political allies of the mayor, however, publicly worried about the perpetuation of a Daley political dynasty in Illinois. "At some point, people begin to say, 'When is enough enough? How much can one person or one family control?'" asked Alderman Patrick O'Connor, one of Daley's close supporters in the Chicago City Council. "If that sentiment begins to take root, people will look at everything the mayor does through a different filter. But the mayor is in a tough place. All the years he's been in public life, his family has been behind him because it was what he wanted to do. If Bill chooses to do this, the mayor would have a difficult time saying, 'Don't do this. It's bad for me.'"

As the youngest Daley brother considered whether to run for governor, Alderman Dick Mell—Rod Blagojevich's father-in-law—threatened to "dirty up" Bill Daley with talk of his messy separation from his wife and his stint as president of Amalgamated Bank, a lending institution with long-time ties to Chicago's unions. After a few weeks of deliberation, Bill Daley withdrew from the race. "I'm not going to run. It's just not the right time," he said. "This has been a tough three weeks and a tough year. But after spending most of the last 20 years in politics, I think I need a break."

With a Daley out of the race, the Democratic field for governor of Illinois had three serious candidates left: Roland Burris, Paul Vallas, and Rod Blagojevich. Burris was an African-American and former Illinois Attorney General who had previously run unsuccessfully for governor in 1994 and 1998. In 1995, Burris had challenged Rich Daley for the office of mayor and had also lost that contest. But Burris had won nineteen out of fifty wards in the mayoral race, demonstrating his popularity with black voters in Chicago. Vallas had different credentials than Burris. He had served as CEO of the Chicago Public Schools, and many voters believed that he was both an effective public administrator and a good-hearted reformer.

Of the three candidates, Vallas seemed like the most logical choice for the mayor of Chicago to support. He had served Daley effectively for six years, and his efforts had strengthened the mayor's reputation as a progressive leader. In fact, according to Vallas, during the previous year Daley confidantes had urged Vallas to step down as CEO of CPS in order to run for governor.

Vallas would later come to believe that Daley and the mayor's political advisers had set him up to fail. "I just think it's ego. They're going to decide your future. You're not going to decide your own. They move people around like chess pieces. . . . This is how they get you out of the [Daley] administration. They ask you to run for a political office that they think you won't win."

Despite indirectly encouraging Vallas to run, Daley did not publicly support Vallas or any other candidate during the Democratic primary for governor. This political vacuum created by the mayor helped one candidate: Rod Blagojevich. Without Bill Daley in the race or Rich Daley openly supporting a political contestant, Blagojevich's campaign for governor had three built-in strengths: name recognition, money, and political muscle. Blagojevich was a popular US Congressman, and Dick Mell had already helped him to raise more than $3 million. He would go on to raise $7.5 million by the end of the Democratic primary. Blagojevich had also collected endorsements from some of the best vote-producing Democratic ward organizations, including those of Ed Burke, Bill Lipinski, Mell, and—just two days before voters went to the polls—John Daley, committeeman for the powerful south-side organization that the Daley family had controlled for fifty years. "We are extremely gratified for the support of John Daley and the people of the 11th Ward organization," said John Wyma, Blagojevich's political director. "We view it as a tremendous boost and help to our campaign." The only noticeable hiccup in Blagojevich's smooth campaign was that media maestro David Axelrod felt uncomfortable with the candidate and refused to join the election drive.

How did the Democratic primary for governor turn out in 2002? Blagojevich eked out a win by 25,000 votes in a state with 12.5 million people, despite losing the voting to Vallas in Chicago and most of the surrounding suburbs. Vallas may have beaten Blagojevich if Mayor Daley had helped him. An endorsement from Daley, as well as help with his political organization and fund-raising, may have not only transformed the Democratic primary but also changed the entire history of state-level politics in Illinois.

In the general election, Blagojevich spent another $16 million, bringing his gubernatorial campaign spending to more than $23 million. This money bought an avalanche of TV ads. He campaigned as a good government candidate—emphasizing the ongoing corruption indictment of the preceding Republican governor George Ryan—and beat his Republican opponent Jim Ryan by more than 250,000 votes. Blagojevich became the first Democratic governor of Illinois in twenty-six years. Rahm Emanuel and most other Illinois Democrats also won. Rich Daley's electoral predictions had turned out to be prescient. "It's going to be a Democratic year from top to bottom," the mayor of Chicago had said the day he warmly endorsed Blagojevich for governor.

A month after the Blagojevich victory, Daley announced in December 2002 that he would run for reelection and seek to win a fifth term in office as Chicago's mayor. His announcement erased speculation that he might retire due to the breast cancer diagnosis that Maggie Daley had received earlier in the year. Despite this family trauma, Daley still had a list of goals for himself and his city. "In the coming weeks I'll lay out the next steps to take to improve education, to make our communities safer and more affordable, and to bring greater hope and opportunities to those Chicagoans who have been left behind," said Daley.

He needn't have bothered. He won the election with 78.5 percent of the vote, crushing three little known politicians. An overwhelming and intoxicating victory. Daley was the undisputed king of Chicago.

But with Rich Daley, as with most men, there was some truth in the old adage that pride comes before the fall. Power and success—by their very nature—tend to corrupt human beings, just as the crashing waves of the ocean tend to break down rocks into sand. At a time when Daley took pride in his recent accomplishments and the renewed vigor of his beloved city, the new millennium began to expose the way in which unchecked power could cloud his judgment. Rich Daley was about to make one of the worst leadership mistakes of his entire career.

The planning started just a few weeks after Daley's landslide reelection victory. The mayor had private conversations with his new chief of staff Sheila O'Grady and a number of other close advisers about closing down Meigs Field Airport, the 3,900-foot runway on Northerly Island just east of downtown Chicago. Daley had first publicly suggested closing Meigs Field in 1994, the year after he and his wife moved nearby the small airstrip. In 1996, Daley had actually succeeded in closing the airport for a while, but the Republican governor and Republican-controlled legislature forced Daley to agree to keep it open until at least 2002. By 1998, the *Chicago Sun-Times* would describe Rich and Maggie Daley as "influential enemies" of Meigs Field. Acquaintances of the Daleys believed that they were bothered by the noise. Surprisingly, in 2001 Daley then cut a deal with another Republican governor to keep Meigs open to at least 2026 if Governor Ryan supported the mayor's O'Hare airport expansion plans.

But now that deal was out the window. Daley wanted the airport closed down and he was ready to take action.

During the last weekend in March, the mayor held a secret meeting with top aides to finalize a strategy designed to knock Meigs Field out of commission before any political opponent could muster defenses or counterattack his plan.

Daley ordered his lieutenants to begin the mission just before midnight on Sunday, March 30. The Chicago public would be sleeping. The city would be dark. The 10 o'clock news would be over. Demolition crews from a private firm—armed with a battalion of steam shovels and giant earthmovers—were told to show up at a secret rendezvous point.

Supervisors there that night then described the mission to the demolition crews and gave the workers strict instructions: "Turn over your cellular phones and pagers. You will get them back at the end of the operation." No one was allowed to leave.

Under cover of darkness, a police escort then chaperoned the demolition crew and the heavy-wheeled equipment as it rolled through downtown Chicago toward Lake Michigan and Meigs Field.

One precaution had already been taken to keep prying eyes from thwarting the mission: knocking out of commission a twenty-four-hour-a-day website camera operated by a pilots association—which enabled citizens to see Meigs Field in real time on the Internet—by shining a bright light at the camera lens.

On reaching Meigs Field, the demolition crew carved gigantic X-shaped gouges in the Lake Michigan airstrip. Each X went down over three feet into the concrete. Mayor Daley stayed up most of the night watching coverage of the Iraq war and waiting for a report back from his demolition crew. At 2 AM a city official phoned the Federal Aviation Administration (FAA) district office and left a message on a telephone answering machine notifying the federal government of the mayor's unilateral decommissioning of the fifty-six-year-old airport.

The next day the mayor said that he had shut down Meigs Field to protect Chicago from terrorist attacks. Later, Daley emphasized that he wanted to build a public park on the Northerly Island land.

Much of the public was outraged, however. "Mayor Daley bull-dozed his way into aviation history this morning by destroying a national treasure," said John Carr, president of the National Air Traffic Controllers Association. "Clearly, the mayor didn't think his policy choices could withstand the light of day." The FAA was also unhappy. It investigated the incident, fined the City of Chicago, and demanded the repayment of $1 million in federal airport development grants that were improperly diverted to destroy Meigs Field.

The destruction of Meigs Field by Daley raised the question of whether during the second half of his career he would become an autocratic ruler like his father. "Dictatorial decision making almost inevitably leads to very bad decisions," said Dick Simpson, a political scientist and former alderman, in commenting on the destruction of Meigs Field.

Jane Byrne, the retired mayor of Chicago, had an even harsher assessment of Daley's actions: "Primarily, I am appalled at the arrogant disregard of due process by whoever ordered the destruction. Due process of law, the most fundamental, precious constitutional right of all citizens, even Chicagoans, was purposely ignored. I say purposely because a few hours after the destruction, the administration stated that its irrational actions had 'prevented the issue from being tied up in the courts.' We are a nation governed by laws, not individuals, and no public servant has the right to place personal opinion or convenience before the laws."

Byrne and Daley had feuded for many years, and so it was easy to question the motives of her letter to the *Chicago Sun-Times*. But she was correct on the merits: Daley's midnight destruction of Meigs Field was indefensible, a complete violation of democratic norms and processes. A terrible break down in leadership had occurred.

And so the first few years of the new millennium had demonstrated the complexity of Daley. He was capable of ego-driven mistakes, as well as elevated leadership and self-serving political actions. What would he do next?

CHAPTER 18

MILLENNIUM PARK

Five years before the destruction of Meigs Field, Rich Daley had sat down with the architect Adrian Smith to review plans to convert the dead Illinois Central rail yard at the northwest corner of Grant Park into a parking garage and transportation center topped with tree-filled public gardens. Smith was a conservative architect and his plans drew on an out-of-date, nineteenth-century Beaux-Arts style. The mayor had no objection to the neoclassical architectural drawings because they mimicked Daniel Burnham's 1909 *Plan of Chicago*, which was an urban-planning talisman for Daley. The mayor focused on two other issues. First, he wanted to get rid of the eyesore in the middle of his city. Second, but importantly, he felt that the city should privatize the financing of the project to make it less costly and to limit any political pushback from voters. In addition to fees from the underground parking garage, Daley thought that he might solve the second problem by partnering with the private sector to pay for the plan's greenery, benches, and statues. Voters would then learn that the city paid for the heavy construction, while the private sector donated the pretty stuff.

The mayor remembered his conversation with John Bryan during the Democratic National Convention and asked the chief executive of Sara Lee to help him by soliciting $30 million from the business community and Chicago's wealthiest families. Daley was comfortable talking with Bryan. He had an easy smile, warm eyes, and a smooth, encouraging voice. The business executive liked the idea for a lakefront Millennium Park and felt that the request was a modest amount of money, and so he agreed to lend a hand to Daley's plan. The mayor eagerly announced the project in March 1998. "Every year, millions of people come to Grant Park to our festivals, gardens, and lakefront," said Daley. "Now they'll have another reason to come. The Lakefront Millennium Project will be free—a place for families and another destination for visitors which will generate convention and tourism jobs for people who live in Chicago's neighborhoods—all at no cost to taxpayers."

The story of Rich Daley and John Bryan and their Millennium Park drama is one worth recounting. World famous architects and artists, wealthy benefactors, and two cultured and persistent wives—each played a part as the media chorus sang its song of shortcomings and failure in the making. But, in life, there is always a story behind the story. A truth that is not widely known. Here, that veiled reality turned out to be a new period of civilizing Richie. Not politically—that had already occurred in the 1970s and 1980s—but aesthetically.

In order to understand the dramatic arc of Daley's continued personal evolution, it is important to know John Bryan, a complicated and compelling man. Bryan grew up in West Point, Mississippi, a small, racially segregated town. His family ran a meat-packing business, Bryan Foods, which was the largest employer in West Point. After graduating from college in the 1960s, Bryan joined the family business. Within two years, his father put the twenty-three-year-old Bryan in charge. "It was an accident of nepotism that led me to control a reasonably sized company at an early age," Bryan recalled frankly. "My father had more confidence in me than I was entitled to." The younger Bryan did not disappoint. Over the next eight years, he doubled Bryan Food's sales and increased profits tenfold before selling the company to Consolidated Foods, a Chicago-based conglomerate.

But Bryan also acted in surprising ways for a fifth-generation Mississippian. The young business owner desegregated his company, making cafeterias, restrooms, and professional jobs open to black employees. He also sent his children to a largely black grade school and personally paid for an integrated swimming pool for the Mississippi town. These progressive acts of leadership resulted from Bryan's social instinct for civil rights, but they deeply angered many of his West Point neighbors.

In 1974, Bryan moved his family to Chicago. Within ten months,

Consolidated Foods named the dynamic businessman as CEO of the $2 billion company. Though large, Consolidated Foods was an unfocused company with relatively low financial returns. Bryan pursued a three-step strategic plan. First, he sold off the company's low-performing business units. Then he focused on branded, nondurable goods, such as Hanes underwear and Jimmy Dean sausage, and changed the company's name to Sara Lee. Finally, Bryan took his traditional, Chicago-based company and focused it on global growth. "In the late 1980s and early 1990s, the world opened up to do business, so we internationalized the company," recalled Bryan. The strategy succeeded and by 1998 Sara Lee reached $20 billion in sales and had operations in over 50 countries around the world. "If you're going to have success over a twenty-five year period, you'd better be willing to change quite a lot," said Bryan in explaining his achievements as a leader.

Like the company he ran, Bryan also evolved personally between the 1970s and late 1990s. Though he had always been instinctively interested in the artistic part of life, he began to more actively cultivate his aesthetic sensibilities. In particular, Bryan became a sophisticated and discerning collector of impressionist and postimpressionist art—both for himself and for the Sara Lee corporate collection. "Growing up, I didn't have much association with the fine arts," recalled Bryan. "There weren't a lot of galleries or museums around for me to wander to. But I took to it very fast."

In 1998, Bryan announced that, as a gift for the new millennium, his company would donate pieces of rare art to forty museums throughout the world. Later that year, he went to the White House and accepted the National Medal of Arts award, one of the nation's highest cultural honors. "The arts enrich society in many ways," said Bryan. "Art is the grandest expression of our creativity and is our most lasting legacy."

Bryan's growing sophistication included a deepening appreciation of global culture. On multiple occasions, he chaired the World Economic Forum, a prestigious group of movers and shakers from business, politics, and universities that met in Davos, Switzerland. The forum was known for its forward-looking ideas and its focus on globalization.

In the early 1990s, Bryan invited Mayor Daley to go to Davos and attend the World Economic Forum with him. Davos is one of Europe's oldest mountain resorts, a scenic town on the east side of Switzerland near the Austrian border. In this idyllic setting, the five-day program was packed with lectures, discussions, and workshops. World leaders socialized and debated issues like European unification and global financial turmoil. According to Bryan, Daley loved meeting the mayors of other international cities. The forum was a transforming moment for Rich Daley, and it kindled in him a great enthusiasm for global cities and travel. He was like a kid who got excited and could not stop talking about his new passion.

Bryan's civic stature continued to grow in Chicago. In the late 1990s he agreed to lead a $100 million fund-raising effort for the Lyric Opera House and Chicago's Orchestra Hall. Due to his people skills and his intimate relationships with Chicago's chief executives and philanthropic families, he was ideally suited to this type of fund-raising. Bryan had an ability to get people to write big checks and feel good about it. One key to his aptitude was that he made donors feel part of an elite, super exclusive club. The second was his talent for communicating to check writers that their money was essential to creating something great that would be part of their personal legacy. Bryan called this "wrapping the civic cloak around the challenge."

Given Bryan's proven skill as a fund-raiser and the prior relationship between the civic leader and the mayor of Chicago, it was natural for Daley to call him in March 1998 and ask him to lead an effort to raise private donations for the building of Millennium Park. Bryan agreed and began to assemble a group of corporate executives to help him raise money. A majority of these original board members of Millennium Park, Inc., were Republicans who lived in the suburbs.

Daley soon added one more key member to the Millennium Park team: Ed Uhlir, a veteran park planner and architect. Uhlir had grown up in Chicago and attended its public schools before working for the Chicago Park District for twenty-five years. He brought design experience and project management skills to the challenge of creating a new park in downtown Chicago. More important, Uhlir was Daley's guy, a person with enough clout to keep the project moving forward.

The nucleus of the team was complete. Daley, Bryan, and Uhlir would work together, each bringing unique talents to the challenge. Under Daley, the city's cultural infrastructure had boomed in the 1990s, and voters knew that he genuinely loved parks. Importantly, the mayor also had enough power to protect the Millennium Park project from bureaucrats and political interference. Bryan brought his vision of creating a world-class development, as well as unique fund-raising skills. He insisted on recruiting the best global artists and designers in order to define Chicago to the world as a city where architecture, art, and design flourish. Uhlir possessed urban planning experience and a calm demeanor. He could translate the varying desires of the donors, architects, businessmen, and politicians.

A great team had come together, but the park's original design was seriously flawed. There were two major problems. First, its creative vision sprung from an out-of-date concept of a park as a place for green trees, sedate recreation, and a few neoclassical statues. Basically, a vision of an unlively place with few people. Second, the design itself had technical, financial, and timing problems. Completing it on budget and on time would be impossible. Over the next several years, Bryan and Uhlir helped Daley to try and solve these problems.

Bryan got off to a fast start with his fund-raising. Based on his prior experience, he established a two-part strategy, which Daley approved. First, he would approach wealthy families and only accept gifts of $1 million—the price of being in the club. Second, he would charge large corporations and the wealthiest families $5–15 million for naming rights. "Your legacy is going to be as a person who made something great happen," he would tell them. Left unsaid was that the naming rights were the equivalent of vanity license plates for the überwealthy. Yet enthusiasm did grow in the right social circles. Many of the affluent potential donors joined the art, garden, or architecture committees that Bryan set up. Others met privately with him.

One of the people that Bryan met with privately was Cindy Pritzker, a member of a wealthy family that owned the Hyatt empire of hotels, as well as real estate and manufacturing companies throughout the world. In the early twentieth century, the patriarch of the family,

A. N. Pritzker, had established the clan's initial riches through astute purchases of real estate and manufacturing companies. A century of investing and generous philanthropic giving by subsequent generations of Pritzkers had transformed the group into one of the leading civic families in Chicago. Cindy Pritzker herself had a track record of civic and cultural involvement. In the early 1990s she had played a leading role in the successful funding and construction of the Harold Washington Library, a grand red-brick structure in the south Loop area of downtown. Previously, in 1979, Cindy and her husband Jay had founded the Pritzker Prize in Architecture, the most prestigious award for achievement in the art of architecture.

The discussions between Bryan and Pritzker in the summer of 1998 focused on her family helping to fund the outdoor music pavilion at Millennium Park.

"It's a beautiful alliteration—the Pritzker Pavilion," Bryan said to her with a suave smile.

"Frank Gehry," Pritzker answered. "If he designs it, we'll pay for it."

Frank Gehry was an internationally known, award-winning architect who had already won the Pritzker Prize in Architecture when his name came up in conjunction with Millennium Park. His style—sculpture-like and funky—was known as post-structuralism, and many people loved it. When his Guggenheim Museum opened in Bilbao, Spain, the previous year, it became an immediate tourist destination, with one critic dubbing it "the greatest building of our time."

Cindy Pritzker greatly admired Gehry and his liberated architectural style. She also abhorred the original Beaux-Arts design that Adrian Smith and his team had put together. "I disliked everything about it," she would later admit. "It was completely traditional."

In Chicago civic circles, the opinion of the Pritzkers mattered. Cindy Pritzker had issued a challenge: if you want our $15 million donation, recruit Frank Gehry.

While Bryan and his fund-raising team contemplated how to meet the Pritzker challenge, Ed Uhlir quietly began to address some of the technical and financial flaws in Millennium Park's original design. The problem according to Uhlir was that Adrian Smith was "a high-rise architect who doesn't know anything about parks." Uhlir persuaded the Millennium Park heavyweights to move the proposed ice skating rink and public plaza to a prominent location along Michigan Avenue. He expanded the size of the restaurant that would become the Park Grill. He also began working with Bryan and others on a novel design for an underground music and dance theater that would not violate Grant Park's height restrictions. Mayor Daley was skeptical about putting a performing arts complex in the park. Uhlir and Bryan, however, kept hammering at it with the mayor until Daley conceded. These three changes eventually had enormous implications for the success of the park. Millions of people would come to Millennium Park in part because they found the revised park plan compelling. Uhlir also incorporated better accessibility and a proper fix of the old underground garage into the plans, leveling with Mayor Daley about the actual cost and timing implications his structural solutions would require. Daley agreed and was confident enough to take the political heat in the media for the resulting cost increases.

But what about Frank Gehry? Adrian Smith had previously telephoned Gehry and asked him to do a fish sculpture for the park. "No, I don't do fish sculptures," Gehry had told him. The busy architect had no problem turning down unattractive assignments.

In December of 1998, Uhlir and one of Bryan's fund-raisers left the cold shores of Lake Michigan and went on a secret mission to Gehry's house in Santa Monica, California. Their goal: convince the acclaimed architect to design the outdoor music pavilion for Millennium Park. Gehry's home—one of his first architectural triumphs—took a conventional suburban Californian design and deconstructed it into a more artistic, expressionistic visual presence.

The architect had white hair, a prominent nose and dark, piercing eyes. As Gehry listened, Uhlir laid out the site plans for the park on the brown wooden table and explained the project. Uhlir emphasized the unique downtown location, its historical importance, and its proximity to Lake Michigan. He offered Gehry a commission to design the music pavilion.

"Aw, come on," replied Gehry. "I don't want to do a band shell in the park. I don't want to come all the way to Chicago to design a little band shell."

"What's your idea?" asked Uhlir as they looked over the drawings.

"If you're going to do a music thing, you've got to make it substantial," answered Gehry. "If I'm going to do it, I'd like to design the relationship between the audience and the stage. That's a magical thing when it works."

"You can do that," agreed Uhlir with quiet enthusiasm while noticing that Gehry's intense eyes seemed to focus on a pedestrian bridge that snaked its way east over Columbus Drive.

"Are you interested in the bridge?" the Chicago native asked.

"I've never done a pedestrian bridge," answered the international architect, his eyebrows rising with interest.

"Frank, if you take the pavilion project, we will throw in the bridge," offered Uhlir. The fund-raiser who had accompanied Uhlir also jumped in the conversation to explain the willingness of the Pritzker family to underwrite the cost. Gehry agreed to accept the commission.

With Gehry and the Pritzkers onboard, the Millennium Park project had cachet. World-famous artists and wealthy benefactors would want to associate their names, talents, and money with the evolving endeavor. The art committee soon selected Anish Kapoor, an Indian-born British artist, to create public art for the park. Kapoor would design a silver, 150-ton sculpture shaped like a gigantic bean. Mayor Daley loved it. Chicagoans would as well. When installed at Millennium Park, the sculpture's sinuous, mirror-like surface reflected visitor's faces along with the Chicago skyline. The urge to take photographs with the massive silver bean became irresistible for both tourists and natives.

The second major piece of public art—which would come to be known as Crown Fountain—also would draw engaged visitors to the park. It is unlikely that these sightseers knew the story of the Crown family: the original patriarch had supposedly completed real estate deals with Jacob Arvey, the machine boss who had mentored Dick Daley. A hundred years of business savvy and liberal philanthropic giving had transformed the Crowns into one of the leading civic families in

Chicago. History did not matter to the sightseers, however. Like the visually stunning "Bean," the colossal Crown Fountain would become a hit with park visitors. They flock to the two fifty-foot tall black glass towers—designed by the Spanish artist Jaume Plensa—that display digital video images of the faces of Chicagoans. In the summer, children splash and shout in the fountain's shallow pool. Smiling adults wade in and snap photos of their children.

The fountain's success remained off in the future, however, and it took a long time for Rich Daley to get comfortable with its sleek interactive design. The mayor did not understand video art and he wanted more trees—*more green, more green* was an urge that sprang from deep within Daley's DNA—to surround the imposing vertical monuments. But John Bryan liked the originality and playfulness of the Crown Fountain design, and he persisted in convincing the mayor to accept it.

Bryan also had another challenge on his desk: convincing Daley not to cancel the pedestrian bridge that Frank Gehry had designed. At Millennium Park planning sessions the mayor had gotten in the habit of taking out his pen and putting an *X* through Gehry's snake-like ambulatory overpass. "No bridge," he would order. Daley's dislike of the bridge was based on his personal tastes at that time in his life. He tended to prefer more traditional, formal designs. The bridge—like most of Gehry's designs—was contemporary, expressionistic.

Bryan had already lined up BP Oil as the bridge's corporate sponsor, and he wanted to prevail on Daley to keep the feature in the park. He therefore invited the mayor and his wife Maggie Daley to return to Davos, Switzerland, and the World Economic Forum. The luxurious private jet carried just two couples, the Daleys and the Bryans. The retired business executive sat near Daley's wife and quietly showed her Gehry's plans for the bridge. Sitting with perfect posture and a warm smile, Maggie listened and nodded her head. She was a cultured woman with good aesthetic sensibilities and she told Bryan that she liked the bridge design. Pleased, Bryan then sat down with the mayor and showed him the plans. Daley frowned and gave the executive a cool reception. Rich Daley was a man who betrays his emotions easily, and he unequivocally did not want to build the bridge in Millennium Park. "John, I'm afraid you're just Gehry-izing the park," said Daley. A few weeks later, construction of the bridge was officially put on hold.

Bryan, however, did not give up. Some time later, he invited Rich and Maggie Daley to visit Crab Tree Farm, the gentleman's estate that he and his wife owned in the suburbs thirty-five miles north of downtown Chicago. The idyllic eleven-acre property was home to swans and sheep, as well as Bryan's world-class collection of arts-and-crafts furniture and other decorative pieces. Its flowering trees and cultivated plants painted the landscape white, pink, and green. Exactly the sort of setting where Daley would be most relaxed.

Through Maggie, the mayor understood that the social visit was somehow tied to Gehry's bridge. The couples barely touched on the subject, however. Instead, they strolled on the grounds of the farm, bantering about the crab trees, the animals, the barn, and the blooming colors. They shared a lovely meal and admired the decorative furniture. After the day was over and the Daleys prepared to depart, the mayor turned toward Bryan and said, "Oh, go ahead and build the goddamned thing." Bryan smiled. Chicago would have the only Frank Gehry–designed bridge in the world.

The city had continued its cultural surge during the more than five years that it took to plan and construct Millennium Park, and popular culture boomed as well. Oprah Winfrey maintained her dominance of daytime television, and her warm and authentic show still brought thousands upon thousands of tourists to Harpo Studios on the west side of the city. In the summer of 1999, Chicago hosted its Cows on Parade exhibit—a highly successful display of public art. Three hundred colorfully painted, life-size cows lined sidewalks, street medians, parks, and lobbies. Some even appeared to be walking up the sides of buildings. Tourists and Chicagoans alike loved the lively, ubiquitous cows. "The cows are such a surprise," said Lois Weisberg, the commissioner of Cultural Affairs who had given her creative blessing to the project. "You smile. Then you want to talk to somebody about them. Then you want to touch them." Colorful cows as public art were fun, and the mayor's city seemed to be morphing into a fun and artsy place.

The city's cultural transformation during Daley's first fifteen years in office also had deeper implications. First, its cultural infrastructure had boomed. In addition to building Millennium Park, the city renovated the Museum Campus, Navy Pier, and Soldier Field, while private institutions had built, rebuilt, or expanded the Museum of Contemporary Art, Chicago Shakespeare Theater, Lookingglass Theatre, Goodman Theatre, Civic Opera House, Chicago Orchestra Hall, and the Notebaert Nature Museum. The Art Institute of Chicago was in the process of raising more than $400 million—with the help of John Bryan—to add a Modern Wing designed by the world-renowned Italian architect Renzo Piano. The Modern Wing would connect to Millennium Park via another visually striking pedestrian bridge. Second, but just as important, Chicago's cultural zeitgeist had also changed. It had not only become more fun, but also more sophisticated—a place where both high and low arts flourished. Rich Daley deserved much of the credit for this cultural renaissance in Chicago. "If you look at Daley's leadership and start to put that in perspective of the last 150 years of Chicago history," explained Bryan, "the cultural infrastructure has boomed like it never has. Every cultural institution is better off—has built new facilities, introduced new programs and has creative initiatives going on. It's an environment that Daley established and it's a unique relationship [with the cultural part of Chicago]."

Daley's string of cultural successes continued with the opening of Millennium Park in July 2004—four years late and more than $300 million over the original budget—to rave reviews. The *Financial Times* described it as "an extraordinary public park that is set to create new iconic images of the city." It also called Millennium Park "a genuinely 21st-century interactive park [that] could trigger a new way of thinking about public outdoor spaces." Chicagoans, as well as architectural critics, agreed. Three million visitors came to Millennium Park in its first year, and some critics considered the park to be the city's most important cultural accomplishment since the World's Columbian Exposition of 1893.

Urban experts began describing the Millennium Park effect, the project's multibillion dollar positive impact on tourism and real estate development. The most visible example of this effect was Trump Tower, a ninety-two-story skyscraper that rose down the street from the new park and Lois Weisberg's Chicago Cultural Center. Trump Tower was the tallest new building in Chicago since the opening of the Sears Tower during the first Mayor Daley's tenure in the 1970s.

Millennium Park reflected Rich Daley's continuing dramatic personal evolution, as well as his innate genius for urban planning. According to Paul Vallas, who worked in the Daley administration for eleven years: "Really, in many respects, he is an urban planner— the consummate urban planner. I also felt that this was his greatest strength: he really understands quality-of-life issues. He was always at his best when he was in the urban-planning phase. He really has a vision for what a modern city should be like." During his first fifteen years in office, Daley physically transformed downtown and the lakefront, while also cultivating an aesthetic sensibility that focused on constantly improving urban quality of life. Millennium Park was the capstone of this achievement, but the process had started shortly after Daley took office in 1989.

The year following Daley's success at Millennium Park, *Time Magazine* named him as one of the best big-city mayors in the United States, writing that many experts considered him the nation's top urban executive. In describing his accomplishments, *Time* noted that Daley "professionalized the city by hiring skilled managers and burnished its business-friendly image by strengthening connections to global firms like Boeing" and that he also "presided over the city's transition from graying hub to vibrant boomtown." The mayor of Chicago was on a roll.

CHAPTER 19

CORRUPTION TAX

But Rich Daley's Chicago was more byzantine than the image portrayed to readers of *Time* magazine. Beneath its civilized surface, the city by the lake contained hustlers and hucksters, money grubbers and power worshippers. In its heart of hearts, Chicago was still a city on the make. Just three months after the opening of Millennium Park, federal prosecutors announced criminal charges against two bribe-taking city officials in an investigation that would become known as the Hired Truck Scandal. "I never cease to be amazed at the level of corruption in this city," said Thomas Kneir, the outgoing leader of the FBI's Chicago office. During the next two years scandal after scandal would unfold, many of which involved Bridgeport natives or other south-siders. These repeated criminal stains deepened the incredulity of many Chicagoans, leading some to wonder if the trail of corruption would lead to the highest levels of government.

The Hired Truck Scandal had first surfaced nine months earlier when the *Chicago Sun-Times* began to print its "Clout on Wheels" special report on corruption in city government. The January 2004 investigative series exposed how the city spent $40 million a year to pay private trucking companies to do little or no work. Many of the private companies had ties to Chicago politicians, including Base Trucking, a company certified by the city as owned and operated by women. The company—which raked in more than $3.6 million beginning in 1999 from the Hired Truck Program —was registered in the names of the wives of two men who helped to run Ed Burke's Fourteenth Ward political operation. Within days of the "Clout on Wheels" articles, the FBI had arrested Angelo Torres, a former gang member who ran the

Hired Truck Program for five years. Torres had close ties to the Hispanic Democratic Organization.

The *Sun-Times* exposé also revealed that three of the largest companies in the Hired Truck Program obtained insurance from the mayor's brother, Cook County Commissioner John Daley, who ran Daley Insurance Brokerage in Bridgeport. His insurance business at 3530 South Halsted was conveniently located just a block down the street from the Eleventh Ward Democratic headquarters, an organization John Daley controlled as committeeman.

Mayor Daley seemed contrite when the Hired Truck Scandal initially hit the news waves. "I am embarrassed," said Daley in his first public comments. "I'm angry, and I'm disappointed because I feel I have let the people down. I am responsible for everything that happens in city government. . . . When problems occur and change is needed, it is my responsibility to ensure that it is complete. In the case of the Hired Truck Program, that did not happen, and, for that, I apologize."

Within weeks, however, Daley was defending Angelo Torres and the Hired Truck Program, saying that the former gang member had worked his way up through city government and "did a good job at the beginning." Daley also reacted angrily to the charge by Alderman Dick Mell that the Hispanic Democratic Organization had an out-of-control influence over city hall hiring. "They don't have any undue influence over anyone," asserted Daley.

When all the dust from the political scandal had settled, Mell's claim turned out to be true. The Hispanic Democratic Organization did have an out-of-control influence at Daley's city hall. Unfortunately, during the first decade of the twenty-first century many other things were also out of control in city government. The Hired Truck Scandal grew and grew to include businessmen from Bridgeport, individuals with mafia ties, members of the Daley extended family, political mercenaries working at city jobs, John Daley's Eleventh Ward organization, and corrupt public officials. Patrick Fitzgerald—a tough federal prosecutor with no ties to the Chicago political establishment—charged forty-nine people with crimes, including bribery, fraud, making false statements, and obstruction of justice. Forty-eight of the criminal defendants were convicted. One—a city employee with mafia and political connections—died bizarrely in a horse-riding accident.

The Jardine Water Filtration plant sat in Lake Michigan, just a half mile east of the Magnificent Mile shopping district. Immediately to the south was Navy Pier, a destination site for millions of visitors who rode its Ferris wheel, visited its IMAX theater, ate, shopped, and played miniature golf. Some of these sightseers looked north and wondered about the enormous, heavily-guarded Jardine plant and its manicured lawns. Nearly one billion gallons of water were processed at the plant each day. The water originated several miles offshore and was brought to Jardine by a pipeline under the bed of Lake Michigan. Jardine's water was used by five million people in Chicago and the suburbs for drinking, bathing, and irrigating lawns and gardens.

The Jardine plant contained the office of Don Tomczak, the first deputy commissioner of the water department. Tomczak was an old-fashioned Chicago operator, a throwback—tough, with a streak of meanness—to a time when hardball was the way politics was played in the city. To reach his office, Tomczak passed by guardhouses and security gates before driving down a winding road and parking his car near the filtration plant. Tomczak walked past the control, the lift pump, and the chlorine rooms as he made his way to grated metal stairs. Up these steps on the top floor was the administrative portion of the facility where Tomczak's large office sat at the end of a long hallway.

Many politically connected businessmen and city workers interested in the Hired Truck Program wanted to get into Tomczak's office and seek his favor. Few did. Instead, Tomczak usually sent one of his bagmen, including the director of finance for the water department, Gerald Wesolowski, to meet with prospective Hired Truck providers and accept bribes from them. These secret meetings occurred in coffee shops, restaurants, and a Mercury Cougar automobile. The bribes included cash, gift certificates, steaks, and free meals. Much of the booty went to Tomczak.

At least one person would meet directly with Tomczak at his office:

John Cannatello from GNA Trucking. The reason that Cannatello received this special treatment was that he had clout: the Cannatellos had Bridgeport roots and went way back with the Daley family. His father, Ross Cannatello, had worked for the city water department and was in charge of hiring private trucks during the reign of Dick Daley. John Cannatello himself was a city truck driver early on in his career.

GNA was registered as a women-owned business, but was actually run by Cannatello. GNA took in more than $6 million through the Hired Truck Program from 1997 to 2003 and another $800,000 from leasing other equipment to the city under a program restricted to businesses owned by women or minorities. The City of Chicago was its only customer.

GNA and the Cannatello family had numerous ties to John Daley, including the purchase of insurance from his Daley Insurance Brokerage in Bridgeport. GNA Trucking was also located in Bridgeport, just down the street from the insurance brokerage and the Eleventh Ward Democratic headquarters. The Cannatellos—who, in addition, gave thousands of dollars to political funds controlled by John Daley—both had low-stress side jobs working for Cook County, among whose commissioners was John Daley. As a result of the Hired Truck investigation, John Cannatello went to jail and his wife was sentenced to two years of probation.

Even as the scandals in Daley's city government continued to grow, the mayor focused on increasing the city's revenues. The reason for this was that Chicago city government had a serious financial problem, though few recognized it at the time. There were at least five forces underlying the city's financial predicament. First, Daley's government lacked financial discipline and produced revenue estimates based on wishful thinking. This was not always the case during Daley's reign and—like a prize fighter past his prime—may have been the result of a softness that he developed after fifteen years at the top. Second, as demonstrated by the Hired Truck Scandal, the City of Chicago wasted millions of dollars a year on corrupt, fraudulent programs. The University of Illinois at Chicago Department of Political Science estimated that these type of activities cost Chicago and Illinois taxpayers $500 million a year. In Chicago, corruption had become a "tax" without any corresponding value: good money flushed down the drain. Third, the city developed an operating deficit in 2002 and this deficit persisted and increased. Again, this was the result of a lack of discipline. Though the city started to reduce its bloated workforce of nearly thirty-nine thousand employees, it had not made deep-enough spending cuts. Fourth, the pensions of more than fifty thousand current and former fire, police, and municipal employees were underfunded by $5.4 billion and the teachers' pension fund was also nearly $1 billion in the hole. These were ticking time bombs waiting to explode. Finally, the City of Chicago—unlike other big cities such as New York—had failed to set aside "rainy day" reserve funds.

Who was responsible for this fiscal imprudence? Rich Daley, the mayor of Chicago. Ed Burke—who still had his city-paid $500,000 a year bodyguard detail and $1.3 million slush fund as chair of the finance committee—also deserved some of the culpability. In his leadership role, Burke had failed to exert a legislative check on the budgeting and spending policies of the Daley administration. In this respect, they both had failed.

But then a gift arrived, as if wrapped in a holiday bow. In October 2004, the city received a $1.8 billion offer to privatize the Chicago Skyway, a 7.8-mile toll road connecting Chicago to northwest Indiana. The Skyway, which was originally built in 1958, had long been a financial problem for the city. Now an international joint venture had offered $1.8 billion to take it off the city's hands. Mayor Daley was thrilled. He recruited John Schmidt, his former chief of staff and an excellent corporate attorney, to advise him. Schmidt proceeded to structure the Skyway deal in a thoughtful, conservative manner. The city used $855 million of the transaction proceeds to pay down debt. The rest of the money went to a variety of programs and so-called reserve funds. Everyone in the mayor's circle was elated, but the high would not last forever. And like any powerful buzz, there now was a risk that this first big privatization deal would create a long-term addiction. The city's need for more revenue would only grow.

A month after the Chicago Skyway deal closed in January 2005, the Chicago Park District awarded a twenty-year lease to run an upscale restaurant at Millennium Park to a group controlled by Matthew O'Malley, a restaurateur whose establishments were frequented by Mayor Daley. The park district awarded the concession to O'Malley's group even though it submitted the least lucrative of three bids. As part of its deal with the park district, the O'Malley group would get free water, gas, and garbage pickup at Park Grill, its Millennium Park restaurant. Among the eighty investors in the Park Grill were friends and neighbors of Mayor Daley, including relatives of Daley's political adviser Tim Degnan.

Three months later, businessman James Duff was sentenced to nearly ten years in prison for a fraud scheme against the City of Chicago. The Duff family, of course, had longtime ties to the Daley family. Patriarch Jack Duff Jr. had worked for the City of Chicago before becoming a tavern owner and union boss. A charming man with a warm singing voice, Duff also had connections to organized crime, including Tony "Big Tuna" Accardo, who ran the mafia in Chicago.

Jack Duff Jr. had three sons: Patrick, John, and James. The first two became senior union officials in Local 3 of the Liquor and Wine Sales Representatives. James went into business, launching Windy City Maintenance one month after Rich Daley became mayor of Chicago in 1989.

Like John Cannatello, James Duff had organized Windy City as an ostensible women-owned business. The new Mayor Daley then allegedly instructed his head of special events to make sure that the Duffs received city work. Windy City received a no-bid contract to clean up after the Taste of Chicago summer festival. Soon, Windy City and other so-called women- and minority-owned businesses set up by Duff would have contracts for Navy Pier, the police department, McCormick Place, the Air and Water Show, and O'Hare Airport. During Daley's tenure, city-related contracts poured nearly $100 million into the Duff's pockets.

The Duffs had clout in Chicago, and every player in city politics knew it. Over the years, James Duff and his brothers contributed money to Rich Daley's campaigns and held fund-raisers for Daley. At one such event in 1999, the mayor put his arm around one of the Duff brothers and walked from table to table greeting his supporters. According to one political insider, "Daley was waving his flag, saying, 'These are my guys.' Everybody got it." When the FBI released its six-hundred-page file on family patriarch Jack Duff Jr. in 2011, Daley was referenced directly or indirectly more than twenty times.

In April 2005, the Hired Truck Scandal kicked into second gear. The FBI arrived at city hall—armed with search warrants—and seized documents and computer hard drives from the mayor's office of intergovernmental affairs. The intergovernmental affairs office oversaw political hiring activity and was headed by mayoral operative Robert Sorich, who had close ties to the mayor's brother, Eleventh Ward committeeman John Daley. Sorich—a Bridgeport native whose father was Dick Daley's photographer during his reign as mayor—spent years as John Daley's personal driver and as the Eleventh Ward secretary. While serving as the second Mayor Daley's unofficial patronage chief, he often still drove John Daley to work.

Within three months, US Attorney Patrick Fitzgerald charged Sorich with orchestrating fraud in city hiring and promotions. Sorich was accused of using his influential position in the mayor's office to manipulate the selection process for certain City of Chicago jobs. According to the US Attorney office, Sorich instructed city employees to conduct sham interviews and falsely inflate interview scores, guaranteeing that certain preselected candidates received jobs. The winners had political pull, through either their efforts on political campaigns or union connections. Qualified candidates lost out. City of Chicago taxpayers picked up the tab. Fitzgerald later characterized the scheme as a corrupt clout machine.

Of course, Sorich did not work alone. Don Tomczak testified at one Hired Truck trial that all promotions in his department had to be approved by Sorich and his boss, Victor Reyes. Tomczak also explained that political organizations were set up within his and other City of Chicago departments and that political activity determined who got jobs and promotions. Also implicated in the second phase of the Hired Truck Scandal was Al Sanchez, a leader of the Hispanic Democratic Organization and a Streets and Sanitation commissioner from the far south side. Back during Rich Daley's 1989 campaign for mayor, Sanchez had met with Tim Degnan and was involved in the founding of the HDO. By the turn of the millennium, Sanchez functioned like an old-school political boss who ordered his people to work on campaigns and then rewarded them with city jobs. Sanchez had clout.

Another Streets and Sanitation employee with political clout was Daniel Katalinic. In 1999, Sorich directed Katalinic to form a new political group of city workers because the mayor's office needed Caucasian political troops to replace the Coalition for Better Government, a political organization focused on getting out voters on election day. Sorich told Katalinic that there was "too much heat" on the Coalition for Better Government and that the mayor's office could no longer use them in campaigns. Katalinic formed his own white political organization, which eventually grew to over two hundred city employees. His political workers allegedly assisted in many Chicago campaigns, including the congressional race of Rahm Emanuel.

In July of 2005, the FBI arrested Sorich. "The dam has broken in terms of a number of people coming forward and cooperating," said US Attorney Patrick Fitzgerald in announcing federal charges against Sorich and another city official from Daley's Bridgeport neighborhood. "More than 30 cooperating witnesses are cited, more than five former commissioners, four former personnel directors and two current personnel directors."

In that same month, the Republican Party of Cook County offered a $10,000 reward to anyone who provided information leading to the conviction of Daley himself. "[That offer] was deeply offensive to me [and] my family," Mayor Daley said with tears in his eyes and a red face. "I understand that things get really dirty and ugly and messy, but this crosses the line."

One month later, the FBI questioned Daley himself with regard to the accusations of pervasive fraud in city hall hiring. The FBI interrogated Daley with his lawyer sitting at his side. John Villa was a low-key and talented hired gun not from Chicago. He practiced law at Williams and Connolly, a Washington, DC, firm known for representing former President Bill Clinton when he faced an independent counsel investigation and an impeachment trial. Maybe the mayor's younger brother, the former US Secretary of Commerce, had made the introduction.

Daley held a news conference after his 2005 FBI questioning. "When there is wrongdoing in my government, I take responsibility for it," Daley said. "I am committed to root it out and do everything I can to prevent it." But Daley had sunk to the low point of his political career. His job approval ratings soon followed, plummeting to 53 percent.

During the same month that the FBI questioned Daley, US Congressman Rahm Emanuel spoke at the City Club of Chicago, a 102-year-old organization focused on providing a public forum for the city's most important policy issues. In his keynote address, Emanuel surprised the audience by publicly defending his old friend Daley while also addressing the mayor's role in the corruption scandals swirling around his administration.

"The mayor deserves criticism—not for what he knew, but for what he did not know. While he focused his attention . . . on the day-to-day work of governing, he should have focused more on how his political agenda was being carried out. If he had done that, he could have avoided some of the problems he is facing today," said Emanuel. "My gut tells me he doesn't really care about the nitty-gritty of politics. It's just not what his interest is. But guess what? In government, there's politics. So you don't get a pass [to] say, 'I gave it to somebody else.' He outsourced it, which is one of the reasons I'm against outsourcing. You're not allowed to outsource your politics."

Basically, Emanuel had posited that Daley was too focused on running city government, and that this had led to the mayor avoiding the nuts and bolts of city politics. Emanuel's clever and full-throated defense of Daley was not surprising, given their friendship and common professional history together. But his thesis was a bit hard to swallow, since Daley was known as both a hands-on micromanager of the city and as the undisputed master of local politics. Emanuel's defense of Daley was also a dramatic contrast to the reaction of Barack Obama, at that time the US senator from Illinois. A few weeks earlier, Obama had hesitated when asked whether he would endorse Daley in the upcoming mayoral election, saying that the Hired Truck and other recent city scandals gave him "huge pause."

Two months later, Daley named David Hoffman as the new inspector general for the City of Chicago. The mayor was still feeling political heat from all of his administration's scandals, and he wanted to project a better image to voters. The inspector general's office was a watchdog organization whose mission was to root out corruption, waste, and mismanagement in city government. Hoffman was a smart, hardworking, clean-cut former federal prosecutor. He was also a protégé of US Attorney Patrick Fitzgerald. He fit the image that Daley wanted to project as the mayor of Chicago struggled to make it through his administration's continuing corruption crisis. Only time would tell, but perhaps the stressed-out mayor had made a mistake: perhaps David Hoffman would be more independent and tougher than Daley had bargained for.

Like the City of Chicago, Cook County government had a long history of corruption. In March 2006, seventy-six-year-old Cook County Board president John Stroger suffered a debilitating stroke shortly before the Democratic primary elections were held. The popular black politician won anyway, beating Forrest Claypool, Mayor Daley's former chief of staff, by a vote of 53 percent to 47 percent.

Stroger had started his political career in the 1950s as a precinct captain in Dick Daley's Democratic machine. A genial tax-and-spend Democrat, Stroger had maintained deep political ties to the Daley family over the next five decades. In 1968, then-mayor Dick Daley made Stroger the Eighth Ward's first black Democratic committeeman, and two years later supported Stroger's run for the Cook County Board. In 1983, Stroger returned the favor by endorsing the late mayor's son Rich, even though at the time Harold Washington was the first black candidate for mayor that was both qualified and capable of winning.

Though Stroger won the primary for what would be his fourth term as Cook County Board president in 2006, within weeks it became clear that his stroke had incapacitated him and that he was not able to serve another term in office. The Democrats needed another candidate before the general election in November. A number of pols floated their names, including John Daley, Congressman Danny Davis, and the incapacitated president's son Todd Stroger, who Rich Daley had appointed to a vacant city council seat in 2001. Reflecting the longstanding view of Chicago politics as a racial/ethnic sweepstakes, some Democratic Party members believed that the office should be reserved for a black leader since the city already had a white mayor. Others wondered why Mayor Daley and other party leaders seemed unwilling to support Forrest Claypool, given his strong showing in the recent primary.

After months of delay and back-room wrangling, the Cook County Democratic Central Committee selected Todd Stroger. "I would be less than honest if I did not express some disappointment in the way this process has been handled," protested Congressman Davis to the Central Committee. "I don't like the idea that family ties and pedigree will continue to trump other kinds of experience and credentials." Many others agreed that this selection of Todd Stroger was a blatant act of nepotism, since the younger Stroger appeared to lack the professional accomplishments and personal attributes necessary to run the county and its $3 billion budget. The *Chicago Tribune* editorialized against Stroger, saying that three other potential black candidates each had "more administrative and budget experience in his pinky finger than Todd Stroger has in his dreams."

Two months later, Forrest Claypool publicly expressed his doubts about the selection process and Todd Stroger's leadership abilities. According to Claypool, local Democratic leaders had "thumbed their nose at the taxpayers" by putting Stroger on the ballot over better choices and had "arrogantly manipulated the system for their benefit and the benefit of outsiders." Claypool also declared that Stroger's record failed to "show he has the executive ability to step up and pursue reform."

Mayor Daley, however, took issue with the perspective of his two-time former chief of staff and delivered an unmitigated endorsement of the younger Stroger. At a joint press conference with the African-American politician, Daley called Todd a "wonderful candidate" and said "he's going to be a great president of the county board." Perhaps Daley was right, but many had doubts. Did Daley really believe in Stroger, or was he just paying back a family for years of political loyalty? Or maybe there was a darker explanation. Maybe Daley knew that Todd Stroger lacked the brain power and toughness to rule independently, and that was exactly why he had backed him.

In the same month that the Cook County Democratic Central Committee selected the inept Todd Stroger to run as its candidate for county president, Robert Sorich and three of his city colleagues were convicted in the second phase of the Hired Truck Scandal. "I think what we saw in this case was the revealing of the Chicago machine, the inner workings of the Chicago machine," said Jay Olshansky, the jury foreman. "There clearly is one. It has been in existence for quite some time."

On the same day, President George Bush was in Chicago to spend his sixtieth birthday with Rich Daley, the mayor of Chicago. The official purpose of the president's visit was to communicate his administration's accomplishments outside the Washington beltway, but some of the local Chicago media speculated that Bush was trying to signal to the aggressive local US Attorney Patrick Fitzgerald that Daley was his friend. Back off, buddy, was the unspoken message according to this theory.

The two hereditary politicians and their guests celebrated together at the Chicago Firehouse Restaurant, a South Loop establishment owned by Daley's friend Matthew O'Malley. O'Malley had purchased a city firehouse and opened the restaurant in 2000 just down the street from the mayor's new home. The Firehouse served steaks, burgers, and seafood, and the mayor dined there frequently.

Daley, Bush and their nine guests were down in the basement gathered around a rectangular, hand-crafted wood table in the restaurant's baroque-style wine cellar room. Daley sat at the president's left. Like Bush, the mayor dressed casually, wearing a white shirt without a tie.

Other guests included business executives from Exelon, Caterpillar, Chicago Board of Trade, Chicago Mercantile Exchange, the Illinois Black Chamber of Commerce, the Illinois Hispanic Chamber of Commerce, and the Illinois Manufacturers Association.

At the Firehouse dinner, Bush ordered Filet Oscar, a cut of steak topped with crabmeat, asparagus, and béarnaise sauce. The attendees sang to the president, who blew out candles on a cake topped with strawberries that read: "Happy 60th Birthday, Mr. President."

The following month, a group of Bridgeport natives hosted a fundraiser for Robert Sorich in the basement of Nativity of Our Lord, the Daley family's home parish. The $100-a-ticket event was designed to help defray the legal bills of the convicted former top mayoral aide. Handwritten signs on the door to the church basement warned against bringing in cameras or recording devices. Attendees included Eleventh Ward committeeman John Daley and Tim Degnan, Sorich's old boss at the mayor's office of intergovernmental affairs. On his way into the Sorich fund-raiser, Degnan ordered a reporter who approached him to "take a hike."

When asked about the event at Nativity of Our Lord, Mayor Daley defended it. "They're still friends of his," said Daley of the contributors. "You think someone makes one mistake that you would kick him all the way down the street? I doubt it." Three months later, after Sorich and three others were sentenced to prison, Daley continued defending the now-convicted scoundrels, "I know all those young men personally, and their families, and they are very fine young men."

PART 7

Legacy

CHAPTER 20

GLOBAL CITY, PAROCHIAL COUNCIL

By the first decade of the twenty-first-century, Chicago would be accepted as one of the most important global cities in the world, an urban center that combined a powerful economy with cultural sophistication. This recognition put Chicago in elite company, along with other metropolises: New York, London, Tokyo, Paris, Hong Kong, and Singapore. Cities such as these drove global markets, technological invention, and the advance of culture. Due to the increasing pace of globalization, these influential cities set the pace of worldwide change and held the ability to create jobs, wealth, and high-quality lifestyles for their citizens.

Chicago had a $460 billion economy, some of the best universities anywhere, and world-class dining, performing arts, cultural attractions, and entertainment. To maintain their competitive edge, global cities such as Chicago required diverse business activity, global information exchanges, rich cultural experiences, and the ability to attract talented people. Daley knew this intuitively, and the pro-business, pro-culture mayor tried to craft policies that facilitated these goals. Unfortunately, the Chicago City Council was quite parochial and had failed to realize that its hometown had become a global city. This blind spot by the legislative body made Daley's job as mayor more difficult.

By 2006, the Daleys—father and son—had dominated the city council for most of the years since 1955. The first Mayor Daley had made the city council compliant when he took steps to dramatically shift the balance of power between the city council and the mayor. Dick Daley achieved this dominance by using his deep knowledge of government to push through structural changes that increased the power of the mayor's office. In 1956, the State of Illinois gave the mayor the right to prepare and propose the city's budgets. It also removed the city council's authority to approve specific city contracts. These legal changes effectively emasculated the city council and gave the elder Daley control of Chicago's finances.

In some ways, his son Rich had his way with the city council even more than the father, almost never losing a roll call vote. After his election to mayor in 1989, Daley reorganized the city council and put allies in charge of all key committees, including the finance, zoning, and rules committees. Any alderman closely aligned with Daley's competitor in the 1989 mayoral contest, Tim Evans, lost out on power. In 1989, Daley also appointed his own Bridgeport alderman Patrick Huels as his floor leader in the council. Huels served Daley effectively in that position until resigning in 1997 in a conflict-of-interest scandal.

Part of the explanation for the younger Daley's legislative dominance is that during the late twentieth century the Chicago City Council lacked both a Republican Party and an independent opposition faction, such as the one led by Alderman Leon Despres during the first Mayor Daley's tenure. More important, Rich Daley also benefited from a structural change in Illinois law, passed by the legislature in 1980, that allowed the mayor of Chicago to fill city council vacancies by appointment rather than by special election. The second Mayor Daley skillfully used his right of appointment to increase his own power over the council. Between 1989 and the end of 2005, Rich Daley seated twenty-eight aldermen, including seventeen who were currently in office at the end of 2005.

"With few exceptions, the current aldermen are a bunch of puppets [of the mayor] doing what they are told," said Judson Miner, the City of Chicago corporation counsel under Mayor Washington. "The mayor is vindictive to anyone who opposes him. There is no thoughtful debate or discussion."

Greed was one of the reasons for a lack of thoughtful debate in the city council. In order to collect multimillion dollar pension benefits, an alderman needed to serve for twenty years, and this milestone was much more likely to be met if an alderman consistently voted with the mayor. In addition, many aldermen, such as Ed Burke, followed in the long Chicago tradition of using their elected position in the city council to generate income for their law practices and realty agencies or to secure perks and jobs for allies who could help their careers in other ways.

Fear was a second reason for a lack of thoughtful debate in Rich Daley's city council. Or more specifically, most aldermen lacked the toughness and confidence to stand up to the second Mayor Daley. The best example of this lopsided match may be Daley's late 1999 appointment of a new fire commissioner. Daley's candidate was a white southsider and third-generation fireman who had worked in the Chicago Fire Department for thirty-four years. Unfortunately, during that time the fire department had consistently discriminated against black employees, and several aldermen expressed concern about the proposed appointment. "The Chicago Fire Department has had a history of insularity and intolerance," said Toni Preckwinkle, an African-American alderman from Hyde Park. "It concerns me that our new fire commissioner has been part of that department for such a long time." The city council confirmed Daley's candidate by a vote of forty-two to five, however, and most of the council gave the new fire commissioner a standing ovation. When the five dissenters remained sitting, Mayor Daley erupted from the podium, "He'll lead the department, with or without your support, and that's why I selected him! This will be a vote we'll remember and I think you will apologize some day!"

This type of public threat by Daley reinforced his reputation for holding grudges, which in turn increased his leverage over many members of the city council. "You don't forget who was with you and who was against you," Daley had told a reporter a few years earlier. "Me? I don't forget."

As 2006 started, however, the Daley family's long-running dominance of the Chicago City Council may have peaked. Due to the Daley administration's recent scandals, the members of the council sensed rare political weakness in Mayor Daley. Restive aldermen found two ways to attack Daley's leadership, one that seemed trivial and the other more substantive. On the surface, the serving of foie gras in restaurants was the less important issue. A potential living-wage law to regulate big-box retailers such as Walmart required more serious consideration. Unfortunately, the long, bumbling history of the Chicago City Council did not give outside observers much hope that the municipal legislators would notice the difference. Even worse, the city council was completely oblivious to the reality that, on a deeper level, each issue was tied up with Chicago's metamorphosis into a global city. In fact, the living-wage issue soon turned into a serious conflict and set the stage for the 2007 Chicago aldermanic elections, an epic political battle between Daley and the labor unions.

Before the living-wage issue surfaced, however, the city council became focused on banning foie gras, a delicacy served in expensive restaurants. This became a political issue, in part, because during Daley's time as mayor Chicago had evolved from a Midwestern city to a global one. This dramatic urban transition tended to benefit the highly educated and the wealthy, while leaving many others behind. The city's new status as a global city also had many secondary impacts, including a significant transformation in the restaurant culture of Chicago. New gourmet restaurants emerged with international reputations, and many of these served foie gras. In order to understand this larger story, it is important to know that Chicago's culinary evolution started with one restaurant: Charlie Trotter's.

Between its 1987 opening and the surfacing of the foie gras political battle in 2005, Charlie Trotter's became internationally known for its unparalleled cuisine and service. During those two decades—as Chicago blossomed into a gourmet foodie enclave—a new generation of superior chefs spent early parts of their careers under Trotter's tutelage. Michael Taus, Bill Kim, Homaro Cantu, Graham Elliot, and Rick Tramonto would move on to success in their own right. During Daley's reign as mayor of Chicago, their restaurants—Zealous, Urban Belly, Moto, Graham Elliot, and Tru, respectively—entered Chicago's expanding gastronomic universe.

In 2005, a culinary controversy developed between Trotter and one of his protégés, Rick Tramonto, when Trotter told a restaurant critic that he no longer served the French delicacy foie gras in his restaurant. Foie gras is a rich, delicious gourmet pleasure made from the fattened liver of a duck or goose. In recent years, foie gras has become controversial with animal rights activists because foie gras producers force-feed corn to fatten their birds. Trotter had, for supposedly ethical reasons, removed it from his menu.

On learning of Trotter's position on foie gras, Tramonto called him "a little hypocritical" since Trotter still served a wide variety of other farm-fattened meats on his menu. A war of words started between the two brilliant chefs. The news media quickly picked up on this culinary controversy, and a national debate between animal rights activists and hardcore food aficionados ensued.

Joe Moore, the Forty-Ninth Ward alderman representing the north-side neighborhoods of Rogers Park and Edgewater, also picked up on the foie gras controversy. Moore was a progressive politician, and one of the few members of the Chicago City Council over the last fifteen years who took positions independent of Mayor Daley's views. Friendly and tall, with a round face and an earnest manner, prior to becoming alderman, Moore had served as a City of Chicago attorney and protégé of former alderman and current Cook County clerk David Orr. "I was the first, and to this day, one of the very few people who defeated a Daley mayoral appointee to become alderman," Moore said proudly. "David Orr's support, along with the Forty-Ninth Ward's independent political tradition, certainly helped."

After the foie gras controversy broke out in the chef community, Alderman Moore introduced an ordinance in the city council in April 2005 to ban the sale of foie gras in Chicago. It was an easy decision for Moore, since his lower-income ward had no gourmet restaurants and quite a few animal rights activists.

"A lot of folks who are concerned about the treatment of animals live in my ward, so I knew that it would have some appeal to those folks," said Moore.

In December, the city council health committee approved the ordinance banning foie gras, and the entire council also passed a bill that banned smoking in restaurants and other public places. Animal rights and healthy living were part of the national zeitgeist, and the city council tended to follow along with popular trends. Worried about their economic impact, Mayor Daley resisted both of the legislative measures and stated that he did not believe that the city should legislate what people eat. "What is the next issue? Chicken? Beef? Fish?" asked Daley.

"Our laws are a reflection of our society's values, and our culture does not condone the torture of small innocent animals," responded Alderman Joe Moore. "It's not a matter of personal choice."

In April 2006, the entire Chicago City Council passed the ban on the sale of foie gras. On passage, Alderman Ed Burke—who usually resisted proposals by independent aldermen—stood to recognize Moore's efforts. "I don't think we should let this pass without noting that the champion of animal rights in the city council has been successful in getting Chicago to be the very first legislative body in the nation to ban this product from restaurants. So Alderman Moore deserves a good deal of credit for being the leader of this movement not only locally but nationwide. It's quite an accomplishment."

Mayor Daley, however, expressed extreme skepticism at the council's foie gras ban. "We have children getting killed by gang leaders and dope dealers. We have real issues in this city. And we're dealing with foie gras? Let's get some priorities." A few months later, Daley added, "I think it's the silliest law that they've ever passed."

Though he may not have communicated the reasons behind his skepticism, Daley was right about the foie gras ban. In a competitive global economy, sophisticated businesses and individuals compared Chicago to Tokyo, London, New York, and Paris—not Detroit or St. Louis. Restricting gourmet restaurants from serving dishes desired by their customers hurt the city's reputation with these important and mobile worldwide constituents.

Before the ban went into effect, many high-end restaurants offered special foie gras–focused menus. The Peninsula Hotel's Avenues restaurant, for example, presented a twelve-course, all foie gras tasting menu for $245 per person. After the ban, many of the finest restaurants in Chicago simply circumvented the regulation by giving away foie gras to customers, rather than selling it to them.

Two months after the food ban went into effect, the Chicago City Council moved onto other matters and passed a groundbreaking new law. The ordinance required big-box retailers, such as Walmart and Home Depot, to pay employees at least $10 an hour, as well as $3 an hour in benefits. The social impact of this new law would be to aid some of Chicago's working poor. Walmart—which wanted to expand into Chicago and other large cities—strongly opposed the living-wage law because it would make the global retailer less competitive.

The Chicago business community and Mayor Daley supported Walmart's position because they believed that the law would dampen job growth and economic expansion. "The aldermen who voted in support of this [bill] . . . helped put the sign up really big that development in Chicago is dead," said Jerry Roper, the president of the Chicagoland Chamber of Commerce. Like the mayor, most business people felt that—in a competitive world economy—the city needed to foster an economic climate that encouraged employers such as Walmart to add jobs in Chicago, rather than creating them in other cities or countries.

Daley's alignment with the business community on this issue was a significant difference between his father and himself. The first mayor Daley had built up his political machine by closely aligning himself with the labor unions supporting the living-wage law.

As expected, unions and community groups strongly backed the new law, declaring that a living wage was an economic justice issue. "The value of the marketplace here in the City of Chicago should not be sold off cheaply," explained Dennis Gannon, president of the Chicago Federation of Labor. "I think that there should be some demands to make sure that people understand that corporations like Walmart have a responsibility to the workers that are here in the city. And that's really where the rubber met the road about the living wage and the Walmart issue."

Fundamentally, the living-wage war—like the earlier foie gras fight—was another symptom of globalization and Chicago's transformation into a world city. Global businesses like Walmart needed to pay low wages in order to stay competitive, but labor unions still acted as if the US economy was shut off from the rest of the world.

The debate was fierce, and the unions threatened to use Chicago as a national test case of their resolve to fight for blue-collar workers and to resist the continued expansion of the union-free Walmart. Joe Moore, who sponsored the living-wage bill in the city council, declared a victory, saying, "This is a great day for the working men and women of Chicago." Mayor Daley disagreed and stated that he might veto the bill, something that he had found no need to do in his previous seventeen years in office.

Before making his decision, however, Daley attended a secret meeting at the Drake Hotel with two union leaders.

The Drake Hotel sits between North Michigan Avenue and East Lake Shore Drive on a piece of land where the Gold Coast neighborhood ends and the Magnificent Mile shopping district begins. Guests of the Italian Renaissance-style hotel, which since 1920 have included many celebrities and heads of state, can look out over Lake Michigan and Oak Street Beach. The Daley family has a long history with the storied Drake Hotel. When Queen Elizabeth II visited Chicago in 1959 and was hosted by the first Mayor Daley, her itinerary included a stop for high tea at the Drake. According to a widely circulated rumor, there was an FBI dossier purporting to describe a secret apartment at the hotel rented by the first Mayor Daley so that he could meet with members of the Chicago mafia. Since becoming mayor in 1989, Rich Daley had also conducted many meetings and attended countless events at the Drake.

More than sixteen years later, however, the meeting Daley hosted at the Drake Hotel was very different—both more private and less lofty than the other receptions held at the Drake since 1989. On August 8, 2006, the second Mayor Daley met in a private suite with AFL-CIO president John Sweeney and Dennis Gannon. At the time, the AFL-CIO was the largest federation of unions in the United States, representing approximately 12 million members. The Chicago Federation of Labor was an AFL-CIO affiliate with more than 500,000 union members. Sweeney asked Gannon to set up a meeting with Daley so that Sweeney could present the mayor with a letter, signed by the heads of all the national AFL-CIO affiliates, urging Daley not to veto the recently passed ordinance requiring big-box retailers such as Walmart to pay their employees a living wage.

Gannon had advised Sweeney that it was not a good time for the unions to meet with Daley. The gray-haired Gannon—a savvy, Irish-Catholic native of Chicago—had a long history with the Daley family and with Chicago politics. "My grandfather was with old Mayor Daley years ago. He was the head of the police pension fund. My uncle, Eddie Fitzgerald, he was the commissioner of the Bureau of Forestry for years. So they all grew up that way. I met the first Mayor Daley on Saint Patrick's Day. I remember meeting the mayor, meaning Rich Daley's father, back at those parades." Gannon's own professional career had started out with the City of Chicago, where for seventeen years he had worked in the Department of Streets and Sanitation as a hoisting engineer, foreman, and general foreman.

There were a number of different reasons why Gannon suggested to Sweeney that the timing was inopportune for a meeting with Daley. Though the immediate issue was the living-wage ordinance, Gannon knew that he would also have to negotiate with Daley on other important issues. "The living-wage issue percolated up over Walmart," said Gannon. "We got wind that Walmart was coming into Chicago, and so we went out there and supported the living wage. Walmart's like public enemy number one for organized labor. It's the biggest corporation in the world, and yet it can't pay its workers a living wage or a comparable wage. But it wasn't just the unions supporting the living wage. It was also the religious community and members of neighborhood communities that got involved with this issue."

At least three other concerns, however, compounded the tension between Daley and Gannon. First, the City of Chicago had waited twenty-eight months before agreeing to give its twenty thousand union workers a new contract in 2005. "That weighed on a lot of people's minds," said Gannon. "The city just kept pushing it back, pushing it back. There was nobody in the room to make the decision. The delay went on way, way, way too long and it was disrespectful to organized labor."

The second concern was Chicago's drive to privatize many city services, which Daley had started in 1989 when the city privatized parts of its towing and janitorial operations. For the City of Chicago the focus was on reducing costs, given that pensions and healthcare benefits for employees had become a huge expense and labor outlays accounted for approximately three-fourths of its corporate budget. In a global economy, forward-thinking mayors—like Ed Rendell in Philadelphia and Rich Daley in Chicago—realized that privatizations were necessary in order to stay competitive. Unlike the first Mayor Daley, this new generation of urban leaders was less focused on maintaining patronage armies of union workers who supported their political organizations. For Dennis Gannon and the unions, however, Daley's drive to privatize city services and to open charter schools was a direct threat to the job protection of union members. "Daley was privatizing water main work, asphalt work—work that was historically done by in-house city employees. Those were the little steps in the privatization drive that really affected our members."

Finally, the Chicago Federation of Labor and its union members had already started to organize aggressively for the upcoming 2007 aldermanic elections in Chicago. The unions planned to take on incumbent aldermen who had supported Daley's positions rather than those of the unions. The unions' nascent political organizing angered Daley, and he was not shy about letting influential political players in Chicago know how he felt about it. "If Dennis [Gannon] wants a fight on the alderman races, tell him to bring it on," fumed Daley on more than one occasion. "I'll give him a fucking fight."

With that backdrop, the August 2006 meeting at the Drake Hotel between Daley, Gannon, and Sweeney seemed primed for confrontation. The private suite where the men met had hosted dignitaries from around the world for many, many years. The three sat down on the overstuffed furniture and quickly got down to business. Daley's position on the living-wage ordinance was that it would hurt economic development in Chicago, giving an advantage to the suburbs. He felt that any living-wage bill should apply to the entire State of Illinois and not just Chicago. Gannon's position, in contrast, was that the unions had loyally supported Daley for many years, and the mayor owed it to them to back the living-wage bill. "This bill will support working men and women and you need to support it," Gannon told Daley.

His anger rising, Daley replied, "No, you need to fuckin' support me on this, Dennis." Underlying Daley's anger was his expectation of loyalty, his deeply internalized sense that other people should bow to his authority.

"I can't do that," replied Gannon, knowing that his interests and responsibilities lay with his union members. A long, shared history mattered only up to a certain point.

With red rising in his face, Daley unleashed another expletive-filled tirade on Gannon. Standing up, Daley told Gannon, "You are a principled man and I will let you know when I decide what to do." Daley then stormed out of the hotel suite.

Approximately a month later, Daley vetoed the living-wage bill. "I understand and share a desire to ensure that everyone who works in the city of Chicago earns a decent wage," Daley wrote in a letter to the city council. "But I do not believe that this ordinance, well intentioned as it may be, would achieve that end."

The unions strongly disagreed. "No American, other than Mayor Daley and the folks at Wal-Mart, believe it's right for corporations to make billions while their workers get paid poverty-level wages and live without affordable health care," said Chris Kofinis, a spokesman for union-affiliated advocacy group Wake Up Walmart.

Two days after Mayor Daley's veto, the city council failed—by three votes—in its attempt to override the veto. "After Daley has taken this position, I don't see how unions could endorse him [in the upcoming 2007 mayoral election]," said Tom Balanoff, president of the Illinois Council of the Service Employees International Union. Balanoff's union, the AFL-CIO, and Chicago's other unions vowed to go after Daley and his pro-business allies in the city council. The fight was on for the upcoming 2007 Chicago elections.

Taking on Daley politically was an ambitious goal for the unions, given his past record of success. Since his election as mayor in 1989, Rich Daley and his allies had achieved a remarkable string of electoral victories. In 2003, the most recent mayoral election, Daley won in a landslide, receiving 78.5 percent of the vote. Over the years, very few anti-Daley or truly independent aldermen had survived in the city council.

However, the dynamics of Chicago politics had changed since 2003, and the 2007 elections would be more competitive. A series of scandals and mistakes—the Hired Truck Scandal, Duff contracting fraud, city hall hiring scheme, and midnight destruction of Meigs Field—had weakened Daley on two levels. First, the mayor's political popularity had peaked and begun to decline. Second, the criminal convictions of people like Donald Tomczak and Robert Sorich had sent a chilling message to other political operatives and sapped the mayor's get-out-the-vote election muscle. Finally, by 2007 the unions were angry and had decided to actively flex their own political muscles. "Working men and women deserve a strong, independent voice in the city council," Dennis Gannon declared. "The CFL will do everything it takes to elect those men and women who will fight for working families and the issues important to them." Gannon's union alliance then endorsed ten aldermanic challengers for the city council and did not endorse Daley for mayor.

The unions put together a formidable political organization and geared up for the elections. "We have a political director that works full time here, but we took it to another level," explained Gannon. "We sat down and talked to all the major unions in the City of Chicago. Asked them if they're going to make an investment in aldermanic elections. They all said okay, so they gave us money and they gave us volunteers. They gave us their organization. They gave us newsletters. They gave us phone banks. They gave us people to do the things that you have to do in order to win elections. . . . We went out and hired five different field directors. We had the phone banks. We had money. We did newspaper. We did radio. We did mailers to all of our members making sure that they understood the importance of the election. Not one or two or three pieces of mail, but as much as we needed per aldermanic district in order to [win]."

The unions did win the fight with Daley, electing six new aldermen to the Chicago City Council, in addition to protecting the independent alderman Joe Moore. The surprising results of the 2007 aldermanic elections and Daley's soured relationship with the unions would have a lasting impact on his political career: he had lost his reputation for political invincibility. Though Chicago electoral politics sometimes seemed like swimming in a large and deep ocean, the local sharks could smell blood in the water from over a mile away.

Thirteen months after the 2007 elections, the Chicago City Council met to conduct its regular business and to consider repealing the ban on the sale of foie gras. Since its passage, the ban had generated significant negative publicity for Chicago, tarnishing its reputation as an attractive and sophisticated global city. Celebrity chef Anthony Bourdain, for example, said that the ban made Chicago appear as "some stupid cow town." The Illinois Restaurant Association pressured the city council and actively campaigned to repeal the foie gras ban. "I'm really searching for the right side of the moral and the ethical," explained Alderman Shirley Coleman. "We are trying to be a global city. I'm not sure it's my job to tell restaurants what they can or cannot sell." When the city council voted, the repeal passed by a vote of thirty-eight to five. Daley had always believed that the ban was a mistake. "I mean, this is what government should be doing? Telling you what you should be putting on toast?" he asked reporters. The foie gras fight ended, but the living-wage battle with Walmart, the union, and the city council would resurface again in two years.

Despite the provincialism of the city council, the transformation of Chicago from the industrial capital of the Midwest into a powerful and sophisticated global city would become Daley's most significant positive legacy. The creation of Millennium Park remained the physical manifestation of this transformation, but the phenomenon also had an impact on the city's economy, universities, cuisine, and cultural zeitgeist. Chicago had evolved, becoming one of the most important urban centers on the planet. Artists, tourists, business people, and world leaders were now drawn to Daley's city, seeing it as an attractive spot to work, to play, and to visit.

CHAPTER 21

ONE TOO MANY

Daley had started his sixth term as mayor of Chicago in May 2007. Since early in the year, his job approval ratings had sunk below 50 percent for the first time in his mayoral career. And it was not just the voters who were unhappy with Daley. The unions, the news media, and the Chicago City Council all still held hard feelings toward him. Daley appeared more and more like a prize fighter past his prime, a once great champion who had stayed in the ring for one fight too many.

His extended family did not help matters. News of an emerging scandal involving his nephew Robert Vanecko soon added to the mayor's growing reputational challenges. Vanecko—the son of Daley's sister Mary Carol and the firstborn grandchild of Dick Daley—had cofounded a real investment company in late 2004 with Allison Davis, a longtime mayoral supporter. The two politically connected businessmen had then raised $68 million from five City of Chicago pension funds.

Davis was a complex character. Well-dressed with a patrician appearance, he had the look and confidence of a blue-blooded Chicago corporate leader. Yet Davis was an African-American who just happened to look white. His father, William Boyd Allison Davis, was a well-known sociologist who had become one of the first black professors to win tenure at the University of Chicago. The older Davis was best known for maintaining that culturally biased IQ tests unfairly penalized minorities. The Davis family was well-connected in liberal Hyde Park and knew influential black families in both Chicago and nationally, including Valerie Jarrett's family and the Washington power broker Vernon Jordan.

The younger Davis had started his professional career as an idealist. After graduating from Northwestern University Law School, he had joined the Agency for International Development where he spent three years in West Africa working on small pox eradication and vocational training.

After returning to Chicago, Davis accepted a legal position at the Metropolitan Housing and Planning Council, a civil rights group often at odds with the first Mayor Daley over slums and the lack of racial integration in Chicago. Two years later, Davis coauthored a report, titled "Dissent in a Free Society," criticizing Dick Daley's administration for its refusal to issue parade permits to protesters who rioted during the 1968 Democratic National Convention. "No one can accurately appraise the extent to which denial of peaceful expression resulted in violent confrontation," said the report.

In 1969, Davis also helped to found the Chicago Council of Lawyers, a progressive group focused on electing judges based on legal skills instead of ties to the local Democratic Party. Its members included a group of young, talented lawyers, such as John Schmidt, Judson Miner, and Michael Shakman. "[At that time] Allison was a reform-minded lawyer, like me and some other young lawyers," said Shakman.

In 1971, Davis helped to found Davis Miner Barnhill and Galland, a boutique law firm that would acquire a solid reputation in civil rights litigation and neighborhood economic development work. Over time, Davis and his firm would represent a number of nonprofit companies that were partnering with private real estate developers to build affordable housing with government subsidies. In 1993, the firm beat out the competition and hired Barack Obama, the first-ever black president of the *Harvard Law Review*. Obama worked at Davis's firm for four years before entering Illinois politics.

While continuing his practice of law during the 1990s, Davis also started dabbling in real estate. In 1991, Mayor Daley appointed Davis to the Chicago Plan Commission, a board on which the politically connected attorney had also served under Mayor Harold Washington. The Chicago Plan Commission was a municipal authority with responsibility for reviewing real estate development proposals in the city. Serving on this influential review panel would help Davis in his growing real estate activities.

By early 1997, Davis had decided to focus all of his professional efforts on real estate, starting out as a for-profit developer and syndicator of low-income housing. Some of Davis's projects were high-minded—combining neighborhood revitalization goals with his own profit-making desires—including a number of developments linked to Mayor Daley's Plan for Transformation. One such undertaking was Davis's redevelopment of Stateway Gardens, the notorious CHA project that had cast its shadows near Comiskey Park and Daley's De La Salle High School. Over the next decade, according to the *Chicago Sun-Times*, Davis received more than $100 million in subsidies to build and renovate fifteen hundred mostly low-income apartments in Chicago.

Some of Davis's other business dealings were not so high-minded, and he seemed to pick his partners poorly. His first real estate partner, William Moorehead, went to jail in 2007 for embezzling from federally funded housing projects he managed, including two buildings co-owned with Davis. In the same year, the US Attorney indicted Tony Rezko—another real estate partner of Davis—for demanding kickbacks from businesspeople working with the Illinois state pension funds.

Rezko was a close adviser to Governor Rod Blagojevich and had recommended that Blagojevich appoint Davis to the Illinois State Board of Investment in 2003. Once on the board, Davis voted to invest $100 million of state workers' retirement money in RREEF America, an investment management firm that specialized in real estate. Months later, Davis joined RREEF's board of directors and accepted $30,000 a year for the part-time post. "It's extremely uncommon to have a [pension] board member serve on the board of a portfolio adviser," said Edward Siedle, a former US Securities and Exchange Commission attorney. "It raises a lot of serious conflict-of-interest questions."

By 2007, the real estate partnership between Davis and Daley's nephew Robert Vanecko also raised conflict-of-interest questions. All of the money garnered by Davis and Vanecko came from City of Chicago pension funds. They had no other investors. This brought up the point of whether their company, DV Urban Realty Partners, was a legitimate investment company or merely two associates of the mayor using political clout to get millions of dollars in pension money from the city. A number of the pension board members who approved funding for DV Urban Realty Partners were senior members of the Daley administration who the mayor himself had appointed to oversee the pension funds. Even worse, one of the pension funds that approved the deal for the mayor's nephew included John Briatta as a fund trustee. The mayor had appointed Briatta—John Daley's brother-in-law who would later go to jail for taking bribes in the Hired Truck Scandal—even though he was a manual laborer who lacked investment expertise.

Unfortunately, this sweet pension deal for Davis and Vanecko brought a sense of deja vu to a number of seasoned political reporters who had covered city hall since Daley took over in 1989. Back in the early 1990s, City Treasurer Miriam Santos accused three of the mayor's closest advisers—Tim Degnan, Frank Kruesi, and Ed Bedore—of pressuring her to invest $5 million in pension funds in a hotel developed by Daley's chief political fund-raiser, Paul Stepan. The mayor then sought revenge on Santos by trying to persuade the Illinois Legislature to remove her from two pension fund boards, but Republican governor Jim Edgar had vetoed Daley's proposal.

There was also a second significant issue with the Davis-Vanecko real estate partnership. A number of its real estate transactions appeared to favor friends of the mayor or to have a political connection that benefited Davis and Vanecko. In August 2007, the mayor's nephew and his partner teamed up with the politically connected restaurant owner Matthew O'Malley in a deal to purchase a building in the South Loop that stood next to O'Malley's Chicago Firehouse Restaurant. According to reports, DV Urban Realty Partners invested $1 million of pension funds, and a bank loan financed the balance of the purchase price. It did not appear as if O'Malley invested any of his own money. Real estate professionals speculated that O'Malley, Davis, and Vanecko would convert the historic building into a restaurant or hotel due to its proximity to the McCormick Place convention center.

Davis and Vanecko landed another sweet deal in November 2007. DV Urban Realty Partners purchased an industrial site that was largely vacant and then immediately started leasing part of the space to the City of Chicago for nearly $23,000 per month. Leases of this type normally required approval of the Chicago City Council, but the Daley administration structured the contract with DV Urban Realty Partners as a month-to-month lease, thereby circumventing the council's right to review the deal. "Things have to be done the right way. Right is right. Wrong is wrong. You can't skirt the rules," said Alderman Ray Suarez, the chairman of the council's Housing and Real Estate Committee, when he later learned that the Daley administration had side-stepped his legislative review.

In the midst of Vanecko and Davis's continued deal making, the Jon Burge police torture scandal resurfaced. In January 2008, the city council voted forty-five to none to pay a $20 million settlement to four black men who alleged that members of the Chicago Police Department had tortured them under the direction of former Commander Burge. "We are going to continue to seek justice in these Burge torture cases, and we will continue to go back to the international arenas until the US government, the City of Chicago and Cook County take responsibility for these human rights violations," said Joey Mogul, the attorney for the four men.

By the middle of 2008, for the first time in his career, more Chicagoans disapproved of Daley's job as mayor than approved. This decline in popularity had started during Daley's prior term, as voters became increasingly disenchanted with the multiple political corruption scandals tarnishing his administration. Some Chicagoans also started to develop the sense that Daley's ego was leading to bad mayoral decisions, such as the destruction of Meigs Field in the middle of the night.

Yet Daley pressed on. In his professional career he had shown a bent for taking big risks, and the mayor now had another plan for his beloved city: Chicago should host the 2016 summer Olympics. Two years earlier, the mayor had announced an exploratory committee to consider the idea. By 2008, Chicago was actively competing to represent the United States in the competition to host the 2016 summer games.

Chicago's Olympic bid organization was stacked with Daley confidantes. His longtime supporter Pat Ryan, the founder of Aon Insurance, chaired the committee. Before the end of the year, Daley's former chief of staff Lori Healey joined the bid committee as its president. The committee's board of directors was also filled with associates of Daley, including Ryan, John Rogers Jr., and Valerie Jarrett. The committee raised $90 million in private funding and gained the support of a wide range of civic and political leaders.

In June 2008, Chicago scored its first victory. The international Olympic committee chose Daley's city—along with Rio de Janeiro, Madrid, and Tokyo—as one of its finalists to become the official Olympic host city in 2016. Daley and Ryan were pleased with the news. Though the event was estimated to cost $5 billion, Mayor Daley believed that all funding could be raised through corporate and philanthropic donations. This claim, along with Chicago's increased chance to become the 2016 Olympic host city, set off a fundamental political clash between groups with opposing visions of Chicago. Those who believed Chicago had become a global city generally supported the Olympic bid. Those who saw Chicago as Midwestern city with limited resources—and a significant population of minorities and poor people—generally opposed the bid. One city with two visions created a wide area for disagreement.

By fall of that year, the campaign for president of the United States was in full swing, and the Democratic candidate was Barack Obama, a black US senator from Daley's hometown. Obama was a phenomenon, a speaker of great charisma who had risen quickly into America's highest political echelons.

Obama had come a long way in a little more than a decade.

Before entering politics, Obama had worked for Allison Davis's law firm. Davis was extremely well-connected in Chicago and he was known for throwing large parties that included a wide cross-section of the city's most influential people: city hall politicians, black professionals, university professors, white progressives, and people from the arts and nonprofit worlds. Obama and his wife attended many of these events and became known in this elite, wealthy circle. "I tried to include Barack and Michelle in everything," recalled Davis.

Obama first won elective office in 1996 as an Illinois state senator, twenty-four years after Rich Daley had been elected to the same position. Like Daley, Obama commuted down to Springfield and began to establish himself as a Democratic legislator. Unlike Daley, however, Obama did not become part of the regular Democratic organization from Chicago. Rather, he performed a difficult balancing act. On the one hand, he positioned himself as a liberal and somewhat independent Democrat. With the other hand, he cozied up to Emil Jones, a powerful old-school Democratic leader in the state senate.

Obama was an ambitious man and he knew that he needed tough and influential friends like Jones if he was ever going to escape Springfield and move up to the next level. One of those new friends was Tony Rezko, a businessman and occasional real estate partner of Allison Davis. Rezko had offered Obama a real estate–development job while he was still at Harvard Law School. Obama turned him down, but the two had stayed in touch. When Obama started campaigning for the Illinois state senate in 1995, Rezko's companies gave the unproven politician $2,000 on the first fund-raising day. Rezko went on to become one of Obama's largest and most consistent fund-raisers.

In 2003, Obama decided to run for an open US Senate seat. The rising politician picked Rezko—along with Allison Davis and Valerie Jarrett—to join his campaign finance committee and help him with fund-raising. Obama faced six competitors in the Democratic primary, but won a surprising 54 percent of the vote. How did Obama do it? Three factors were key.

First, Obama got lucky with respect to his Democratic rivals. Gery Chico—former school board president and chief of staff to Mayor

Daley—struggled with his television presence and was distracted by the insolvency of his law firm, Altheimer and Gray. Dan Hynes—the son of Thomas Hynes, a Democratic power broker and Daley's longtime ally—served as Illinois state comptroller, but lacked personal charisma. Despite endorsements from major unions and old-school politicians such as John Stroger, Hynes soon bored voters and they would search for alternative candidates. Blair Hull, a wealthy businessman with no prior experience in public office, spent millions of his own money on the campaign, but eventually was hobbled by accusations of abusive behavior toward his ex-wife.

The second factor was Obama himself. He was attractive, radiated personal charisma, and had begun to develop into a skillful campaign speaker. Moreover, he seemed to possess a personal integrity that voters picked up on.

Finally, Obama had selected capable advisers, such as Jarrett and David Axelrod, to help in his US Senate campaign. Both of these advisers had long and deep ties to Mayor Daley and they helped Obama to persuade many of the mayor's financial donors that Obama was also a good investment. Axelrod, in particular, served an invaluable role in helping Obama to craft his media message. The theme of Axelrod's appealing television ads was "Yes, we can." In one commercial, for example, Obama approached the camera and said, "Now they say we can't change Washington? I'm Barack Obama and I am running for the United States Senate to say, 'Yes, we can.'" Voters found this classic change-agent message irresistible, and the advertisements were very effective during the last three weeks of the primary campaign.

On election night, it was clear that Obama had clobbered his opponents. Axelrod—with nearly twenty years of campaign experience in Chicago and Illinois politics—knew that something historic was about to happen. "The most surprising and gratifying thing was when those numbers rolled in on primary night," Axelrod later said. "I was covering Chicago politics when the issue of race was at a jagged edge here. And I was around when Harold Washington went to Saint Pascal's Church on the Northwest Side and was roundly booed and the hatred was palpable. And [on Obama's] primary night I was moved . . . by watching numbers come across a computer screen. What those numbers meant was that we had passed a Rubicon in the politics of this state, where a guy could come along who was an African-American candidate, but who had universal appeal and people were willing to look beyond race."

Obama got lucky again in the general election. News reporters discovered that his Republican opponent Jack Ryan had, despite her protestations, taken his ex-wife to sex clubs. Ryan soon dropped out of the race and was replaced by Alan Keyes, a bombastic conservative who had not previously lived in Illinois. Such a weak opponent, combined with Obama's increasing popularity, created the impression that Obama would easily win the Senate seat. He stood a good chance of becoming only the third African-American US senator in more than a hundred years.

Obama had previously prepared for this moment by reaching out to the Daleys. During the primary campaign, he had crafted a conciliatory letter to the mayor. "You're with Hynes, I understand that," Obama had written. "I just hope that after the primary you can help me if I was to win this thing." Bill Daley would later comment on Obama's political savvy: "[The note to my brother] was a very smart thing to do. I think [Obama] did that with a lot of people."

Just a few days before the general election, Obama reached out again to Mayor Daley. Obama was smart enough to know that having the mayor of Chicago in his corner would increase his chances of winning the election. But what was in it for Daley? The answer was that a victory would send Obama to Washington, DC, thereby eliminating him as a potential African-American rival to Daley's mayoral office. "There were very few people at [city hall] who had given much thought to Barack [Obama] until then," recalled the political strategist Pete Giangreco. "But the modern Daley world revolved around racial divisions, which are as large and nasty in Chicago as anywhere in the country. It was always No. 1 on their agenda to make nice with black politicians in a way Old Man [Daley] never really did."

The senatorial candidate set up a lunch at Manny's Coffee Shop and Deli with Daley and the two men agreed to invite the media.

Manny's—a longtime favorite spot of local politicos, such as Rahm Emanuel and David Axelrod—was known for its Jewish comfort food, including corned beef sandwiches, brisket, potato pancakes, and chicken pot pie. Daley and Obama ate corned beef sandwiches and matzo ball soup. Though their lives had very different starting points, the two Chicago politicians appeared to enjoy their conversation.

"I think he has enough confidence to know that if he thinks something is important, that I am going to be responsive," Obama said after the lunch. "I'm not, hopefully, going to be the US senator from Chicago. I will be the US senator from Illinois."

Obama was right. He easily won the general election, garnering 70 percent of the vote.

Two years later in November 2006, the US senator from Chicago drove to the offices of David Axelrod's consulting firm in an off-the-beaten-track River North location. Obama was to share a private lunch with Bill Daley and seek his advice on running for president.

"Yeah, you gotta run," advised the political consigliore. "Why not? What have you got to lose? Can you win? I think you can." The youngest Daley brother also told Obama that he would have no problem raising money and that he should therefore carefully prepare before launching his campaign. Once launched, Hillary and Bill Clinton would come after him big time.

A few hours later, Obama began plotting his campaign in Axelrod's fourth-floor conference room. His closest confidantes were all invited, including Axelrod, Valerie Jarrett, and his wife Michelle. This was the beginning of Obama's two-year campaign to become the first black president of the United States.

Two months later, Obama endorsed Mayor Daley's 2007 bid for re-election. This decision was a significant change for Obama since 2005 when he had declined to endorse Daley and said that the Hired Truck Scandal gave him "huge pause." But Obama's flip-flop was not surprising. The mayor had endorsed Obama a few weeks earlier in his bid for the US presidency and Bill Daley was now one of Obama's national campaign advisers. In politics, changing circumstances usually called for new alliances. New beds sometimes needed new bedfellows.

Obama and his team ran a brilliant campaign and won the presidential election in 2008 by a comfortable margin. The candidate had a political formula that was hard to beat: charisma, a smart strategy, great speeches, and record-breaking campaign donations. His national finance committee—which included Chicago business and political heavyweights John Rogers Jr., Penny Pritzker, Bill Daley, Neil Bluhm, and Mellody Hobson—helped Obama to raise $750 million. Neither Hillary Clinton nor John McCain was up to the challenge of beating him.

Obama's November 2008 victory celebration in Grant Park brought out a crowd of nearly 250,000 energized supporters. Music blared, cameras flashed, and people hugged and celebrated in Chicago's front yard as they waited for the president-elect. Numerous celebrities and politicians attended, including Oprah Winfrey, Brad Pitt, Governor Rod Blagojevich, and Jesse Jackson. Blagojevich, who only stayed thirty minutes and left before Obama took the stage, may have been jealous of the US senator's political victory. Obama would soon become the nation's first black president, as well as the first big-city president in many decades. And Chicago would have an achievement of its own. One of its own politicians had finally made it into the nation's highest office.

One month later, the FBI arrested Blagojevich and John Harris, the governor's top aide who had worked in the Daley administration for a decade before becoming Blagojevich's chief of staff. US Attorney Patrick Fitzgerald accused the two men of a vast criminal conspiracy. "The breadth of corruption laid out in these charges is staggering," said Fitzgerald. He also specifically accused Blagojevich of attempting to "sell" the US Senate seat that president-elect Obama had left open. Tape recordings made by the FBI later revealed that in one phone conversation Blagojevich had said that the opportunity to leverage Obama's vacated Senate seat in return for financial gain was "fucking golden." It would also come out that Rahm Emanuel spoke about the open seat with both Blagojevich and Harris and suggested that the governor should appoint Valerie Jarrett. But Blagojevich was arrested before he could appoint anyone. Weeks later on January 9, 2009, he was impeached by the Illinois House of Representatives, making him the first governor in the nearly two-hundred-year history of the state to suffer such a humiliation.

Eleven days later, Barack Obama was inaugurated. Obama took many Daley protégés with him to Washington: David Axelrod as senior adviser to the president, Rahm Emanuel as chief of staff, Valerie Jarrett as senior adviser to the president, and Arne Duncan as US secretary of education. The Chicago crew was now playing in the big leagues. Only time would tell if they would be successful at this higher level of competition.

One week before the FBI arrested Blagojevich, the Daley administration announced another privatization deal. The city would lease its system of thirty-six thousand parking meters to a private firm for seventy-five years in exchange for approximately $1.2 billion.

Two days later, on December 4, 2008, the Chicago City Council voted forty to five to approve the transaction, even though some members privately admitted to not understanding the terms of the agreement. Dissenters included Toni Preckwinkle and Scott Waguespack, who argued that the city was not getting a good deal and that the decision-making process should be more deliberative and transparent. A number of older aldermen disagreed. Eighty-one-year-old Bernie Stone, for example, favored the deal because he thought that "this money is not going to be spent like a drunken sailor."

Two of the primary motivators of the city council, of course, were greed and fear. The parking meter vote was a casebook example of fear-driven decision making by the legislative body. When faced with a "fight-or-flight" situation, the Chicago City Council failed to weigh the pros and cons of an important long-term decision rationally. Instead, it simply ratified Daley's deal and felt relieved that the city had averted a budgetary crisis.

The council's fear was understandable. Six weeks earlier, Lehman Brothers—a 158-year-old investment bank with over $600 billion in assets—had filed for bankruptcy. A full-scale banking and credit crisis ensued, and stock markets around the globe panicked. The US government then bailed out the financial system by authorizing the Treasury to spend up to $700 billion to purchase distressed assets such as mortgages and mortgage-backed securities.

The City of Chicago's finances were also a mess. The city ran a $95 million deficit in fiscal 2007 and then had its proposed 2008 budget publicly rejected by the Civic Federation, a respected fiscal watchdog group. In opposing the proposed 2008 budget, the Civic Federation stated that "the city must continue to move forward on its efforts to contain costs and better manage its existing resources" while also demanding that the city's "pension funding crisis and chronically underfunded emergency reserve fund" be immediately addressed. Mayor Daley and the Chicago City Council did not listen, however. The budget deficit would increase to $218 million the next year, even as municipal pension and reserve funding levels became alarmingly low. Unfunded pension liabilities for local government employees in Chicago and Cook County had risen to $18.5 billion! Any reasonably competent financial manager would be seriously alarmed.

"Now Daley's selling city assets in order to raise the money to enable him to balance his budget," said Paul Vallas, "while avoiding making the real tough decisions that need to be made if he's going to bring governmental expenditures in line with projected long-term revenues. As a result, the city is becoming more and more an unpleasant place to do business, and yet city services are going to continue to diminish. And the city's long-term structural deficits are huge . . . , not to mention the unfunded, long-term mandates. . . . My view is that he's left the city a financial train wreck. The city has some serious, long-term financial issues."

Though the city council's fear was understandable, its decision to approve Daley's parking meter deal was a serious mistake. Initially, many Chicagoans were angered by steep new parking rates and meters that malfunctioned, leading to unfair parking tickets. Though these problems were relatively minor and short-lived, they created the perception in voters that perhaps the Daley administration had negotiated a flawed, short-sighted deal. The voters were right, though not for the reasons initially suspected. Within six months, the inspector general of Chicago, David Hoffman, publicly released a report highlighting damning long-term flaws in Daley's parking meter pact. By that time, the voters' memory of operating snafus and pocketbook issues would be compounded by a real financial crisis in Chicago and questions about the Daley administration's reckless spending of the parking meter proceeds.

A political issue was brewing.

CHAPTER 22

SISYPHUS

In Greek mythology, Sisyphus was a leader condemned by the gods to an eternity of frustration. According to legend, when Sisyphus ruled over Corinth, a city-state in ancient Greece, he committed certain unnamed crimes against the gods. Sisyphus was punished for this when he died. In the afterworld, he was made to push a great boulder to the top of a steep hill, where it rolled back to the bottom and he would be forced to start over. His fate was to labor endlessly over the same task without ever quite achieving his goal.

And so it seemed with Rich Daley as his tenure as mayor of Chicago passed the nineteen-year milestone. Daley continued to toil with economic development, schools, budgets, crime, and public housing, while old scandals resurfaced.

In September 2008, Oprah Winfrey kicked off her twenty-third television season by inviting 175 US Olympic athletes to the pavilion at Millennium Park for a welcome-home tribute from the Beijing games. The medalists stood on stage as the crowd cheered and Oprah introduced the rock singer David Cook who performed "Time of My Life." American flags and Olympic symbols draped the stage as confetti floated down on the audience. The moment seemed to capture what the architect Frank Gehry had originally envisioned for the pavilion: a magical place that creates a special relationship between the audience and the stage. Oprah's extravaganza also served as a rally for Chicago's bid to host the 2016 Olympics, and Mayor Daley and his wife Maggie attended their first Oprah Winfrey show. Daley seemed worn-down and tired, but he was a persistent man, and the Olympic bid represented an opportunity for him to showcase Chicago on the world stage while also jumpstarting economic development in the city.

Many observers believed he was thinking of his political legacy as he pressed forward with Chicago's effort to host the Olympics.

Four months after Oprah's show, Arne Duncan resigned his position as chief executive of the Chicago Public Schools and moved to Washington, DC, to become President Obama's first secretary of education. Duncan had served in his role for over seven years and his appointment by Mayor Daley as CEO of the public school system in 2001 had represented an important signpost in Daley's evolution as a leader. Whereas his predecessor Paul Vallas had been a no-nonsense administrator and financial expert, Duncan was an educator and an avowed liberal who socialized with many African-Americans.

Duncan had a different background and personality than his predecessor. He had grown up in Hyde Park, a diverse neighborhood near the University of Chicago, and had attended the University of Chicago Laboratory School. At Lab, Duncan met John Rogers Jr., one of the school's basketball stars. Duncan, who was six years younger than Rogers, followed around the older, African-American teen like a puppy dog. Rogers became a mentor to Duncan and one of his most important lifelong friends.

Duncan's parents were educators. His father was a psychology professor at the University of Chicago. His mother ran Sue Duncan's Children's Center, a free after-school program for African-American children on Chicago's south side. The center—which was one room in a church in the Kenwood neighborhood—focused on development of the whole child, including academic, emotional, and social growth. When he was not playing basketball, Arne Duncan worked with his mother at the center and spent years tutoring black kids after school. He then attended Harvard University, where he was co-captain of the basketball team and an Academic All-American.

After playing professional basketball in Australia for four years, Duncan returned to Chicago and began working for his friend Rogers at Ariel Investments, one of the largest minority-run investment firms in the United States. Duncan did not have financial expertise, but was passionate about education. Rogers, therefore, took the extraordinary step of funding a nonprofit education foundation called the Ariel Education Initiative and allowed his friend Duncan to run it. This foundation mentored a class of African-American sixth graders for six years and helped to pay their college tuition under the "I Have a Dream" program.

In 1999, Rogers phoned Gery Chico, who served as the chairman of the board of the Chicago Public Schools, and suggested that Duncan would be a great addition to CPS. Chico knew Rogers well from his six years of service as president of the Chicago Park District and was receptive to the solicitation. Maggie Daley, the mayor's wife, was also a big fan of Duncan. She had met him at various social events, including functions at the Lab School, and put in a good word for Duncan with her husband. One of the mayor's nephews, who worked for Rogers at Ariel Investments, also spoke favorably to his uncle about Duncan, who soon joined the Daley team as deputy chief of staff to Paul Vallas, the CEO of the schools. After leaving Ariel, Duncan maintained his close relationship with Rogers, and the two former basketball standouts played on a winning three-on-three hoops team with Craig Robinson, a Hyde Park native who was also the brother-in-law of then Illinois state senator Barack Obama.

When Paul Vallas decided to leave the Daley administration in mid-2001, Daley appointed Duncan as CEO. It was a surprising choice since Duncan had little administrative experience and the Chicago school system had 420,000 students and more than twenty thousand teachers. But Duncan was passionate about the education of kids—he did not have any political aspirations whatsoever—and he interpreted the mayor's selection as a pure mandate to improve schools and the lives of students.

One of the first directives the mayor gave Duncan as the new CEO of the school system was, "Just do the right thing for children." Daley exemplified these words with actions of his own. The mayor constantly visited schools—sometimes as many as three times per week—and was relentless in rallying the city behind his efforts to improve public education. This impressed Duncan tremendously, especially since 90 percent of the students in Chicago public schools were minorities and 85 percent lived below the poverty line.

Duncan had another opportunity to observe Daley's passion for his city and its children when, just three months after Daley selected Duncan to run Chicago's public schools, two airplanes struck and destroyed the World Trade Center in New York on September 11, 2001. On that morning, Duncan was out visiting a school when he began to receive urgent messages telling him to report immediately to the city's 911 emergency center. He ended up spending most of the day in lockdown mode, alone in a room with Mayor Daley as the tragic events unfolded. There were rumors that Chicago was a terrorism target, and neither Duncan nor the mayor knew what would happen. Duncan sat and worried about the kids in his schools, feeling a heavy responsibility. During his quarantine period with Daley, the school chief also had an absolute feeling that the mayor had the weight of the entire city—nearly 3 million Chicagoans—pressing down on him. When at last their quarantine period ended, Duncan left with a profound impression of what Chicago meant to Daley.

As the terror of 9/11 began to recede and life normalized again for those outside of New York, Duncan and Daley pressed forward with their efforts to improve the city's public schools. Under Vallas, the administration and infrastructure of the school system had improved significantly, while performance standards and accountability had been instituted for student achievement. This had led to higher math scores and modest improvements in reading scores for grade school students. Despite this progress, high school dropout rates remained high and the average graduate fell well below the benchmarks for college readiness.

Duncan, as the CEO of Chicago schools, focused on three initiatives: instructional excellence, professional development of teachers and principals, and new school creation. The first prong of the strategy concentrated on having an effective curriculum in reading and mathematics, while also training teacher specialists in these subjects. The second initiative emphasized fostering top-rate principals and also developing teachers who achieved national board certification, the gold standard for teacher quality. Finally, Duncan and his team experimented with many different strategies for new school creation, but ended up putting most resources behind Renaissance 2010, a plan announced in 2004 to open a hundred new schools over a ten-year period while also closing poor performers.

During its seven-year tenure serving Mayor Daley, the Duncan administration developed many innovative policies and achieved some real accomplishments before Arne Duncan headed off to Washington, DC. But its Herculean efforts led to mixed success in improving the academic achievement of Chicago students. Graduation rates advanced substantially, but reading scores and college readiness did not. Much of this achievement gap could rightly be blamed on the poverty and challenging home life of the city's public school students, rather than on any deficiency in Duncan or Daley. There were no easy answers to the socioeconomic problem.

But Daley and Duncan also deserved significant criticism for an action they failed to take: confronting the teachers' union. Chicago had the shortest school day of all American big cities and neither the mayor nor the chief executive of the schools had gone to battle to try and fix this serious structural flaw. This lack of will by the Daley administration failed the mayor's own leadership test—just do the right thing for children—and perhaps was responsible for the mixed results of Chicago's school reform efforts. But giving a politically active municipal union a cushy contract and a free pass on reform was characteristic of Daley in his later years in office. The formerly bold mayor had lost some of his will to take on risky fights.

In June 2009, Inspector General David Hoffman released a forty-six-page report criticizing Daley's parking meter deal. Hoffman focused on the lack of a deliberative process in the Chicago City Council, as well as the defects of the transaction itself. His analysis had two primary conclusions. First, Daley and his team had negotiated a bad deal for the city. The inspector general estimated that Chicago should have received $1 billion more than it did. The transaction also had another significant flaw: its seventy-five-year length. "It's a mistake to rush into a deal for such a long period of time without a full public accounting of the pros and cons," said Hoffman. The city could have received nearly the same amount of proceeds for the parking meters with a forty-year deal. The second major problem that Hoffman identified was that the privatization of the parking meter system was not even needed to improve the city's fiscal outlook. The City of Chicago could have kept its meters, raised rates to market levels and retained 100 percent of the revenues for itself. Daley's deal was unnecessary. Hoffman's report ignited a firestorm of outrage that burned across Chicago for the next two years.

But the inspector general was not finished with making Daley's life uncomfortable. The week before Hoffman's parking meter report was released, a federal grand jury issued four subpoenas to city pension funds—including those representing police and fire employees—that had invested $68 million with the real estate firm run by the mayor's nephew, Robert Vanecko. Hoffman had recruited prosecutors from US Attorney Patrick Fitzgerald's office to help out after the city pension funds refused to cooperate with his inspector general office's investigation. "I'm running this office as an independent entity—period," explained Hoffman. "People need to believe that you're independent of every other part of city government. Especially the mayor."

Within two weeks, the legal pressure from Hoffman and the US Attorney led to the announcement by Vanecko that he was resigning as Allison Davis's partner in DV Urban Realty Partners. Michael Shields—a police officer who served as a pension trustee and the only city professional to cooperate with Hoffman's investigation—said the police fund should demand its money back. "Nine percent of an officer's salary goes into the pension fund," said Shields. "This is not the Daley family's personal piggy bank." Over the next two years, the investments of DV Urban Realty Partners experienced many problems: one would end up in bankruptcy, one in foreclosure, and half would suffer financial difficulties. Politically connected investing apparently did not always lead to high returns.

After ten years, Daley's Plan for Transformation had made a large and positive impact on the neighborhoods surrounding the former public high-rises in Chicago. Ghettos started to disappear as new communities replaced them. This neighborhood revitalization was most evident in the area surrounding Cabrini-Green, a notorious public-housing development on the north side of the city.

The site of Cabrini-Green was known as Little Hell in the early 1900s because of its pervasive poverty and crime. During World War II, the Chicago Housing Authority demolished Little Hell and constructed low-rise apartments for defense-industry workers. The CHA named the site the Frances Cabrini Homes in honor of the first American canonized as a saint by the Catholic Church.

In the late 1950s and early 1960s, the CHA constructed the large high-rise buildings that were named in honor of labor leader William Green. The entire project became known as Cabrini-Green. The original population of the public-housing development was a mix of Italians, Irish, Puerto Ricans, and blacks. In the early 1960s, however, racial segregation in the Chicago housing market contributed to Cabrini-Green becoming an almost exclusively African-American population. By the 1970s, the public project had a reputation for crime and poverty that mirrored the Little Hell image from decades earlier. Residents of Cabrini-Green were significantly more likely to be robbed, assaulted, raped, and murdered than other Chicagoans. The area surrounding Cabrini-Green soon became a no-man's land for law-abiding citizens, who would drive circuitous routes to avoid it.

The US Department of Housing and Urban Development had begun the demolition of Cabrini-Green high-rises in 1995, but the process proceeded slowly. As the vertical ghettos were gradually razed, the surrounding neighborhood began to improve. One of the first signs of change was a large Dominick's grocery store, which opened in 1999 a few blocks from Cabrini. Two years later, Mayor Daley dedicated a new 47,000-square-foot police station within the projects' shadows. As he had done in Bronzeville and other communities located near public housing, Daley wisely sought to make the large law enforcement facility an anchor of the neighborhood redevelopment process.

As the neighborhood gradually improved, schools, businesses and stores started to arrive. In 2008, the British School of Chicago—a private international-style institution with strong academics—opened a 75,000-square-foot facility in the area. Later in that same year, a startup company called Groupon moved in down the street from the police station. Within three years, it would employ nearly ten thousand people. In April 2009, Apple picked the locale to build a 15,000-square-foot glass-cube Apple Store like the one it had opened on Fifth Avenue in Manhattan. By fall of 2009, when only three of the public high-rises remained at Cabrini, it was clear that the neighborhood had transformed.

Neighborhood revitalization succeeded near Cabrini-Green and some other public-housing sites in Chicago, but the rest of Daley's Plan for Transformation experienced somewhat mixed results. Though many Chicagoans agreed that the new low-rise mixed-income units were preferable to the vanquished vertical ghettos, the pace of new construction had lagged behind the original plan. This left some of the original CHA residents using housing vouchers rather than living in redeveloped mixed-income units. The encouraging news, however, was that a good portion of the former residents using vouchers had an improved quality of life, primarily from living in a lower crime area. Others felt dislocated from friends and community and continued to live a life challenged by crime and poverty.

Daley's bid to bring the 2016 Summer Olympics to Chicago seemed to have great promise in the fall of 2009, with many predicting that the International Olympic Committee would choose the city when it met in Copenhagen, Denmark, in October. Olympic bid experts generally agreed that Chicago had put together a strong bid package and that Pat Ryan and Mayor Daley had rallied significant civic support for the games. Some prognosticators also believed that the backing of the president of the United States for his home city would make a crucial difference.

But then tragedy struck one week before the Olympic meeting in Copenhagen. A sixteen-year-old Fenger High School student named

Derrion Albert was beaten to death near school. The brutal teenage brawl that followed on Chicago's south side was captured on video and aired throughout the world. Though it was unclear if the news coverage of this violent event would have an impact on the Olympic Committee's upcoming decision, Mayor Daley used his White House connections to arrange a summit in Chicago where US Attorney General Eric Holder and US Secretary of Education Arne Duncan would discuss ways to limit school violence.

In the meantime, Mayor Daley and a large Chicago delegation had boarded a charter plane for the upcoming Olympic Committee meeting. The mayor's group included his wife Maggie, his brother Bill, Chicago 2016 CEO Pat Ryan, presidential adviser Valerie Jarrett, and US education secretary Arne Duncan, as well as Olympic gold medalists and businesspeople with close ties to Mayor Daley and President Obama. Two famous Chicagoans would also join the delegation in Denmark: First Lady Michelle Obama and television star Oprah Winfrey. The press also speculated as to whether President Obama himself would attend.

"You know, I would love to go, because Chicago is my hometown," the president had said a few weeks before the Olympic meeting. "The track and field stadium, if we got the Olympics here in the United States, would actually be about three blocks from my house [in Chicago], so I could walk over. . . . We are deeply invested in getting this done. Michelle is definitely planning to go to Copenhagen, and she's, I think, the best Obama representative that we have."

In the end, Obama did attend the Olympic meeting in Copenhagen. His decision had two political perils for the president. If Chicago won, Obama risked association with any corruption or misconduct that might occur as Daley's city prepared for the Olympic Games over the next seven years. If Chicago lost, Obama's personal appeal exposed the White House to an erosion of prestige and even diplomatic damage on the world's stage.

When the team from Chicago made its presentation to the International Olympic Committee, the president sat on stage between his wife and Mayor Daley. The Obamas' appeals tried to link the Olympic

Committee's decision to their own personal and political history with Chicago, as well as their sense that America had a unique ability to inspire the rest of the world. Afterward, Daley's Olympic team celebrated at the Admiral Hotel, feeling that Chicago had a good chance of advancing toward its goal. However, the American city soon learned that it had been knocked out in the first round and that Rio de Janeiro had won the right to host the 2016 Olympics.

Mayor Daley had an uncharacteristically philosophical reaction to the disappointing news. "I get emotional about it," said the mayor. "I love my job, Chicago really shined here. I just want to make sure people realize that. People did a tremendous job. You don't have to win everything in life to be victorious." These were surprising words from a normally hot-tempered man who had not lost an election in twenty-six years.

Why did Chicago suffer such a decisive loss? One unresolved issue seemed most significant: a long-running financial dispute in which the US Olympic Committee refused to take a smaller share of the global Olympic sponsorship revenues and US broadcast rights. This hardheaded position by the Americans had left bruised feelings in some Olympic delegates, which were heightened by President Obama's high-security, somewhat imperial visit.

By the time Mayor Daley and the Olympic delegation returned to the United States, many in Chicago speculated that Daley would retire at the end of his term in May 2011. Despite an all-time low approval rating of 35 percent for the mayor, his brother Bill discounted the political rumblings. "Win or lose, the Olympics were never going to determine what Rich Daley was going to do," said the political consigliore. "I believe he runs again. I just assume he does. He still has the enthusiasm for the job." But shrewd political operators like Bill Daley were not always known for their candor. Only time would tell if his statement was sincere or a head fake designed to keep the Daley clan's opponents off balance.

Two months later, the Chicago City Council ignored a $520 million structural budget deficit and voted to pass the mayor's proposed

$6.1 billion budget by a vote of thirty-eight to twelve. Money to close the budget gap came from a supposedly long-term fund set up by the seventy-five-year parking meter privatization transaction. This financial sleight of hand infuriated a number of aldermen. "You cannot break a contract in 12 months that's supposed to last for 75 years," said Alderman Tom Allen. "It's unconscionable, and it's disingenuous, and it's intellectually dishonest." Allen then voted against Daley's budget for the first time in his sixteen-year career as an alderman. The Civic Federation also rejected Daley's budget and did not mince words: "It is unsustainable and relies too heavily on one-time reserve funds to close a $520 million budget deficit. The proposed drastic draw down of long-term reserves allows for increased spending in Fiscal 2010 but does not properly plan for the future." The issue identified by the Civic Federation was known as "sudden-wealth syndrome"—typical of lottery prize winners—a malady where a person comes into an unexpected windfall and then loses all sense of compass and dissipates the proceeds. But Daley and the city council were not listening. They had unfortunately punted on leadership, kicking the problem down the road for future generations to address.

CHAPTER 23

BLOODLINES

In January 2010, White House chief of staff Rahm Emanuel reportedly informed certain Washington, DC, insiders that his service to President Obama was an eighteen-month job and that he was contemplating running for mayor of Chicago. This statement surprised many since Emanuel was considered close to the Daley family, and the current mayor had not publicly indicated an inclination to retire. Three months later, Emanuel again brought up his Chicago desire on the eponymous show hosted by Charlie Rose. "First of all, let me say it this way, I hope Mayor Daley seeks reelection. I will work and support him if he seeks reelection. But if Mayor Daley doesn't, one day I would like to run for mayor of the City of Chicago. That's always been an aspiration of mine even when I was in the House of Representatives."

For followers of Chicago politics, this second statement by Emanuel raised the question of what private conversations were occurring between three friends: Emanuel, Bill Daley, and Rich Daley. Had Rich discussed retiring with his brother Bill? Did Bill tip off Rahm? Or was the assertive Emanuel simply marking out his territory, like a big dog raising his leg at every tree and fire hydrant on his block? It was hard to know if such speculation had any basis.

But there were clues for those paying attention. First, Emanuel and Bill Daley had a close and long-standing relationship. In 2004, then US Congressman Emanuel had told a reporter, "I trust Bill . . . with my life. [We] talk constantly." The close rapport between Emanuel and Bill Daley meant that it was unlikely that the disciplined Emanuel would be publicly discussing running for mayor of Chicago unless he had some basis for thinking that the office might soon have a vacancy. The second clue was more visible and more important. In April

2010—one week after Emanuel went on *Charlie Rose*—the White House chief of staff flew to Chicago and attended the Richard J. Daley annual Global Cities Forum at the University of Illinois at Chicago. The prestigious event included mayors from cities around the world, as well as prominent business, civic, and academic leaders. Mayor Daley himself welcomed the mayors and other leaders from over a hundred cities to the event that honored his father. During the panel discussions that followed, Rahm Emanuel sat near the front with the mayor, his wife Maggie, and other members of the Daley family. During the official break, Emanuel laughed, hugged, and shook hands with the Daley clan and their entourage. It was a warm and very public display of affection for a man who had just said his life goal was to succeed Daley as mayor of Chicago.

Two and a half months later, the Chicago Blackhawks hockey team defeated the Philadelphia Flyers and won the Stanley Cup championship. The last time the Blackhawks were champions was in 1961 when the first Mayor Daley had started to revitalize Chicago during his second term in office. Now forty-nine years later, his son, the second Mayor Daley, joined thousands of Chicagoans for a victory celebration.

Nearly two million people attended the raucous event, which included screaming fans, flag-waving jersey wearers, and a tickertape parade. At the end of the procession, Mayor Daley and Governor Quinn went up onstage with the team for a rally. The two politicians were greeted with strong boos from the otherwise happy crowd. The mayor recovered and went on to speak words consistent with his personal philosophy. "The Blackhawks' success this year has been a great life lesson for the people of Chicago. It shows that with teamwork, dedication and a commitment to never give up—no matter what—you can achieve your goals," said Daley. "It proves that if people continue to work together as a team, great things can happen." A nice address— short and honest—but the hearty boos from thousands of Chicagoans must have hurt. Daley was an experienced politician, but also a man with a somewhat thin skin for criticism. It was likely that the jeers of the Blackhawks crowd left him heavy in both mind and heart.

A few weeks later, the Chicago City Council voted to approve the second Walmart store in the city. The unanimous vote came one week after unions dropped their longstanding opposition to the company's expansion plans. This dramatic change in the perspective of the city council resulted from a negotiated deal in which Walmart agreed to pay an hourly wage at least fifty cents more than the legal minimum. Two years of job losses and a bad economy had worn down the negotiating position of the unions and their backers in the city council. Mayor Daley approved of the compromise. "Wal-Mart will be good for our neighborhoods, good for our workers," said Daley. "The No. 1 issue in America is jobs. You hear from people [that] they just want something [to do]." In addition to the second store on the city's south side, Walmart promised to develop a plan that would bring dozens of additional stores to Chicago. "Over the next several months, we look forward to working with the city to help ensure our stores are part of the solution in terms of creating jobs, stimulating economic development and eradicating food deserts here," said Walmart executive Hank Mullany.

During the late summer and early fall of 2010, the Daley brothers performed a series of political head fakes that created uncertainty for their professional rivals. In August, the mayor delivered a forceful annual state of the city address in which he highlighted municipal priorities, such as reducing violent crime and trimming the budget deficit. "There is more to be achieved. We face major challenges which together we can all solve," said Daley. Local politicians and the media failed to recognize his skillful misdirection move, and instead widely interpreted the mayor's resolve as a sign that he intended to seek reelection. Daley did not publicly reveal his plans, however, and tended to bristle when questioned. "The election is in February," he snapped at a reporter who inquired about his reelection intentions. Shortly after Labor Day, Bill Daley told a reporter that he expected his brother to seek a seventh term as mayor, specifically downplaying the retirement speculation in Chicago. "We've seen this movie six times [before]," said Bill. Another Chicago head fake, beautifully executed.

Mayor Daley had already decided to retire months earlier.

A few days later, at a city hall press briefing, the mayor announced that he would step down the following May after more than twenty-two years in office. The Daley era was ending. "I have always known that people want you to work hard for them," said Daley. "Clearly, they won't always agree with you. Obviously, they don't like it when you make a mistake. But at all times, they expect you to lead, to make difficult decisions, rooted in what's right for them. For 21 years, that's what I've tried to do. But today, I am announcing that I will not seek a seventh term as Mayor of the City of Chicago."

Up onstage with the mayor stood his wife Maggie—a cancer survivor supporting herself with a crutch—his daughters Nora and Lally, and his son Patrick. Family only. The mayor, who wore a tailored gray suit, light blue shirt, and sophisticated striped tie, had started his announcement by professing his great love of Chicago and its people. "I am here today to say what I hope you already know, I love Chicago. I love the 'I will' spirit of the place, and most of all, I love the people. Throughout this great city, in every neighborhood and on every block, there are people who give unselfishly, unbending in their determination, bold in the belief that they can make a difference. And they have. Together as a city, we have moved past our differences to reach real progress. We are Chicago—in my view, the greatest city on earth."

When the short speech ended, the Daley family left the stage and filed out of the room without answering questions. Why had he chosen to retire now? Some in the media speculated that Daley was retiring to spend more time with his ailing wife Maggie. The mayor himself said that this was not the case and close friends of the Daleys confided that his spouse had given him the green light to run again. Maggie was not the reason.

Daley had kept his thinking to himself, but there were at least three factors that explained his decision. First, his political popularity had reached an all-time low. This fact would make even a champion pol such as Daley worry about a reelection battle. The thought of losing his last fight would be excruciating to a man with Daley's temperament. Second, the mayor had conversations with his brother Bill and other friends about how lucrative the private sector could be for him. At the age of sixty-nine, perhaps it was time to bulk up his retirement accounts. Finally, the prospect of four more years could do nothing to aid his political legacy. Rich Daley had already surpassed his father to become the longest-serving mayor in the history of Chicago. He had taken big risks, persisted over many years, and made substantial improvements to his city. With a weak economy and without the prospect of the 2016 Summer Olympics, no impetus existed for taking Daley's legacy up a notch.

After he finished his retirement announcement, the media in Chicago began immediately to speculate on the likely nature of Daley's professional legacy. His admirers focused on how he had transformed a Rust Belt town into a global city, created Millennium Park and beautified downtown, improved race relations, and taken political risks to improve public schools and housing. They emphasized his love of, and commitment to, Chicago. Daley's detractors focused on a growing pension crisis, the midnight destruction of Meigs Field, persistent corruption within city government, high levels of crime, and the mayor's financial mismanagement during his last years in office. There was truth in both points of view, but the passage of time would likely lead to history's judgment that Daley's achievements had outweighed his mistakes.

The following month, the Chicago City Council met to discuss the mayor's final budget. Despite a worsening structural budget deficit of $655 million and the city's $16.5 billion of unfunded pension liabilities, the aldermen approved the city's financial plan for 2011 by a forty-three-to-seven vote. Both the Civic Federation and certain aldermen strongly objected, especially to the use of nonrecurring revenue sources—such as money from the parking meter deal and other privatization transactions—to fund current-year operations. Moody's, Standard and Poor's, and Fitch rating agencies had already downgraded the city's bond ratings due to such poor financial practices. "It's a ticking time bomb for the future of the city," agreed Alderman Robert Fioretti. "The way we're dealing with the budget is not sustainable." But Mayor

Daley differed, depicting his budget plan as the only practical option in a tough economy, and a majority of the city council went along with his proposal. It was clear that Daley had left the city's financial mess as a problem for his successor to tackle.

The fall weather in Chicago was unusually warm in 2010, and the campaign to follow Daley as mayor soon was in full swing. On the first day of October, Rahm Emanuel announced that he would give up his White House chief-of-staff position to campaign for the mayor's office. At a packed press conference, President Obama praised Emanuel. "This is a bittersweet day here at the White House," said Obama. "On the one hand, we are all very excited for Rahm as he takes on a new challenge, for which he is extraordinarily well qualified. But we are also losing an incomparable leader of our staff, and one who we are going to miss very much." After the news conference, Obama went even further, coming close to endorsing Emanuel for the highest leadership position in his hometown Chicago. "I think he would make an excellent mayor, and he would bring an incredible energy to the job," said the first Chicago politician to become president of the United States.

The other candidates for mayor probably disagreed. After Mayor Daley had announced his intention to retire, a pack of local politicians expressed an interest in running to replace him: James Meeks, Danny Davis, Carol Moseley Braun, Miguel del Valle, Tom Dart, and Gery Chico. Each represented different constituencies in a city where blacks, whites, and Hispanics persistently jostled for political power.

Meeks, Davis, and Braun are African-American. Meeks was both an Illinois state senator and an admired preacher presiding over a megachurch. Davis was a long serving US Congressman who had started his political career in the Chicago City Council. Braun had also grown up in city politics, before going on to become the first female African-American in the US Senate.

Del Valle, of Puerto Rican descent and a former state legislator, was the Chicago City Clerk. Though not a high-profile politician, he had a solid reputation and was popular within the fast-growing Hispanic demographic.

Dart was the Cook County sheriff and a former member of the Illinois state senate. As sheriff, he had made national headlines during the 2008 financial crisis with his refusal to enforce court-ordered foreclosure evictions. Otherwise unexceptional, Dart ignited the hopes of a classic segment of Chicago voters: white south-siders.

Gery Chico was more complicated than the other candidates who considered challenging Rahm Emanuel. After leaving the Daley administration in 2001, he had experienced both setbacks and success. His disappointments included the insolvency and dissolution of the Altheimer and Gray law firm, as well as an unsuccessful candidacy for the US Senate. His achievements included the founding of Chico and Nunes, a boutique law firm that used savvy and connections to lobby city hall for more than forty corporate clients, including Exelon, Cisco Systems, and Clear Channel Communications. Intelligence and a strong work ethic had aided Chico in his professional comeback, but perhaps more important were his relationships with a wide swath of Chicago politicos. Chico had bloodlines running from deep in the Daley administration, as well as from Alderman Ed Burke, the mayor's lifelong rival. His lineage could be traced back to the earliest days of the Chicago machine.

Even as the mayoral campaign started, Mayor Daley made a major announcement: the president of China, Hu Jintao, would visit Chicago following his official state visit with President Obama at the White House in January 2011. China's leader would only visit one US city outside of Washington, DC, and Daley called Hu's selection of Chicago a "big, big, big, big, big deal."

After meeting with Obama at the White House, President Hu arrived in Chicago, the hometown of the US president. By coming to the city, Hu was not only trying to ingratiate himself with a powerful world leader, he was also acting in China's self-interest. More than three hundred Chicago area businesses had a presence in China, and the economically vibrant Asian country generally viewed Chicago as the capital of the Midwest's significant manufacturing capabilities.

The Chinese delegation's visit confirmed Chicago's place as a global city. Saskia Sassen—an influential thinker who coined the term "global city"—took note of the Chinese visit to Chicago in *Foreign Policy*'s 2011 year-end issue, and cited it as an example of a global city that was "becoming more important geopolitically than the United States is as a country."

From his entry into the mayoral contest, Emanuel—who voters almost immediately perceived as the front runner—faced a difficult balancing act. He had to deal respectfully with the substantial legacy of a mayoral predecessor, namely Rich Daley, while also establishing himself as a forward-looking problem solver. Daley's legacy was two decades of leadership and stability for Chicago. As a candidate, Emanuel paid homage to that legacy and refrained from any public criticism of Daley, while simultaneously working to demonstrate that a new era of city government would begin under his mayoral administration. In this respect, Emanuel closely followed Daley's own playbook from the 1989 election.

In 2011, Emanuel skillfully maneuvered during the campaign by proposing new ideas, such as a longer day at public schools, while repeatedly acknowledging Daley's more than two decades of service. Emanuel organized his campaign around four significant issues: fiscal solvency for the city, continued education reform, crime reduction, and transparent, accountable government. Left unsaid by Emanuel was the fact that none of these topics would be relevant campaign concerns had not the outgoing mayor—Richard M. Daley—neglected to take on big challenges during his last years in office.

Emanuel's disciplined, high-energy balancing act looked like it was working, and none of the other mayoral candidates had captivated Chicago voters. But then a controversy arose that threatened his entire campaign. On November 26, 2010, attorney Burt Odelson filed an official objection to Emanuel's candidacy, arguing that Emanuel was not a resident of Chicago and therefore was ineligible to become mayor. Odelson asked that Emanuel's name be removed from the upcoming February 22, 2011, ballot.

The basis of Odelson's argument was that Emanuel had lived in

Washington, DC, while serving as White House chief of staff and therefore could not be a Chicago resident. He also noted that the former Illinois congressman had rented out his home while serving the president of the United States.

Those were the official facts of the dispute, but the real story was much more interesting—and complicated. It went deep into the bloodlines of Chicago Democratic politics. Since the assassination of Mayor Anton Cermak in 1932, Chicago had had eight full-term mayors, five of whom were Catholics from Bridgeport's Eleventh Ward. These white south-side men—including Dick Daley and his son Rich—controlled city hall for sixty-nine of those seventy-nine years. Rahm Emanuel—like an adopted firstborn son—ended up as the likely successor to the Eleventh Ward's royal line.

For much of the twentieth century, however, the Fourteenth Ward stood as a political counterweight to the Bridgeport-dominated Eleventh Ward. In the 1950s, the Fourteenth Ward power brokers essentially ruled Chicago during the weak reign of Mayor Kennelly. In 1953, these Fourteenth Warders challenged Dick Daley for the chairmanship of the Democratic Party, but their coup failed when one of their leaders died in a weekend automobile accident. In 1968, Ed Burke acceded to the head of the Fourteenth Ward and he has held on to power for more than forty years.

Burke had long believed that he should be mayor of Chicago. His problem was that his leadership role in the racially divisive Council Wars during the 1980s made him unsupportable by voters who valued diversity and fairness. He needed a proxy candidate, and Gery Chico seemed like the best fit. The two men had known each other well and for a long time, and there was no question that Burke would retain his kingpin role in city council if Chico became mayor.

In 2011 political circles, it was widely believed that Ed Burke was behind the attempt to knock Rahm Emanuel off of the ballot. The legal process dragged on for nine weeks. Emanuel won the first two rounds, receiving positive rulings from the Chicago Board of Election Commissioners and a Cook County judge. But then the appellate court, by a vote of two to one, ruled against him and ordered his name stricken from the ballot. Both judges responsible for tossing Emanuel from the ballot were slated for election by the Cook County Democratic Party judicial slating committee chaired by Ed Burke, the boss from the Fourteenth Ward. Burke had the power to make or break the career of Chicago judges, and ambitious magistrates were well aware of that fact.

By the end of January, the case challenging Emanuel's residency ended up before the Illinois Supreme Court. The high court was composed of seven justices, including Anne Burke, the wife of Eddie Burke himself. This set up a potential conflict of interest in the Emanuel ballot case.

Anne Burke had had an unusual legal career, which was greatly facilitated by her husband's political clout. Born in 1944, she grew up in a Catholic family and was a self-described poor student. After getting married, she became a stay-at-home parent for many years. At the age of thirty-nine, however, she graduated from law school and passed the Illinois bar. She then established a neighborhood law practice that took on a wide range of civil and criminal matters for clients. In 1987—after a mere four years of legal experience—Governor James Thompson appointed her judge to the Illinois Court of Claims. In 1995, Burke received another surprising appointment: Illinois Appellate Court, First District, for an interim term. This is a prestigious plum for attorneys, and the Chicago Council of Lawyers strongly objected to the selection of Anne Burke, rating her not qualified due to insufficient legal experience.

The following year, the political maneuvering of her husband and his friend Fast Eddie Vrdolyak became even more apparent. Anne Burke needed to stand for judicial reelection, and the 1996 sequence of events gave the impression that the two Eddies, as they were sometimes known, were up to their old tricks. Two of Vrdolyak's law partners—Michael Casey and Michael McCafferty—filed to run against Anne Burke, giving the judicial race the appearance of a crowded field. Potential competitors migrated to other election contests. After the filing deadline had passed, however, both of Vrdolyak's partners dropped out of the race, allowing Burke an uncontested victory. A decade later, Anne Burke was appointed—not elected—to the Illinois Supreme Court.

So the stage was set, and during the first month of 2011 the Illinois Supreme Court would decide if Emanuel would get his chance to succeed Daley and become the next mayor of Chicago. When the decision came down on January 27, the high court not only strongly reversed the appellate court decision but also emphasized that the key legal question "had been settled in this State for going on 150 years." The unanimous vote by the court was a complete judicial slap down of the lower court's opinion. It was surprising, therefore, that Justice Burke and one other judge wrote a special concurring opinion that sounded remarkably like a dissent.

It was unlikely that Emanuel would forget the role that the Burkes had played during the campaign.

But a win was a win. Emanuel's name would stay on the ballot. "The voters deserved the right to make the choice of who should be mayor," said Emanuel after the ruling. "And I think what the Supreme Court said was basically, in short, that the voters will make the decision who should be mayor."

From a political perspective, the divisive legal fight may have actually helped Emanuel for two reasons. First, he received free and frequent publicity. More important, the transparent escapades of old school Chicago politicians left many voters with the sense that perhaps a victorious Emanuel would bring a much needed housecleaning to city government. Voters favored him by a two-to-one margin over his next closest rival.

Over the next month, Emanuel strengthened his lead with voters by pushing his fund-raising total over $12 million and increasing his campaign visits to more than a hundred Chicago el stops. Emanuel also did well in the candidate debates, coming across as intelligent and decisive. In the final debate, Emanuel seemed to indicate that as mayor he would reform the structure of the city council and go after longstanding excesses, such as Ed Burke's bodyguard detail. "There will be a shared sacrifice, including for Ed Burke and all the City Council," said Emanuel. "If Ed Burke has six police officers, that just can't continue."

Immediately before the February 22 election, Emanuel started a "50 Wards in 50 Hours" tour that would take the candidate to every neighborhood in Chicago. He visited restaurants, el stops, grocery stores, barbershops and old people homes. When voters went to the polls, he won handily with 55 percent of the vote. Emanuel had won forty of the fifty wards, including every lakefront and African-American ward. After twenty-two years, Chicago had a new mayor-elect.

At his victory celebration at a union hall near the United Center stadium, Emanuel declared that Daley had "earned a special place in our hearts and our history." In the rafters above stood David Axelrod—the political consultant with the magical touch who had guided Rich Daley to victory in 1989 and Barack Obama to victory in 2008—alone, quietly watching. Axelrod and Emanuel knew each other well. They had grown up professionally together in Daley's Chicago and had served together in Obama's White House. Now they were both back in the city by the lake.

Two months later, on a sunny May morning, Rahm Emanuel was inaugurated as the forty-sixth mayor of Chicago. The ceremony took place at the Millennium Park pavilion designed by Frank Gehry. On stage with Emanuel and his wife Amy were Rich and Maggie Daley, as well as the Chicago City Council and other elected officials. The audience included White House chief of staff Bill Daley, as well as Vice President Joe Biden, Transportation Secretary Ray LaHood, Treasury Secretary Timothy Geithner, and Emanuel's old friends David Axelrod and Forrest Claypool, who would become president of the Chicago Transit Authority under the new mayor. Also in attendance were many members of the Chicago Consular Corps, including representatives from Monaco, France, Thailand, Mexico, and the United Kingdom.

The new mayor's speech almost immediately genuflected to the outgoing mayor's accomplishments. "When Richard M. Daley took office as mayor 22 years ago, he challenged all of us to lower our voices and raise our sights," said Emanuel. "Chicago is a different city today than the one Mayor Daley inherited, thanks to all he did. This magnificent place where we gather today is a living symbol of that transformation." After that homage to Daley's legacy, the balance of Emanuel's speech focused on the need for change and his plans for tackling the city's problems.

When the ceremony was over, the new mayor went to his office at city hall. Emanuel then quickly signed six executive orders focused on ethics, including a two-year prohibition on appointees lobbying city hall after they leave municipal government. "Chicagoans want to see change in the way their city government does business," said Mayor Emanuel. "My first official act as Mayor sends a clear message that all operations of City government must be guided by a spirit of public service."

Two days later, Emanuel convened his first meeting of the Chicago City Council. For nearly a month, the media had speculated whether the new mayor would use his powers of office to inflict retribution on Alderman Ed Burke, the longstanding chairman of the finance committee. It did not happen. Instead, Emanuel's first session with the council seemed just like hundreds of similar events during the reign of former Mayor Daley: grandstanding by Burke, ceremonial speeches by Burke, and a small amount of substantive business. The city council committees were reorganized, and Alderman Patrick O'Connor—a close ally of Emanuel and a longtime legislative leader—was given more authority, but the meeting was otherwise unexceptional. Burke stood and spoke, preened and smiled. He had outlasted Rich Daley in office, and as a man who held onto political power. Emanuel chose not to fight an unnecessary battle, since there was work to be done.

The new mayor's first calendar year in office was marked by energy and decisiveness. Emanuel cut Daley's final budget by $75 million. He recruited jobs to Chicago through his own corporate connections. He lobbied Illinois legislators to pass an education reform bill that would allow him to lengthen the classroom time at schools. He landed the hosting of the prestigious NATO summit for Chicago. He began trying to settle the decades-old Jon Burge police torture cases.

He reduced the expensive bodyguard protection provided to Ed Burke and the now retired Mayor Daley. He proposed a tough 2012 budget, taking a first step in stabilizing the city's fiscal profile. Chicagoans abhorred a political vacuum, and it was now clear that Emanuel would govern with a strong hand.

Rich Daley refrained from second-guessing the new mayor and, instead, stayed busy in retirement. He became a senior fellow at the University of Chicago's Harris School of Public Policy Studies. He joined the firm Katten Muchin where one of his closest friends had long practiced law. He began to help his son Patrick put together a business venture. He resisted depositions seeking him to testify in the ongoing police torture scandal cases. He gave speeches on governing, leadership, and public-private partnerships.

Despite his largely low profile, Daley suffered from the public's growing sense that his positive legacy might be tarnished by Chicago's pension crisis. Unfunded pension liabilities had risen to more than $20 billion, which was equal to nearly $7,500 for every man, woman, and child living in the city. Moreover, within a year of his retirement a *Chicago Tribune* investigation would reveal that in 1991 Daley—along with Tim Degnan, his political adviser and close friend—had personally taken advantage of a loophole in the pension laws. This maneuver had led to Daley receiving an eventual pension of more than $180,000 for life, while allowing him to avoid paying $400,000 into the pension plan. The revelation of this slick, self-serving move would begin to create deep resentment with Chicago voters. "People are raw with anger, that's all they've been talking about is the *Tribune* story," one knowledgeable insider would say. "They're just raw with it. It's like the parking meter deal. $180,000 a year pension after all the money the Daleys made? For life? That's overkill."

However, before the public would become completely aware of this scandal, death came into Daley's life once again. On Thanksgiving, six months after his retirement as mayor, his wife Maggie died. She had lived nine years after her diagnosis of breast cancer.

Three days after Thanksgiving, thousands came to grieve for Chicago's First Lady at the Chicago Cultural Center that she had helped to rejuvenate and make a special place. The former mayor—looking tired and sad—and his family stood patiently and greeted the many mourners. A beautiful photograph of Maggie, along with her closed casket, stood in front of the giant third-floor windows of Preston Bradley Hall. Mourners waiting in line could look out the windows and see the pavilion and sculptures of Millennium Park, as well as Lake Michigan in the blue distance beyond. The prayer cards given out by the Daley family included a photo of Maggie smiling, along with her favorite quote from Margaret Mead: "Never doubt that a small group of thoughtful, committed people can change the world; indeed, it is the only thing that ever has."

The funeral was held the next morning at Old Saint Patrick's Church in the west Loop. Founded by Irish immigrants in 1846, Saint Pat's was the oldest Catholic church in Chicago and one of the few downtown buildings to survive the Great Chicago Fire of 1871. It had become the Daleys' principal place of worship, and their grandchildren attended its grade school, Frances Xavier Warde School, which Maggie Daley had helped to found in 1989.

Attendees at the funeral included a wide swath of politicians from both the national and local stages. First Lady Michelle Obama, Vice President Joe Biden, Chief of Staff Bill Daley, senior adviser to the president, Valerie Jarrett, and Secretary of Education Arne Duncan had all flown in from the White House. Mayor Rahm Emanuel sat near the front of the cathedral with his wife Amy. Chicago politicos from Daley's peer group—such as Ed Burke, Dick Mell, and Mike Madigan—were also in attendance. The rest of the largely gray-haired pew fillers were friends, family, and professional associates of many years. The funeral ceremony was not merely a religious rite and a personal milestone. It was also a generational event for a certain group of Chicagoans born during or just after World War II. An important and much loved member of their cohort had passed from this world.

The ceremony itself was lovely. Beautiful music. A wise, warm-hearted priest. Short and dignified readings. A well-delivered eulogy. Rich Daley carried himself with discipline and grace during the ritual, though the wet sadness in his eyes was clear for all to see. At the end of the mass, Daley bent and kissed his wife's casket.

Daley then drove with his family and the funeral hearse and buried Maggie at the family plot at Holy Sepulchre Cemetery south of the city. He had now put to rest his wife, along with his son and his father.

CHAPTER 24

SUNRISE, NOVEMBER 29, 2011

Tuesday, November 29, 2011, 6:56 AM. The sun rose in the east, though it was hidden behind thick clouds. The waters of Lake Michigan roiled as if disturbed by unhappy gods rumbling in its depths. Strong winds blew ten-foot-tall waves toward the shore. The chilly forty-three-degree temperature was evidence of another Chicago winter in the making.

To the south and west, the sky appeared yellow and purple and gray, like a bruised thigh.

The city was quiet, except for the wind. Millennium Park was empty. Children and teachers had not yet arrived at schools. But planes at O'Hare and Midway Airports were preparing for their flights. Chicago would soon awake and start its morning rituals.

Rich Daley would wake up by himself. His Maggie—graceful, gracious Maggie—was gone. Nearly thirty-five years had lapsed since the death of Daley's father, and now he felt alone again. But he still had the rest of his family, and there was new work to be done. Daley would go out and face his day as he always had. He would do his best.

The sky above Lake Michigan glowed pinkish and then grew white. Another day had dawned in Chicago, the city by the lake.

APPENDIX A

CHICAGO MAYORS SINCE 1900

CARTER HARRISON II	1897–1905, 1911–15
EDWARD DUNNE	1905–7
FRED BUSSE	1907–11
WILLIAM H. THOMPSON	1915–23, 1927–31
WILLIAM DEVER	1923–27
ANTON CERMAK	1931–33
FRANK CORR	1933
EDWARD KELLY	1933–47
MARTIN KENNELLY	1947–55
RICHARD J. DALEY	1955–76
MICHAEL BILANDIC	1976–79
JANE BYRNE	1979–83
HAROLD WASHINGTON	1983–87
DAVID ORR	1987—interim mayor for one week after Harold Washington died in office
EUGENE SAWYER	1987–89
RICHARD M. DALEY	1989–2011
RAHM EMANUEL	2011–

APPENDIX B

Election Results of Rich Daley's Political Campaigns

Campaign	Date	Result/Comments
Delegate to the Illinois Constitutional Convention of 1970	1969	Daley is high vote getter in a low turnout election; Michael Shakman, an attorney and unsuccessful independent candidate for a convention delegate seat, files a lawsuit against the Chicago machine claiming that the Democratic Party's system of patronage politics puts nonmachine candidates at an unconstitutional disadvantage
Illinois State Senate District 23	November 7, 1972	Daley wins 74.1%, defeating Republican Robert Urbanek
Illinois State Senate District 23	November 2, 1976	Daley wins running unopposed
Illinois State Senate District 23	November 7, 1978	Daley wins running unopposed
Cook County State's Attorney—1980 Democratic Primary	March 18, 1980	Daley defeats machine politician Ed Burke, who had the support of Mayor Jane Byrne and much of the local party; the Daley versus Burke contest represented a near civil war within the Chicago Democratic organization
Cook County State's Attorney—1980 General Election	November 4, 1980	Daley wins 50.4%, defeating Bernard Carey, the sitting Republican state's attorney; this is arguably the most important electoral victory of Daley's career
Chicago Mayor—1983 Democratic Primary	February 22, 1983	Daley loses, receiving only 29.7% of the vote; Harold Washington became the first African-American mayor of Chicago
Cook County State's Attorney—1984 Democratic Primary	March 20, 1984	Daley wins 63.9%, defeating Larry Bloom, a white alderman who represented Hyde Park and other south-side neighborhoods
Cook County State's Attorney—1984 General Election	November 6, 1984	Daley wins 66.0%, defeating Republican Richard Brzeczek, the former Chicago superintendent of police
Cook County State's Attorney	November 8, 1988	Daley wins 66.7%, defeating the Republican Terrance Gainor, a candidate with a law enforcement and legal background
Chicago Mayor—1989 Democratic Primary	February 28, 1989	Daley wins 55.4%, defeating Mayor Eugene Sawyer, the black politician who succeeded Harold Washington after his death
Chicago Mayor—1989 General Election	April 4, 1989	Daley wins 55.4%, defeating Tim Evans, a black alderman and member of the Harold Washington party who wins eighteen out of the fifty wards

Campaign	Date	Result/Comments
Chicago Mayor—1991 Democratic Primary	February 26, 1991	Daley wins 63.0%, defeating former Mayor Jane Byrne and Danny Davis, a black alderman; Daley refuses to debate his challengers, correctly believing that his wide popularity and strong approval ratings would ensure his reelection
Chicago Mayor—1991 General Election	April 2, 1991	Daley wins 70.6%, defeating former Judge Eugene Pincham, an African-American and member of the Harold Washington party who wins nineteen out of the fifty wards
Chicago Mayor—1995 Democratic Primary	February 28, 1995	Daley wins 65.8%, easily beating the Metropolitan Water District commissioner, Joseph Gardner; more than a hundred black ministers, including the one from Gardner's own church, support Daley; like the 1991 election, Daley refuses to participate in debates
Chicago Mayor—1995 General Election	April 4, 1995	Daley wins 60.1%; his competitor, Roland Burris, a black Illinois attorney general, wins nineteen out of the fifty wards
Chicago Mayor	February 23, 1999	Daley wins 71.9%; his competitor, Bobby Rush, a black US congressman, wins seventeen out of the fifty wards
Chicago Mayor	February 25, 2003	Daley wins 78.5%, defeating three little-known politicians; in a few weeks, Daley will instruct workers to demolish the runway at Meigs Field in the middle of the night—perhaps the greatest election victory of his career had caused hubris in the mayor
Chicago Mayor	February 27, 2007	Daley wins 70.7%, defeating Circuit Court Clerk Dorothy Brown, an African-American politician; receives the endorsement of Barack Obama, a US senator with presidential ambitions

APPENDIX C

Timeline of Events in Rich Daley's Life

April 24, 1942	Eleanor "Sis" Daley gives birth to Rich Daley
1947	Dick Daley becomes the Eleventh Ward Democratic committeeman and political Boss of the Bridgeport neighborhood in Chicago; Rich Daley is five years old
August 9, 1948	Birth of Bill Daley, youngest brother of Rich Daley
July 21–26, 1952	Chicago hosts the 1952 Democratic National Convention at the International Amphitheatre near Bridgeport; the Democrats choose Adlai Stevenson, the governor of Illinois, who loses to Dwight D. Eisenhower in the general election for US president
1955	Joe Rostenkowski, father of Dan Rostenkowski, supports Dick Daley for mayor over a well-known Polish politician
April 20, 1955	Dick Daley begins his first term as mayor of Chicago; Rich Daley turns thirteen-years-old four days later
Late Spring 1956	Rich Daley graduates from Nativity of Our Lord Grammar School
August 13–17, 1956	Chicago hosts the 1956 Democratic National Convention at the International Amphitheatre near Bridgeport; the Democrats choose Adlai Stevenson, the governor of Illinois, who loses to Dwight D. Eisenhower in the general election for US president
January 3, 1959	Thirty-one-year-old Dan Rostenkowski becomes a member of the US House of Representatives from Illinois
September 22, 1959	The Chicago White Sox wins its first American League baseball pennant in forty years
Fall 1959	Rich Daley runs for president of his high school class at De La Salle Institute; he loses
Late Spring 1960	Rich Daley graduates from De La Salle Institute, the same Catholic high school his father had attended
July 11–15, 1960	Rich Daley attends the Democratic National Convention in Los Angeles with his father and other family members
1960–62	Daley attends Providence College, a Catholic school in Rhode Island
1962	Daley transfers to DePaul, a Catholic college in Chicago, to complete his undergraduate education
1966	Martin Luther King Jr. moves to Chicago, and his Chicago Freedom Movement group focuses on eliminating urban blight and improving living conditions for black Americans; he is unsuccessful
April 4, 1968	Martin Luther King Jr. is assassinated in Memphis, Tennessee, and the black ghetto on the west side of Chicago suffers forty-eight hours of burning and looting; Dick Daley, the mayor of Chicago, issues his infamous "shoot to kill" statement

Late Spring 1968	Daley graduates from DePaul School of Law and takes three attempts to pass the Illinois bar exam
August 26–29, 1968	Dick Daley hosts the infamous 1968 Democratic National Convention in Chicago; Rich Daley attends as his guest
February 1969	*Gautreaux v. Chicago Public Housing*, a landmark legal decision, rules that the CHA had engaged in decades of racial discrimination by only building public housing in black neighborhoods
1969	Michael Shakman files a lawsuit against the City of Chicago, the mayor of Chicago, and the Cook County Democratic Party, alleging that Chicago's Democratic Party used patronage politics to unfairly disadvantage candidates who were not part of the Democratic machine
December 1969–September 1970	Rich Daley, Mike Madigan, and Dawn Clark Netsch serve as delegates at the Illinois Constitutional Convention of 1970; the new constitution passes
December 1970	Rich Daley meets Maggie Corbett at a Christmas party and asks her out on a date
1972	Rich Daley is elected to the Illinois State Senate
June 1972	Rich Daley marries Maggie Corbett; the couple settles in Bridgeport
Early 1970s	Dawn Clark Netsch coins the nickname "Dirty Little Richie" for Daley; the nickname sticks
August 9, 1973	Maggie Daley gives birth to Nora Daley
1975	Rich Daley is appointed chair of the Illinois Senate Judiciary Committee
June 10, 1975	Maggie Daley gives birth to Patrick Daley
December 20, 1976	Dick Daley dies while serving his twenty-first year as mayor of Chicago; more than twenty-five thousand Chicagoans attend the wake at Nativity of Our Lord Church in Bridgeport
December 1976	Rich Daley is named Eleventh Ward Democratic committeeman
February 1977	Tom Hynes, a key ally of Rich Daley, becomes president of the Illinois Senate
September 1977	Rich Daley makes a surprise visit to the Forty-Third Ward softball game fund-raiser hosted by Dawn Clark Netsch
June 1978	Maggie Daley gives birth to Kevin Daley who is born with spina bifida, a crippling disease
February 1979	Jane Byrne becomes the first female mayor of Chicago
November 1979	Rich Daley declares his candidacy for Cook County state's attorney; he goes on to defeat Ed Burke in the Democratic primary
February 4, 1980	In his run for state's attorney, Daley receives the endorsements of a group of prominent lawyers, including John R. Schmidt, former president of the Chicago Council of Lawyers
March 1, 1981	Kevin Daley dies
November 1980	Daley wins general election for Cook County state's attorney versus Republican Bernard Carey; Ronald Reagan wins election as the fortieth president of the United States
Late 1980	John Daley replaces his brother Rich as the Eleventh Ward Democratic committeeman; Tim Degnan becomes the Illinois state senator from Bridgeport
February 1982	Chicago Police Chief Brzeczek forwards a letter to Cook County state's attorney Daley describing possible police torture of Andrew

	Wilson, a black man accused of murder; Daley does not respond to Brzeczek
1982–83	Daley runs for mayor of Chicago; he loses to Harold Washington who becomes the city's first African-American mayor
November 17, 1983	Maggie Daley gives birth to Elizabeth Lally Daley
November 6, 1984	Daley wins reelection as Cook County state's attorney
November 25, 1987	Harold Washington dies at his desk while serving as mayor of Chicago
November 8, 1988	Daley wins reelection as Cook County state's attorney
April 4, 1989	Daley is elected mayor of Chicago, winning approximately 56% of the vote; key campaign advisers include Bill Daley, David Axelrod, Jeremiah Joyce, Rahm Emanuel, David Wilhelm, Tim Degnan, and Forest Claypool
April 24, 1989	Daley starts first term as mayor of Chicago; he names John Schmidt as his first chief of staff
April 26, 1989	Daley chairs his first Chicago City council meeting; his proposals include an overhaul of city council committees and a water- and sewer-rate tax increase; both proposals pass the council
October 1989	The city erects barricades around the Block 37 downtown site and begins demolition of the block near city hall in order to prepare for the planned site redevelopment
February 15, 1990	Daley unveils a $5 billion plan for a third airport in the Lake Calumet neighborhood on the south-east side of the city
Late Spring 1991	Comiskey Park is demolished and a new White Sox baseball stadium opens in Daley's Bridgeport neighborhood
May 6, 1991	Daley starts his second term as mayor of Chicago
June 1991	Daley initiates sweeping reorganization of his administration, naming David Mosena as chief of staff and Valerie Jarrett as planning and development commissioner
July 1991	The Illinois legislature gives its approval for $1 billion expansion of the McCormick Place convention center and the creation of a Museum campus along the lakefront
October 7, 1991	The Harold Washington Library Center opens as the new main branch of the Chicago library system
1992	Sears Corporation moves its headquarters from the Sears Tower to Hoffman Estates, Illinois
March 2, 1992	Daley cries at a press conference when discussing a violent fight at a party hosted by his teenage son in his family's Grand Beach, Michigan, vacation home
April 13, 1992	Underground tunnels in the loop rupture and flood downtown with millions of gallons of water
1992	Bill Daley serves as Illinois chairman of Bill Clinton's campaign for president; David Wilhelm and Rahm Emanuel are also, respectively, the national campaign manager and campaign finance director for the governor of Arkansas; Clinton wins
July 1992	Daley pulls the plug on planned third airport in Lake Calumet after failing to get support in the Illinois Senate
April 1993	Daley institutes a new crime reduction program called Chicago Alternative Police Strategy (CAPS)
April 1993	Rich and Maggie Daley move from their home in Bridgeport to a new row house in the South Loop's trendy Central Station development

May 1993	The Clinton administration proposes federal empowerment zones for community development in inner-city neighborhoods; Daley puts Valerie Jarrett in charge of Chicago's application, and the city is named a recipient of $100 million in funding
June 2, 1993	Daley proposes an $800 million riverboat gambling facility but his plan fails to win approval from the Illinois General Assembly
August 1993	Bill Daley becomes special counselor to President Clinton for the North America Free Trade Agreement; it becomes law four months later
June 1994	Chicago serves as a host for the World Cup Soccer championship in the United States
1994	The original Maxwell Street market is demolished for the expansion of University of Illinois at Chicago; real estate development accelerates in the South Loop
1994	Daley first publicly suggests closing Meigs Field
May 1, 1995	Daley starts his third term as mayor of Chicago
May 30, 1995	The Republican-led Illinois General Assembly gives Daley control of the Chicago Public Schools; Daley names Paul Vallas as CEO of the schools and Gery Chico as president of the school board
May 30, 1995	The US Department of Housing and Urban Development takes control of the Chicago Housing Authority; one of its first steps is to begin demolishing some of the public high-rises at Cabrini-Green
July 1995	More than seven hundred Chicagoans die in a heat wave
July 12, 1995	Navy Pier reopens after $150 million in improvements, including the fifteen-hundred-seat outdoor Skyline Stage, restaurants, shops, and exhibition facilities
October 19, 1995	Daley endorses Rod Blagojevich in his bid to become a US congressman
August 26–29, 1996	Chicago hosts the Democratic National Convention
December 1996	The new south hall opens at the 2.6 million-square-foot McCormick Place convention center
January 30, 1997	Bill Daley becomes US secretary of commerce under President Clinton
October 1997	The first major scandal of the Daley administration erupts; Patrick Huels, Daley's floor leader in the city council and friend from Bridgeport, resigns
1997	The estimated annual attendance at Navy Pier reaches 7 million
June 4, 1998	Daley dedicates the new Museum Campus along the lakefront
1998	The *Chicago Sun-Times* describes Rich and Maggie Daley as "influential enemies" of Meigs Field
March 1998	Daley announces the Lakefront Millennium Project, a plan that will evolve into Millennium Park
February 1999	Daley proposes a $1 billion expansion of O'Hare Airport, including two new terminals and twenty gates
March 1, 1999	Daley starts his fourth term as mayor of Chicago
April 27, 1999	Daley names Julia Stasch chief of staff, while the imminent takeover of the CHA by the City of Chicago is delayed
June 1999	City of Chicago takes back control of the CHA, and Daley appoints Rahm Emanuel to the CHA board
Summer 1999	Chicago hosts its Cows on Parade exhibit, a highly successful

	display of public art: three hundred colorfully painted, life-size cows lined sidewalks, street medians, parks, and lobbies
July 1999	A newspaper investigation reveals that the Duff family had won nearly $100 million of city contracts by violating a minority contracting program; the FBI begins an investigation
September 30, 1999	The CHA announces a Plan for Transformation to tear down most public high-rises and replace them with Mixed-income communities
December 15, 1999	The Chicago City Council votes forty-two to five to confirm the city's new fire commissioner; Daley gets publicly angry at the five aldermen who did not support the old-school white fire chief he nominated
January–February 2000	Housing and Urban Development approves the Plan for Transformation in January and signs the agreement in February
April 2000	Daley gets sick and his chief of staff Julia Stasch runs the show while he is incapacitated; other members of the Daley administration work to undermine her authority
September 20, 2000	Groundbreaking held for rooftop garden at city hall
November 7, 2000	Beginning of five-week legal dispute between George Bush and Al Gore over the 2000 presidential electoral contest; Bush wins
November 29, 2000	Julia Stasch resigns as chief of staff
March 7, 2001	New 678,000-square-foot terminal building opens at Midway Airport
December 4, 2001	Daley announces an additional $6 billion expansion of O'Hare Airport, including new and extended runways
June 2001	Paul Vallas and Gery Chico resign from the Chicago Public Schools; Daley names Arne Duncan as the new CEO of CPS
August 3, 2001	Daley unveils One Book, One Chicago, a citywide reading program; the first selection is *To Kill a Mockingbird* by Harper Lee
September 11, 2001	Two airplanes strike and destroy the World Trade Center in New York City
September 2001	Boeing Corporation decides to move its worldwide headquarters to Chicago
2002	The City of Chicago begins running at an operating deficit and will continue to do so for the next decade under Daley
January 19, 2002	Renovation begins on Soldier Field sports stadium
April 2002	Daley agrees to become general chairman of Rod Blagojevich's campaign to become governor of Illinois, but does not support the campaign of Paul Vallas, his former aide who served for years as the CEO of Chicago Public Schools
June 7, 2002	Mayor Daley announces that his wife Maggie has breast cancer
Fall 2002	Rahm Emanuel runs to represent the Illinois Fifth District in the US House of Representatives (the old seat of Rod Blagojevich and Dan Rostenkowski); for the only time in his career, Daley goes "all in" to support another politician
January 13, 2003	Rod Blagojevich becomes the first Democratic governor of Illinois in twenty-six years
February 16, 2003	Eleanor "Sis" Daley dies
March 30–31, 2003	Daley orders the middle-of-the-night demolition of the runway at Meigs Field airport
May 5, 2003	Daley starts his fifth term as mayor of Chicago
September 25, 2003	Two members of the Duff family are indicted for fraud schemes

	related to $100 million in contracts obtained by sham women- and minority-owned businesses
October 2003	Daley announces that the city will privatize the Chicago Skyway, a 7.8-mile toll road connecting Chicago to northwest Indiana
January 2004	The Hired Truck Scandal begins to become public
June 2004	The $927 million renovation of Midway Airport is complete
June 2004	Daley and public schools CEO Arne Duncan announce Renaissance 2010, a plan to open a hundred new schools over a ten-year period while also closing poor performers
July 16, 2004	Millennium Park officially opens
October 27, 2004	Chicago agrees to privatize the Chicago Skyway in a $1.8 billion ninety-nine-year lease transaction
Late 2004	Robert Vanecko—nephew of mayor Daley and the firstborn grandchild of Dick Daley—founds DV Realty, a real estate investment company, with Allison Davis, a longtime Daley supporter; the two businessmen later receive $68 million from five CIty of Chicago pension funds
January 4, 2005	Barack Obama, a politician from Chicago, becomes a US senator
April 2005	The FBI arrives at city hall, armed with search warrants, and seizes documents and computer hard-drives from the mayor's office of intergovernmental affairs
April 25, 2005	*Time* magazine names Daley as one of the best mayors in the United States
May 2005	James Duff is sentenced to nearly ten years in prison and ordered to pay more than $22 million in forfeitures and restitution for his role in minority contracting fraud against the City of Chicago
July 2005	Robert Sorich, Daley's longtime patronage aide from Bridgeport, is arrested by the FBI
July 2005	The Republican Party of Cook County offers a $10,000 reward to anyone who provides information leading to the conviction of Daley
August 2005	The FBI questions Daley with regard to fraud in city hall hiring
August 2005	Barack Obama, US senator from Chicago, hesitates when asked whether he would endorse mayor Daley for reelection, saying that the city's recent scandals gave him "huge pause"; a few weeks later, Congressman Rahm Emanuel speaks at the City Club of Chicago and defends Daley with respect to the scandals
October 2005	Daley names David Hoffman as the new inspector general for the City of Chicago
April 2006	The Chicago City Council passes a ban on the sale of foie gras at restaurants
June 1, 2006	John Briatta—a City of Chicago employee and brother-in-law of John Daley—is sentenced to eighteen months in prison for his role in the Hired Truck Scandal
July 6, 2006	Robert Sorich, Daley's longtime patronage aide, is convicted; on the same day, President George Bush celebrates his sixtieth birthday in Chicago with Daley at the Chicago Firehouse Restaurant, one of the mayor's favorites
July 18, 2006	Daley supports Todd Stroger, the son of John Stroger, to replace the elder Stroger as the Democratic candidate for Cook County Board presidency, but does not support Forrest Claypool, his two-time chief of staff

September 11, 2006	Daley vetoes a living-wage ordinance, passed by the city council, which requires big-box retailers to pay workers more than the minimum wage; the veto is Daley's first in more than seventeen years in office
November 9, 2006	Donald Tomczak, a Bridgeport native, is sentenced to forty-seven months in prison for taking $400,000 in bribes in the Hired Truck corruption case
January 2007	Barack Obama endorses Daley's bid for reelection as mayor of Chicago
Early 2007	Daley's job approval ratings sink below 50% for the first time in his mayoral career
May 21, 2007	Daley starts his sixth and final term as mayor of Chicago
Late 2007	After running a $95 million deficit in fiscal 2007, the city's proposed 2008 budget is publicly rejected by the Civic Federation, a respected fiscal watchdog group
January 2008	The Chicago City Council votes forty-five to none to pay a $20 million settlement to four black men who alleged that members of the Chicago Police Department had committed torture against them while in custody
April 25, 2008	Daley hosts an antiviolence summit in Chicago after nine people are killed in thirty-six shootings one weekend
Mid 2008	For the first time in his mayoral career, more Chicagoans disapprove of Daley's job as mayor than approve
June 2008	The International Olympic Committee chooses Chicago—along with Rio de Janeiro, Madrid, and Tokyo—as one of its finalists to become the official host city for the 2016 Summer Olympics
Fall 2008	The campaign for president of the United States is in full swing; Barack Obama is one of the Democratic candidates
September 2008	Oprah Winfrey kicks off her twenty-third television season by inviting US Olympic athletes to Millennium Park; Rich and Maggie Daley attend, as the mayor presses forward with Chicago's efforts to host the 2016 Summer Olympics
September 15, 2008	In the midst of a global financial crisis, Lehman Brothers—a 158-year-old investment bank with over $600 billion in assets—files for bankruptcy
November 2008	The first phase of the O'Hare Airport expansion project is completed
November 4, 2008	Barack Obama beats John McCain in the election for US president; the victory celebration is held in Chicago's Grant Park, just west of Lake Michigan
December 4, 2008	With minimal oversight, the Chicago City Council votes to approve Daley's $1.2 billion privatization of the city's thirty-six thousand parking meters
January 9, 2009	Rod Blagojevich becomes the first governor in the nearly two-hundred-year history of the state to be impeached by the Illinois House of Representatives
January 20, 2009	Barack Obama becomes first African-American president of the United States; Rahm Emanuel is named chief of Staff, David Axelrod and Valerie Jarrett are named senior advisers to the president, and Arne Duncan becomes US secretary of education
June 2009	City of Chicago inspector general, David Hoffman, releases a forty-six-page report criticizing Daley's parking meter privatization deal

June 2009	Robert Vanecko, the nephew of Mayor Daley, resigns from DV Urban Realty Partners within weeks of pressure from the City of Chicago inspector general
October 2, 2009	Chicago fails in its bid to host the 2016 Summer Olympic Games, despite personal pleas from President Obama and First Lady Michelle Obama
October 2009	Daley's public approval ratings sink to an all-time low of 35%
December 2009	The Chicago City Council ignores a $520 million structural budget deficit and votes to pass Daley's proposed $6.I billion budget
April 2010	White House chief of staff Rahm Emanuel goes on the show *Charlie Rose* and explains that running for mayor of Chicago is one of his lifetime aspirations; one week later, Emanuel flies to Chicago and attends the Richard J. Daley Global Cities Forum, sitting up front with the Daley family
June II, 2010	At the tickertape parade celebrating the Chicago Blackhawks' Stanley Cup championship, Mayor Daley is jeered at and booed by Chicagoans
June 28, 2010	The US Supreme Court strikes down Chicago's gun ban
June 30, 2010	The Chicago City Council votes to approve the second Walmart store in the city; the long political battle over living wages in Chicago ends
September 7, 2010	Daley announces that he will not seek reelection as mayor of Chicago
October I, 2010	Rahm Emanuel declares his candidacy for mayor of Chicago; President Obama states that he believes Emanuel would be an excellent mayor of his hometown
November 17, 2010	Despite a structural budget deficit of $655 million and growing unfunded pension liabilities, the Chicago City Council approves Daley's final budget
November 26, 2010	Attorney Burt Odelson seeks to remove Rahm Emanuel's name from the mayoral ballot, saying that Emanuel was not a legal resident of Chicago
December 26, 2010	Rich Daley surpasses the tenure of his father Dick Daley to become the longest-serving mayor in the history of Chicago
January 13, 2011	Bill Daley becomes White House chief of staff under President Obama
January 27, 2011	The Illinois Supreme Court rules that Rahm Emanuel is a legal resident of Chicago and that his name should stay on the ballot in the upcoming mayoral election
February 22, 2011	With 55% of the vote, Rahm Emanuel wins the mayoral election to replace Rich Daley; Emanuel captures forty of the fifty wards, including every lakefront and African-American ward
May 4, 2011	Daley attends his last meeting of the Chicago City Council
May 16, 2011	Rahm Emanuel is inaugurated as mayor of Chicago; Rich and Maggie Daley attend the ceremony, sitting on stage
May 18, 2011	Mayor Emanuel presides over his first city council meeting; the council approves everything Emanuel wants during the ninety-minute session
May 24, 2011	Former Mayor Daley becomes a senior fellow at the University of Chicago's Harris School of Public Policy Studies
June I, 2011	Rich Daley joins the firm Katten Muchin, where one of his closest friends has long practiced law

November 24, 2011   Maggie Daley dies

December 2011   Along with his son, Daley announces the formation of Tur Partners, an investment and advisory firm focused on sustainable urban Development; Daley also joins the board of directors of the Coca-Cola Company

ACKNOWLEDGMENTS

Thanks again to Robert Devens and his colleagues at the University of Chicago Press for shepherding me through the book creation process. I have found Robert's editorial and publishing guidance to be consistently skillful and balanced and am lucky to have found him. Thanks to Brad Hunt for making the introduction.

I could not have written this book without the support of my family. Claire, you're the best. No words could do justice to how much you mean to me. Penn and Drake have had a curious, upbeat perspective on my Daley project, and I have had fun seeing them grow and mature over the last few years. I have also learned from them that homework, cooking, soccer games, and going to the park are a good balance to writing a book. Mom and Dad have always supported my crazy pursuits, and for that I am deeply grateful.

Special thanks to Jean Baldikoski—a talented reader, a wise listener, and a disciplined crafter of sentences. You are my secret weapon.

Thanks also to the many individuals who have either sat for an interview or introduced me to other interviewees. My deepest thanks to all of you.

I am also deeply grateful for the encouragement and support of many colleagues. In particular, I would like to recognize Larry Bennett, an expert on Chicago politics, author of *The Third City*, and my periodic conversational partner at the Local Option on Webster Avenue. The brilliant and high-energy Andy Shaw has also been a source of insights, great introductions, and continuing enthusiasm. I would also like to express gratitude to Brad Hunt for his eager support and his Chicago public-housing expertise. In addition, I would like to acknowledge Tim Gilfoyle for his wise editorial guidance and his deep insights into Chicago's history, politics, and culture. Marilyn Katz is smart, tough, and independent—a completely original person—and her advice and encouragement has been invaluable. Thanks are due as well to Ellen Skerrett for her early encouragement and her resourceful assistance in selecting photographs for the book.

I would like to express thanks, too, to other friends who gave me encouragement and assistance during my solitary journey of writing a book, including Jeff Levick, Mike O'Brien, Katie Spring, Steve Edwards, Beth Daley, J. D. Cronin, Kris Mackey, Mike Fortin, and Brian Hand.

Finally, I would like to thank my seventh-grade English teacher, Kate Janush. When I was young and rambunctious, Mrs. J. allowed me to ignore her and the rest of the class in order to explore the world of literature at my own pace. I read scores and scores of books, and the world opened up to me. For that wise permission, I am deeply grateful.

NOTES

Every attempt has been made to keep citations as concise as possible. Quoted or controversial material is cited, but citations for facts that are widely known and accepted are omitted. The following abbreviations appear in these notes:

AMER   Adam Cohen and Elizabeth Taylor, *American Pharaoh* (New York: Little, Brown, 2000)

BOSS   Mike Rokyo, *Boss: Richard J. Daley of Chicago* (New York: E. P. Dutton, 1971)

BRIDGE   David Remnick, *The Bridge: The Life and Rise of Barack Obama* (New York: Alfred A. Knopf, 2010)

CD   Paul Kleppner, *Chicago Divided: Making of a Black Mayor* (DeKalb: Northern Illinois University Press, 1985)

CHI   Dominic A. Pacyga, *Chicago: A Biography* (Chicago: University of Chicago Press, 2009)

CM   *Chicago Magazine*

CPW   David K. Fremon, *Chicago Politics Ward by Ward* (Bloomington: Indiana University Press, 1988)

ENCY   James Grossman et al., eds., *Encyclopedia of Chicago* (Chicago: University of Chicago Press, 2004)

FOIE   Mark Caro, *The Foie Gras Wars* (New York: Simon and Schuster, 2009)

GRIM   William Grimshaw, *Bitter Fruit: Black Politics and the Chicago Machine, 1931–1991* (Chicago: University of Chicago Press, 1992)

HUNT   Bradley Hunt, *Blueprint for Disaster* (Chicago: University of Chicago Press, 2009)

MAYR   Paul Green and Melvin Holli, eds., *The Mayors* (Carbondale: Southern Illinois University Press, 1995)

MP   Timothy Gilfoyle, *Millennium Park: Creating a Chicago Landmark* (Chicago: University of Chicago Press, 2006)

NYT   *New York Times*

OR   off-the-record interviews or confidential sources

READ   *Chicago Reader*

ROST   Richard Cohen, *Rostenkowski: The Pursuit of Power and the End of Old Politics* (Chicago: Ivan R. Dee, 1999.)

RRR   Dick Simpson, *Rogues, Rebels, and Rubber Stamps: The Politics of the Chicago City Council from 1863 to the Present* (Boulder, CO: Westview Press, 2001)

SUN   *Chicago Sun-Times*

TRIB   *Chicago Tribune*

WAVE   Milton Rakove, *Don't Make No Waves—Don't Back No Losers: An Insider's Analysis of the Daley Machine* (Bloomington: Indiana University Press, 1975)

YARD   Robert Slayton, *Back of the Yards* (Chicago: University of Chicago Press, 1986)

PROLOGUE

P. xv   "We want all our young people": City of Chicago press release, January 6, 2011.

P. xv   "Chicago mafia": *Politico*, January 6, 2011.

P. xvi   "genetic trait": White House Press briefing on YouTube, January 6, 2011.

P. xix   "It's not his nature": OR.

CHAPTER 1

P. 3   "great open sewer": Upton Sinclair, *The Jungle* (New York: Penguin Books, 1906), 115.

P. 4   "very serious boy": AMER, 25.

P. 4   "behind painted green": Eugene Kennedy, *Himself!* (New York: Viking Press, 1978), 35.

P. 5   "student enrollment at Catholic": ENCY, 122.

P. 5   "De La Salle": Interviews with Ted Villinski and Ron Gralewski; BOSS, 28–29.

P. 6   "white school as an island": AMER, 26.

P. 6   "hated the goddamn niggers": interview with Ned Kennan.

P. 7   "extreme ethnic and racial parochialism": BOSS, 30–32; AMER, 27–30.

P. 7   "inflamed the fears": AMER, 35–36.

P. 9   "went out dancing every night": BOSS, 35.

P. 9   "Only lazy precinct captains steal votes": AMER, 52.

P. 10   "$1.5 million in cash": AMER, 51.

P. 11   "best exhibit of the hard-working": Frank Sullivan, *Legend, the Only Inside Story about Mayor Richard J. Daley* (Chicago: Bonus Books, 1989), 120.

P. 12   "three new avenues of expansion": MAYR, 111–25.

P. 13   "a largely cynical move": MAYR, 111–25, 126–43; BOSS, 54–58.

P. 14   "I guess we wanted him": BOSS, 83.

P. 14   "nothing wrong with politics": AMER, 120.

P. 15   "most notorious rascals": AMER, 141.

P. 15   "one tough sonofabitch": AMER, 141.

P. 15   "they're not gonna run nothing": AMER, 141.

P. 16   "de-fanged the Chicago City Council": BOSS, 92–93; AMER, 142–46.

P. 17   "Don't worry if they're Democrats": YARD, 157.

P. 17   "total value of $8 billion": David Bernstein, "Daley vs. Daley," CM, September 2008.

P. 18   "golden age of building": David Bernstein, "Daley vs. Daley," CM, September 2008.

P. 18   "$38 billion": "About the O'Hare Modernization Program," *City of Chicago: The City's Official Site*, www.cityofchicago.org/city/en/depts/doa/provdrs/omp/svcs/about_the_omp.html.

CHAPTER 2

P. 20   "most wonderful smile, robust laugh": interview with Bill Marovitz.

P. 21   "I'll take credit for that": SUN, December 7, 1986.

P. 21   "strong communities built on": Alan Ehrenhalt, *The Lost City: Discovering the Forgotten Virtues of Community in the Chicago of the 1950s* (New York: Basic Books, 1995), 8–154.

P. 21   "city's archdiocese": ENCY 122–123, 600, 690–696.

P. 22   "Neighborhood locals described Bridgeport": interview with Ted Villinski.

P. 23   "Here he is, kids!": AMER, p.128.

P. 23   "I shall conduct myself": AMER, p.128.

P. 23   "We never used our home": SUN, December 7, 1986.

P. 24   "quintessential Catholic grammar school": interview with Ted Villinski.

P. 25   "My dad loved": TRIB, September 12, 1982.

P. 25   "childhood was rather unremarkable": TRIB, September 12, 1982.

P. 26   "influence of my dad ever wears off": interview with Ed Burke.

P. 26   "The Daleys never saw Rich": interview with Ned Kennan.

P. 26   "Christian Brothers were very stern": interview with Ron Grawlewski.

P. 27   "Rich and I once both got paddled": the story that follows is based on an interview with Ron Grawlewski.

P. 27   "like the three seasons": interview with Ron Grawlewski.

P. 28   "newly constructed Dan Ryan Expressway": John F. Bauman and Roger Biles, *From Tenements to the Taylor Homes: In Search of an Urban Housing Policy in Twentieth-Century America* (University Park: Pennsylvania State University Press, 2000), 149; BOSS, 133; ENCY, B16.

P. 28   "it was a black neighborhood": interview with Ron Grawlewski.

P. 28   "Isolated from racial tension": interview with Ted Villinski.

P. 29   "Blacks never crossed Wentworth": interview with John Monacella.

P. 29   "attitudes toward racial minorities": CHI, 307.

P. 29   "powder keg of racial tensions": CHI, 307.

P. 29   "wasn't exactly blessed with great athletic skills": TRIB, September 12, 1982.

P. 30   "out there with the boys": interview with Ron Grawlewski.

P. 30   "wanted to be a politician": interview with Ron Grawlewski.

P. 31   "Richie was rather shy": interview with Ray Flynn.

P. 31   "Banks study group": Interview with Bill Banks.

P. 32   "I know who I am": SUN, February 21, 1999.

CHAPTER 3

P. 33   "expected these patronage workers": AMER, 156–59.

P. 34   "While the Daley boys": TRIB, September 12, 1982.

P. 34   "thinking of my four sons": Sullivan, *Legend*, 150.

P. 35   "We want Stevenson": RB, 70.

P. 35   "It's too late": Richard Ciccone, *Daley: Power and Presidential Politics* (Chicago: Contemporary Books, 1996), 39.

P. 35   "That was a special day": TRIB, September 12, 1982.

P. 35   "politicians invented jokes": AMER, 278.

P. 36   "Rich needs a haircut": June 9, 2009, conversation with Abner Mikva at a Cory Booker talk in Chicago.

P. 36   "relationship with Jane Byrne": Jane Byrne, *My Chicago* (New York: W. W. Norton, 1992; reprint, Evanston, IL: Northwestern University Press, 2004), 13–17, 192–204, 246–47; Sullivan, *Legend*, 1–24.

P. 36   "Jane Byrne was the supreme misjudgment": Sullivan, *Legend*, 24.

P. 36   "Resentful of Byrne": interview with Ned Kennan; phone conversation with Ed Kelly; OR.

P. 37   "rare, very valuable talent": interview with Ned Kennan.

P. 37   "started off as political allies": GRIM, 97–112.

P. 38   "Black voters passively accepted": GRIM, 108–27.

P. 38   "lost the white vote in 1963": GRIM, 109–34; BOSS, 127.

P. 38   "inflamed the black community": GRIM, 115; BOSS, 138–39.

P. 38   "The more blacks picked on Willis": BOSS, 139.

P. 39   "shallow understanding from people of good will": Martin Luther King, Jr., April 16, 1963.

P. 39   "King decided to come to Chicago": BOSS, 145–46.

P. 39   "The door is always open": AMER, 353–56.

P. 40   "our objective will be to bring": AMER, 356.

P. 40   "White power!": AMER, 393.

P. 40   "Two, four, six, eight": AMER, 395.

P. 40   "I've been in many demonstrations": AMER, 396.

P. 41   "It seemed to me": Godfrey Hodgson, *Martin Luther King* (Ann Arbor: University of Michigan Press, 2009), 183.

P. 41   "Never before have such": AMER, 420.

P. 41   "whole lot of lies": AMER, 423.

P. 42   "spoke on the phone from his Bridgeport home": AMER, 451.

P. 43   "blood is on the chest and hands": ENCY, B36.

P. 43   "No thousands will come": TRIB, January 9, 1968.

P. 43   "important sign of faith to the American people": BOSS, 167–68.

P. 43   "I was an organizer": interview with Marilyn Katz.

P. 44   "Unfortunately, Mayor Daley's recent actions": David Farber, *Chicago '68* (Chicago: University of Chicago Press, 1988), Kindle edition, chap. 6; Richard Ciccone, *Rokyo: A Life in Print* (New York: Public Affairs, 2001), 147; Roger Biles, *Richard J. Daley* (DeKalb: Northern Illinois University Press, 1995), 152–53.

P. 44   "most public cultural disputes": Farber, *Chicago '68*, Kindle edition, preface; Sullivan, *Legend*, 36; AMER, 481; interview with Marilyn Katz.

P. 44   "pigs eat shit!": Farber, *Chicago '68*, Kindle edition, chap. 7.

P. 45   "You could see them at the edge": interview with Marilyn Katz.

P. 45   "police state terror": BOSS, 184.

P. 45   "Gestapo in the streets of Chicago": BOSS, 184–85.

P. 45   "Fuck you, you Jew son of a bitch": BOSS, 185. Some Daley supporters claim that Dick Daley shouted "faker" at the 1968 Democratic National Convention rather than "fuck you." While theoretically possible, this claim appears highly dubious.

P. 46   "bumper stickers on cars": AMER, 483.

P. 46   "worked through these conflicting ideas": interview with Dick Devine; interview with David Axelrod; interview with Ed Kelly; interview with Bernie Hanson; interview with Ray Flynn.

CHAPTER 4

P. 49   "The mayor's clout": TRIB, September 12, 1982; TRIB, November 20, 1979; TRIB, July 11, 1970.

P. 49   "blessing of a fine wife and family": AMER, 495.

P. 50   "We never had a chance": TRIB, September 12, 1982; TRIB, July 11, 1970.

P. 50   "I hope and pray to God": WAVE, 52–53.

P. 50   "glass shelter around him": interview with Dawn Clark Netsch.

P. 51   "I would say that he influenced me": TRIB, December 10, 1970.

P. 51   "Mayor Daley thought long and hard": interview of David Kenney on September 18, 1987, by Cullom Davis in *Illinois Constitutional Convention Memoir, 1969–70*, vol. 2, University of Illinois at Springfield Oral History Collection, http://www.uis.edu/archives/memoirs/ILCONCONvII.pdf.

P. 52   "hundreds and hundreds of patronage workers": interview with Michael Shakman.

P. 52   "None of this has ever been personal though": interview with Michael Shakman.

P. 52   "benefited from their dad's citywide clout": AMER, 526; TRIB, September 12, 1982.

P. 53   "more than $1 million in no-bid": Sullivan, *Legend*, 6–9, 111–13.

P. 53   "I make no apologies to anyone": AMER, 526.

P. 54   "Rich didn't have the luxury": TRIB, September 12, 1982.

P. 54   "Rich Daley introduced the artist": the story that follows is based on an interview with John Schmidt.

P. 56   "to enhance the opportunity for vote fraud": TRIB, September 12, 1982.

P. 56   "I would do a lot of things differently": TRIB, February 13, 1983.

P. 56   "I was furious": interview with Dawn Clark Netsch.

P. 57   "I guess that doesn't make for great popularity": TRIB, December 2, 1979; TRIB, February 13, 1983.

P. 57   "favorite story illustrates": *Orlando Sentinel Sunday Magazine*, August 25, 1996.

P. 59   "Look, you're name is Nudelman": *Illinois Issues*, December 1975; TRIB, May 2, 1975.

P. 59   "Katz is just another phony liberal": GRIM, 210.

P. 59   "pretty awful back then": TRIB, September 12, 1982.

P. 60   "We had just bought our house": TRIB, December 9, 1975; SUN "Mayor Daley Remembered," 1987, 1.

P. 60   "Chicago's future mayor Jane Byrne": Sullivan, *Legend*, 12.

P. 61   "Mayor Daley was a man who": ROST, 98–99.

CHAPTER 5

P. 63   "description of the leading candidates": RRR, 160–67.

P. 63   "how the pie was split": RRR, 167.

P. 63   "The committeemen respected Rich": interview with Ed Kelly.

P. 64   "cautious, lawyerly Hynes": SUN, December 11, 1986; GRIM, 211; *Illinois Issues*, May 1977.

P. 64   "resisted Hynes and Daley fiercely": interview of Dawn Clark Netsch; Dempsey Travis, *"Harold": The People's Mayor* (Chicago: Urban Research Press, 1989), 107–8; *Illinois Issues*, May 1977.

P. 64   "sleeping giant in Chicago": Biles, *Richard J. Daley*, 234.

P. 64   "a third-rate boss Daley": Travis, *"Harold,"* 111.

P. 65   "mean little prick": interview with Don Rose.

P. 65   "civilizing Richie": interview with Don Rose.

P. 65   "any human being who doesn't change": READ, July 12, 1991.

P. 66   "I was amazed": TRIB, September 12, 1982.

P. 66   "Rich Daley got very interested": interview with Dawn Clark Netsch.

P. 66   "very interesting to see Frank": interview with Dawn Clark Netsch.

P. 67   "lost much of the mean edge": interview with Dawn Clark Netsch; TRIB, March 20, 1979.

P. 67   "They say Rich isn't bright": TRIB, September 12, 1982.

P. 67   "I didn't for one minute think Rich": interview with Dawn Clark Netsch.

P. 68   "simple and complex political forces": TRIB, February 27, 1979; Biles, *Richard J. Daley*, 223–37.

P. 68   "When Richie and I met": Byrne, *My Chicago*, 274.

P. 69   "Daley and I didn't speak": Byrne, *My Chicago*, 283.

P. 69   "announcing that he would run": TRIB, October 19, 1980.

P. 69   "grown into a feverish paranoia": March 1980 interview of Jane Byrne by Bob Crawford on WBBM Radio from the Bob Crawford Audio Archive at the University of Illinois at Chicago.

P. 69   "Byrne could see Rich Daley over her shoulder": interview with Ed Burke.

P. 70   "Rich was running as an independent": interview with Ed Kelly.

P. 70   "civil war": OR.

P. 70   "Visitation parish was so central": interview with Ed Burke; YARD, 33–38, 150–71; CPW, 100–106.

P. 71   "Chicago neighborhood politics": interview with Ed Burke.

P. 71   "Politics was kind of in my blood": interview with Ed Burke.

P. 72   "Through his acquaintance with Rich": *Chicago Life Magazine*, August 1, 2005.

P. 72   "what would have happened": *Chicago Life Magazine*, August 1, 2005.

P. 72   "In those days people looked for": interview with Ed Burke.

P. 73   "most charismatic and most persuasive individuals": interview with Ed Burke.

P. 73   "As Daley was wont to do": AMER, 544.

P. 74   "For twenty-one years, I represented": Ehrenhalt, *The Lost City*, 8.

P. 74   "John Fary was a temporary seat warmer.": AMER, 544.

P. 75   "Burke has got a glorified vision of himself": TRIB, January 29, 1984.

P. 75   "The youngest Daley brother had great judgment": interview with John Rogers.

P. 75   "became known as Daley's political enforcer": TRIB, May 30, 2007; SUN, May 26, 1995; SUN, May 14, 1993; TRIB, March 18, 2009.

P. 76   "personality of a Doberman pinscher": SUN, December 3, 1986; CPW, 129–34.

P. 76   "would have kissed Rich Daley's ass": READ, July 14, 1989.

P. 76   "I'd stayed in touch with Dick Devine": CM, August 1992.

P. 77   "Rich Daley's campaign": the following story is from CM, August 1992.

P. 77   "re-asserting their parochial interests": RRR, 161–62, 198; MAYR, 168–73; CD, 125–27.

P. 77   "You break it all the way down to the precinct level": OR.

P. 78   "bare-legged shivering cheerleaders": the following story is based on TRIB, March 18, 1980.

P. 78   "Rich Daley not only beat Burke": CD, 127–28; TRIB, September 19, 1980.

P. 78   "believed that Byrne even lent her behind-the-scenes support": TRIB, October 19, 1980; CD, 131.

P. 79   "ruthless desire for power": TRIB, October 29, 1980.

P. 79   "There isn't a precinct captain": TRIB, October 29, 1980.

P. 79   "A tidal wave hit us": James Patterson, *Restless Giant* (Oxford: Oxford University Press, 2005), 151.

P. 80   "What went wrong was": TRIB, November 14, 1980.

P. 80   "Rich Daley's face turned bright red": TRIB, December 20, 1981.

P. 80   "That's Richie Daley, you idiot": TRIB, December 20, 1981.

P. 81   "Rich has a lot of ideas": interview of Dick Devine.

P. 81   "I've found that this job": TRIB, September 12, 1982.

P. 81   "Daley's performance has been a pleasant surprise": TRIB, December 20, 1981.

P. 81   "I think his political judgment was": interview with John Schmidt.

P. 82   "failing to prosecute voting fraud": GRIM, 213.

P. 82   "Kevin affected us in a good way": TRIB, September 12, 1982.

P. 82   "I'm forty years old now": TRIB, November 5, 1982.

P. 83   "woman he disliked intensely"; interview with Ed Kelly; interview with Ned Kennan; OR; SUN, April 28, 2005; SUN, January 19, 1987; Byrne, *My Chicago*, e.g., 333

P. 83   "Brzeczek had forwarded him a letter": G. Flint Taylor, "Chicago Police Commander Convicted of Lying about Torture," *Police Misconduct and Civil Rights Law Report* 9, no. 17 (September–October 2010); February 2, 2006 Office of Professional Standards Memorandum from Robert D. Boyle concerning his questioning of Mayor Richard M. Daley; the "Goldston Report" by the Chicago Police Department Office of Professional Standards, November 2, 1990.

P. 83   "the doctor's letter concerned the physical mistreatment": letter from Dr. Raba, February 17, 1982, stamped received on February 22, 1982 by the Chicago Police Office of the Superintendent; a copy was provided to me by attorney G. Flint Taylor via e-mail on October 28, 2010.

P. 84   "his boat, dubbed *The Vigilante*": Steve Bogira, *Courtroom 302: A Year behind the Scenes in an American Criminal Courthouse* (New York: Vintage Books, 2006), 175.

P. 84   "official police investigation": the "Goldston Report" by the Chicago Police Department Office of Professional Standards, November 2, 1990.

P. 85   "torture of black suspects in Chicago police stations": Taylor, "Chicago Police Commander Convicted of Lying about Torture"; the "Goldston

Report" by the Chicago Police Department Office of Professional
Standards, November 2, 1990; Bogira, *Courtroom 302,* 174–77.

P. 85   "No record Daley ever responded": February 2, 2006, Office of Professional
Standards Memorandum from Robert D. Boyle concerning his
questioning of Mayor Richard M. Daley; the "Goldston Report" by the
Chicago Police Department Office of Professional Standards, November
2, 1990.

P. 86   "Dunne advised Doctor Raba not to get involved": Taylor, "Chicago Police
Commander Convicted of Lying about Torture."

CHAPTER 6

P. 87   "part of his evolving character": Irving J. Rein, "The Transformation of a
Candidate: Richard M. Daley," *American Communication Journal* 2, no. 1
(Winter 2000).

P. 88   "great sense of entitlement to the office": Rein, "The Transformation of a
Candidate."

P. 88   "three strategic mistakes": CD, 140–45; GRIM, 156–64.

P. 88   "It is better to boycott with dignity": Travis, *"Harold,"* 145.

P. 88   "People are worried about the future": CD, 150.

P. 89   "Black voters hate Ronald Reagan": CD, 135; Travis, *"Harold,"* 143–69.

P. 89   "Chicago is a divided city": CD, 157.

P. 89   "I have compassion for the terrible plight of our people": CD, 157.

P. 89   "They saw Harold Washington": interview with Ned Kennan.

P. 89   "I've been a Daley man right along": TRIB, November 6, 1982.

P. 90   "I'm a very strong supporter of Rich": TRIB, December 15, 1982.

P. 90   "Racial, ethnic, religious and sexist slurs": MAYR, 224.

P. 90   "The fear, the hysteria he's using": CD, 178–79.

P. 90   "Byrne's campaign workers began scaring voters": CD, 162, 173–79.

P. 92   "That's Rich. He's the eldest": TRIB, January 30, 1983.

P. 92   "I make no apology for my name": TRIB, February 13, 1983.

P. 92   "We have to recognize that racism reduces": TRIB, February 3, 1983.

P. 92   "I'm an old friend of Rich Daley's": TRIB, February 3, 1983.

P. 93   "Jane, I'm not so happy to say this": based on an interview with Ned
Kennan.

P. 93   Statistical information taken from "Chicago Mayor—D Primary" at http://
www.ourcampaigns.com/RaceDetail.html?RaceID=6469.

P. 93   "We learned a lot about what not to do": CD, 166–71.

P. 94   "all neighborhoods and all people": CD, 187–88.

P. 94   "By your vote": Travis, "Harold," 179.

P. 94   "NIGGER DIE on the church doors": CD, 209.

P. 94   "The big thing is fear": CD, 209.

CHAPTER 7

P. 97   "All Hell Breaks Loose": Adapted from the quote by Paul Green, a public policy professor and political writer, who said, "If Harold Washington dies, all hell breaks loose": CPW, 343.

P. 97   "Well, I loved Harold": interview with Marilyn Katz.

P. 97   "a bunch of white men ran the city": interview with Marilyn Katz.

P. 98   "black-versus-white political civil war": RRR, 210–20.

P. 98   "bitter or hateful person": interview with Ed Burke.

P. 98   "bodyguards and gangster-looking black sedan": Charles Thomas and Ben Bradley, "Court Records Shed Light on Burke's Bodyguards," June 28, 2011, http://abclocal.go.com/wls/story?section=news/politics&id=8220005.

P. 98   "chilly 45 degree temperature": "November 25, 1987," The Old Farmer's Almanac, www.almanac.com.

P. 99   "beat the whole god-damn machine singlehanded": MAYR, 168.

P. 99   "A vote for Daley is a vote for Washington": CD, 177.

P. 100   "The mayor is dead": READ, March 11, 1988.

P. 100   "Burke was a living relic": OR; interview with Ed Burke; Chicago Life Magazine, August 1, 2005; CPW, 100–106.

P. 101   "this man was like a god": READ, March 11, 1988.

P. 101   "holding secret meetings": READ, March 11, 1988.

P. 101   "he'd stab you in the chest": RRR, 228.

P. 101   "support from various aldermanic colleagues": GRIM, 197–99; CPW, 343–58.

P. 102   "Dick Mell called me several times": READ, March 11, 1988.

P. 102   "designed to unite black aldermen behind Evans": CPW, 343–58.

P. 102   "I could support a black man": CPW, 350.

P. 103   "they were attracted to his flaws": GRIM, 198–99.

P. 103   "He loved people—black, white, brown": NYT, December 1, 1987.

P. 103   "became a political rally for Evans": CPW, 351–52.

P. 103   "had already agreed on a deal" CPW, 352–58; MAYR, 205–6.

P. 103   "What a sham! What a sham!": CPW, 357.

P. 104   "started to receive death threats": MAYR, 206.

P. 104   "But you should tell the people who backed you": RRR, 230.

P. 104   "Rich Daley, Cook County state's attorney, controlled the abstaining alderman": OR; CPW, 358.

P. 104   "I said to former Mayor Washington": SUN, February 8, 1989.

P. 104   "Political insiders knew, however": interview with Alderman Pat O'Connor, April 2010.

P. 104   "It was a ruse to get him": RRR, 230-31.

P. 105   "Sawyer did have some quick successes": MAYR, 210-11.

P. 105   "took active steps to reassert their control": MAYR, 216; RRR, 233-34.

CHAPTER 8

P. 106   "This is a great victory": SUN, November 22, 1988.

P. 106   "I had a closer relationship with Harold": SUN, November 22, 1988.

P. 106   "the Seven Dwarfs": READ, December 23, 1988; SUN, November 22, 1988.

P. 106   "Eight months later": CM, August 1992.

P. 107   "It's not just important to win elections": interview with Bob Crawford.

P. 107   "Billy [Daley] is a political genius": CM, August 1992.

P. 107   "Billy was the smartest of them all": interview with Phil Krone.

P. 108   "We were just the best":CM, August 1992.

P. 108   "established his liberal bona fides": *Illinois Issues*, June 1997.

P. 108   "slow, funny-talking south-side guy": CM, August 1992.

P. 109   "They want to be on the list": CM, August 1992.

P. 109   "We're not out to buy a piece of Chicago": READ, March 31, 1989.

P. 109   "They thought that they were buying their way in": CM, August 1992.

P. 110   "Five thousand dollars": CM, August 1992.

P. 110   "big old pair of brass balls": *Rolling Stone Magazine*, October 20, 2005; TRIB, November 12, 2006.

P. 111   "You've got to have a thirst for winning": TRIB, November 22, 2006; TRIB, November 12, 2006; NYT, November 6, 2008.

P. 111   "Rich has a very hearty and wonderful laugh": SUN, February 23, 1989.

P. 113   "When I was a state senator": SUN, December 16, 1988.

P. 113   "This should be the essence of the campaign for mayor": "Improving Education in Chicago," speech by Richard M. Daley, Friday, January 13,

1989, in "Daley Agenda for Chicago's Future," Chicago Municipal Reference Library, April 28, 1989.

P. 113   "Education is the top priority for Richard M. Daley": "Richard M. Daley's Education Platform," *The Daley Agenda for Chicago's Future*, Chicago Municipal Reference Library, April 28, 1989.

P. 113   "I want each school in Chicago to be the heartbeat": *The Daley Agenda for Chicago's Future*.

P. 114   "If you want to win": August 13, 2002, speech at the University of Edinburgh, Scotland. Retrieved at popular-today. com/2008/2/13/43/2008-2-13-43-2.html.

P. 115   "My expertise is in the areas": READ, July 12, 1991.

P. 115   "Every campaign begins with essentially the same process": READ, July 12, 1991.

P. 115   "We made one adjustment at the beginning": READ, July 12, 1991.

P. 116   "He is the master of the short bite": Green and Holli, eds., *Restoration 1989*, 1991, 156.

P. 116   "The thing about the Daley operation": READ, July 12, 1991.

P. 117   "some of the white politicians": READ, March 31, 1989; READ, March 10, 1989; SUN, November 12, 1988.

P. 117   "[Daley] certainly has the money": SUN, December 28, 1988; SUN, December 23, 1988.

P. 118   "You want a white mayor to sit down with everybody": Green and Holli, eds., *Restoration 1989*, 23.

P. 119   "Campaigning citywide is brutal": READ, February 24, 1989.

P. 119   "I think people want some peace and tranquility": READ, February 24, 1989.

P. 119   "Politics: Gays and Daley" *Chicago Reader*, November 17, 1989; "The 1989 Mayoral Primary Election"; Greg Hinz, "Lakefronters"; Jorge Casuso, "Hispanics"—all in *Restoration 1989*, ed. Green and Holli, 25–31; 74–77; 70–73, respectively.

P. 120   "Come with me": based on an interview with Ned Kennan.

CHAPTER 9

P. 122   "heart of Robert Taylor homes": adapted from Sudhir Venkatesh, *American Project: The Rise and Fall of a Modern Ghetto* (Cambridge, MA: Harvard University Press, 2000).

P. 123   "I've not had any problems": Mary Patillo, *Black on the Block* (Chicago: University of Chicago Press, 2007), 86.

P. 123   "My old man—I remember around the table": "Life after Steel: The Life and Death of a Chicago Steel Mill" an oral history by Dan Collison; retrieved at www.talkinghistory.org/collison.html.

P. 124   "Tener un hambre canina": The phrase means "to be as hungry as a wolf"; retrieved at http://www.spanishdict.com/translate/hungry.

P. 124   "The money can come from desegregation funds": READ, May 19, 1989.

P. 124   "What the Board of Education": Lois Wille, *At Home in the Loop* (Carbondale: Southern Illinois University Press, 1997), p. 155.

P. 124   "Two boys, aged fourteen and eleven": adapted from Alex Kotlowitz, *There Are No Children Here* (New York: Anchor Books, 1991).

P. 125   "We know the signs won't stop": READ, February 23, 1990.

P. 126   "In the last ten years": READ, July 14, 1989.

P. 126   "We take a giant step forward today": Miller, Ross. *Here's the Deal.* (New York: Alfred A. Knopf, 1996), p. 193.

CHAPTER 10

P. 127   "should not be a pigpen": SUN, May 12, 1989.

P. 127   "needed to overcome many challenges": SUN, May 19, 1989.

P. 128   "One day does not an administration make": SUN, April 26, 1989.

P. 129   "no other agenda other than Rich Daley's interest": interview with Forrest Claypool.

P. 130   "original source of the tension": SUN, May 18, 1989.

P. 130   "lucrative, politically connected law practice": SUN, May 18, 1989; TRIB, January 22, 2010.

P. 131   "the City's back in business folks": interview with Forrest Claypool.

P. 132   "an inside deal on the towing contract": TRIB, March 23, 2003; SUN, April 6, 2001; SUN, August 1, 1997; TRIB, November 5, 2003; OR.

P. 132   "politically questionable deal for Daley": TRIB, March 23, 2003; SUN, April 6, 2001; SUN, August 1, 1997; TRIB, November 5, 2003; OR.

P. 133   "take part in this parade to show my support of the gay community": SUN, June 26, 1989.

P. 133   "most dramatic transformation was with the gay-lesbian issue": interview with Dawn Clark Netsch.

P. 134   "Many political insiders believe": OR.

P. 134   "As finance committee chair": SUN, November 12, 1988; SUN, October 26, 1997; SUN, December 22, 1990; SUN, May 22, 1997.

P. 134   "garbage is votes": SUN, October 15, 1989.

P. 135   "Are steel mills coming back?": SUN, August 1, 1989; SUN, August 2, 1989.

P. 135   "I don't get so disappointed": Bob Crawford Audio archive from the University of Illinois at Chicago, Richard M. Daley tape 4, track 34.

P. 136   "private army of political operatives": interview with Bernie Hanson; interview with Danny Solis; interview with Don Rose; TRIB, May 10, 2006; interview with Bob Crawford.

P. 136   "white ethnic aldermen were still furious": interview with Bernie Hanson.

P. 136   "an unnecessary evil": interview with Bernie Hanson.

P. 136   "[Voters] have their own opinions about candidates": Bob Crawford Audio archive from the University of Illinois at Chicago, Richard M. Daley tape 3, track 44.

P. 136   "own parallel political organization": interview with Bernie Hanson; interview with Danny Solis; interview with Don Rose; interview with Bob Crawford; Bob Crawford Audio archive from the University of Illinois at Chicago, Richard M. Daley tape 3, track 44.

P. 137   "exact birth of the Hispanic Democratic Organization": *ChicagoBreakingNews.com*, March 17, 2009; SUN, June 12, 2005; SUN, July 3, 2008; TRIB, December 2, 2006; SUN, March 23, 2006; SUN, December 15, 2006; TRIB, March 10, 2009; interview with Danny Solis; interview with Bernie Hanson; OR.

P. 137   "Al Sanchez met with Tim Degnan" *ChicagoBreakingNews.com*, March 17, 2009.

P. 137   "took place at a bar called G's": SUN, June 12, 2005.

P. 137   "We're going to build a Hispanic organization": SUN, June 12, 2005.

P. 137   "That's beautiful": SUN, June 12, 2005.

P. 137   "These strategy sessions included politicians": SUN, June 12, 2005; *ChicagoBreakingNews.com*, March 17, 2009; SUN, June 12, 2005; SUN, July 3, 2008; TRIB, December 2, 2006; SUN, March 23, 2006; SUN, December 15, 2006; TRIB, March 10, 2009; interview with Danny Solis; interview with Bernie Hanson; OR.

P. 138   "You're talking about 20 years ago": TRIB, March 10, 2009.

P. 138   "committed Daley loyalist in the 1990s": TRIB, May 10, 2006; SUN, January 12, 2000; TRIB, February 3, 2005; TRIB, February 10, 2005.

P. 138   "similar roots as Rich Daley": SUN, June 6, 2006; SUN, November 10, 2006.

P. 139   "Dan Rostenkowski convinced Daley": SUN, November 10, 2006; SUN, October 22, 2004.

P. 139   "key factors in Daley's political organization": SUN, July 30, 2005; SUN, April 17, 2008; TRIB, May 10, 2006; TRIB, February 3, 2005;

SUN, June 24, 2005; SUN, June 1, 2006; SUN, June 6, 2006; SUN, November 10, 2006; SUN, October 22, 2004.

P. 140   "buy off political opposition": TRIB, May 1, 2012.

P. 140   "$58 million into the pockets of alderman": TRIB, May 1, 2012.

P. 140   "Chicagoans had lowered their voices": *Illinois Issues*, June 1991 v. 17.

CHAPTER 11

P. 143   "You gotta do this!": OR.

P. 143   "getting a beating": OR.

P. 143   "playing basketball for Bobby Knight": OR.

P. 143   "dealing with the economic recession": *Albany Times Union*, June 18, 1989; SUN, December 28, 1989; SUN, October 16, 1991; SUN, November 24, 1991.

P. 144   "Air and Water Show": the following story is based on various confidential sources.

P. 146   "unauthorized party": SUN, March 4, 1992; SUN, March 2, 1992.

P. 146   "I'm very disappointed as a parent": *Post-Tribune* (Northwest Indiana), March 3, 1992; SUN, August 31, 1998.

P. 147   "one of its worst civic disasters": SUN, February 23, 1994; *Washington Post*, April 25, 1992; *Nation's Cities Weekly*, April 27, 1992.

P. 147   "These people are going to be held accountable": *Post-Tribune* (Northwest Indiana), April 14, 1992; SUN, February 23, 1994.

P. 147   "He was really pissed off at me": interview with John LaPlante.

P. 148   "Sometimes you have to face reality": SUN, July 2, 1992.

P. 148   "For politicians to come in": SUN, February 21, 1992.

P. 148   "Daley did not get along with Jim Edgar": OR.

P. 149   "city's recent increase in violent crime": Wesley G. Skogan, *Police and Community in Chicago: A Tale of Three Cities* (Oxford: Oxford University Press, 2006).

P. 149   "increase in violent crime": SUN, October 11, 1991; SUN, November 10, 1991; SUN, November 9, 1991.

P. 150   "a piece of human garbage": SUN, March 20, 1992.

P. 150   "[They] come in all the time high as a kite": READ, January 7, 1993.

P. 150   "one day in early 1993 was typical": READ, January 7, 1993.

P. 151   "Possession of controlled substance": READ, January 7, 1993.

P. 152   "experimenting with 'community policing'": Skogan, *Police and Community in Chicago*; SUN, April 30, 1993.

P. 153   "my relationship with my wife": *Washington Post*, December 26, 1993; SUN, April 4, 1993.

P. 153   "I think it's empowered people": Skogan, *Police and Community in Chicago*, 79–80.

CHAPTER 12

P. 155   "chairman of the School Finance Authority": the following story is based on an interview with Mike Koldyke.

P. 156   "tore at the very social fabric of Chicago": interview with Mike Koldyke; interview with Bill Singer; interview with Terry Mazany.

P. 156   "damaged the Chicago school system": interview with Paul Vallas; Dorothy Shipps, *School Reform, Corporate Style: Chicago, 1880–2000* (Lawrence: University Press of Kansas, 2006), 60–88.

P. 157   "What Daley senior was doing": interview with Paul Vallas.

P. 157   "decade of chaos ensued": interview with Paul Vallas; Shipps, *School Reform, Corporate Style*, 89–129.

P. 157   "harsh assessment of CPS was justified": *Economic Perspectives*, May 1, 1995; *Newsweek*, June 22, 1998; *Washington Post*, August 26, 1996.

P. 158   "Rich was very much interested": interview with Bill Singer.

P. 158   "Singer used his talents": interview with Bill Singer.

P. 159   "Koldyke also put forth ideas": SUN, October 13, 1993; SUN, April 5, 1994; SUN, April 3, 1994.

P. 159   "small-minded ex-marine": interview with Mike Koldyke; *Daily Herald*, December 5, 2002; *Catalyst*, February 29, 2000.

P. 160   "Written reform proposal": SUN, April 23, 1995.

P. 160   "He never wanted anybody to say": interview with Mike Koldyke.

P. 160   "I think his greatest accomplishment": interview with Arne Duncan.

P. 161   "He appointed Paul Vallas": interview with Paul Vallas; interview with Gery Chico; *Philadelphia Weekly*, October 16, 2002; *Newsweek*, June 22, 1998; *Newsweek*, November 11, 1996; "Paul Vallas in New Orleans," episode 1, pt. 1 of a series of special reports by John Merrow on PBS's *NewsHour*, http://www.youtube.com/watch?v=FLVpKpaYtRI.

P. 161   "Chico had other strengths": interview with Paul Vallas; interview with Gery Chico; *Newsweek*, June 22, 1998; *Newsweek*, November 11, 1996; SUN, March 31, 1996; SUN, May 25, 2001; SUN, November 14, 2010.

P. 161   "inherited a gigantic mess": interview with Paul Vallas; interview with Gery Chico; *Philadelphia Weekly*, October 16, 2002; SUN, June 30, 1996.

P. 162   "more than $1.5 billion": TRIB, November 16, 2010.

P. 162   "Daley always flew air cover": interview with Paul Vallas.

P. 162   "Vallas was biased toward action": interview with Paul Vallas; *Philadelphia Weekly*, October 16, 2002; SUN, June 30, 1996.

P. 163   "Just go in there and stick to our": the following story is based on a number of confidential interviews.

P. 164   "ethical lapses seemed to center around Ed Burke": SUN, January 29, 1998; SUN, May 4, 1997; SUN, May 5, 2005; SUN, June 10, 1997; NYT, October 22, 1997.

P. 164   "both Burke and Huels were implicated": SUN, October 26, 1997; SUN, October 18, 1997.

P. 165   "allegations against Huels": SUN, October 20, 1997; *Crain's Chicago Business*, October 27, 1997; SUN, October 22, 1997; SUN, October 16, 1997; NYT, October 22, 1997.

P. 165   "friends and longtime political allies": SUN, October 20, 1997; *Crain's Chicago Business*, October 27, 1997; SUN, October 22, 1997; SUN, October 16, 1997.

P. 165   "nondescript Huels": SUN, January 23, 2006; SUN October 22, 1997.

P. 165   "Daley tried to distance himself": SUN, September 28, 2003; SUN, October 26, 1997; *Chicago Life Magazine*, August 1, 2005.

P. 166   "What is working in Chicago must blow": SUN, October 29, 1997.

P. 166   "the city that works now has a school system": SUN, October 29, 1997.

P. 166   "another large political scandal arose": SUN, October 23, 1997; SUN, January 23, 2006.

P. 167   "reported student test scores also rose": *Philadelphia Weekly*, October 16, 2002; interview with Paul Vallas: interview with Arne Duncan.

P. 167   "Don't ever believe that one person": SUN, May 30, 2001.

P. 167   "I like to think that we have started an education revolution": SUN, June 8, 2001.

CHAPTER 13

P. 171   "very important to Daley that the convention function smoothly": OR; SUN, August 5, 1994.

P. 172   "walked over to the window": interview of John Bryan; Scott Jacobs, "The New Burnham," *The Week Behind: Inside the Chicago Art Scene*, http://www.theweekbehind.com/2009/06/04/the-new-burnham/.

P. 172   "We should build a park": interview with John Bryan; MP, 81–133.

P. 173   "Weisberg was a super creative": SUN, May 6, 1998; SUN, March 8, 2006; *New Yorker*, January 11, 1999.

P. 173   "Lois Weisberg is one of those unique people": SUN, May 6, 1998.

P. 173   "Daley family had a long history": TRIB, March 11, 1999; "Chicago Public Library/Cultural Center," City of Chicago Department of Planning and Development, Landmarks Division 2003, http://webapps.cityofchicago .org/landmarksweb/web/landmarkdetails.htm?lanId=1274.

P. 174   "That's a beautiful site where it is": TRIB, March 11, 1999.

P. 174   "It's important to the quality of life in the city": SUN, January 19, 2001.

P. 174   "ideas for using Block 37": the following story is based on SUN, December 22, 1999, and SUN, April 11, 2004.

P. 175   "This was one of the most boring city blocks": *Washington Post*, August 16, 1991.

P. 175   "The artists bring their culture with them": SUN, July 16, 1996.

P. 177   "political liability to the second Mayor Daley": OR; Toni Helen Hartrich and Neville Dowell, *The Chicago Park District: An Independent Appraisal of its Form and Function*, Bulletin no. 1088 (Chicago: Civic Federation, 1993); Civic Federation and Friends of the Parks, *The Chicago Park District: A Progress Report on Decentralization* (Chicago: Civic Federation and Friends of the Parks, September 1995).

P. 177   "serious political concern for Daley": OR.

P. 177   "problems at the parks were severe": interview with Forest Claypool; interview with John Rogers; James G. Clawson, "Chicago Park District (A)," Case Study UVA-OB-0618 (Charlottesville: Darden Business Publishing, University of Virginia, 1996).

P. 178   "told us there are no sacred cows": SUN, July 9, 1993; SUN, July 16, 1993

P. 178   "In moments of crisis, normal politics cannot": interview with Forest Claypool.

P. 179   "former critics of the Chicago parks began": *Daily Herald*, August 3, 1999; *American Forests*, June 22, 1999.

P. 179   "I love this city and": "National Convention: 1996 Host City," August 4, 1994, C-Span video library, http://www.c-spanvideo.org/ program/59264–1.

P. 179   "It's important for us to recognize": "National Convention: 1996 Host City," August 4, 1994, C-Span video library, http://www.c-spanvideo.org/ program/59264–1.

P. 180   "1996 convention was really important to Daley": OR.

P. 180   "very important for Rich Daley to redo the 1968 convention": OR.

P. 180   "One focus of convention preparations was urban beautification": OR; *Daily Herald*, August 25, 1996; *NPR Morning Edition*, August 23, 1996; SUN, August 24, 2000.

P. 180   "some cities that are resolutely turned toward the future": SUN, February 4, 1996; SUN, February 2, 1996.

P. 181   "one who cares deeply about the issues": SUN, February 4, 1996; SUN, February 2, 1996.

P. 181   "Daley attended a healing ceremony": *Economist*, August 17, 1996; *Washington Times*, August 26, 1996.

P. 182   "If you embrace the idea of Chicago playing host": *Daily Herald*, August 25, 1996; *Washington Times*, August 26, 1996; *Washington Times*, August 29, 1996.

CHAPTER 14

P. 183   "Housing without hope": I would like to thank D. Bradford Hunt, author of *Blueprint for Disaster: The Unraveling of Chicago Public Housing* (Chicago: University of Chicago Press, 2009), for his comments on this chapter.

P. 183   "the boys they run everything": Susan Popkin, ed., *The Hidden War: Crime and the Tragedy of Public Housing in Chicago* (New Brunswick, NJ: Rutgers University Press, 2000), 126.

P. 183   "HUD announced that it was taking over control": interview with Julia Stasch; interview with Joseph Schuldiner; June 21, 2011 comments on manuscript by D. Bradford Hunt, author of *Blueprint for Disaster*; Larry Bennett and Janet Smith, eds., *Where Are Poor People to Live? Transforming Public Housing Communities* (Armonk, NY: M. E. Sharpe, 2006), 93–236; Popkin, ed., 1–38; Alexander Polikoff, *Waiting for Gautreaux* (Evanston, IL: Northwestern University Press, 2006),304–10.

P. 184   "Daley worried that the charismatic black leader": OR.

P. 184   "sweeping reorganization of his administration": SUN, June 1, 1991.

P. 184   "One of Jarrett's early decisions": BRIDGE,272–74.

P. 185   "Barack felt extraordinarily familiar": BRIDGE, 273.

P. 185   "Jarrett developed into an influential player in Chicago": BRIDGE,271–74.

P. 185   "Valerie is the one": BRIDGE, 274.

P. 186   "The political issue that developed": interview with Jerry Reinsdorf; interview with Earnest Gates; interview with Julia Stasch; "Earnest Gates Stayed Rooted, Helps Community Do the Same," *Near West Side Community Development Corp.*, October 31, 2011, http://www .nearwestsidecdc.org/news/1631.

P. 186   "The priority will be dealing with the people living there": SUN, May 24, 1989; SUN, June 8, 1987.

P. 186   "a fourteen-point plan": interview with Jerry Reinsdorf; interview with
          Earnest Gates; READ, September 19, 1996.

P. 187   "she put together a program": interview with Andrew Mooney; SUN,
          February 1, 1995; SUN, January 3, 1994; SUN, February 9, 1993; SUN,
          June 10, 1992; SUN, March 30, 1993.

P. 187   "I was just walking through the North Kenwood": CM, August 2000.

P. 188   "We've had some rocky days": SUN, May 15, 1995.

P. 188   "cumulative track record was mixed": OR; TRIB, March 22, 1998.

P. 188   "The national system of public housing is on trial in Chicago": TRIB,
          December 27, 1998.

P. 188   "heat wave struck the city": Eric Klinenberg, *Heat Wave: A Social Autopsy of
          Disaster in Chicago* (Chicago: University of Chicago Press, 2002).

P. 189   "relationship between Daley and Jarrett had become frayed": SUN,
          September 15, 1995; *Bond Buyer*, September 18, 1995; BRIDGE, 259–75;
          interview with Marilyn Katz; interview with Andrew Mooney; OR.

P. 189   "She has been great in a tough job": SUN, September 15, 1995.

P. 190   "high-clout appointment": SUN, June 5, 1996; SUN, November 16, 2008;
          SUN, September 17, 1995.

P. 190   "two decades dragging its feet": Polikoff, *Waiting for Gautreaux*, e.g., 7,
          37–50, 166–69, 182–88; interview with Andrew Mooney; interview
          with Joseph Schuldiner; comments on manuscript, June 21, 2011, by
          D. Bradford Hunt, author of *Blueprint for Disaster*.

P. 191   "The whole program was a joke": interview with Joseph Schuldiner.

P. 191   "significant changes with respect to public housing": interview with Joseph
          Schuldiner; HUNT, 259–95.

P. 191   "Visible changes in public housing": interview with Joseph Schuldiner;
          Polikoff, *Waiting for Gautreaux*, 288–328; Pattillo, *Black on the Block*,
          217–57; Bennett and Smith, eds., *Where Are Poor People to Live?*
          93–236.

P. 192   "Daley and I said that we willing": interview with Julia Stasch.

P. 192   "the only thing possible was to reimagine or reinvent": interview with Julia
          Stasch.

P. 193   "It's not just money, it's a variety of issues": *Daily Herald*, April 29, 1999.

P. 193   "She's definitely no-nonsense": SUN, April 27, 1999.

P. 193   "Daley appointed ten new board members": SUN, June 28, 1999.

P. 194   "another potentially big political scandal": OR; "Mayor Daley's Name Turns
          Up in FBI Files on Embezzler John F. Duff Jr.," May 9, 2011, http://
          www.bettergov.org; TRIB, July 25, 1999; SUN, January 29, 2000.

P. 194   "new initiative called the Plan for Transformation": interview with Julia Stasch; HUNT,259–95; Henry Cisneros and Lora Engdahl, eds., *From Despair to Hope* (Washington, DC: Brookings Institution Press, 2009), 85–91.

P. 194   "plan was not only radical, but also risky": comments on manuscript, June 21, 2011, by D. Bradford Hunt, author of *Blueprint for Disaster*.

P. 195   "What kind of bullshit is this?": *Newsweek*, May 15, 2000.

P. 195   "There was some pressure coming from the White House": interview with Julia Stasch; OR.

P. 196   "political culture would soon threaten to take over": OR.

CHAPTER 15

P. 197   "I have some news to share with all of you":"Bill Daley Addresses Pro-Gore Crowd, Election Night 2000," November 7, 2000, http://www.youtube .com/watch?v=c5kQwuNIbhA.

P. 198   "Bill Daley is really, really smart": OR.

P. 199   "He was savvy about watching how things got done": interview with Bob Crawford.

P. 199   "gregarious personality and political connections": interview with Ed Burke; interview with Bob Crawford; SUN, September 25, 2008.

P. 199   "I am sure that Billy will tell you": interview with Ed Burke.

P. 199   "Billy was also a dealmaker": interview with Ed Burke; interview with John Schmidt; interview with John Rogers; interview with Bob Crawford; interview with Forrest Claypool; interview with Ned Kennan; OR.

P. 200   "alienated many of the alderman's Polish supporters": ROST, 19–22.

P. 200   "Loyalty was the heart of my Dad's support": ROST, 29.

P. 201   "As much as people criticize the back room": NYT, August 11, 2010; "Dan Rostenkowski: Obituary," http://www.legacy.com/obituaries/fosters/ obituary.aspx?n=dan-rostenkowski&pid=144620376.

P. 201   "When Bill was in Washington": *The Nation*, February 3, 1997.

P. 201   "Bill is obviously not a lawyer whose strength": CM, February 2005.

P. 202   "built up his standing within national Democratic circles": SUN, November 9, 1988; CM, February 2005; SUN, November 27, 1992; SUN, November 6, 1992.

P. 202   "Bill Daley seriously considered running for mayor": interview with Ned Kennan; SUN, March 12, 2001.

P. 203   "person who is loyal to his brother": interview with Ned Kennan.

P. 203   "In his brother's 1989 campaign for mayor": interview with David Axelrod;

interview with Ed Burke; interview with John Schmidt; interview with John Rogers; interview with Bob Crawford; interview with Forrest Claypool; interview with Ned Kennan; OR; SUN, August 22, 1993.

P. 204   "believed that NAFTA could pass": *The Nation*, February 3, 1997.

P. 204   "Rostenkowski became the key to success": CM, February 2005; *The Nation*, February 3, 1997; "Clinton Signs NAFTA–December 8, 1993," *American President: A Reference Resource*, http://millercenter.org/academic/americanpresident/events/12_08; ROST,218–44.

P. 204   "but he was able to pull it out of the bag": CM, February 2005.

P. 205   "Rich has always been a loner": SUN, August 27, 1995.

P. 205   "Public service often is demeaned": SUN, December 14, 1996.

CHAPTER 16

P. 209   "Crossing the River": based on a well-known fable of unknown origins. Adapted from http://allaboutfrogs.org/stories/scorpion.html.

CHAPTER 17

P. 210   "The idea of the dinner": SUN, November 4, 1999.

P. 211   "It's going to be a radical change": NYT, February 25, 2001.

P. 211   "Boeing Company initiated a search": the following story is based on an interview with John Warner and *Harvard Business Review*, October 2001.

P. 213   "Today's decision confirms to the world": *Site Selection*, June 2001.

P. 214   "We had one of the most wonderful meals": interview with John Warner.

P. 214   "aggressively pushing for a modernization program at O'Hare": *Business Travelers News*, September 23, 2002; "Passenger Traffic 2000 Final," Airports Council International, November 1, 2001, http://www.aci.aero/cda/aci_common/display/main/aci_content07_c.jsp?zn=aci&cp=1-5-54-55-189_666_2__.

P. 214   "Daley soon began aggressively pushing for a modernization program at O'Hare": *PRNewswire*, June 29, 2001.

P. 215   "Chicago is known for making big plans": *PRNewswire*, June 29, 2001.

P. 215   "A win-win deal": "Statement of Samuel K. Skinner, Chairman, President and CEO, USfreightways and Member of the Civic Committee of the Commerical [*sic*] Club of Chicago," Hearing on the National Aviation Capacity Expansion Act (S. 1786) before the Subcommittee on Aviation, Committee on Commerce, Science, and Transportation, U.S. Senate, March 21, 2002, http://www.civiccommittee.org/initiatives/aviation/Aviation%20Skinner%20Testimony.pdf; *Illinois Issues*, December 20, 2001.

P. 215   "Mayor Daley helped to bring a glass exhibit": interview with John Warner.

P. 216   "I'll do anything Rod wants me to do": SUN, May 1, 2002.

P. 216   "Everyone wanted to touch him": CM, November 2003.

P. 216   "This is how hard I work": CM, November 2003.

P. 217   "an ease talking to everyone": CM, November 2003.

P. 217   "Mell is interested in the game": CM, November 2003.

P. 218   "Mr. DuMont, which one is Patti Mell?" CM, June 2009.

P. 218   "If you go out with me, I'm going to show you the time of your life": CM, November 2003.

P. 218   "You know, Rod has always wanted to run for some office": CM, February 2008.

P. 218   "I don't give a fuck about that": READ, September 21, 2009.

P. 218   "team of Mell and Blagojevich": CM, November 2003; READ, May 6, 2004; READ, September 21, 2009; CM, June 2009.

P. 218   "accomplished little but became known as an exceptionally personable": CM, November 2003.

P. 219   "Dick Mell is a longtime ally": SUN, February 16, 1996.

P. 219   "David Axelrod signed on": CM, June 2009.

P. 220   "Axelrod gradually began to worry": CM, June 2009.

P. 220   "Blagojevich saw Rahm Emanuel": CM, June 2009; READ, February 15, 2002.

P. 220   "Who's going to run": READ, February 15, 2002.

P. 220   "Rahm, you should run": CM, June 2009.

P. 220   "Emanuel met with Daley": READ, February 15, 2002; OR.

P. 221   "Rich was a big supporter of Rahm's": Naftali Bendavid, *The Thumpin': How Rahm Emanuel and the Democrats Learned to Be Ruthless and Ended the Republican Revolution* (New York: Doubleday, 2008), Kindle edition, chap. 2; OR.

P. 221   "Word got around town": OR; BRIDGE, 365: Bendavid, *The Thumpin'*, Kindle edition, chap. 2.

P. 221   "benefited from a militia of political mercenaries": OR; Bendavid, *The Thumpin'*, Kindle edition, chap. 2; testimony by Donald Tomczak in federal court, *United States of America vs. Robert Sorich*, Transcript of Proceedings, June 5, 2006, 2444; *Chicago Daily Observer*, March 11, 2011.

P. 221   "Chicago media speculation": SUN, August 15, 2001.

P. 221   "Rich Daley is a very strong": SUN, August 15, 2001.

P. 221   "I didn't take over the United States": SUN, August 15, 2001.

P. 222 "When is enough enough?": SUN, August 15, 2001.

P. 222 "dirty up Bill Daley": CM, February 2005.

P. 222 I'm not going to run": SUN, August 28, 2001.

P. 222 "Daley confidantes had urged Vallas": interview with Paul Vallas.

P. 223 "I just think it's ego": interview with Paul Vallas.

P. 223 "go on to raise $7.5 million": *Illinois Issues*, December 2008.

P. 223 "We are extremely gratified": SUN, March 18, 2002.

P. 223 "Blagojevich eked out a win": retrieved at http://www.uselectionatlas.org/ RESULTS/state.php?year=2002&off=5&elect=1&fips=17&f=0.

P. 223 "Blagojevich spent another $16 million": *Illinois Issues*, December 2008.

P. 224 "It's going to be a Democratic year": SUN, May 1, 2002.

P. 224 "In the coming weeks": *Bond Buyer*, December 10, 2002.

P. 224 "78.5% of the vote": "Chicago Mayor," *Our Campaigns*, http://www .ourcampaigns.com/RaceDetail.html?RaceID=52636.

P. 224 "mayor had private conversations": OR; SUN, April 26, 2003; TRIB, Business sec., April 1, 2003.

P. 225 "influential enemies": OR; SUN, December 10, 1998.

P. 225 "mayor held a secret meeting: TRIB, Business sec., April 1, 2003.

P. 225 "to begin the mission just before midnight": SUN, April 1, 2003; *Daily Herald*, December 1, 2003.

P. 225 "turn over your cellular phones": *Daily Herald*, December 1, 2003.

P. 226 "bright light at the camera lens" SUN, April 1, 2003.

P. 226 "Mayor Daley stayed up": SUN, April 1, 2003.

P. 226 "the mayor said": SUN, May 13, 2003.

P. 226 "Mayor Daley bulldozed his way": TRIB, Business sec., April 1, 2003.

P. 226 "Dictatorial decision making": *Christian Science Monitor*, April 7, 2003.

P. 226 "I am appalled at the arrogant disregard": SUN, August 17, 2003.

CHAPTER 18

P. 228 "mayor focused on two other issues": interview with Ed Uhlir; MP, 81–133.

P. 228 "Every year, millions of people": MP, 90.

P. 229 "It was an accident of nepotism": *Mississippi Business Journal*, July 16, 1990.

P. 230 "the world opened up to do business" *Mississippi Business Journal*, April 12, 2004.

P. 230   "Growing up, I didn't have much association": *Mississippi Business Journal*, April 12, 2004.

P. 230   "Celebrating the Art of Giving," Sara Lee Corporation, 1998 National Medal of Arts Recipient, http://www.saraleefoundation.org/history/ nmabrochure.pdf; "Sara Lee Chairman John H. Bryan to Accept National Medal of Arts at White House Ceremony" *Business Wire*, November 4, 1998.

P. 231   "wrapping the civic cloak around the challenge": interview with John Bryan; TRIB, December 26, 2004.

P. 232   "two major problems": interview with Ed Uhlir; interview with John Bryan; MP, 81–133.

P. 232   "Your legacy is going to be": interview with John Bryan.

P. 232   "Cindy Pritzker, a member of a wealthy family": MP, 114–116; interview with John Bryan; interview with Ed Uhlir; Gus Russo, *Supermob* (New York: Bloomsbury USA, 2006),137–39.

P. 233   "It's a beautiful alliteration": TRIB, December 26, 2004.

P. 233   "Frank Gehry": interview with John Bryan; TRIB, December 26, 2004; interview with Ed Uhlir; MP, 114.

P. 233   "disliked everything about it": MP, 114.

P. 233   "issued a challenge": MP,114–16; interview with John Bryan; interview with Ed Uhlir.

P. 234   "high-rise architect who doesn't know anything about parks": interview with Ed Uhlir.

P. 234   "Mayor Daley was skeptical": interview with John Bryan; interview with Ed Uhlir.

P. 234   "No, I don't do fish sculptures": "AIA Award for Millennium Park Slights Uhlir, Plumps for SOM," *ArchitectureChicago Plus*, http://www. lynnbecker.com/repeat/millennium/millennium.htm.

P. 234   "offered Gehry a commission": the following story is based on: interview with Ed Uhlir; interview with John Bryan; MP,117–18; "AIA Award for Millennium Park Slights Uhlir, Plumps for SOM," *ArchitectureChicago Plus*, http://www.lynnbecker.com/repeat/millennium/millennium.htm.

P. 235   "supposedly completed real estate deals": Peter Dale Scott, *Deep Politics and the Death of JFK* (Berkeley: University of California Press, 1993), 155.

P. 236   "long time for Rich Daley to get comfortable": interview with John Bryan; interview with Ed Uhlir.

P. 237   "John, I'm afraid you're just Gehry-izing the park": interview with John Bryan.

P. 237   "invited Rich and Maggie Daley to visit Crab Tree Farm": interview with John Bryan; interview with Ed Uhlir.

P. 237   "Oh, go ahead and build the goddamned thing": interview with John Bryan; interview with Ed Uhlir.

P. 237   "The cows are such a surprise": "Chicago Milks Exhibit for the Humor," http://www.chicagotraveler.com/cows_usa_today.htm.

P. 238   "If you look at Daley's leadership": interview with John Bryan.

P. 238   "an extraordinary public park": *The Financial Times*, July 20, 2004.

P. 239   "in many respects, he is an urban planner": interview with Paul Vallas.

P. 239   "professionalized the city by hiring skilled managers": *Time Magazine World*, April 17, 2005.

CHAPTER 19

P. 240   "I never cease to be amazed": SUN, October 7, 2004.

P. 240   "Base Trucking": SUN, January 6, 2005.

P. 240   "the FBI had arrested Angelo Torres": SUN, January 26, 2004.

P. 241   "insurance from the mayor's brother": SUN, February 4, 2004.

P. 241   "I am embarrassed": SUN, January 31, 2004.

P. 241   "did a good job at the beginning": SUN, February 12, 2004.

P. 241   "They don't have influence over anyone": SUN, February 12, 2004.

P. 241   "would charge 49 people with crimes": SUN, July 23, 2010.

P. 242   "usually sent one of his bagman": *United States v. Donald Tomczak*, Plea Agreement, July 29, 2005; US Department of Justice press release, February 24, 2005; SUN, May 3, 2005.

P. 243   "the Cannatellos had Bridgeport roots": *Herald News*, January 26, 2005.

P. 243   "was actually run by Cannatello": *US v. John Cannatello*, Plea Agreement, July 21, 2005; *Herald News*, January 26, 2005.

P. 243   "numerous ties to John Daley": *Herald News*, January 26, 2005.

P. 243   "Chicago city government had a serious financial problem": Civic Federation analyses of City of Chicago proposed budgets for fiscal 2002 through fiscal 2011; Thomas J. Gradel and Dick Simpson, "Patronage, Cronyism and Criminality in Chicago Government Agencies," Anti-Corruption Report no. 4, Department of Political Science, University of Illinois at Chicago.

P. 244   "bodyguard detail and slush fund": Better Government Association, August 5, 2011; City of Chicago Annual Appropriation Ordinance for the year 2011, 30.

P. 244   "$1.8 billion offer to privatize the Chicago Skyway": interview with John Schmidt; Civic Federation analysis, November 10, 2010.

P. 245   "friends and neighbors of Mayor Daley": SUN, February 11, 2005.

P. 245   "longtime ties to the Daley family": TRIB, July 25, 1999; TRIB, July 26, 1999.

P. 245   "connections to organized crime": TRIB, July 25, 1999; TRIB, July 26, 1999.

P. 245   "one month after Rich Daley became mayor of Chicago": TRIB, July 25, 1999; TRIB, July 26, 1999.

P. 245   "instructed head of special events": TRIB, July 25, 1999; TRIB, July 26, 1999.

P. 245   "$100 million into the Duff's pockets": sentencing of James Duff, Case #: 03-CR-922–1, May 18, 2005, US Department of Labor, www.dol.gov/ olms/regs/compliance/criminal_enforce/criminal_2005/USvsDuff0705.htm.

P. 246   "these are my guys": TRIB, July 26, 1999.

P. 246   "FBI released its 600-page file": Case ID#: 159A–CG-New (Pending); "Mayor Daley's Name Turns Up in FBI Files on Embezzler John F. Duff Jr.," Better Government Association, May 9, 2011, www.bettergov.org /mayor_daley%E2%80%99s_name_turns_up_in_fbi_files_on_embezzler _john_f_duff_jr/.

P. 246   "close ties to the mayor's brother": TRIB, June 13, 2006; SUN, July 19, 2005.

P. 246   "corrupt clout machine": NYT, July 7, 2006.

P. 246   "Don Tomczak testified": *Patrick McDonough v. City of Chicago*, videotaped deposition, July 15, 2008.

P. 247   "got involved with the founding of the HDO": SUN, June 12, 2005.

P. 247   "allegedly assisted in many Chicago campaigns": *United States v. Daniel Katalinic*, Plea Agreement, November 15, 2005; TRIB, June 1, 2006; OR.

P. 247   "the dam has broken": TRIB, July 19, 2005.

P. 247   "deeply offensive to me": SUN, July 28, 2005.

P. 247   "FBI questioned Daley himself": SUN, August 27, 2005.

P. 248   "When there is wrongdoing": SUN, August 27, 2005.

P. 248   "job approval ratings": NYT, January 6, 2006.

P. 248   "The mayor deserves criticism": SUN, August 25, 2005.

P. 249   "huge pause": SUN, August 25, 2005.

P. 249   "maintained his deep political ties": SUN, January 24, 2008; *Jet Magazine*, February 4, 2008.

P. 250   "I would be less than honest": *Chicago Defender*, July 19, 2006.

P. 250   "than Todd Stroger has in his dreams": TRIB, June 29, 2006.

P. 250   "arrogantly manipulated the system": SUN, September 8, 2006.

P. 251   "wonderful candidate": TRIB, October 26, 2006.

P. 251   "revealing the Chicago machine": NYT, July 7, 2006.

P. 251   "Chicago media speculated": TRIB, July 6, 2006, TRIB, July 8, 2006, Daily Herald, July 8, 2006; OR.

P. 252   "fund-raiser for Robert Sorich": TRIB, August 23, 2006.

P. 252   "They're still friends of his": TRIB, August 23, 2006.

P. 252   "very fine young men": SUN, November 29, 2006.

CHAPTER 20

P. 255   "one of the most important global cities": "2012 Global Cities Index," *Chicago Council on Global Affairs*, www.thechicagocouncil.org/files/ Studies_Publications/TaskForcesandStudies/GlobalCitiesIndex2012 .aspx.

P. 256   "almost never losing a roll call vote": RRR,247–90.

P. 256   "Rich Daley had seated 28 alderman": RRR,247–90.

P. 256   "With few exceptions, the current alderman": Quoted by Judson Minor in RRR, 282.

P. 256   "such as Ed Burke": RRR,273–77.

P. 257   "history of insularity and intolerance": RRR, 283.

P. 257   "you will apologize some day!": RRR, 283.

P. 257   "Me? I don't forget": RRR,247–90.

P. 259   "a little hypocritical": FOIE, 1.

P. 259   "defeated a Daley mayoral appointee": interview of Joe Moore.

P. 259   "appeal to those folks": FOIE, 126.

P. 260   "Chicken? Beef? Fish?": FOIE, 137–138.

P. 260   "reflection of society's values": *Christian Science Monitor*, December 13, 2005.

P. 260   "very first legislative body in the nation": FOIE,139–40.

P. 260   "gang leaders and dope dealers": FOIE, 142.

P. 260   "silliest law that they've ever passed": FOIE, 142.

P. 261   "development in Chicago is dead": *AP Online*, July 27, 2006.

P. 262   "great day for working men": *International Herald Tribune*, July 28, 2006.

P. 262   "FBI dossier purporting to": Jay Robert Nash, *Citizen Hoover* (Chicago: Nelson-Hall, 1972), 284.

P. 263   "My grandfather was with old Mayor Daley": interview of Dennis Gannon.

P. 263   "living wage issue percolated up": interview of Dennis Gannon.

P. 263   "At least three other concerns": interview of Dennis Gannon.

P. 264   "I'll give him a fucking fight": OR.

P. 265   "support working men and women": OR; interview of Dennis Gannon.

P. 265   "fuckin' support me on this": OR.

P. 265   "You are a principled man": OR.

P. 265   "I understand and share a desire": *USA Today*, September 11, 2006.

P. 265   "workers get poverty level wages": *USA Today*, September 11, 2006.

P. 265   "After Daley has taken this position": TRIB, September 12, 2006.

P. 266   "message to other political operatives": undated plea agreement between Donald Tomczak and US attorney for the District of Illinois in case 04 CR 921-1.

P. 266   "strong, independent voice in the city council": Mike Dumke, "The CFL Endorsements: A 'Strong, Independent' City Council?" January 17, 2007, http://www.chicagoreader.com/Bleader/archives/2007/01/17/the-cfl-endorsements-a-strong-independent-city-council.

P. 266   "we took it to another level": interview of Dennis Gannon.

P. 267   "some stupid cow town": TRIB, June 7, 2006.

P. 267   "We are trying to be a global city": FOIE, 301.

P. 267   "this is what government should be doing?": FOIE, 312.

CHAPTER 21

P. 268   "then raised $68 million": SUN, June 28, 2010.

P. 268   "Davis was an African-American": *Crain's Chicago Business*, January 13, 1997; BRID, 269.

P. 269   "denial of peaceful expression": SUN, November 11, 2007.

P. 269   "Allison was a reform-minded lawyer": SUN, November 11, 2007.

P. 269   "the firm hired Barack Obama": SUN, November 11, 2007.

P. 270   "$100 million in subsidies to build": *Boston Globe*, June 27, 2008.

P. 270   "seemed to pick his partners poorly": *Boston Globe*, June 27, 2008.

P. 270   "lot of serious conflict-of-interest questions": SUN, June 26, 2008.

P. 271   "John Daley's brother-in-law who would go to jail": SUN, February 17, 2006.

P. 271   "accused three of the mayor's closest advisers": SUN, June 16, 2009.

P. 271   "according to reports": SUN, August 29, 2011.

P. 272   "circumventing the council's right to review": SUN, June 17, 2009.

P. 272   "Right is right. Wrong is wrong": SUN, June 17, 2009.

P. 272   "to seek justice in these Burge torture cases": Ashahed M. Muhammad, "Chicago Police Torture Victims Share $20 Million Settlement,"

FinalCall.com News, January 28, 2008, www.finalcall.com/artman/
publish/article_4342.shtml.

P. 273   "stacked with Daley confidantes": TRIB, December 10, 2008; *Time,*
September 30, 2009.

P. 274   "I tried to include Barack and Michelle": BRIDGE, 270.

P. 274   "$2,000 on the first fundraising day": *Boston Globe,* June 27, 2008.

P. 275   "Yes we can": BRIDGE, 371.

P. 275   "Most surprising and gratifying thing": David Mendell, *Obama: From
Promise to Power* (New York: Amistad, 2007),243–44.

P. 276   "I just hope that after the primary": BRIDGE, 407–8.

P. 276   "very smart thing to do": BRIDGE, 408.

P. 276   "had given much thought to Barack": BRIDGE, 408.

P. 277   "going to be the US senator from Chicago": TRIB, October 30, 2004.

P. 277   "What have you got to lose?": John Heilemann and Mark Halperin, *Game
Change* (New York: HarperCollins, 2010), 61.

P. 277   "Obama's flip-flop": WLS-TV ABC7 News, January 22, 2007.

P. 278   "breadth of corruption": US Department of Justice, press release,
December 9, 2008; Patrick Fitzgerald press briefing on YouTube,
December 9, 2008.

P. 278   "fucking golden": Wiretaps from the trial of Rod Blagojevich on YouTube,
July 9, 2010.

P. 278   "come out that Rahm Emanuel spoke": SUN, December 17, 2008; SUN,
December 18, 2008; SUN, December 24, 2008.

P. 279   "spent like a drunken sailor": TRIB, December 4, 2008.

P. 280   "unfunded pension liabilities": Civic Federation analysis, "Status of
Local Pension Funding Fiscal Year 2008: An Evaluation of Ten Local
Government Employee Pension Funds in Cook County," March 8, 2010.

P. 280   "Chicago's finances were a mess": Civic Federation's budget analyses for
2002 through 2008.

P. 280   "pension funding crisis": Civic Federation budget analysis for the proposed
FY2008 budget.

P. 280   "avoiding the real tough decisions": interview of Paul Vallas.

CHAPTER 22

P. 283   "like a puppy dog": "A Night with John Rogers Jr.," video, www
.arielinvestments.com/historymakers/.

P. 284   "Rogers phoned Gery Chico": interview of John Rogers Jr.

P. 284   "put a good word in for Duncan with her husband": interview of John Rogers Jr.

P. 284   "Just do the right thing for children": interview of Arne Duncan.

P. 285   "85% below the poverty line": interview of Arne Duncan.

P. 285   "the mayor had the weight of the entire city": interview of Arne Duncan.

P. 285   "dropout rates had remained high": "Trends in Chicago's School's across Three Eras of Reform," Consortium on Chicago School Research, September 2011 report.

P. 285   "focused on three initiatives": interview of Arne Duncan; interview of Barbara Eason-Watkins.

P. 286   "efforts led to mixed success": Consortium on Chicago School Research, September 2011 report.

P. 286   "municipal union a cushy contract": SUN, August 30, 2007.

P. 286   "report criticizing Daley's parking meter deal": "Report of Inspector General's Findings and Recommendations: An Analysis of the Lease of the City's Park Meters," Office of the Inspector General, June 2, 2009 report.

P. 287   "It's a mistake to rush into a deal": *Bloomberg*, November 15, 2010.

P. 287   "People need to believe you're independent": TRIB, June 7, 2009.

P. 287   "Daley family's personal piggy bank": TRIB, June 10, 2009.

P. 288   "Ghettos started to disappear": Lawrence J. Vale and Erin Graves, *The Chicago Housing Authority's Plan for Transformation: What Does the Research Show So Far?* Final Report (Cambridge: Department of Urban Studies and Planning, Massachusetts Institute of Technology, 2010), http://web.mit.edu/dusp/dusp_extension_unsec/people/faculty/ljv/vale_macarthur_2010.pdf.

P. 288   "robbed, assaulted, raped and murdered": HUNT, 173.

P. 288   "police station within the projects' shadows": interview of Andrew Mooney.

P. 289   "somewhat mixed results": Vale and Graves, *The Chicago Housing Authority's Plan for Transformation*.

P. 290   "Chicago is my hometown": SUN, September 14, 2009.

P. 291   "I get emotional about it": WLS-TV ABC7 News, October 3, 2009.

P. 291   "long-running financial dispute": OR; "USOC, IOC Revenue Agreement Talks Taking Longer Than Expected," *Sports Business Daily*, December 5, 2011.

P. 291   "Olympics were never going to determine": TRIB, October 7, 2009.

P. 292   "cannot break a contract in 12 months": TRIB, December 3, 2009.

P. 292   "unsustainable and relies too heavily": Civic Federation budget analysis for the proposed FY2010 budget.

CHAPTER 23

P. 293   "reportedly informed certain Washington, DC, insiders": SUN, January 5, 2010.

P. 293   "I hope Mayor Daley seeks reelection": TRIB, April 19, 2010.

P. 293   "I trust Bill": CM, September 29, 2010.

P. 294   "life lesson for the people of Chicago": "Mayor Daley Proudly Proclaims Chicago Blackhawks Day," *Examiner.com*, June 12, 2010.

P. 295   "Wal-Mart will be good for our neighborhoods": *Chicago News Cooperative*, February 24, 2012.

P. 295   "There is more to be achieved": WLS-TV ABC7 News, August 5, 2010.

P. 295   "The election is in February": *Chicago News Cooperative*, February 24, 2012.

P. 295   "seen this movie before": NYT, September 4, 2010.

P. 296   "not seek seventh term as Mayor": *Huffington Post*, September 7, 2010.

P. 296   "I love Chicago": *Huffington Post*, September 7, 2010.

P. 296   "his spouse had given him the green light": OR.

P. 297   "ticking time bomb for the future of the city": CBS Chicago, November 17, 2010.

P. 298   "bitter-sweet day here at the White House": White House, press release, October 1, 2010.

P. 298   "he would make an excellent mayor": *Los Angeles Times*, October 1, 2010.

P. 299   "Chico had bloodlines": interview of Gery Chico; TRIB, December 21, 2010.

P. 299   "big, big, big deal": SUN, January 12, 2011.

P. 300   "more important geopolitically than the US": *Foreign Policy Magazine*, December 2011.

P. 300   "Closely followed Daley's own playbook": *Huffington Post*, October 19, 2011.

P. 301   "unsupportable by voters": TRIB, January 17, 1988.

P. 301   "known each other well": interview of Gery Chico; TRIB, December 21, 2010.

P. 301   "widely believed that Ed Burke": OR; NBC Chicago, January 27, 2011; TRIB, February 8, 2011.

P. 302   "facilitated by her husband's political clout": SUN, April 6, 2006.

P. 302   "self-described poor student": "Anne M. Burke: Cornelius Amory Pugsley National Medal Award, 2009," *American Academy for Park and Recreation Administration*, http://www.aapra.org/Pugsley/BurkeAnne .html.

P. 302   "rating her not qualified": SUN, April 6, 2006.

P. 302   "up to their old tricks": SUN, April 6, 2006.

P. 303   "had been settled in this State": Illinois Supreme Court ruling on January 27, 2011, *Walter Maksym v. Board of Election Commissioners of the City of Chicago*, Docket No. 111773.

P. 303   "voters deserve the right to make the choice": TRIB, January 28, 2011.

P. 304   "shared sacrifice, including for Ed Burke": SUN, February 14, 2011.

P. 304   "special place in our hearts": TRIB, February 22, 2011.

P. 305   "Chicago is a different city today": TRIB, May 16, 2011.

P. 305   "Chicagoans want to see change": *Huffington Post*, May 16, 2011.

P. 306   "Unfunded pension liabilities had risen": Civic Federation analyses of the City of Chicago Fiscal 2012 proposed budget and the Chicago Public Schools Fiscal 2012 recommended budget.

P. 306   "This maneuver had led to Daley receiving": TRIB, May 2, 2012.

P. 306   "People are raw with anger": TRIB, May 3, 2012.

CHAPTER 24

P. 309   "chilly 43 degree temperature": weather.com and http://chicago.cbslocal.com/2011/11/29.

INDEX

abandoned automobiles, 127, 131–32, 135, 152
Adamowski, Benjamin, 38, 200
AFL-CIO, 262–63, 265–67
Air and Water Show, 144–45, 245
Aon Center, 18, 171–72
Ariel Investments, 283–84
Art Institute of Chicago, 54, 212–13, 238
Arvey, Jacob, 12, 235
Axelrod, David: as adviser to Daley, 111, 114–17, 129, 203, 219; as adviser to Emanuel, 221, 304; and Blagojevich, 223; and connections to Daley and Obama, xvi, 275–76, 277, 279; and insights into Daley, 25, 34, 65; and Manny's Coffee Shop, 276–77

Battle of Michigan Avenue, 45
Bauler, Paddy, 15
beautification, xviii–xix, 125–26, 174–82, 228–39
Bedore, Ed, 129, 271
Bennett, William, 157
Biden, Joe, 202–3, 304, 307
Bilandic, Michael, 63–64, 67–68, 74, 99, 153
Blagojevich, Patti, 218
Blagojevich, Rod, 101, 138, 215–20, 222–24, 270, 278–79
Block 37, 126, 174–75
Boeing Company, 211–14, 215, 239
Braun, Carol Mosely, 298
Briatta, John, 271
Bridgeport: and Daley, Dick, 3–11, 16, 60; and the Daley brothers, 53–54; and Degnan, 75, 80, 252; and the Democratic machine, 33–34, 57, 62–63, 70–71, 99; as influence on Rich Daley, xix, 20–28, 49, 118–19; and inside deals, 132, 139, 165–66, 240–43; and political career of Rich Daley, 92, 104, 116,

128–29, 134, 139, 199, 203, 256, 301; and tolerance for corruption, 246–47, 252; and White Sox baseball team, 122
British School of Chicago, 289
Bryan, John, 172, 180, 228–31, 232–34, 236–38
Brzeczek, Richard, 83, 86
budgeting: and Chicago Park District, 177; and Chicago Transit Authority, 190; and Cook County, 250; and deficits, 69, 127, 143–45, 291–92, 295, 297–98, 305–6; and Daley, Dick, 8; and ineffectiveness of Burke, 244; and Millennium Park, 232, 238; and 1989 budget of Daley, 129–35; as a political weapon, 16, 161–62, 256; and Sawyer, 105; and shenanigans, 157, 161–62; and stress, 154, 172–73, 279–80, 282; and union contracts, 264
Burge, Jon, 84–86, 149–50, 272, 305
Burke, Edward "Ed": and Blagojevich, 223; and Byrne, 69–70, 74–75, 78, 198; and Chicago City Council role, 244, 260, 305; and Chico, 161, 299; and Council Wars, 97–98, 100–102; and Daley, Bill, 199; and Democratic machine, 69–70, 198; and Emanuel, 301–3, 306; and Fourteenth Ward politics, 70–71, 301; and his father, 26; history of, 69–75; and ineffectiveness as legislative check on the mayor, 244; mayoral ambitions of, 63, 106, 117, 301; personal qualities of, 72–73, 74–75; and questionable practices, 244, 256–57; and racial views, 97–98, 105, 105n; as rival of Rich Daley, xviii, 26, 69–75, 83, 134, 307; and scandals, 164–66, 240; and Visitation parish, 70–71; and Vrdolyak, 73–74, 77, 98, 302; and Washington, 100–102
Burnham, Daniel, 214, 228

Burris, Roland, 222
Bush, George, 198, 251
Byrne, Jane: and Burke, 74–75, 100; and Daley, Dick, 36–37, 60; and Daley, Rich, 36–37, 68–70, 74–75, 77–80, 83, 130, 226–27; and mayoral election of 1979, 67–68, 74, 77, 99; and mayoral election of 1983, 88–93, 99, 203; and mayoral election of 1991, 140; as mayor of Chicago, 74; and state's attorney election of 1980, 77–80, 198

Cabrini-Green, 126, 152, 191, 288–89
Callaway, John, 116
Cannatello, John, 243, 245
Carter, Jimmy, 60, 202
Catholic parish, 5, 21–22, 24, 36, 70–71, 153, 200, 252
Cermak, Anton, 9–10, 11–12, 301
Charlie Rose, 293–94
Charlie Trotter's restaurant, 125–26, 213–14, 258
Chicago Alternative Policing Strategy (CAPS), 152–53
Chicago City Council: and Burke, 72–74, 77, 134, 164–66, 199, 256–57, 260, 301, 305; and corruption, 13; and Council Wars, 97–98; and Daley, Dick, 8, 10–11, 16, 63–64, 174, 255–56; and Daley, Rich, 68, 70, 118, 134, 140, 250, 256–58, 268; and Degnan, 129, 134; and elections of 2007, 265–68; and Emanuel, 303–5; and Fourteenth Ward, 71; and ineffectiveness as legislative check on the mayor, 244, 272, 279–80, 286, 291–92, 297–98; and mayoral election of 1989, 106; and parking meter privatization, 279–80, 286; and parochial nature of, 255–67; and police torture, 272; and scandal, 139, 164–66; and Vrdolyak, 77; and Walmart, 295; and Washington's death, 100–105
Chicago Cultural Center, 171, 174, 239, 307
Chicago Daily News, 15
Chicago Defender, 29, 140
Chicago Firehouse Restaurant, 251–52, 271
Chicago flood of 1992, 146–47
Chicago Housing Authority (CHA), 88, 124, 126, 183–84, 188, 190–96, 220, 270, 288–89
Chicago Laboratory School, 188, 283
Chicagoland Chamber of Commerce, 261

Chicago Park District, 76, 102, 144, 176–79, 231, 245, 284
Chicago School Finance Authority, 155, 157, 159
Chicago Sister Cities International, 176
Chicago Skyway, 244–45
Chicago Transit Authority (CTA), 68, 147, 190, 216, 304
Chicago Tribune, 56, 92, 250, 306
Chico, Gery, 161–62, 166–67, 274, 284, 298–99, 301
Chihuly glass exhibit, 215
China, 299–300
Chirac, Jacques, 180–81
City Club of Chicago, 248
Civic Federation, 135, 177, 280, 292, 297
Civil Rights Act, 42
Claypool, Forest, 109–10, 114, 116, 131, 144, 178, 193, 249–50, 304
Clinton, William J. "Bill": and the Clinton Crime Bill, 151–52; and Daley, Bill, 202–5, 277–78; and Daley, Rich, 166, 195; and the Democratic National Convention of 1996, 181–82; and Emanuel, 110, 151–52, 193, 195; and empowerment zones, 187–88; and Obama, 277–78; and presidential decision making, xvi; and Stasch, 193; and Williams and Connelly, 248
"Clout on Wheels," 240–41
Coalition for Better Government, 137–39, 219, 247
Comiskey Park, 5, 20, 24–25, 27–28, 122, 125, 270
Commercial Club of Chicago, 97, 212, 214
Cook County Criminal Courts, 80, 150–51
corruption: and Blagojevich, 278; and the city council, 134; in city government, xix, 12–13, 138, 240–52; and Cook County government, 249; and disapproval of Daley, 272, 297; risk of, 240; and state government, 224; tolerance of, 87, 133, 166
Council Wars, 97–105, 301
Cows on Parade, 237
Crawford, Bob, 107, 199
crime: and abandoned automobiles, 132; and Burge police scandal, 149–50; and community policing, 152–53; and Cook County courts, 150–51; Daley's attempts to reduce, xvii, 154, 282, 295, 300; and fears of whites,

28; high levels of, xix, 177, 297; and mayoral
race of 1989, 112; and political instability,
127; and the state's attorney office, 82; and
the state's attorney race, 79; and west side of
Chicago, 125
Crown, Lester, 214, 235–36
culture war, 44, 58–59
Cuomo, Andrew, 192

Daley, Eleanor "Sis," 20–21, 23, 49, 58, 91–92,
120, 173
Daley, John, 53–54, 153, 223, 241, 243, 246, 250,
252, 271
Daley, Kevin, 82, 135
Daley, Lillian Dunne, 3–4
Daley, Margaret "Maggie": and cancer, 224;
and Chicago Cultural Center, 174; and
Daley, Rich, 111, 120, 294, 296, 304; death
of, 306–9; and Duncan, 284; marriage
of, 57–58, 82, 152–53; and Meigs Field,
225; and Millennium Park, 236–37; and
Olympic bid, 290; and the Oprah Winfrey
show, 282; and Saint Patrick's Day parade,
78; and Weisberg, 175
Daley, Patrick, 145–46, 296, 306
Daley, Richard J. "Dick": career, 7–19; and
Chicago City Council, 16, 255–56; and
Chicago Public Schools, 156–57; and Dawson, 37; death of, 60–61; and Democratic
National Convention of 1968, 41–46; family
of, 20–21, 23; flaws of, xvi; and King,
Martin Luther, Jr., 39–41; and nepotism,
52–54; and political power, xvi; and race,
37–41; and Shakman, 52; youth of, 3–7
Daley, Richard M. "Rich": and artist protection
bill, 54–56; and Axelrod, xvi, 114–17, 279;
and Blagojevich, 216–24, 270; and Boeing,
212–13; and Burke, xviii, 70–75, 117, 134,
164, 305, 307; and Bush, 251–52; and Byrne,
36–37, 69, 88; and Chicago City Council,
256–62, 267; and Chicago Public Schools,
156–64; and China, 299–300; and Daley,
Bill, xv, 75, 107, 198, 203; and Daley, Maggie,
57–58, 152–53, 236–37, 282, 296, 307–9;
and the Daley Agenda for Chicago's Future,
111–13; and Democratic machine, 136; and
Democratic National Convention of 1968,
41–46; and Democratic National Conven-

tion of 1996, 171, 179–82; and DePaul
University, 31–32; and "Dirty Little Richie"
nickname, 56–57; and Emanuel, xvi–xvii,
110–11, 195, 220–21, 293–94, 300, 304; and
the FBI, 247–48; and fiscal irresponsibility,
140, 162, 280–81, 292, 297–98; and health
issues, 195; and his father, xvi–xvii, xx,
22–31, 33–34, 36–37, 41–46, 49–66, 76,
78, 82–83, 87, 89–90, 92, 107–8, 120–21,
122, 126, 128, 133–34, 136, 144, 156, 158, 171,
173, 176, 178, 179, 180, 181, 186, 195, 199, 202,
205, 226, 255–56, 261, 294, 297, 308–9;
and Hispanic Democratic Organization,
137–38; and hubris, 33, 56, 87–88, 224–27,
250–51, 257; and Huels, 165–66; and Illinois
Constitutional Convention of 1970, 49–52;
and Jarrett, xvi; legacy of, xvi, xviii–xix, 158,
238–39, 267, 283, 297, 300, 305, 306; and
mayoral election of 1983, xviii, 74, 87–94,
99, 136; and mayoral election of 1989, 104,
106–7, 111, 117–20, 134, 136–37, 176, 202–3,
256; and mayoral election of 1991, 140, 203;
and mayoral election of 2003, 221, 224; and
mayoral election of 2007, 249, 258, 264–67,
277; and Millennium Park, 228–39; and
nepotism, 52–54, 59; and Obama, xvi–xvii,
276–77, 279; and Olympic bid, 273, 289–91;
personality of, 56–57, 59, 62; personal
transformation of, 65–67, 82, 87–88, 94, 172,
229, 239; and political skill, 78, 135–40; and
retirement, 296–97, 306; and rooftop garden,
210; and state's attorney office, 80–86; and
state's attorney race, 74–80; temper of,
143–45, 264–65; and tolerance for corruption, 132–33, 240–52, 268, 270–72, 287;
and Tomczak, 138–39; and unions, 261–67;
and Washington, xviii, 113, 127–28; youth
of, 23–30
Daley, William M. "Bill": and Burke, 199; and
Clinton, 203, 205; and Democratic convention of 1996, 205; and Emanuel, 203–4,
293; and Gore presidential campaign,
197–98; and mayoral race of 1983, 199; and
mayoral race of 1989, 203; and NAFTA,
203–4; and Obama, xvi, 277–78; political
ambitions of, 202–3, 221–22; political
skill of, 198–99; and Rostenkowski, Dan,
200–202, 204

Dawson, Bill, 14, 37
Davis, Allison, 268–72, 274, 287
Davis, Danny, 106, 117, 128, 140, 250, 298
Davis, Dantrell, 152, 191
Degnan, Tim: and Daley, Rich, 75, 80, 111, 116, 129–30, 134, 137–38, 178, 196, 247, 271, 306; and Huels, 165; and Koldyke, 155–56; and the Park Grill, 245; and personal characteristics, 75, 116, 129; and Sorich, 252
De La Salle Institute, 5–6, 26–30, 49, 83, 138, 165, 270
Democratic machine: and black voters, 64, 68; and Burke, 71–73, 161, 299; and Byrne, 68–69, 77–80; and Daley, Dick, xvii, 8–15, 33, 38, 52–53, 61, 235, 249, 261; and Daley, Rich, xviii–xix, 33, 52–53, 56, 59, 75, 77–80, 99, 136, 158; and the Hired Truck Scandal, 246, 251; and Madigan, Mike, 51; organization of, 8; and the park district, 176, 218; and Rostenkowski, Dan, 61, 105, 200; and Tomczak, 138–39; and Washington, 64, 99–101
Democratic National Convention, 34, 41–44, 87, 108, 158, 171, 179–81, 228, 269
DePaul University, 31, 49, 71–72, 126, 213
Despres, Leon, 256
Devine, Richard "Dick," 76, 81
Drake Hotel, 262–64
Duff, James, 194, 245–46, 266
Duncan, Arne, xvi, 160, 279, 283–86, 290, 307
Dunne, George, 86
DV Urban Realty Partners, 271–72, 287

economic development: and Daley, Dick, 17–19; and Daley, Rich, 112, 130, 135, 154, 261–62, 264, 282; and Davis, Allison, 269; and the Democratic National Convention of 1996, 180; and Midway Airport, 211; and NAFTA, 203; and O'Hare Airport, 17–19, 214–15; and the Olympic bid, 282; and Walmart, 261–62, 264, 295
Edgar, Jim, 148, 154–55, 271
education reform, 157–63, 166–67, 300, 305
Eleventh Ward: and Bilandic, 63, 99; and Byrne, 74; and Daley, Dick, 7–8, 10–11, 13, 50, 139; and Daley, John, 153, 241, 243, 246, 252; and Daley, Rich, 33–34, 50, 57, 74, 99, 104, 137, 165; and Degnan, 137; and

the Democratic machine, 63, 301; and the Fourteenth Ward, 71; and Huels, 165; and Tomczak, 139
Emanuel, Rahm: and Blagojevich, 200, 278; and the CHA, 193, 195; and the Clinton Crime Bill, 151; and Daley, Bill, 204; and Daley, Rich, xvii, 111, 129, 193, 195, 220, 248–49, 293–94, 300, 307; and desire to win, 111; and his congressional campaign, 220–21, 224, 247; and Manny's Coffee Shop, 277; as mayor, 304–6; and the mayoral campaign of 1989, 110, 114, 116, 118; and the mayoral campaign of 2011, 300–304; and NAFTA, 204; and relationships with Obama and Rich Daley, xvi, 279, 293–94, 298
Environmental Auto Removal, Inc., 132–33
Epton, Bernard, 90, 94
Evans, Timothy "Tim," 101–5, 117, 120, 256

Fary, John, 73–74
Federal Bureau of Investigation (FBI), 139, 240–41, 246–48, 262, 278–79
fiscal irresponsibility, 140, 162, 280–81, 292, 297–98
Fitzgerald, Patrick, 241, 246–49, 251, 263, 278
Flynn, Ray, 30–31
foie gras, 257–61, 267
Fourteenth Ward, 70–72, 240, 301–2
Friends of the Parks, 177

Gabinski, Terry, 105
Gallery 37, 174–76
Gannon, Dennis, 261–66
Gates, Earnest, 186–87, 193
Gautreaux v. CHA, 190
gay community, 105, 116, 118–20, 133–35, 140, 218
Gehry, Frank, 233–37, 282, 304
Giangreco, Pete, 276
Gingrich, Newt, 181
GNA Trucking, 243
Gore, Al, 198, 202
graffiti, 163–64
Gralewski, Ron, 26–28, 30
Grand Beach, Michigan, 145–46
Grant Park, 12, 152, 171, 173, 212, 228, 234, 278

Great Migration, 6, 12
Gutierrez, Luis, 102, 118, 138

Habitat Company, 189–90
Hamburg Athletic Club, 6–7, 10
Hansen, Bernie, 136
Harold Washington Library, 173, 233
Harris, John, 278
Harrison, Carter H., II, 3
Harvard, 185, 269, 274, 283
heat wave, 40, 188–89
Henry Horner projects, 124, 183
Hired Truck Scandal, 240–43, 246–47, 249,
    251, 266, 271, 277
Hispanic Democratic Organization (HDO),
    137–39, 241, 247
Hoffman, David, 249, 281, 286–87
Huels, Patrick, 104, 164–66, 256
Hynes, Thomas, 63–64, 275

Illinois Central rail yard, 126, 171, 173, 228
Illinois Constitutional Convention of 1970,
    49–52, 54, 56, 65, 198
inauguration, 122, 175, 304–5
International Amphitheatre, 33–34, 43

Jackson, Jesse, 42, 88, 91–92, 102, 108, 117, 181,
    202, 220, 278
Jardine Water Filtration plant, 242
Jarrett, Valerie, xvi, 128, 184–85, 187–90,
    273–75, 277–79, 290, 307
Johnson, Lyndon, 42–43, 46, 114
Jones, Emil, 274
Joyce, Jeremiah, 75–76, 111, 116, 129, 132, 137,
    198

Kapoor, Anish, 235
Katalinic, Daniel, 247
Katten Muchin, 306
Katz, Marilyn, 44–45, 97
Keane, Tom, 14–15
Kelly, Ed (mayor), 11–13, 15, 153
Kelly, Edward "Ed," 63, 70, 106, 117, 177, 218
Kennan, Ned, 26, 89, 92–93, 120–21, 203
Kennedy, John F., xvi, 34–35, 42–43, 122, 201
Kennedy, Teddy, 60, 78, 202
Kennelly, Martin, 13–14, 71, 153, 301
King, Martin Luther, Jr., 37, 39–44, 124

Klutznick, Philip, 109
Koldyke, Mike, 155, 159–60
Krone, Phil, 76, 116
Kruesi, Frank, 65–67, 75, 81, 111, 116, 129, 271
Kunkle, Bill, 81

Lake Calumet, 123, 135, 137, 148–49, 154, 211
Lake Michigan: and Burge, 84; and the Daley
    family, 23; and the Deep Tunnel project,
    201; and the Drake Hotel, 262; and Grand
    Beach, Michigan, 145; and the Jardine
    Water Filtration plant, 242; and Meigs
    Field, 225–26; and Navy Pier, 131, 179; as a
    prominent physical feature of Chicago, 98,
    120, 122, 125–26, 152, 171, 210, 234, 307, 309;
    and the race riot of 1919, 7
Lane, Vince, 184
LaVelle, Avis, 116
Lehman Brothers, 279–80
legacy, xvi, xviii–xix, 158, 238–39, 267, 283,
    297, 300, 305, 306
Lincoln Park, 44–45, 125, 177, 213
Little Hell, 288
Little Village, 80, 124
living wage, 258, 261–65, 267
Loop, 17, 124, 126, 147, 173, 174–75, 307
Lycée Français de Chicago, 176

Madigan, John, 212
Madigan, Michael "Mike," 51, 77, 130, 148,
    177, 307
Magnificent Mile, 171, 242, 262
Manny's Coffee Shop, 276–77
mayoral election: of 1983, xviii, 74, 87–94,
    99, 136; of 1989, 104, 106–7, 111, 117–20,
    134, 136–37, 176, 202–3, 256; of 1991, 140,
    203; of 2003, 221, 224; of 2007, 249, 258,
    264–67, 277
McCormick Place Convention Center, 17, 122,
    131, 272
McDonough, Joseph, 7–10
Meigs Field Airport, xix, 152, 171, 215, 225–28,
    266, 272, 297
Mell, Richard "Dick," 101–5, 138, 217–20,
    222–23, 241, 307
Midway Airport, 123, 148–49, 189, 211, 213, 309
Millennium Park, xix, 228–40, 245, 267, 282,
    297, 304, 307, 309

Millennium Park effect, 238–39
Mondale, Walter, 79, 92
Moore, Joe, 259–60, 262, 267
Mosena, David, 128, 147, 149, 161, 175, 184, 190

Nash, Pat, 11–12, 15
Nativity of Our Lord: and Daley, Bill, 53–54; and Daley, Dick, 5, 10, 20, 33, 60; and Daley, John, 53–54, 153, 252; and Daley, Rich, 23–24, 26, 33, 49; and Sorich, 252
Navy Pier, xix, 88, 131, 179, 182, 238, 242, 245
Netsch, Dawn Clark, 50, 56, 59, 64–67, 92, 133
North American Free Trade Agreement (NAFTA), 182, 203–4

Obama, Barack: and Axelrod, 275–77, 279, 304; and Blagojevich, 278; and Daley, Bill, xvi, 276–78; and Daley, Rich, 249, 275–77, 290, 299; and Davis, Allison, 269, 274; and Duncan, 160, 279, 283–84; and Emanuel, 110, 249, 293, 298; and Jarrett, 185, 275, 279; and Jones, 274; and the Olympic bid, 290–91; and Rezko, 274
Obama, Michelle, 184–85, 274, 277, 290, 307
O'Connor, Patrick, 222, 305
Odelson, Burt, 300–301
O'Hare Airport, 17–18, 68, 105, 125, 133, 149, 214–15, 225, 245, 309
Old Saint Patrick's Church, 307
Olympic bid, 273, 282–83, 289–91, 297
Orr, David, 75, 98–99, 101–5, 259

Park Grill restaurant, 234, 245
parking meter privatization, 279–81, 286–87, 292, 297, 306
pension funds: and budget maneuvering, 162, 263–64; and Daley, Rich, 140; and Davis, Allison, 268, 270–71, 287; and the legacy of Rich Daley, xix, 306; and the pension crisis, xix, 244, 280, 297, 306; and political crony-ism, 109, 140, 256, 268, 270–71; and Rezko, 270; and unions, 263–64; and Vanecko, 268, 271, 287
Pincham, Eugene, 140
Plan for Transformation, 194–96, 270, 288–89
Plensa, Jaume, 236
Preckwinkle, Toni, 257, 279
Pritzkers, 90, 232–33, 235, 278

privatization, 154–55, 244–45, 264, 279–81, 286–87, 292, 297, 306
public housing: and Cabrini-Green, 126, 152, 191, 288–89; and the CHA, 88, 124, 126, 183–84, 188, 190–96, 220, 270, 288–89; as challenge for the mayor, xvi, xviii, 127, 282, 297; and the Plan for Transformation, 194–96, 270, 288–89; and race, 28, 38, 123–24
public schools, xvi–xviii, 38, 127, 154–67, 183, 222, 282–86, 289, 297

race: Axelrod's view of politics and, 275–76; and Bilandic, 68; and Bridgeport, 28–29, 118; and Byrne, 88; and Burke, 105, 105n; and the Council Wars, 99, 105, 105n, 275; and Daley, Dick, 37–38, 87, 156; and Daley, Rich, xviii, 90–92, 118, 191, 297; and Dawson, 37–38; and housing, 12–13, 28; and King, Martin Luther, Jr., 39–41; and Obama, 275–76; and politics, 12–13, 14–15, 103, 105; and race riots, xvi, 7, 42; and racial tension, 28–29; and Sawyer, 103
Reagan, Ronald, xvi, 79, 89
Reinsdorf, Jerry, 185–86
Rezko, Tony, 270, 274
Ribicoff, Abrahm, 45
Robert Taylor homes, 122–23, 184
Rogers, John., Jr., 178, 273, 278, 283–84
rooftop garden, 210
Roosevelt, Eleanor, 35
Roosevelt, Franklin Delano, 20, 55
Rose, Don, 65, 79–80, 204
Rosenberg, Tom, 186
Rostenkowski, Dan, 61, 90, 105, 139, 149, 200–202, 204, 218–19
Rostenkowski, Joseph, 200
Rush, Bobby, 192
Ryan, George, 212, 215, 224–25
Ryan, Jack, 276
Ryan, Pat, 108, 171, 273, 289–90

Saint Stanislaus Kostka Parish, 200
Sanchez, Al, 137–38, 247
Santos, Miriam, 109, 271
Sawyer, Eugene, 100–106, 117–19, 130
Schmidt, John, 65–67, 81, 108, 129, 201, 203, 244, 269

SDI Security Inc., 164–65
Sears, Roebuck and Co., 144
Sears Tower, 18, 126, 144, 171, 239
Shakman, Michael, 52, 82, 269
Shuldiner, Joseph, 188–91
Simpson, Dick, 226
Singer, William "Bill," 108, 158
Skinner, Sam, 149
Smith, Adrian, 228, 233–34
Solis, Danny, 124, 138
Sorich, Robert, 246–47, 251–52, 266
South Loop, 5, 124, 173, 233, 251, 271
Stasch, Julia, 192–96
Stateway Gardens, 270
Strategic Action Neighborhood Pilot Program
    (SNAPP), 187
Strautmanis, Mike, 185
Stepan, Paul, 76–77, 93–94, 106–8, 116, 118,
    271
Stevenson, Adlai, 11, 13, 34–35, 122
Stroger, John, 199, 249–50, 275
Stroger, Todd, 250–51

Thompson, Big Bill, 8, 120
Thompson, Jim, 69, 109, 130–31, 148, 302
Tomczak, Donald, 137–39, 221, 242, 246, 266
Torres, Angelo, 240–41
Trotter, Charlie, 213–14, 258–59
Trump Tower, 239

Uhlir, Ed, 231–35
unions: and Amalgamated Bank, 222; and
    Byrne, 69; and Chicago Public Schools,
    177–78; and the City of Chicago, 127; and
    Daley, Bill, 222; and Daley, Dick, 156–57,
    261; and Daley, Rich, 140, 158, 261, 265–68,
    295; and DePaul alumni, 31; and the Duff
    family, 245–46; and educational reform,
    155–61, 286; and elections of 2007, 258,
    266–67; and Emanuel, 304; and globaliza-
    tion, 261–68, 295; and NAFTA, 203–4;
    and politics, 140, 156–57, 295; and Sorich,
    246; and strikes, 69
Union Stock Yards, 3, 6, 22
University of Chicago, 65–66, 116, 123, 184, 188,
    268, 283, 306

University of Illinois at Chicago, 17, 91, 103, 131,
    218, 243, 294
US Department of Housing and Urban Devel-
    opment (HUD), 183–84, 188, 192, 195

Vallas, Paul, 157, 161–64, 166–67, 222–23, 239,
    280, 283–85
Valle, Miguel del, 298
Vanecko, Robert, 268, 271–72, 287
Villinski, Ted, 24, 28
Visitation parish, 70–71
Vrdolyak, Edward "Ed": and Blagojevich, 217;
    and Burke, 73–74, 77, 302; and Byrne, 74;
    and the Council Wars, 98–99; and Lake
    Calumet, 123; the mayoral election of 1983,
    90; the mayoral election of 1989, 106, 117,
    120; racial views of, 90, 98–99; and the
    Seven Dwarfs, 106; succession politics in
    1976, 63

Walmart, 258, 261–67, 295
Warner, John, 211–15
Washington, Harold: and the Council Wars,
    97–104; and Daley administration appoin-
    tees, 128, 161, 172, 184, 269; and the Daley
    Agenda for Chicago's Future, 111, 113, 127;
    and Evans, 106; and the Harold Wash-
    ington Party, 118; and the Illinois senate
    president race of 1977, 64; and the mayoral
    election of 1983, xviii, 88–91, 93–94, 199,
    249; and the mayoral election of 1989,
    117–18, 202; and Obama, 275; and west side
    development, 186
Weisberg, Lois, 128, 172–77, 210, 237
White Sox baseball team, 5, 20, 24, 119, 137, 186
Wilhelm, David, 111, 114, 116, 129, 179, 203, 204
Willis Wagons, 38
Wilson, Andrew, 83–86
Windy City Maintenance, 194, 245
Winfrey, Oprah, 237, 278, 282, 290
Wirtz, Bill, 185–86
World Economic Forum, 195, 230–31, 236
World's Columbian Exposition of 1893, 212,
    238

Zum Deutschen Eck, 217